Archaeological Mexico

DESIGN MOTIFS OF ANCIENT MEXICO

ARCHAEOLOGICAL MEXICO

A TRAVELER'S GUIDE TO
ANCIENT CITIES AND SACRED SITES

Second Edition

Andrew Coe

PHOTOS BY
DANIELLE GUSTAFSON

**AVALON
TRAVEL**

Archaeological Mexico
Second Edition

Andrew Coe

Published by
  Avalon Travel Publishing
  5855 Beaudry St.
  Emeryville, CA 94608, USA

Please send all comments,
corrections, additions, amendments,
and critiques to:

Archaeological Mexico
AVALON TRAVEL PUBLISHING
5855 BEAUDRY ST.
EMERYVILLE, CA 94608, USA
email: atpfeedback@avalonpub.com
www.travelmatters.com

Printing History
  1st edition–October 1998
  2nd edition–November 2001
          5 4 3 2 1

ISBN: 1-56691-321-7
ISSN: 1095-8886

Editor: Erin Van Rheenen
Series Manager: Angelique Clarke
Copy Editor: Karen Bleske
Graphics: Erika Howsare, Melissa Sherowski
Production: Jacob Goolkasian, Amber Pirker, Dave Hurst
Interior Design: Amber Pirker
Cover Design: Jane Musser, Jacob Goolkasian
Map Editor: Naomi Dancis
Cartography: Mike Morgenfeld, Ben Pease, Bob Race
Proof and Index: Leslie Miller
Illustrations: Bob Race (where noted)

Front cover photo: Susan Kaye

Distributed by Publishers Group West

Printed in China through Colorcraft Ltd., Hong Kong

This book is dedicated to my father,
Michael D. Coe.

CONTENTS

INTRODUCTION 2

The Land 3; The Cultures 5; Visiting the Ruins 15

VALLEY OF MEXICO 22

The Land 25; History 29

CHIAPAS 240

THE SOCONUSCO COAST

THE USUMACINTA BASIN

YUCATAN PENINSULA 322

CHRONOLOGIES

The following are considered the most important periods of occupations for these major sites, though they may have been founded and continued as minor sites for hundreds of years before and after. Frequently evidence is fragmentary and all scholars may not agree on starting dates.

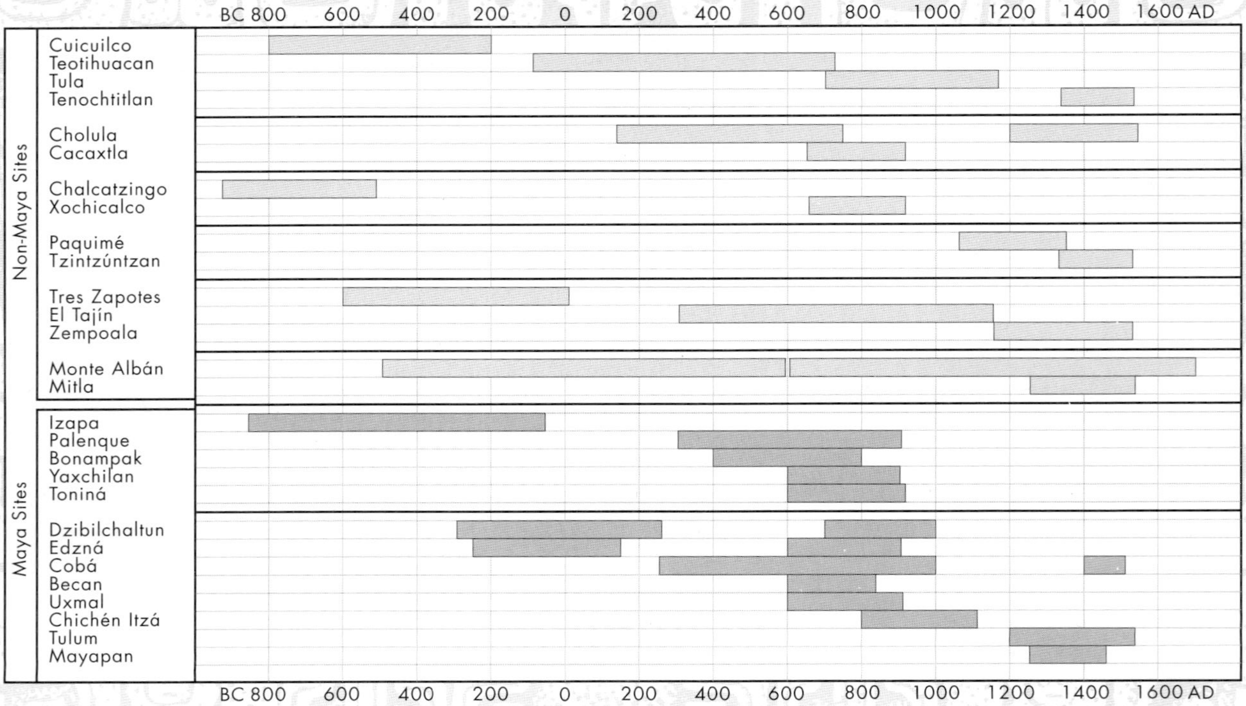

Non-Maya Sites

Cuicuilco
Teotihuacan
Tula
Tenochtitlan

Cholula
Cacaxtla

Chalcatzingo
Xochicalco

Paquimé
Tzintzúntzan

Tres Zapotes
El Tajín
Zempoala

Monte Albán
Mitla

Maya Sites

Izapa
Palenque
Bonampak
Yaxchilán
Toniná

Dzibilchaltun
Edzná
Cobá
Becan
Uxmal
Chichén Itzá
Tulum
Mayapan

BC 800   600   400   200   0   200   400   600   800   1000   1200   1400   1600 AD

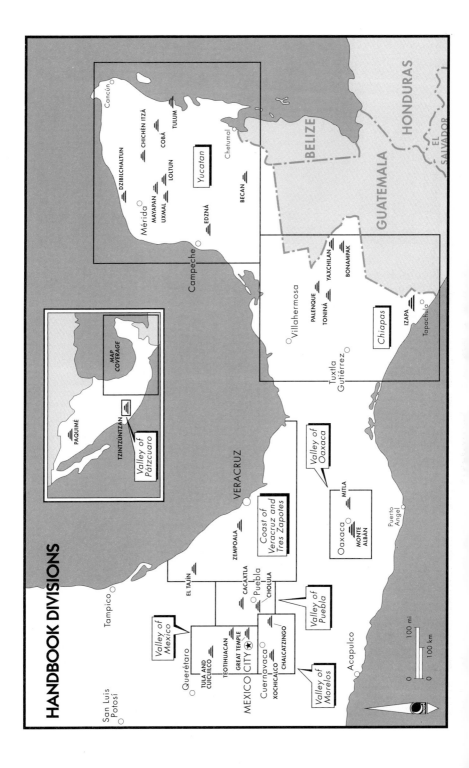

HANDBOOK DIVISIONS

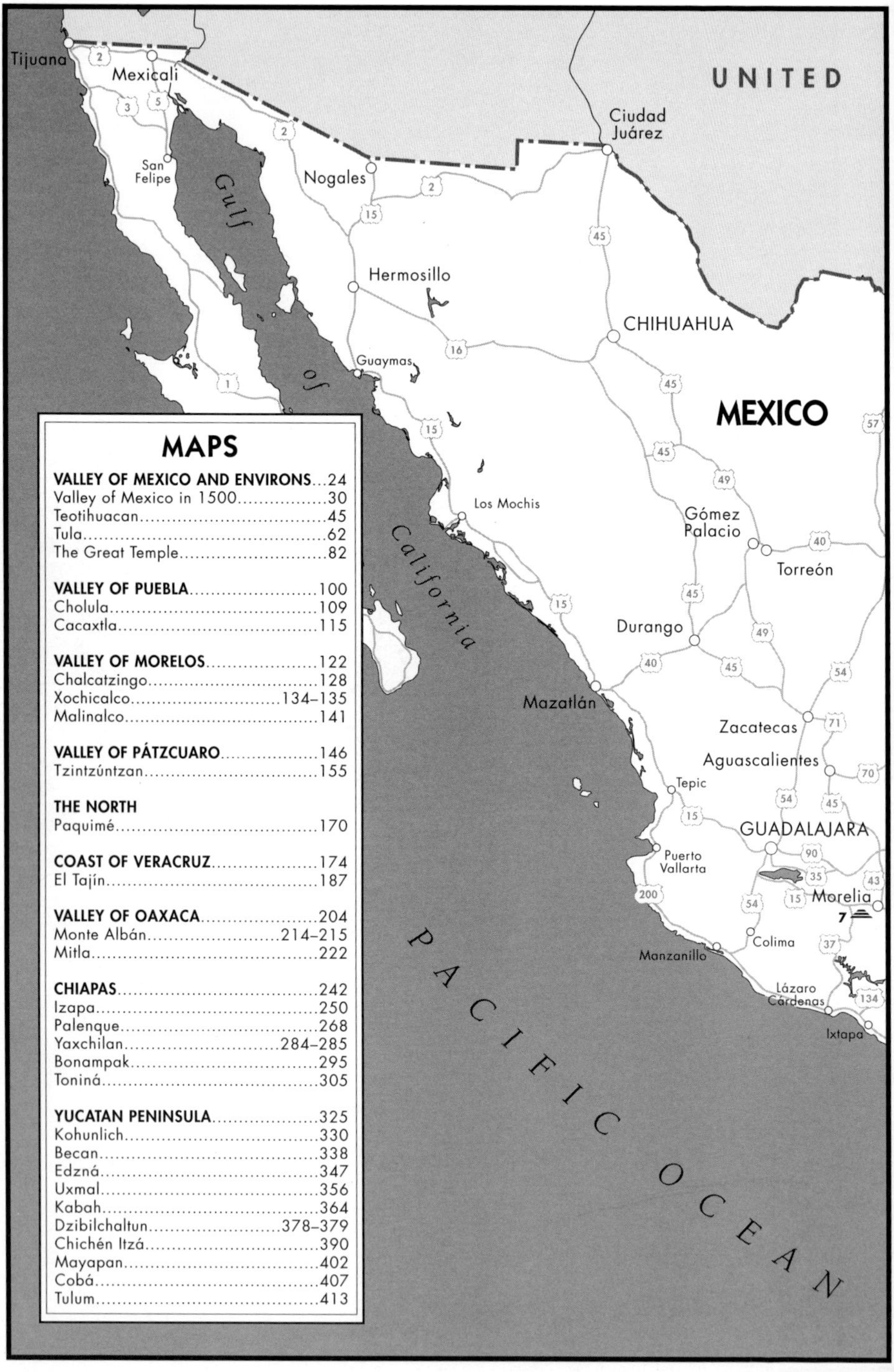

MAPS

Tijuana

Mexicali

San Felipe

Nogales

Ciudad Juárez

UNITED

Hermosillo

CHIHUAHUA

Guaymas

MEXICO

Los Mochis

Gómez Palacio

Torreón

Gulf

of

California

Durango

Mazatlán

Zacatecas

Aguascalientes

Tepic

Puerto Vallarta

GUADALAJARA

Morelia

Colima

Manzanillo

Lázaro Cárdenas

Ixtapa

PACIFIC OCEAN

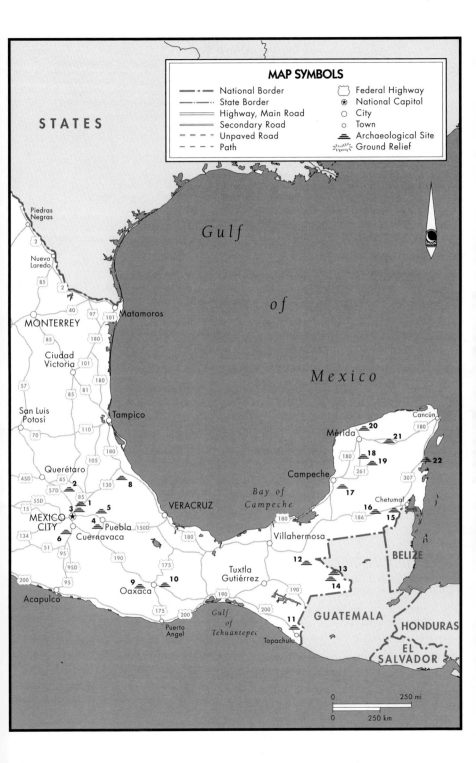

MAP SYMBOLS

— · — National Border
— · · — State Border
═══ Highway, Main Road
═══ Secondary Road
- - - Unpaved Road
- - - Path

⬭ Federal Highway
⊛ National Capitol
○ City
○ Town
🜚 Archaeological Site
Ground Relief

STATES

Gulf

of

Mexico

Piedras
Negras

Nuevo
Laredo

MONTERREY

Matamoros

Ciudad
Victoria

San Luis
Potosí

Tampico

Querétaro

2

1

3

5

4

8

MEXICO
CITY

6

Cuernavaca

Puebla

VERACRUZ

Bay of
Campeche

Mérida

20

21

18

19

22

Campeche

17

16

15

Chetumal

9

Oaxaca

10

7

Tuxtla
Gutiérrez

Villahermosa

12

13

14

BELIZE

Acapulco

Puerto
Angel

Gulf
of
Tehuantepec

11

Tapachula

GUATEMALA

HONDURAS

EL
SALVADOR

Cancún

0   250 mi

0   250 km

SITE RANKINGS

KEY: **Four Trowels:** A world-class site, a must for every visitor
Three Trowels: A major site, possessing great historic and/or artistic value
Two Trowels: Worth a detour, and generally of regional importance
One Trowel: For the indefatigable archaeological tourist, or if you happen to be in the neighborhood

VALLEY OF MEXICO

Cuicuilco
Teotihuacan
Tula
Tenayuca
Great Temple
Tlatelolco
Santa Cecilia Acatitlán

VALLEY OF PUEBLA

Cholula
Xochitécatl
Cacaxtla

VALLEY OF MORELOS

Chalcatzingo
Xochicalco
Malinalco

VALLEY OF PÁTZCUARO

Tzintzúntzan
Ihuatzio

THE NORTH

Paquimé

COAST OF VERACRUZ

Tres Zapotes
El Tajín
Quiahuiztlan
Zempoala

VALLEY OF OAXACA

Monte Albán
Mitla
Yagul
Lambityeco
Dainzú
Zaachila

CHIAPAS

Izapa
Palenque
Yaxchilan
Bonampak
Toniná
Chinkultic
Comalcalco

YUCATAN PENINSULA

Kohunlich
Xpujil
Becan
Chicanná
Edzná
Uxmal
Kabah
Sayil
Labná
Xlapak
Loltun Cave
Dzibilchaltun
Izamal
Chichén Itzá
Balankanché Cave
Mayapan
Cobá
Tulum
Muyil
El Rey

PREFACE

hy visit Mexico's ancient ruins? On my first few trips to Mexico as a child, the question would not even have come up. My parents were anthropologists, and my siblings and I were taken to dozens of Mesoamerican sites every year as a matter of course.

For us, it was an adventure. The road to the site was usually some terrible track hugging a cliff, and we spent the trip wondering if the next rock would be the one to pierce the oil pan and strand us for days. At the ruins, we were set loose on the ancient temples to scramble up stairways, explore tunnels, or scour the surrounding fields for potsherds and obsidian (a pursuit that is now prohibited by law).

Today it may seem as if the possibilities for archaeological adventure have disappeared. Decades of urban development and the rise of mass tourism have made many sites more accessible to individual travelers and bus tours alike. Nevertheless, there remain a number of destinations, such as the amazing jungle ruins of Yaxchilan and Bonampak, that still pose a significant challenge to visit, providing an extra measure of satisfaction for the intrepid traveler. Even in Mexico City, it is possible to escape the touristic horde by visiting such obscure but still impressive ruins as Tenayuca and Cuicuilco.

And there are other satisfactions. Once I began traveling to Mexico on my own, it became increasingly apparent to me that the ancient wonders of Mesoamerica are not simply the ruins of dead civilizations, but living works of art. From the refined stucco reliefs at Palenque to the Sun God masks covering the main temple at Kohunlich, the art and architecture of Mesoamerica are forms of communication, full of fear, anger, sadness, and beauty. There are also historical lessons to be learned: for example, many Mesoamerican cultures declined because of ecological disasters resulting from overpopulation, a danger we still face today. Perhaps the most important thing we can learn from visiting archaeological Mexico is humility. Mesoamerican art, learning, and culture were developed without any apparent influence from Europe, Africa, or Asia. Truth and beauty are not the exclusive provinces of any civilization.

This book is a guide to 53 of the largest and most spectacular ancient ruins in Mexico. This is by no means all of them: archaeologists have identified well over 10,000 sites in Mexico, and new discoveries are being made every week. Nor are my selections intended to be definitive, and specialists will notice the unavoidable omission of a handful of significant sites, such as Calakmul and La Venta. Nevertheless, the present volume is arguably the most complete travel guide to Mesoamerican sites ever published, and it should provide a starting point for countless journeys of discovery.

Geography was destiny for most ancient Mesoamerican cities, hence the sites are presented geographically, from the Valley of Mexico to the Yucatan Peninsula. Each region is introduced separately, followed by coverage of individual sites. Most entries include a brief **Introduction** to the site and its general significance; a **History** of the development of the site and of its ancient inhabitants; and a review of the **Archaeological Record,** from earliest discovery to most recent excavations. Individual attractions and travel recommendations are covered in **Touring the Site.**

This book seeks to de-Hispanicize many originally Indian words. Thus, the accent has been taken off all names ending in -an—for example, Yucatan instead of Yucatán—and off names ending in -on or -un, since there is no way of knowing whether the originators of these words actually accented them. Also, archaeologists are introducing a "new orthography" for Maya names, and these have been adopted wherever practicable.

In every instance I have attempted to include the most recent archaeological theories on each site, and on Mesoamerican cultures in general. During the last three decades, researchers have overturned many of the old verities, such as viewing the Maya as a race of peaceful star-gazers. Unfortunately, many discredited theories live on as a kind of folklore that is passed on to tourists by guides, out-of-date museum displays, and even a few guidebooks. This new edition of my guidebook is designed to bring the newest and most exciting information to archaeological tourists, and, I hope, make their visits to Mexico's ruins that much more interesting an adventure.

INTRODUCTION

ceremonial doorway at Chicanna

THE LAND

The great cultures of Mexico rose in a distinct landscape, one that combined extremes of abundance with awful poverty. Much of the land is composed of almost uninhabitable deserts and steep mountainsides. Around them and between them, however, are nestled green coasts and valleys that contain many of the resources necessary for human settlement. It was these extremes of arid and lush, cold and hot that drove bands of early nomadic hunters to develop the skills, such as the domestication of plants and animals, that allowed the eventual development of an agrarian society and the rise of a complex civilization.

Mexico is shaped like a funnel—some say a cornucopia—with its widest part opening at the north along the border with the United States. From here, it slowly narrows southward to its slimmest part at the Isthmus of Tehuantepec before turning east toward Guatemala and Central America. The east and west sides of the funnel are bordered by two mountain ranges, the Sierra Madre Oriental and Sierra Madre Occidental. These both descend toward saltwater—the Gulf of Mexico or the Pacific Ocean—ending at narrow bands of flat, hot coastal land. Between them, these two ranges enclose a broad, dry plateau that slowly ascends from north to south.

This plateau reaches its summit in central Mexico, where the two mountain ranges meet at the Transverse Volcanic Axis, a band of geological faults and volcanoes running from southern Veracruz to Colima on the Pacific. This a region of towering, snow-capped volcanoes and pine-covered ridges. The mountains are separated by a series of wide, protected valleys containing rich soils and ample supplies of water.

The most important of these valleys is the Valley of Mexico, home to today's Mexico City. It is surrounded to the east, west, and south by the Valleys of Puebla, Toluca, and Morelos respectively. Each of these became home to important intermediary cultures between the great civilizations of the Valley of Mexico, such as Teotihuacan or the Aztecs. To the north of the Valley of Mexico extends the central plateau, the main route by which "barbaric" tribes of nomads entered, and threatened, Mesoamerica.

As the mountains descend, sometimes sharply, to the Isthmus of Tehuantepec, they open on two very different regions that saw the birth of early cultures. Along the Veracruz coast lies a wide strip of swamps and steamy lowlands rich in plant and animal resources. This abundance fostered the development of the Olmecs, Mesoamerica's first civilization. On the opposite side of the mountains, you find the Valley of Oaxaca lying just inland from the Pacific Coast. Here, the early Zapotecs were forced by the relative scarcity of resources to develop early agriculture and probably the first writing system and calendar.

East of the Isthmus of Tehuantepec rise the two sharply serrated ridges of the Chiapas Highlands, which merge as they head east into Guatemala. The rich rainforests along Chiapas's Pacific Coast saw the rise of the Izapan civilization that linked the Olmecs with the later Maya. To the north, the highlands descend to the hot coastal plains of Tabasco and, inland, the basin of the Río Usumacinta, home to dozens of splendid Classic Maya cities, including Palenque.

From the Guatemala Highlands, a vast swath of forest extends hundreds of kilometers northward. The thick jungle of the Petén grades imperceptibly into the drier forests of the Yucatan Peninsula, a broad, flat limestone shelf bulging out between the Gulf of Mexico and the Caribbean Sea. Although this peninsula possesses almost no supplies of surface water, the Maya white limestone cities such as Chichén Itzá were home to tens of thousands and the center of large city-states.

The defining feature of all these regions of Mexico is that, although they con-

a temple on the North Platform at Monte Albán, Oaxaca

tained enough resources for small- and medium-sized settlements, they did not maintain a favorable enough combination of soil, water, and climate to support great cities. All these regional cultures needed trade to survive, varying from raw materials—iron ore and cotton cloth—to luxury goods such as quetzal feathers and jade. It was through trade that the disparate regions and cultures of Mexico were bound together into what's now known collectively as Mesoamerica.

THE CULTURES

Humankind first entered Mexico at the end of the Ice Age, when much of North America was locked in a band of ice and snow that circled the Northern Hemisphere. A land and ice bridge between Far Eastern Siberia and Alaska became a crossing for nomadic Asian hunters. Some researchers believe others may have trekked across ice floes that linked Europe with eastern Canada. Following herds of now-extinct mammals, including mastodons, horses, giant sloths, and antelopes, these hunters headed south into Mexico and on to South America.

In the Valleys of Mexico and Puebla, archaeologists have found what may be early tools amid piles of extinct mammal bones dated 21,000–24,000 years ago. Clearer evidence of early hunters emerges from around 9500 B.C., when a type of finely crafted flint arrowheads called Clovis points suddenly appeared across North America. In Mexico, Clovis points have been discovered in rock shelters in Tamaulipas and Durango and among mastodon bones found along the now-disappeared lakes of the Valley of Mexico.

This early Mexico was far wetter, cooler, and lusher than it is today. Thick vegetation filled the Valley of Mexico and spread across the high plateau to the north. After 7000 B.C., however, the land began to dry out, and the huge mammals—originally a near-limitless supply of protein—gradually dwindled into extinction, perhaps because of overhunting or the climatic changes. The hunters were forced to learn new strategies for survival, becoming hunter-gatherers who foraged for wild fruits, seeds, and roots to supplement the game. Archaeologists have named this distinctive way of life the Desert Culture; it continued into the 20th century in some parts of northern Mexico.

During the millennia that followed, these nomads gradually settled down, limiting their treks between semipermanent seasonal encampments within one valley. Their culinary habits began to focus increasingly on plant material, and they learned that they did not have to be dependent on the whims of the natural world but could influence plant growth and form. Between 5000 and 3400 B.C., the residents of the Tehuacan Valley between Puebla and Oaxaca cultivated the first domestic plant, maize, which would grow into the Mesoamerican staff of life. Other important regions for early settlers were the Valley of Oaxaca and the Grijalva Basin in Chiapas.

During the **Archaic era (3000–1800 B.C.)**, improved cultivation and food-storage techniques allowed the early farmers to build the first permanent hamlets and small villages. These have been found from Tamaulipas in the northeast all the way down to the Soconusco region of Chiapas's Pacific Coast. The end of this period also brought the crafting of the first ceramic pots for storage and food preparation. The best of these, such as those from the Barra culture of Chiapas, were not crude pots but thin-walled vases and dishes covered with beautiful geometric designs.

Up to this point, archaeologists have found only the slightest hint that there was much interchange between the regions. During the **Early Preclassic era (1800–1000 B.C.)**, however, this situation dramatically changed, with ritual goods bearing similar religious motifs appearing from the Maya region to Oaxaca and the Valley of Mexico. The source of these objects, mainly jade and ceramic figurines, was the coast of Veracruz, where a group named the Olmecs was building Mesoamerica's first great center at San Lorenzo. Their religion, which included the cults of the cave, the World Tree, and jaguars, appears to have been the basis for many of the Mesoamerican beliefs that followed.

This Olmec colossal head, from Villahermosa's La Venta Park Museum, is probably a portrait of a deceased ruler.

The other centers for early cultures were Tlatilco on the lakeshore of the Valley of Mexico, Chiapa de Corzo (Chiapas), and the "shaft-tomb" villages of Nayarit, Jalisco, and Colima, where archaeologists have found thousands of beautiful ceramic burial offerings. In the Valley of Oaxaca, San José Mogote grew into a small town built around a raised, stucco-covered platform. By the **Middle Preclassic era (1200–400 B.C.)**, its rulers had subjugated the surrounding villages and commemorated their victories in stones depicting dead chieftains. On one, the glyph "One Earthquake" represents not only his name but one of the earliest examples of Mesoamerican writing.

The Olmec influence, now emanating from La Venta in Tabasco, continued to be felt throughout Mesoamerica until about 400 B.C. Olmec emissaries even built an outpost in far-off Morelos; Chalcatzingo was covered with fine carvings that acted as a gallery of the Olmec religion for their central Mexican audience.

During the **Late Preclassic era (300 B.C.–A.D. 250)** that followed, however, many regions of Mexico began to go their separate ways. San José Mogote was supplanted by the growing Oaxaca metropolis of Monte Albán, which shows remarkably few signs of outside influences during its early years. On the coast of Chiapas, the lush jungle site of Izapa became the pivot between the Olmec and the later Maya civilizations. Stelae around its ceremonial center were decorated with scenes from the Popol Vuh (the later mythological text of the Maya) and dated inscriptions written in early forms of the Maya calendar.

In the valley of Mexico, the early city of Cuicuilco was destroyed by a volcano. Its replacement was Teotihuacan to the northeast, which was built on top of a narrow volcanic tube. Around this cave, the Teotihuacanos built a cult whose power lasted through the Spanish Conquest. Their small side valley lacked in natural resources, forcing them to travel extensively and forge trade ties with more powerful states while subjugating weak ones. During the **Early Classic era (A.D. 150–600)** Teotihuacan grew into Mesoamerica's greatest trade and tribute empire (many followed) with connections as far south as Copán in Honduras.

In the regions of southern Mexico and Yucatan, the Teotihuacanos built trade routes that connected many perhaps isolated groups. After the fall of Izapa in Chiapas, the primary Maya heartland became southern Guatemala around the great early city of Kaminaljuyú. The core traits of Maya culture—commemorative stelae, steep temple pyramids, the long-count calendar—spread from here north into the Petén Jungle and then beyond to Yucatan. Cities such as Tikal and El Mirador built trade routes along Yucatan's east coast to Kohunlich and later Cobá, both of which were built in traditional Maya style.

Teotihuacan stone mask

The influence of the Petén region also spread northwest toward the early center of Dzibilchaltun. Here, however, the residents also had strong ties to central Mexico via Gulf Coast trade routes. In the Río Bec and Chenes regions, the Maya built cities that appear to contain cartoon images of the Petén centers—towers that look like pyramids with impossibly steep steps—while also encompassing central Mexican traits. These traditions reached their highest form in the beautiful cities of the **Late Classic era (A.D. 600–900)**, such as Uxmal of the Puuc region in Mexico.

Just to the west of the Petén, more "orthodox" groups of Maya began to build a series of astounding cities along the banks of the Río Usumacinta. Their development was spurred by a dynastic system whose main tenet was the deification of its dead rulers. To aid in this cult, the living rulers built huge temples covered with ste-

Jaina Island burial figurine of ballplayer

lae, stone panels, and murals; these were adorned with long inscriptions glorifying their forebears and, by association, themselves. The largest of these cities, such as

© JORGE PEREZ DE LARA

DANIELLE GUSTAFSON

WARRIORS VS. ASTRONOMERS: VIEWS OF PRE-COLUMBIAN MEXICO

Expert opinions about the pre-Columbian cultures have varied, as have the experts. The first Europeans to enter Mexico were the early 16th-century equivalent of the U.S. Marines; they firmly believed that they had landed in Asia, perhaps China. The product of the late Middle Ages, they expected they would see the beings they had read about in the old Greek geographies: races of giants, dwarves, and men with heads below their shoulders. They also hoped to find the Fountain of Youth and the mythic city of El Dorado made all of gold. Nevertheless, the conquistadors had firsthand knowledge about pre-Hispanic Mexico, and, while biased, their eyewitness accounts are some of the most important sources for modern study.

In the century or so after the Conquest, the mythic Mexico of giants and El Dorado dissolved for lack of proof. The main argument became whether the land's rapidly dwindling and often enslaved native population had descended from those who built the ancient pyramids. The extreme negative position was taken by a Spanish priest who denied that they were even human (he did not want to be bothered with converting them to Christianity). On the other side, priests such as Fray Bernadino de Sahagún, Bishop Diego de Landa, and Diego Durán devoted years to documenting native histories and religious beliefs. They had no doubt that Mexico's indigenous groups were the same as the ones who built the pre-Columbian cities.

Mexico City's intellectual elite lost interest in the pyramids and those who built them for the next century and a half. Then, as the European Enlightenment finally reached Mexico in the late 18th century, scholars suddenly realized that they were sitting among the ruins of an ancient civilization about which they knew nothing. Their interest was spurred by the 1790 discovery of the Aztec Sun Stone and Coatlicue sculpture beneath Mexico City's Zócalo. They pulled

what dusty copies of earlier scholarship remained on library shelves—many had been destroyed by the Inquisition—and published a whole series of articles speculating on the cultures of the Aztec, Maya, and other groups.

When these articles reached Europe and the United States, they launched the era of the great expeditions to Mexico's ruins. The most important explorations were led by Guillermo Dupaix, Alexander von Humboldt, and John Lloyd Stephens and Frederick Catherwood. Their accounts were published with copious illustrations that sparked the imagination of scholars in both hemispheres. The great debate became, "Where did these ancient peoples come from?" The answers included ancient Israel, Carthage, Egypt, India, China, Africa, and even Atlantis. (Adherents to many of these theories still write polemics, with the addition of flying saucers.)

In the 19th century, most experts divided Mesoamerica into two main fields, the Maya and the Aztecs. The Maya were identified with the ancient Greeks; the period when they were carving dated monuments became the "Classic" era. The Aztecs, on the other hand, whom they knew from eyewitness accounts, were associated with Rome, the successor to Greece; they were considered barbarous, given to warfare and human sacrifice. Other cultures, such as the Olmecs and Zapotecs, were banished to the sidelines and considered of marginal importance.

During this time, the pendulum had slowly been swinging away from the 16th-century priest who denied that Mexico's native residents were even human. Scholars such as William H. Prescott in his *History of the Conquest of Mexico* romanticized the Aztecs as a noble race that created both great works of art and admirable social and political institutions. Motecuhzoma II, once a depraved despot, became a brave but tragic leader with the fatal flaw of hesitancy. Désiré Charnay said that the Toltecs lived in a "perpetual spring" and gave offerings of flowers, not human hearts. In the 1880s, Adolph Bandelier extolled Aztec society as a harmonious collective ruled by an elected leader. This view was avidly taken up by intellectuals associated with Mexico's early Marxist movements. By the 1920s, many called Cortés an evil syphilitic sadist, the advance guard of an hegemonistic feudal society, who toppled a great communitarian civilization.

These beliefs were the apogee of a trend of formulating theory first and then looking at the evidence. Luckily, there were many serious explorers who preferred collecting information to indulging in these speculations. Scholars such as Alfred Maudslay and Eduard Seler pored over the ruins and noticed substantial differences between the regions and traces of a long chronology (as opposed to many who had theorized a relatively recent and abbreviated timeline for human occupation in Mexico, beginning around A.D. 1100).

By the late 19th century, amateur and professional Mesoamericanists had unearthed hundreds of native and early Spanish accounts, including Sahagún's, in archives in both Mexico and Europe and were rapidly bringing them into print. In the 1880s, Ernst Förstemann of Dresden deciphered the system of the Maya Long Count calendar, and a few years later the American journalist J. T. Goodman correlated it to the Christian calendar. Experts discovered that all the stones found in the Maya region were dated A.D. 907 or before—far earlier than theorized.

In 1909, the Mexican archaeologist Manuel Gamio was the first to use the techniques of stratigraphic excavations at a site. Although it took some years for the practice to be completely accepted, archaeologists now could unearth the true chronology of cultures at a site rather than base one on supposition. In the Valley of Mexico, for instance, this completely overturned the accepted notions of the relative ages of Tula, Teotihuacan, and Tenochtitlan. A

huge body of new information became available, and experts began to realize that the cultures of Mesoamerica were far more original than they had previously thought. Scholars began to realize that they would have to understand the cultures of Mesoamerica on their own terms, not on their preconceived ideas.

In the Maya region, early 20th-century scholarship was dominated by Sir Eric Thompson. Through the 1950s, many believed that the Maya were the "mother culture" of Mesoamerica, the formulators of the calendar, religion, and hieroglyphic writing, just as the ancient Greeks were the supposed founders of Western civilization. Thompson proposed that Maya cities were relatively empty centers of learning built so that Maya priest-astronomers could study the stars and discuss their significance. On the hundreds of Maya reliefs, he saw depictions of Maya gods and purely religious subjects—abstractions—and not a drop of history or genealogy. The Maya were a peaceful and contemplative civilization that did not know war or sacrifice (unlike the barbarous 20th century embroiled in a succession of world wars).

After World War II, a series of breakthroughs began to chip away at Thompson's romanticization of the Maya. Carbon 14 tests showed that the Olmecs, not the Maya, were the earliest Mesoamerican civilization. Aerial photographs of the Yucatan Peninsula revealed traces of widespread ancient fields, the first clue that Maya cities had a far larger population than Thompson believed. Then, in the 1960s, experts began to realize that Maya reliefs were historical in content and not scenes of gods and mythic animals.

The spur for this revolutionary idea was the translation of Maya hieroglyphs. This did not happen all at once (as with Egyptian hieroglyphs and the Rosetta Stone) but incrementally. Scholars working independently in many parts of the world, including Yuri Knorosov in

continued on page 10

continued from page 9

the Soviet Union, began to work out the mixture of phonetic and ideographic components in the glyphs. In the 1970s, a group of epigraphers that included Linda Schele, David Kelley, and Floyd Lounsbury used this earlier work to make the first complete translations of Maya texts. With this breakthrough many of the old verities about Maya culture toppled.

The ancient texts were not abstract at all; their subjects were rulers, genealogy, war, bloodletting, sacrifice, and tribute. Thompson said that they did not record self-glorification of rulers; in contrast, self-glorification appears to be their principle topic. The evidence now shows that the Maya region was populated with hundreds of large towns and cities with as many as 50,000 inhabitants. The people were bound to the centers by a cult of the deified ruler; it was the ruler's interaction with the gods that brought rains and good crops. To feed his subjects, the aristocracy had to perform ritual bloodletting and wage war to acquire sacrificial victims—the Universe continued to revolve only with the shedding of blood.

Interestingly, these new accounts of Maya culture strongly resemble the descriptions of the Aztecs found in the conquistadors' writings. Scholars now believe that the glorification of rulers, warfare, tribute, and sacrifice were primary attributes not only of the Maya but of all Mesoamerican cultures. While traces of romanticization continue—a group of anthropologists recently denied that any Mesoamericans performed human sacrifices—most experts now subscribe to this new, nuanced reading of Mexico's pre-Hispanic cultures. Despite all the work that has been done, many discoveries and breakthroughs (such as the translation of Zapotec writing) are still waiting to be made.

Palenque and Yaxchilan in Chiapas, are among the most beautiful sites in the Western Hemisphere.

In central Mexico, meanwhile, disaster struck at Teotihuacan. Around A.D. 725, the city (at the time one of the largest in the world) was sacked, burned, and abandoned. Archaeologists do not understand all the repercussions of this event, but it is clear that they were largely negative. Although Teotihuacan probably had kept some cultures from growing too aggressively, there is evidence that its emissaries were honored more than vilified. A series of reliefs at the booming city of Monte Albán shows the arrival of near-deified envoys from Teotihuacan. Perhaps this connection was Monte Albán's fatal flaw: by A.D. 750, it too was abandoned.

The centuries following Teotihuacan's fall were marked by unrest and militarism. Some cities did prosper—El Tajín on the Veracruz coast grew into a crowded metropolis—but their temples were covered with images of warfare and bloody sacrifice (not that sacrifice was unknown before).

Clovis points are finely carved arrowheads used by the early hunters who stalked large game across North America during the Late Pleistocene era.

Where once people had built towns in the middle of valleys, they now built them on protected hilltops. In Morelos, the city of Xochicalco is a glorified fortress surrounded by rings of defensive walls. It was built by Putún Maya traders from the Tabasco and Campeche coasts taking advantage of the central Mexican vacuum to extend their own trade and tribute empire.

Unrest also struck the Maya region. Between the end of the 8th and the beginning of the 10th centuries, every Classic Maya center was abandoned. Archaeologists have speculated for decades on the reasons for the Maya "collapse." They now seem to agree that environmental degradation—there were simply too many people for the land—led to political unrest and internal uprisings. When the old ruler cults could not bring rain and good crops, there was nothing to tie the people to the cities, and they left.

During the **Early Postclassic era (A.D. 900–1200)**, Mexico's cultures were characterized by militarism, strong influences from northern Mexico "barbaric" groups, and the deification of those who built the now-abandoned cities. Teotihuacan, Cobá, and dozens of other empty ruins became important pilgrimage centers. New peoples moved in and claimed that the ruins had either been built by the gods or by their own forebears.

Many of these groups were Chichimecs (People of the Dog) originating in the deserts of the northern plateau. Fierce fighters, they quickly carved out a role for themselves as mercenaries working for the more established tribes and, later, as warriors fighting on their own account. The most successful of the early Chichimecs were the Toltecs, who after a long nomadic period built a great city at Tula, just north of the Valley of Mexico. From here, they dominated central Mexico through warfare, and their reach extended as far as the trading center of Casas Grandes in Chihuahua, and perhaps to northern Yucatan as well. It is hotly debated, but some archaeologists believe that Chichén Itzá was captured and settled by a Toltec army that introduced its central Mexican gods, particularly the Feathered Serpent, to the Maya.

The unrest continued, and by A.D. 1150 Tula and Chichén Itzá were abandoned, both apparently after an outbreak of arson and destruction. There followed another period of political vacuum, fighting, and the entrance of wandering tribes. The Maya area never really recovered, although in the Yucatan a group of Itzá did build a regional center at Mayapan. The wandering tribe that came to dominate central Mexico, the Mexica—better known as the Aztecs—entered as one of the poorest and most bedraggled of the nomadic groups.

In A.D. 1325, the Aztecs founded a settlement on a muddy island in the middle of one of the Valley of Mexico's lakes. Through a combination of political maneuvering and skill at warfare, they managed to parlay that foothold, called Tenochtitlan,

the Aztec Calendar Stone

MESOAMERICANISTS

The following is a list of the most influential explorers, priests, and archaeologists who added to our knowledge of Mexico's ancient cultures. No living figures are included.

Andrews IV, E. Wyllys (1916–1971): Much of what we know about the archaeology of the Yucatan Peninsula we owe to Andrews, who worked for the Carnegie Institution and then for Tulane's Middle America Research Institute. Among the sites he reported on are Becan, Dzibilchaltun, and Balankanché Cave.

Batres, Leopoldo (1852–1926): As director of all Mexico government archaeological projects, Batres was the pioneer of official archaeology in Mexico and was the first to acquire government funds for an excavation. He led the first large-scale explorations of Mitla and Teotihuacan, where he also began restoration of the Pyramid of the Sun.

Caso, Alfonso (1896–1970): Caso was the colossus of 20th-century Mexican archaeology. He is best-known for his work in the Valley of Oaxaca, where he dug all the major sites and directed the excavation of Monte Albán from 1931 to 1943. At the latter site, Caso found more than 180 tombs, including the famous Tomb 7 with its hoard of jewels and carvings. He published ground-breaking works on Mixtec and Zapotec codices, religion, and history. He also helped organize modern Mexican archaeology through his work at the anthropology museum and as a founder of the Escuela Nacional de Antropología. Finally, Caso was a fierce defender of the rights of Indians in a country ruled by its Ladino majority. He both illuminated the cultures of their ancestors and, as director of the National Indigenous Institute, sought to improve their place in Mexican society without destroying Indian culture.

Covarrubias, Miguel (1904–1957): First famous as a celebrity caricaturist, Covarrubias became passionate about Mexico's indigenous cultures. In books such as *Mexico South* and *Indian Art of Mexico*, he explored the links between modern-day Indians and their ancient ancestors, always emphasizing the great artistic merit of what they produced.

Díaz del Castillo, Bernal (1495–1583?): One of Cortés's conquistadors, Díaz later wrote a remarkable eyewitness account of his adventures in his *True History of the Conquest of New Spain,* one of the best—and only—sources of first-person testimony about the Late Postclassic Mexicans.

Dupaix, Guillermo (1748–?): The king of Spain gave Dupaix, an Austro-French officer, the commission to explore the ruins of his Mexican colony. The publication of Dupaix's heavily illustrated 1805, 1806, and 1807 journeys was the catalyst for numerous European explorers to travel to Mexico.

Gamio, Manuel (1883–1960): Gamio was Mexico's first scientific archaeologist and one of the greats in the field. The head of the first official archaeological organization, he pioneered stratigraphic excavations and the study of ceramic typologies. The results of his Teotihuacan dig helped prove that the city predated the Aztecs and Toltecs.

Landa, Bishop Diego de (1524–1579): In 1549, just three decades after the conquest of Yucatan, a Franciscan priest named Diego de Landa was assigned to the Maya town of Izamal. Landa was shocked by the persistence of the Maya religion and crusaded to erase every vestige of native paganism. He ordered the imprisonment and torture of its practitioners and collected more than 5,000 idols and at least 27 codices and destroyed them in a great bonfire at Maní in 1561. These actions were not necessarily against the policy of Spain, then in the throes of the Inquisition, but they were a clear overstepping of Landa's authority—only the bishop could authorize those punishments. He was recalled to Spain to answer for his sins. As an atonement, he wrote down every fact about Maya culture and religion that he had learned, calling his work the *Relación de las Cosas de Yucatan*—the "Account of the Affairs of Yucatan." Eventually absolved, Landa was named Bishop of Yucatan and lived there from 1572 until his death. Though the original of Landa's manuscript disappeared, a condensed copy made a century later was finally published in 1864 and immediately revolutionized the nascent field of Maya studies. Landa not only gave information on nearly every aspect of Maya life and history, he included careful descriptions of the Maya calendar (with a correlation to our own) and of the writing system. This information would be used during the 20th century as part of the key to finally decipher Maya hieroglyphs. Landa is the great double-edged character of Mesoamerican studies—he destroyed indigenous culture but also gave us the means to rebuild it.

Maler, Teobert (1842–1917): In the late 19th and early 20th centuries, this Austrian photographer traveled through Guatemala and Chiapas recording dozens of Maya sites for Harvard's Peabody Museum. His plates are a priceless resource for Mayanists studying inscriptions before they were destroyed by time and vandalism.

Maudslay, Alfred (1850–1931): An English explorer, Maudslay trekked through the Maya jungles to document ancient art and architecture with photos, drawings, and plaster casts. He discovered a number of sites and published a highly valued study of Maya inscriptions.

Morley, Sylvanus (1883–1948): For many years, Morley led the Carnegie Institution's explorations in Mexico and Central America, personally leading excavations at Chichén Itzá and Copán in Honduras. He was also one of the great experts on Maya hieroglyphs.

Proskouriakoff, Tatiana (1909–1985): This chain-smoking Russian émigré started out as an architectural artist for the Carnegie Institution, producing remarkable drawings of sites such as Piedras Negras in Guatemala and Copán in Honduras. Her close attention to detail served her well, because she noticed that the dates on Maya stelae had a pattern. And what this pattern meant was that the stelae's hieroglyphic texts were not about religion or astronomy, as was the prevailing wisdom, but that they referred to historical events such as battles, marriages, and ascensions to the throne. In one stroke—an article that appeared in 1960—she changed the direction of Maya studies, pointing it toward the eventual translation of Maya hieroglyphs.

Río, Captain Antonio del (??–??): In 1787, this Spanish military officer was sent from Guatemala City to explore a rumored lost city in the jungles of Chiapas. Reaching his destination near the village of Palenque, he discovered that the buildings were obscured by towering trees and closely interwoven vines. He hired some local Chol Maya to chop down the vegetation and then set it on fire, finally exposing one of the greatest ancient Maya cities. Del Río and his artist, Ricardo Almendáriz, then set out to explore every inch of Palenque's ruins. Almendáriz sketched the four-story tower, among other structures, and also the numerous stone and stucco reliefs they unearthed. Some of these del Río removed and sent back to Spain for study by royal historians. Del Río finally wrote a detailed report, accompanied by Almendáriz's illustrations, and sent it to Madrid. When his work was finally published, in an English translation in 1822, it gave scholars their first look at Maya hieroglyphs carved on stone. In his untutored but methodical way, del Río was in some ways the first Mesoamerican archaeologist.

continued on page 14

continued from page 13

Ruz Lhuillier, Alberto (1906–1979): Ruz made one of the great finds of Mesoamerican archaeology: the discovery of Pakal's tomb in Palenque's Temple of the Inscriptions. He led the Mexican excavations at Palenque for almost a decade and is now buried on the site.

Sahagún, Bernardo de (1499?–1590): This Franciscan priest taught young Aztec nobles at the Colegio de Santa Cruz de Tlatelolco in Mexico City and collected information for his *General History of the Things of New Spain,* a monumental work about Aztec history, religion, and culture.

Schele, Linda (1942–1998): Trained as an artist, in 1973 Schele played a pivotal role in the first translation of Maya hieroglyphs. She then became one of the preeminent scholars of ancient Maya culture, helping to totally revise the old conception of them as peaceful astronomers into a picture of them as builders of large, complicated warrior states. With the help of many collaborators, she wrote dozens of books and articles that elucidated the history of the major Maya cities.

Seler, Eduard (1849–1922): A brilliant German Mesoamericanist, Seler spoke many Indian languages and was one of the great experts on pre-Hispanic codices. He helped show that the Maya and central Mexican pre-Columbian states were part of one great Mesoamerican culture.

Stephens, John Lloyd (1805–1852) and **Frederick Catherwood** (1799-1854): Respectively, an American lawyer and an English architect and artist, Stephens and Catherwood in 1839 embarked on the first of two remarkable journeys to explore all the major ruins in Mexico and Central America that they could find. Fighting mosquitoes, ticks and tropical ailments, they visited and carefully described Copán, Quiriguá, Palenque, Chichén Itzá, Uxmal, Kabah, Sayil, Edzná, Mayapan, and numerous smaller sites. Aided by a *camera lucida,* Catherwood drew what he saw—not, like so many of his predecessors, what he wanted to see. Scholars of their day theorized that the cities had been built by Atlanteans, Israelites, Carthaginians, and so on; Stephens and Catherwood believed that they were built by one indigenous culture whose descendants were the same Maya Indians they met living among the ruins. They published the results of

into the center of the last great Mesoamerican empire. Aztec armies conquered domains from the Veracruz coast to the Pacific, including the Valley of Oaxaca; the only group they failed to defeat were the fierce Tarascans who controlled Michoacan. Tenochtitlan, the Aztec capital, grew into a city of at least a quarter million—one of the largest in the world. Its Great Temple was the navel of their Universe, the axis between the upper and lower realms and the start of the four cardinal directions.

A **stela** (the plural form is stelae) is an upright stone slab carved with a historical or mythological scene.

In 1521, the Aztec empire came to an end, and with it, Mesoamerica. Hernán Cortés's conquest of Tenochtitlan was more destructive than the Aztec's worst prophecies. The Spaniards brought with them European diseases to which the Mexicans had no immunity. Millions died of infectious diseases, and in the decades that followed, Spanish priests tried to erase all vestiges of Mesoamerican religions and forcibly converted the native peoples. It is only since the late 18th century that the New World's European inhabitants realized what

their expeditions in two books, *Incidents of Travel in Central America, Chiapas, and Yucatan* and *Incidents of Travel in Yucatan,* whose great scholarly value and fresh prose style keep them in print today.

Stirling, Matthew (1896–1975): An indefatigable explorer whose wanderlust took him to the Amazon and New Guinea, among many other parts of the world, Stirling was the long-time chief of the Bureau of American Ethnology, which studied indigenous cultures throughout the Americas. Stirling's greatest fascination was with the Olmecs of Mexico's Gulf Coast. Between 1939 and 1946, he explored and excavated at Tres Zapotes, Cerro de las Mesas, La Venta, and San Lorenzo, which he discovered. Among his discoveries are Stela C at Tres Zapotes, the stone tombs and jade offering at La Venta, and the massive colossal head, known as

Matthew Stirling with an Olmec head

Monument 1, from La Venta. Along with Miguel Covarrubias, he believed that the Olmec predated the Maya and indeed were Mesoamerica's "mother culture." Subsequent research, including carbon 14 dates, proved him correct, much to the embarrassment of prominent Mayanists.

Thompson, Sir Eric (1898–1975): From his post at the Carnegie Institution, Thompson dominated the field of Maya archaeology for most of the 20th century. He specialized in the study of Maya hieroglyphs and was the most vociferous proponent of the school propounding that Maya reliefs were purely mythological and/or astronomical in content and that the hieroglyphs had no phonetic component.

treasures they had destroyed. The long, slow process of reconstructing the world of ancient Mesoamerica has only just begun.

VISITING THE RUINS

Before You Go

The days of the great expeditions are over. You do not need to carry supplies of food and medicine and hack your way to the ruins using machetes. Almost all the sites in this guide (except Bonampak and Yaxchilan) are easily accessible by paved road and lie within a few hours, or minutes, from hotels, restaurants, and other services. You should still, however, make a few preparations before visiting the ruins.

What To Bring

Good shoes are a must. For most ruins, athletic shoes are enough; at sites, such as Cobá, where more walking and climbing are involved, I recommend lightweight

C. 1400, CODEX BOTURINI

hiking boots, especially if you have a tendency toward foot or ankle problems. As most sites lie within the "torrid zone," you should bring cool but sturdy cotton clothing. Wear long pants if you plan to explore ruins in the bug- and thorn-infested bush, but for the most part bush-whacking is not necessary at any of the sites.

The broiling tropical sun makes hats a must, preferably the wide-brimmed straw hats available in Mérida and many other cities. A hatless visit to an enormous site such as Teotihuacan can easily lead to a case of sunstroke. Sunblock should be copiously applied before entering the ruins. Most sites have shops selling ice-cold soda and water at the entrance (the days of roving soda vendors on the ruins are mostly over). At larger sites and at remote ruins such as Bonampak, you should consider bringing a canteen or water bottle in one of those over-the-shoulder slings. You may also want to bring an inexpensive compass to help yourself get oriented and (let us hope not) find your way back to civilization.

In southern Mexico, many ruins lie among forests and lush jungles; these are beautiful but filled with mosquitoes, ticks, and other bugs. Although you should be careful applying it (it can cause rashes and eye irritation), I recommend any repellent containing large amounts of DEET—most other formulas are not effective against clouds of tropical mosquitoes. Malaria has been mostly eradicated but still lingers in the remote lowland jungles of Chiapas and parts of Veracruz.

Safety

Mexico's archaeological sites are generally safe. You should, however, take a few basic precautions such as locking valuables in the car trunk while you are visiting the ruins. While in the site itself, you can best protect your safety by watching your footing and not climbing where climbing is forbidden. Snakes are common in much of rural Mexico but rarely encountered on daytime jaunts through the ruins. Stay off pyramids and other exposed ruins during thunderstorms (an archaeologist was killed by lightning while climbing Chichén Itzá's Castillo).

When to Go

Mexico has a two-season climate, with a winter dry season and a summer rainy season. Regionally, there are many variations on this model. It hardly rains at all in parts of the North, while in the Soconusco along the Chiapas coast, the "dry" season lasts only from January to March. Generally, December through

May is dry, with the latter months being quite arid and dusty. Winter "Nortes" are days-long storms that bring clouds, wind, and cool drizzle to even the tropical jungles. Hurricanes are possible along both the east and west coasts from July through November. In 1988, Hurricane Gilbert slightly damaged many of Yucatan's archaeological sites.

Most visitors tour the ruins during the winter. The summer rainy season, however, should not be forgotten as a good time to visit Mexico. The rains generally fall as afternoon thunderstorms; the air is clearer (better for photography) and the vegetation is a deep green and covered with flowers. The only difficulty in summer is that rains make some rural roads impassable in places such as Chiapas and the Yucatan Peninsula.

Traveling to the Sites

Some of the sites in this book are easily accessible by public transportation. Most of the ruins in the Mexico City area are best reached by subway, bus, or taxi. In heavily touristed areas such as Yucatan and Oaxaca, many travel agencies offer one- or two-day tours of archaeological sites. For the most mobility, however, a rented car is by far the easiest way—in some cases the only way—to reach the ruins. In places such as Yucatan and Chiapas, a car such as a Jeep (or even Volkswagen Beetle) with a rugged suspension is highly recommended. The only other option to a car is taking slow, overcrowded rural buses and then perhaps hiking a few kilometers. As driving in a foreign country brings its own set of concerns, it is recommended that the traveler be well-rehearsed in the vagaries of driving in Mexico and at minimum sure to acquire Mexican auto insurance as foreign insurance is not valid within the country.

Guides and Vendors

Until the last few years, visitors to the major archaeological sites were constantly approached by roving "antiquities" (almost always fake) vendors and self-proclaimed guides peddling dubious theories about the ancient peoples. Many of these were impoverished residents of nearby towns for whom this was the best source of income. The Mexican government now has largely banished them from the ruins and built artisans' markets where they can sell their wares to tourists. Officially authorized guides

INAH: OVERSEEING THE SITES

The Instituto Nacional de Antropología y Historia main office in Mexico City should be able to answer questions regarding site information and video and photo permissions as well as guide you to its regional offices. It also has a good bookstore with many choice books on archaeology and anthropology.

INAH
Cordoba 45
Colonia Roma, Mexico DF
tel. 5/533-2263

Aztec relief carving

DANIELLE GUSTAFSON

THE POLITICS OF ARCHITECTURAL RESTORATION

When you tour an archaeological site, are the buildings that you are admiring really the same ones that the ancient peoples saw? On the surface, no. Almost all important Mesoamerican ceremonial structures were coated with plaster and painted with bold colors, mainly red and blue. They were also adorned with brightly hued murals and elaborate stucco decorations. What you see now is like Times Square without the lights: a dim reflection of its real self.

A deeper question is: are the structures themselves the same as the originals? The answer would have to be no. No perfectly preserved Mesoamerican structures have ever been found (the closest is a beautiful small temple found at Copán in Honduras). The buildings at every archaeological site in Mexico are either in ruins or are partial or complete restorations based on theories of how they originally looked. These theories have changed over the years and so have the methods of reconstruction. Mexico's great temples and pyramids are to a larger or smaller extent works of the imagination. Unfortunately, a visitor does not always know how much is fantasy and how much is original.

Archaeologists only began restoring Mesoamerican monuments a little more than a century ago. During the second half of the 19th century, as the study of ancient Mexico became more organized and more scientific, researchers realized that the ruins were rapidly being destroyed by pothunters, excavations, urban development, and locals seeking building material. A movement began to conserve the ancient sites. One of the first to put this into practice was Alfred Maudslay, who in 1888 cleared and repaired part of the Great Ballcourt at Chichén Itzá at the same time that he studied it.

Two occasionally conflicting traditions of archaeological restoration soon appeared. Beginning in 1894, a team from Harvard University's Peabody Museum began work on the famous hieroglyphic staircase at Copán in Honduras. After clearing the steps, they carefully studied the stones and surrounding structures and then planned their restoration on paper before beginning work. This work was one part of a much larger scientific excavation project that spent decades at Copán.

The second tradition contains aspects of archaeological science but is also closely related to politics and tourism. Between 1905 and 1910, the controversial Leopoldo Batres excavated and restored the Pyramid of the Sun and nearby structures at Teotihuacan. This was a special project approved by the dictatorial president of Mexico himself, Porfirio Díaz. A self-trained archaeologist, Batres did not emphasize the connection between the careful study of the ruins and restoration. He cleared the entire south face of the Pyramid of the Sun, misread the archaeological evidence and decided that the pyramid had a fifth level on top when it did not. This flight of the imagination—one of a number he engraved on the pyramid—is now accepted as fact by most visitors to Teotihuacan. (It should be noted, however, that some archaeologists believe that the pyramid did indeed have five levels, the same as the Pyramid of the Moon.)

When Batres was done, Díaz visited the site and had himself photographed in front of the pyramids. This began what some call the official "archaeology of pyramids." Mexican presidents wanted archaeologists to find pyramids so they could be shown standing in front of these massive monuments, tapping into their ancient glory. If the archaeologists could not find the pyramids, they were encouraged to build them out of concrete.

In the 1920s, a number of powerful Mexican businessmen began promoting foreign tourism. They realized that the country's colonial and pre-Columbian monuments were a major draw and pressured the government to restore the ancient cities. Work began at a number of sites in central Mexico, Oaxaca, and Yucatan, including Teotihuacan, Tenayuca, Cuicuilco, and Mitla. Two projects at Chichén Itzá are a good example of the conflicting methods of restoration. In the early 1920s, the Carnegie Institution performed an exemplary reconstruction of the Temple of the Warriors as part of a scientific study of that part of the site.

A few years later, a totally nonscientific team decided to completely rebuild the famous Castillo. The base that you see today is largely a fantasy in concrete; there is no proof for the designs on the side of the tiers, and the famous Kukulcan shadow is probably a product of the reconstruction. One of the goals was to make the building as open as possible to tourists, which unfortunately made it easier for them to damage the sculptures. The leaders of this project had no idea that an earlier temple could be hidden inside the base; 10 years later, archaeologists had to break through the concrete to find it. A number of voices within the Mexican archaeological establishment, such as Manuel Gamio, were beginning to say that all restorations should be part of larger scientific studies and should clearly mark the difference between the original work and modern additions. Unfortunately, these criticisms were lost in the rush to open the sites to tourism.

During the next four decades, numerous important sites were damaged by overenthusiastic restorations. At Tula, Pyramid B's main staircase and placement of the warrior columns are based on guesswork; the columns in the Burnt Palace replace originals of which archaeologists found no traces. The Pyramid of the Magician at Uxmal was encased around the base in a stone sheath for which there is no earlier evidence. The west face of Cholula's main pyramid is a fantasy in concrete for presidential photo opportunities. At Teotihuacan, the work since Leopoldo Batres has unfortunately not been exemplary. The Palace of the Quetzal Butterfly is based on largely hypothetical reconstructions, and the buildings around the Plaza of the Moon have been turned into a sterile stage set. Perhaps the most artificial of all is the tiny Aztec site of Santa Cecilia, where restorers turned a literal mound of rubble into a perfect little (wholly imaginary) temple.

The tide began to turn against this tradition of aggressive reconstruction in the late 1960s. After intense debate, the new goal became "consolidation": to protect the structure from further collapse and to restore it using the original stones with as little as possible architectural fantasy. The reconstruction also had to be accompanied with a careful archaeological and art-historical study of the ruins.

A good example of these new methods is Cacaxtla, where the murals and structures have been carefully protected but no hypothetical reconstructions have been attempted. Different colored stones or plaster show the difference between the original work and the restoration. The public is guided along paths that allow visitors to view the ruins without clambering all over and destroying the structures. Another example is the Great Temple in Mexico City, where archaeologists have luckily not succumbed to the temptation to rebuild the original edifice (the city already has a theme park). It may be confusing to look at, but at least you know that it is not a fabrication.

now offer their services to visitors at sites such as the Great Temple and Chichén Itzá. Their information is more grounded in reality than the amateurs' but may contain a few factual errors. Visitors to the caves at Loltun and Balankanché must be accompanied by a guide or will not be allowed entry.

Regulations

Mexico's archaeological sites are administered by the Instituto Nacional de Antropología y Historia (INAH), which is an agency of the federal government. It sets the hours and entrance fees and regulates the use of cameras. Hand-held cameras are permissible everywhere; in some areas, you may not use a flash because of potential damage to ancient artwork. INAH heavily regulates the use of tripods and video cameras; you have to pay extra at the entrance or in some cases receive special permission for their use at a regional INAH office. Off-site most locals don't mind if you wish to include them in a photo as long as you ask their permission first. The exception is in the Indian towns of highland Chiapas, where local beliefs preclude picture-taking. Most ruins are open 0800–1700; some sites stop letting visitors enter an hour before closing. Smaller sites are often closed on Monday.

Mexican federal law prohibits the removal of any type of archaeological artifact from ancient ruins. And the penalties are severe if you are caught trying to carry them out of the country.

VALLEY OF MEXICO

Santa Cecilia Acatitlán: pyramid with temple on top

The Valley of Mexico lies at the center of the Mexican landmass, encompassing the Federal District, the eastern half of the State of Mexico and part of southern Hidalgo. Now home to Mexico City—the most populous city in the world—the valley saw the rise of three of the most influential cultures of Mesoamerica, the Teotihuacanos, the Toltecs, and the Aztecs. Their development was aided by a number of the region's unique geographical features: its strategic position in the center of Mexico, the natural defenses provided by a ring of mountains, and the fertile environment found around a system of lakes that used to exist on the valley floor.

Over the centuries, roughly 500 B.C.–A.D. 1521, the Valley of Mexico was an important meeting point for the "barbarians" from the northern deserts and the more advanced cultures to the south. The origin myths of many of the valley's cultures are strikingly similar: after years of wandering, a group of nomadic hunter-gatherers from the northern deserts arrives in the valley; the wanderers intermarry with the sedentary agriculturists they find there; and from that mix comes a new, vibrant, and aggressive culture that quickly flourishes. The valley's inhabitants were also determined traders, penetrating as far south as Guatemala and north to the southwest of the United States. From cultures such as the Olmecs, Zapotecs, and Maya, they brought back advanced writing and calendrical systems and new forms of religious belief adopted as their own.

Without exception, each of the valley's most important cultures came to its end violently, whether by nature or at the hands of fellow humans. Cuicuilco was buried under a lava flow; Teotihuacan and Tula were burned and looted; and Tenochtitlan was razed by the Spanish. This history has not been forgotten by the Valley of Mexico's current residents; the 1985 earthquake and the recent rumblings from the Popocatépetl volcano were both reminders of the precariousness of life in this region.

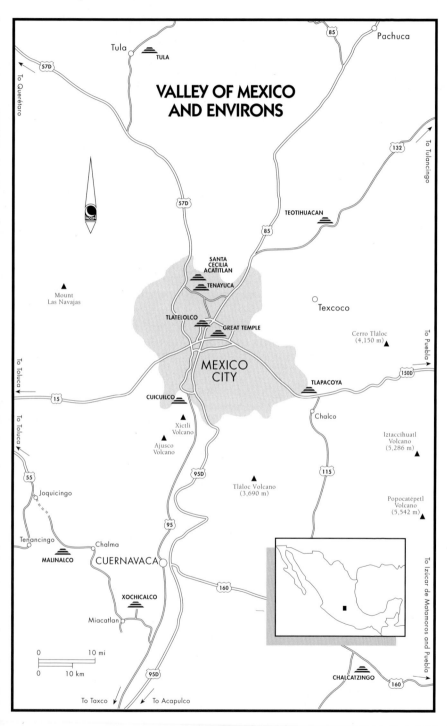

VALLEY OF MEXICO AND ENVIRONS

Tula

TULA

Pachuca

To Querétaro

57D

85

132

To Tulancingo

57D

85

TEOTIHUACAN

Mount Las Navajas

SANTA CECILIA ACATITLAN

TENAYUCA

Texcoco

TLATELOLCO

GREAT TEMPLE

Cerro Tláloc (4,150 m)

To Puebla

150D

MEXICO CITY

To Toluca

15

CUICUILCO

TLAPACOYA

Xictli Volcano

Chalco

Iztaccíhuatl Volcano (5,286 m)

Ajusco Volcano

To Toluca

55

95D

Tláloc Volcano (3,690 m)

115

Popocatépetl Volcano (5,542 m)

Joquicingo

95

Tenancingo

Chalma

MALINALCO

CUERNAVACA

160

To Izúcar de Matamoros and Puebla

XOCHICALCO

Miacatlan

0   10 mi

0   10 km

95D

CHALCATZINGO

160

To Taxco

To Acapulco

LODGING AND FOOD
IN THE VALLEY OF MEXICO

The Valley of Mexico contains Mexico City and more than 20 million inhabitants. As the capital of a highly centralized country, Mexico City is the terminus for all major air, train, bus, and auto routes. Visitors have the choice of hundreds of hotels, varying from cheap guesthouses to ultramodern high-rises.

Archaeological tourists may find that the most appropriate place to stay is near the Zócalo downtown; the center of modern Mexico, this also lay at the heart of ancient Tenochtitlan (you find the Great Temple a few steps to the north). A good budget choice is the **Hotel Catedral,** which stands behind the cathedral at Donceles 95, tel. 05/518-5232. The more expensive **Hotel Majestic** directly overlooks the Zócalo at Madero 73, tel.

05/521-8600. A few doors south at 16 de Septiembre 82, the **Howard Johnson Gran Hotel** contains a beautiful, early 20th-century vaulted lobby, tel. 05/521-0202.

The Zócalo area is also home to a number of restaurants serving classic Mexican dishes with occasional pre-Hispanic touches. At Belisario Domínguez 72, the **Hostería de Santo Domingo,** tel. 05/510-1434, bills itself as Mexico City's oldest restaurant; in season, it serves maguey worms and other Aztec specialties. The excellent **Café de Tacuba** at Tacuba 28, tel. 05/512-8482, serves regional specialties and excellent hot chocolate; the back wall is adorned with a mural illustrating the history of chocolate from pre-Columbian times to the modern era.

A visitor to the Valley of Mexico will find that most traces of the spectacular pre-Columbian cities have been obliterated. After the Spanish Conquest in 1521, almost all Aztec structures were razed. Pyramid stones were used to build churches and palaces; Aztec idols were either destroyed or, if too large, buried; the shallow lakes were drained, forever altering the area's ecology. During the 20th century, Mexico City's rapid industrialization and explosive growth literally paved over many ancient sites. At first glance, modern Mexico has not only destroyed the pre-Hispanic past but the colonial one as well.

However, it is one of Mexico City's special qualities that no matter how much the past is erased, it still lives on, sometimes in surprising ways: you turn a corner and you are face to face with a carved Aztec stone set into the facade of an 18th-century palace. Workers repairing an electrical line discover the spectacular Coyolxauhqui stone that marked the hub of the Aztec Universe.

With a little imagination—and the help of some excellent museums—you can still recreate the pre-Hispanic world in the Valley of Mexico.

THE LAND

The Valley of Mexico lies at the southern confluence of Mexico's two great mountain ranges, the Sierra Madre Oriental and Occidental. These ranges end at a high, mountainous plateau called the Mesa Central, which is also the heart of a volcanic belt running from the state of Colima on the Pacific Coast to Ver-

THE ANTHROPOLOGY MUSEUM

Every visitor to Mexico City must tour the **Museo Nacional de Antropología,** one of the world's greatest museums, situated in enormous Chapultepec Park a few steps north of the boulevard of Paseo de la Reforma. Open daily except Monday 0900–1900, this dramatic structure contains most of the greatest artifacts collected from Mexico's archaeological sites. The exhibits, which are divided by region, include Pakal's tomb from Palenque, numerous Maya stelae, Olmec colossal heads, the Aztec Sun Stone, and on and on. Many of the labels are out-of-date; nevertheless, they cannot hide the brilliance of the artworks. Allow at least a day to make your way through the bounty of exhibits. Entrance fee is 38 pesos. Both the metro and the bus make frequent stops.

acruz on the Gulf. Known as the Transverse Volcanic Axis, this is a zone of earthquake-producing faults and snow-capped volcanoes flanking a series of broad valleys. The largest and most important of these is the Valley of Mexico, covering 7,000 square kilometers at the center of the Mesa Central.

Geologists believe that the Valley of Mexico's origins lie under the sea. During the Cretaceous Era (the climax of the dinosaurs 140 to 65 million years ago), this region was the floor of a shallow tropical sea between the North American continent and the Caribbean landmass. In the millennia that followed, seven phases of volcanic activity raised the valley floor to its present height of 2,240 meters. These forces also produced today's geological features, including the minor sierras that divide the valley into smaller units and the two large sierras to the east and west. The last major phase was the Pleistocene (1.8 million to 10,000 years ago), when a lava flow from a particularly violent volcanic eruption slid across the valley's outlet southeast of Mexico City.

Because of this blockage, the Valley of Mexico has no natural outlet. Technically, it is not a valley at all but a closed hydrographical system, commonly called a basin. When lava closed the valley, runoff from springs, snowmelt, and rain began to accumulate in a network of lakes and marshes along the valley floor. At the time of the Conquest (1521), these covered upward of 1,000 square kilometers. Without this lush lakeshore environment—abundant flora and fauna and rich soil for farming—the valley never could have supported the dense pre-Columbian populations.

Although the valley's geological features are largely unchanged since the Aztec era, its physical appearance is drastically different. The extensive forests have disappeared, and what is left of the lakes are a few swampy puddles.

Perhaps the least changed region is the pine-covered sierra. Three mountain ranges, the Sierra de Nevada, Sierra de Las Cruces, and the Sierra de Ajusco, guard the valley to the east, west, and south respectively. Too cold for crops, their higher altitudes were visited mainly by pre-Columbian travelers, hunters, and priests on ritual business. The three volcanoes that border the valley to the southeast were objects of awe and reverence to the Aztecs. Mount Tlaloc, the shortest of the three (3,690 meters) and named after the Rain God, was the site of annual ceremonies to bring the rain for the corn crop. Iztaccíhuatl (White Woman, 5,286 meters) and Popocatépetl (Smoking Mountain, 5,542 meters), the second- and third-highest mountains in Mexico, are both embodiments of figures in Aztec myths. Today there are some small towns along the highways crossing the lower passes of the sierras, but most of this region is still too cold and too high for intensive habitation.

From the sierras, the slopes drop into the Valley of Mexico. During pre-Conquest times, much of this was covered with oak and pine forests (soon chopped down by the Spaniards) rich in white-tailed deer and rabbit. Four smaller ranges of hills extend from the sierras into the valley, dividing it into smaller valleys, such as the one containing Teotihuacan. The conical shapes of many of these hills—the Cerro de Chimalhuacan, for example—indicate that they were formed by volcanic action. The last major eruption within the valley was the Xictli Volcano (west of Ciudad Universitaria) that destroyed Cuicuilco in A.D. 100.

At the bottom of the Valley of Mexico lie the remnants of the original lake system, now largely covered by the streets and slums of Mexico City. Before the Conquest, these lakes were fed by rain, springs, and snowmelt from the volcanoes. The system's southernmost lakes, Chalco and Xochimilco, were closest to the water sources; their water was the freshest and their ecosystems the richest. From here, the water flowed into Lake Texcoco, occupying the center of the valley and, at 2,235 meters, its low point. Lake Texcoco lost water only through evaporation; consequently, it had the highest salt and chemical content of the lakes, and only microscopic shrimp and algae grew in its waters. No vegetation could grow around its shores, but the saltworks here supplied much of central Mexico. (You can still see swampy remnants of Lake Texcoco to the northeast of Mexico City's airport.) The northernmost parts of the system were the slightly briny Lakes Zumpanco and Xaltocan, which were shallow, marshy, and slowly drying out even during Aztec times.

After a series of devastating floods, in the mid-17th century the colonial government began a massive excavation project to drain the valley's lakes through the Grand Canal heading to the north. This has protected Mexico City from floods but caused numerous deleterious side effects, including the slow collapse of many colonial buildings and the gradual diminution of the water supply. The drainage was completed in 1900.

Climate

Ten thousand years ago, the Valley of Mexico was a very different place. The temperature was on average six degrees warmer and twice the amount of rain fell as today. Lush forests ringed the valley, attracting herds of mammoths and, in their wake, early hunters. In the succeeding millennia, the valley became progressively drier because of climatic changes as the Ice Age receded. The draining of the lakes and the destruction of the pine and oak forests since the Conquest have speeded up this process of dessication.

Despite these changes, many of the other weather patterns remain the same. There has always been a cool dry season from October to April and a warmer rainy season during the summer. These annual cycles were of crucial importance to the pre-Columbian cultures, because their well-being was dependent on the success of their staple crop, maize (corn). Two crops a year would have meant prosperity and plenty, but wintertime frosts frequently killed the plants. The summer rains normally fall between June and mid-September with torrential, highly localized afternoon downpours that still flood Mexico City's streets. Some years the rains are weeks or even months late; summer droughts devastated the pre-Columbian maize harvest. When droughts and frosts occurred during the same year, such as happened between A.D. 1450–54, thousands died of famine and whole societies trembled.

The Valley of Mexico is large enough to have significant climatic differences within its confines. The rainiest region is the southwest, where the lush gardens of the towns of Coyoacan and Xochimilco to the east are always green. Far less rain falls in the northeast. Teotihuacan was almost totally dependent on springs for its water supply; the lack of flowing water had a severe effect on the city's sanitation and disease was rampant. Today, cacti and maguey are the only plants that thrive in the surrounding hills.

Flora and Fauna

Faced with the smog, the cinderblock slums, and the gleaming towers of modern Mexico City, it takes a determined act of the imagination to conjure the Valley of Mexico's biota (its ecosystem of plant and animal life) at the time of the Conquest.

The now dried-up lakes once teemed with life. They were an important winter resting spot for migratory waterfowl, and the ducks, coots, and other birds played a large role in the pre-Columbian diet. From the lakes, they also harvested small fish, frogs, salamanders, crayfish, tiny shrimp, insects, and spirulina, a nutritional algae that was dried and sold in cakes. When the Aztecs were just another semibarbaric tribe attempting to gain a foothold in the valley, they were forced to live in a swampy area infested with snakes. Always ingenious, they prepared the snakes "roasted and stewed in a thousand manners and tastes" and confounded the ruling tribe by thriving on this diet.

The shores of the salt lakes were barren. To the south, the shallows of the freshwater lakes Chalco and Xochimilco were devoted to intensive farming using the *chinampa* system. *Chinampas* are tiny blocks of arable land constructed in shallow lakes on a base of brush and vegetation and covered with mud. You can still see them along the canals of the town of Xochimilco. Highly fertile, the *chinampas* were the breadbaskets of the Valley of Mexico. Among the crops grown here and in the nearby terraced fields were the principal staple, maize, as well as beans, *chía* (used for its tiny seed), amaranth, chile, squash, tomatillos, chayote, jicama, avocado, and many types of green herbs. The pre-Columbian inhabitants also harvested wild rice and reeds from the swampy areas. In the drier areas away from the lakes, maguey—a plant with a thousand uses as food, drink, textile, and even building material—and the nopal cactus were important crops.

The lands that ascended from the lakeshores were covered with oak and grassy open areas to the south and scrub oak and maguey in the drier north. Farther up the hillsides, the oak forest closed in. The woods were filled with deer, rabbit, squirrel, antelope, gopher, peccary, and quail, all of which the omnivorous Aztecs used to supplement their animal diet of domesticated turkey, Muscovy duck, and edible dog (a special kind of fat hairless canine that was fed a vegetarian diet). They also collected many wild vegetables and edible weeds. As the hills rose to the sierras, pine supplanted oak, covering the slopes up to the 4,000-meter (12,000-foot) timberline. Above was grass, rock, and the snow of the volcanic summits.

HISTORY

Man came early to the Valley of Mexico. The warmer and wetter climate of the Late Pleistocene era (50,000–10,000 years ago) produced lush vegetation on the hillsides and fed lakes that were far larger than their extent at the Conquest. The valley teemed with now-extinct mammals, including mammoths, camels, early horses, and giant bison and sloths, and early hunters followed in their wake.

Evidence of the valley's earliest inhabitants is fragmentary at best. Researchers have found the remains of a crude flint workshop tentatively dated 21,000 to 24,000 years ago in the town of Tlapacoya, just north of Chalco off the Mexico-Puebla Highway 150. More compelling pieces of evidence have been found along the shores of the now-disappeared lakes to the north. In 1870, a Mexican naturalist discovered a fossilized camelid sacrum (part of the pelvis) carved in the shape of an animal head, possibly a dog, in Tequixquiac due north of the city. This remarkable piece was not excavated under the most rigorous conditions, but scientists believe it may date to around 9000–7000 B.C.

The eastern shores of Lake Texcoco, particularly around Tepexpan (just before Acolman on the Teotihuacan road, Highway 132D), are the site of more recent and exciting discoveries. In 1949, Mexican researchers discovered the fossilized remains of a woman who appeared to have been buried during the same era as nearby extinct mammal bones (9000–7000 B.C.). She was interred in a flexed position, leading some to say that she dated from the far later Archaic era, but recent tests point to the original hypothesis.

Three years later, workers digging a drainage ditch a few kilometers to the south stumbled on the bones of a mammoth that had obviously been killed at the spot. Scientists believe that the early hunters drove the mammoth into the soft mud of the lake, where they killed and butchered it on site. Six tools, including a stone point and a knife, scraper, and blade, all of obsidian, were found among the bones, as if they had been dropped in the mud and lost. The remains of other slaughtered mammoths and more tools lost in the butchering process have been found in the area. Based on the radiocarbon dates of a fireplace found at the side of one, researchers assign a date of around 7710 B.C. to the mammoth kills.

Between the early hunters and the first settlements of the Preclassic era, there is a gap in the Valley of Mexico's archaeological record. Humans undoubtedly occupied the area during the Archaic era, but the evidence is rapidly being destroyed by urbanization. If the patterns of the nearby Tehuacan Valley hold true, the

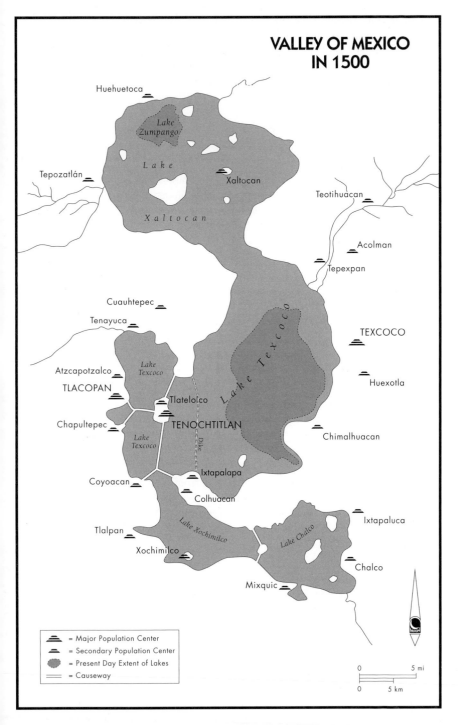

VALLEY OF MEXICO IN 1500

Huehuetoca

Lake Zumpango

Lake

Tepozatlán

Xaltocan

Xaltocan

Teotihuacan

Acolman

Tepexpan

Cuauhtepec

Tenayuca

TEXCOCO

Atzcapotzalco

Lake Texcoco

Lake Texcoco

TLACOPAN

Tlatelolco

Huexotla

Chapultepec

TENOCHTITLAN

Lake Texcoco

Dike

Chimalhuacan

Coyoacan

Ixtapalapa

Colhuacan

Ixtapaluca

Tlalpan

Lake Xochimilco

Lake Chalco

Xochimilco

Chalco

Mixquic

= Major Population Center
= Secondary Population Center
= Present Day Extent of Lakes
= Causeway

0   5 mi

0   5 km

Valley of Mexico's Archaic residents were hunter-gatherers who moved between established dry and rainy season camps. One of the first permanent settlements was found at Tlapacoya, the same site as the above-mentioned Pleistocene flint workshop, where archaeologists have excavated remains of a small village with circular huts dated around 2300 B.C.

By 1500–1200 B.C., there were well over a dozen communities in the valley. Most were hamlets, but some were villages with a few hundred inhabitants. The largest was Tlatilco, first settled around 1300 B.C. on the western shores of Lake Texcoco. Now buried under factories about 10 blocks northwest of Mexico City's Buenavista railway station, Tlatilco was rediscovered in 1936 by brickworkers digging for clay. Here they found more than 340 burials accompanied with elaborate offerings, including figurines that were obviously based on Tlatilcan daily life–children, couples, dancers, acrobats, and ball players. Some of the offerings showed distinct signs of Olmec influence, the first evidence of the intense cross-fertilization between the cultures of the valley and beyond.

The **radiocarbon dating system** is a method for dating objects of organic material such as wood or bone. The presence and quantity of carbon 14 atoms is measurable and known to decay at a set rate. The longer an organism has been dead, the greater likelihood less carbon 14 will be present.

Tlatilco faded within a few hundred years, but during the Middle Preclassic (1200–400 B.C.) the valley's population continued to grow. Much of the expansion was concentrated along the southwestern shores of the lakes. Here villages became small towns, a few with a population reaching 1,000 inhabitants. To the northeast, in places such as the Teotihuacan Valley, the settlements remained impoverished hamlets. The main artifacts found from this era are ceramics, mainly simple vessels and small figurines representing a woman, perhaps a deity. Despite this growth, there is little evidence of social stratification or an advanced civic or religious life. The Valley of Mexico still lagged behind the Olmec area and the Zapotecs of Oaxaca.

CUICUILCO

INTRODUCTION

The home of the Valley of Mexico's first great culture is not the first place one would look for archaeological remains. The Pedregal (Rocky Plain) is a vast sweep of volcanic flow that covers the southwestern corner of the valley. Until the 20th century, the Pedregal was an arid, scrub-covered wasteland occupied only by snakes, scorpions, criminals, and escapees from political repression hiding out in its lava caves. In the 1920s, quarries began

CUICUILCO

How to get there: The ruins lie at the south end of busy Av. Insurgentes Sur just beyond the Periférico (a few kilometers south of Ciudad Universitaria). Without a car, the best way to reach them is to take the Metro to the Universidad stop and from there take a taxi or minibus marked "Cuicuilco."

Hours: Tues.–Sun. 0900–1700.

Admission fee: Free.

How long to tour: Two hours. If you want to see the lesser ruins of Cuicuilco B (only for diehards) in the Villa Olimpica across Insurgentes Sur, add another 45 minutes.

Recommended gear: Hats. Rain gear during rainy season.

Museum: The exhibition is compact but interesting, with photographs of the Fire God figures and numerous artifacts found in burials. These include skeletons with deformed skulls and dental mutilation, ornate jewelry such as nose plugs, figurines with bulging legs, and black and red ceramic pots. These burials show evidence of trade ties with other regions of Mexico, such as shells from the Pacific and jade from the Olmec region along the Gulf of Mexico.

to mine this vast store of lava to provide building material for modern Mexico City. Buried beneath the stone, they discovered a series of ancient, primitive settlements that appeared to predate the rest of the valley by many thousands of years. By far the most impressive of these—the others included Copilco and Zacatenco—was Cuicuilco, which was dominated by a massive, circular pyramid.

Today, Cuicuilco sits half-forgotten amid the apartment buildings and highways of one of Mexico City's southern suburbs. Two millennia ago, its Great Pyramid was one of the largest structures in central Mexico, and, with more than 40,000 inhabitants, it had the highest population of any settlement in the valley up to that time. Most of the ceramics found here were small and relatively crude—not so different from Tlatilco-style figurines. Nevertheless, the site is worth visiting to wonder at the mysterious altars and to ponder the fate of a culture that came to such an abrupt and violent end, covered by lava spewed from the nearby Xitli Volcano eight kilometers to the southwest.

H I S T O R Y

The main difficulty in providing an accurate chronology and description of Cuicuilco has always been the cap of lava that covers the site. Since the Great Pyramid was uncovered in the early 1920s, very little excavation has been done aside from a few exploratory trenches. Nevertheless, the information from those trenches combined with a comparison of neighboring sites has produced a relatively in-depth historical outline of Cuicuilco.

The site was first settled between 2100 and 1800 B.C.; its inhabitants, probably farmers, produced simple clay pots and figurines, among the earliest found in the Valley of Mexico. After this, there is a gap in the archaeological record until about 1000 B.C., when the Cuicuilcans built simple oval temple platforms, including the base of the Great Pyramid, and had trade contacts with Chalcatzingo over the mountains to the south. For the next millennium, it was the largest settlement in the Valley of Mexico, growing from 5,000 to perhaps as many as 40,000.

By 800–600 B.C., Cuicuilco was a regional center with clear links to a number of satellite villages. The temple-platforms became round, and the Great Pyramid was given a stepped construction. For the next 400 years, Cuicuilco dominated the valley; its ceramic styles spread through the region. The final cap was added to the Great Pyramid, and Superimposed Altars in its center were raised to their current height.

After 200 B.C., activity in Cuicuilco began to decline. A new city to the north—Teotihuacan—was growing rapidly, and perhaps it took over Cuicuilco's trade routes. This was also the era of increased seismic activity in the valley, and some researchers believe that either an earthquake or a volcanic eruption precipitated the city's slow collapse. Incense burners in the form of a fire god dating from this era hint at a preoccupation with conflagrations and perhaps volcanoes.

Cuicuilco A—the region around the Great Pyramid—was abandoned first, followed by Cuicuilco B by about A.D. 150. People still visited the site—a Teotihuacano-style offering cache dating to A.D. 150–200 was found near the Great Pyramid—but the population was drastically reduced. Around A.D. 400, the Xitli Volcano eight kilometers to the southwest erupted, sending a huge flow of lava downhill toward the lakes and numerous settlements, including Cuicuilco. The site's residents may have tried to protect the Great Pyramid from impending destruction. At the pyramid's base, archaeologists found rows of stone slabs possibly placed to block the flow. The attempt was unsuccessful; molten lava covered Cuicuilco, leaving only the tops of a few temples exposed and erasing almost all trace of the city from the valley's history.

ARCHAEOLOGICAL RECORD

In the late 19th century, Mexico City's antiquarian community became excited by news of burials and prehistoric artifacts discovered beneath the Pedregal in the southwestern zone of the Valley of Mexico. They believed the Xitli lava flow to be ancient, perhaps many thousands of years B.C., and thus any sites buried below would be by far the oldest in Mexico. Because of the difficulties of penetrating the lava cap—in places 7.5 meters thick—the first excavations of the Pedregal area did not take place until 1917. That year Manuel Gamio (who succeeded Leopoldo Batres as director of all Mexico government archaeological projects) discovered house foundations, fire pits, and a five-meter-deep refuse pit at the bottom of a lava quarry in nearby Copilco.

In his explorations of the Pedregal, Gamio had noticed a circular hill called San Cuicuilco rising out of the lava nearby. He became convinced that the hill was an artificial construction and in 1922 invited Byron Cummings, a University of Arizona expert on Southwestern American archaeology, to dig the site.

Between 1922 and 1925, Cummings spent 22 months at Cuicuilco uncovering the Great Pyramid and clearing the lava away from the base. To achieve this task, he used explosives to blast his way through the many feet of volcanic rock. He has since come under attack for these efficient but crude methods—dynamite is the great taboo of modern archaeology. The vast majority of the Cuicuilco discoveries date to the Cummings excavations. He wrote up his finds in *National Geographic,* positing that the site dated to 5000 B.C., far before the pyramids of Ancient Egypt.

The excavations since Cummings have been few, minor, and mostly unpublished. In 1939, Eduardo Noguera, who did publish his results, discovered 12 bodies buried along the base of the Great Pyramid. He also rebuilt the altars in the top, unfortunately not following Cummings' photos from the original excavation. The altars had a staggered top, not flat as you see today.

In 1940, George Vaillant made a comparative study of artifacts found in Cuicuilco and other central Mexico sites. The parallels between the areas could not be coincidental. Vaillant stated, and it has since been accepted, that Cuicuilco dates from the Preclassic era and not from the early Archaic. This was confirmed in 1957 excavations by Robert Heizer and J. A. Bennyhoff in which they laid out a firm ceramic sequence and conducted some of the first radiocarbon dating.

The last major excavations at Cuicuilco occurred during the construction of the Villa Olimpica for the 1968 Olympics just west across Av. Insurgentes Sur. When they cleared away the lava, they found the remains of a number of small temples as well as numerous house foundations and ballcourts. Unfortunately, much of this was destroyed to make way for the athletes' housing, now apartment complexes, and little of the research has been published.

Archaeologists believe that as little as 5 percent of Cuicuilco has been uncovered. Until the thick cap of lava is removed, many of the details of Cuicuilco's history and culture will remain mysteries.

TOURING THE SITE

You enter the site through a gate next to a small parking lot on the east side of Insurgentes Sur immediately south of the Periférico Sur highway. Mexico City's building boom has covered the Pedregal with superhighways and apartment buildings sprouting satellite dishes. It is rather disconcerting to see Cuicuilco's ancient pyramid surrounded by these emblems of modernity.

From the gate, it is about a half-kilometer walk over the 7.5-meter-thick lava field to the Great Pyramid. A nature trail meanders off the main path and takes you on a tour of the Pedregal's scrub fauna. The spiky maguey plants were one of the Central Highlands' most important crops, producing pulque (a beerlike beverage), textiles, and paper among dozens of other products.

The Great Pyramid rises in four tiers from a circular base 116 meters in diameter. The exterior

Cuicuilco: the Superimposed Altars on top of the Great Pyramid

walls are rough stone, while the interior is sand and rubble fill. The original base of the pyramid lies about six meters below your feet—the depth of the ancient lava flow here.

Facing you is the main ramp leading up the pyramid's west side. As you walk up it, you can see the different stages of the ramp's construction; the last stage was roughly one meter higher than what you see today. The pyramid and its ramps were expanded at least twice from the first construction around 800–600 B.C. On either side of the ramp, excavations cut through the lava to the original ground level 23 meters below the pyramid's summit.

The top of the Great Pyramid is now a grassy dome. Through this dome cuts a path dug by archaeologists leading to the structure's center. Here you find a roughly circular pit whose walls were originally plastered and painted red. From the center of the pit rise the Superimposed Altars, one of Cuicuilco's most unique features, now protected by a plastic roof.

The Superimposed Altars are an oval structure with three distinct levels. The earliest, now buried beneath the floor of the pit, was a flat surface made of clay. Next, a rock pedestal rises to another clay platform on which traces of red ochre were found. On top of this, another pedestal holds a very different platform, this time constructed of round river stones. Photos from Cummings's excavation show this top layer to be built on two levels, but the reconstruction gives it only one. This layer is also connected to the side of the pit, perhaps for support and easier access. The Superimposed Altars have an obvious ritual function, but how they were used researchers do not know.

Returning to the top of the pyramid, you will be rewarded with an excellent view of the site. On the east side look for another, smaller ramp heading down. About 36 meters to the east you will see the top of Structure E-1, a small, late temple platform dating to A.D. 150–250 and notable mostly for its staircase.

Retrace your steps and descend the western ramp. If you turn left at its base and walk along the path skirting the pyramid, you come to a wooden roof covering the Circular Chamber, another of Cuicuilco's unique altars. This is a series of rough stone slabs propped in an inward-leaning circle. The inside of the rocks is painted with faint red ochre pictographs that are little more than patterns of wavy and twisting lines. Researchers have seen crude animal heads in the paintings, but it takes a very good imagination. Again, a ritual use is evident, but the specific activity remains a mystery.

From here you can walk down a flight of steps to the bottom of the trench circling the pyramid. These are Byron Cummings's original excavations, and when you look up the wall of lava rising eight meters in places you can sympathize with his use of dynamite. Along the base of the lava, you can see caves and tunnels dug by archaeologists and pothunters seeking artifacts.

Between the lava and the pyramid, Cummings unearthed four rows of stone slabs placed like barriers to protect the pyramid. These are almost all covered by debris—your path walks over them—but the tops of some are still visible. Cummings believed these slabs were a futile attempt to stop the lava from overwhelming the pyramid.

Cuicuilco B

Of the 11 small temple-platforms discovered during the 1967 Villa Olimpica excavations, only a handful are still standing. You reach them by crossing Insurgentes (carefully) and walking in the Villa Olimpica entrance. Two temple-platforms stand behind a chain-link fence on the north side of the apartment buildings. To reach a third, you must enter the Tlalpan sports complex and ask permission from the director's office. Most of these temples were first built around 800–600 b.c. and were expanded between 100 b.c. and a.d. 100, when the main area of Cuicuilco began to show signs of abandonment.

TEOTIHUACAN

INTRODUCTION

Cuicuilco's successor was Teotihuacan, one of the most spectacular sites in the New World. It lies in the Teotihuacan Valley less than an hour's drive from Mexico City and just beyond the city's smog. Teotihuacan is best known for its Pyramids of the Sun and the Moon, two massive constructions that rival nearby hills in size. From the top of the pyramids, you have an excellent view of what makes the city unique: its sheer size, the sophistication of its city planning, and the brilliance of its architecture and applied arts, particularly mural painting.

Uniquely among Mesoamerican sites, Teotihuacan has never been forgotten, even after its near-total destruction between A.D. 650 and 750. The Toltecs and

DESIGN MOTIFS OF ANCIENT MEXICO

TEOTIHUACAN

How to get there: The ruins lie about 50 kilometers northeast of downtown Mexico City. To reach them by car, take Highway 85 toward Pachuca but turn onto the Teotihuacan highway just before you enter the State of Mexico. This toll road runs to the site 22 kilometers farther on. You can also catch an inexpensive bus (frequent departures) next to the Indios Verdes Metro station; the bus will drop you at the side of the ruins before continuing into the town of San Juan Teotihuacan.

Hours: Daily 0700–1800.

Admission fee: 50 pesos.

How long to tour: To see *everything* at Teotihuacan, you need at least two days. For an abbreviated, one-day tour, limit yourself to the Pyramid of the Sun, the Ciudadela, the Pyramid of the Moon, and the nearby Palace of the Quetzal Butterfly. The extremely energetic may prefer to park at one entrance and see the entire site on foot. For those with cars, it may make more sense to see the ruins near each site entrance and then drive to the next entrance. This is particularly advisable between the Pyramid of the Moon and the Ciudadela, which is otherwise a three kilometer walk. (Your admission ticket is good for unlimited reentries on the same day.)

Recommended gear: Hats, sunblock, bottled water, sturdy shoes or sneakers.

Museum: Just south of the Pyramid of the Sun and semihidden in a small depression, this building is "camouflaged" with lush plantings on its tilted roof and a Hanging-Gardens-of-Babylon motif around the eaves. At the entrance stands a stone relief of the Great Goddess. Inside, the dramatically lit rooms feature many fine pieces from recent excavations. The first two exhibits orient you to Teotihuacan's environment and historical phases. Next, the "Social and Economic Organization" room contains some brilliantly colored mural fragments, followed by a technology exhibit with elaborate Tlaloc incense burners.

The museum's north end is devoted to a diorama of the site under a glass floor that you walk over like a god. The main wall is a picture window framing a stunning view of the Pyramid of the Sun's south face. The next room, "Burials," features many of the objects found in the mass interments from the Temple of the Feathered Serpent (Quetzalcoatl). The necklace made from shell carved in the form of animal and human teeth is the high point. Next you come to the religion room, displaying objects dedicated to the Feathered Serpent and Tlaloc, followed by "Aesthetics" with a beautiful greenish alabaster basin. The focal point of the last room, "Contact with Other Cultures," is a photograph of the Aztec Sun Stone flying through space like the monolith in *2001: A Space Odyssey.*

Food and accommodations: Although Teotihuacan is an easy daytrip from Mexico City, you may want to spend more time at the site. Just south of the ruins stands the excellent **Hotel Villas Arqueológicas Teotihuacan,** tel. 595/6-0909 or 6-0728, fax 6-0244. It offers a/c, a pool, tennis courts, and a restaurant, all for about 595 pesos for one or two.

You will find a few overpriced family restaurants on the ring road around the site; on weekends, dozens of open-air barbecue eateries suddenly appear.

Aztecs revered it as "the place where the gods were conceived." For the Spanish, it was too close to Mexico City to ignore and too big to destroy. Despite this long history, it is remarkable what we don't know about the Teotihuacanos. Huge gaps remain in our knowledge about their history, culture, and society. We can only guess about the main tenets of their religion, and the identity of any of their rulers is unknown. Much of our ignorance is due to the final conflagration that destroyed the city, all of its records, and nearly all of its artwork. Also, despite an almost uninterrupted series of excavations since the early 1900s, the site is so huge that much work remains to be done.

HISTORY

Teotihuacan lies in the Teotihuacan Valley, which is in the relatively arid northeastern corner of the Valley of Mexico. At first glance, it is an unattractive site for a major metropolis. The shores of the pre-Conquest lakes were at least 10 kilometers away, and rainfall was far less than along the Valley of Mexico's lush southern rim. On the other hand, there were good springs nearby, and the soils were rich. Most important, the nearby hills contained large deposits of obsidian, the volcanic glass from which they could make razor-sharp arrowheads, blades, and other tools.

Human settlement in the Teotihuacan Valley lagged behind the rich lakeshores to the south and west. By 200 B.C. the valley held about 25 small villages and hamlets with a total population of 5,000–6,000. Inhabitants lived in simple houses clustered together by family or clan groups and farmed the surrounding valley. Those settlements occupying the rich lands at the center of the valley, where Teotihuacan is today, were noticeably better off than their neighbors, and the first signs of social stratification appear. Small workshops for carving obsidian sprang up, and their wares began to spread through the valley. By 100 B.C., the western part of present-day Teotihuacan was home to a large town of 7,000 people covering six square kilometers. There were no permanent structures, yet.

What caused the phenomenal explosion of this town into a city of 200,000 people, one of the largest in the world at the time? Archaeologists believe that the spur was the discovery, shortly after 100 B.C., of a cave, actually a volcanic tube, under the present Pyramid of the Sun. The cave runs east to west, and its entrance lines up with various astronomical phenomena, including the setting sun and the rising of the Pleiades constellation on the equinoxes. Caves were holy places throughout Mesoamerica, and the Teotihuacan cave may have been considered a place of emergence, the womb from which the sun, the moon, and all of humankind were born.

The cave became the center of the cult of Teotihuacan, a creed mixing religion and politics and lasting, in one form or another, until the Conquest. In one of the first acts of urban planning in the New World, a city was laid out. The main avenue, now called the Street of the Dead, was built perpendicular to the cave's sight line and extended almost a kilometer north to the first phase of the Pyramid of the Moon. Continuing north, this axis lines up with the notched summit of Cerro Gordo, the hill dedicated to the Great Goddess that marked the northern limit of the valley. Massive labor was needed to complete these building projects; almost the entire population of the Valley of Mexico was moved, perhaps forcibly, to Teotihuacan. About 100 years later, the avenue was continued another kilometer to the south, and the Pyramid of the Sun was begun exactly on top of the holy cave. Neither of the two pyramids was actually dedicated to the Sun or the Moon. Researchers believe they were actually devoted to the Great Goddess and the Rain God (Tlaloc), the city's principal deities.

This early Teotihuacan, which had a population of 20,000–25,000 spread over 13 square kilometers, defined the future civilization. Priest/monarchs ruled the city; they based power on the cult of the cave—the center of the Universe—and built a city to reflect their beliefs. These early rulers designed Teotihuacan as an urban world, one of the first in Mesoamerica, in which people lived in an elaborate social hierarchy and practiced one of a number of specialized trades. Agriculture was still important during these early days, but, as the city grew, trade and the manufacture of obsidian tools and ceramics became increasingly important.

Between A.D. 150 and 300, all the great edifices of Teotihuacan were completed. The Pyramids of the Sun and the Moon were enlarged to their final states. The Street of the Dead was extended three kilometers to the south, and a major east-west avenue was constructed, dividing the city into four quadrants. This avenue met the Street of the Dead at the Great Compound on the west and, on the east, the Ciudadela, one of the city's most important structures.

The heart of the Ciudadela, a large rectangular space surrounded by low temple-platforms, is the Temple of the Feathered Serpent (Quetzalcoatl). Archaeologists recently found buried within the temple the remains of at least 120 ritually sacrificed men and women; some of them were evidently placed there at start of construction and others at the temple's inauguration. This discovery demolished a long-held belief about Teotihuacan: that this culture, unlike the rest of Mesoamerica, was a relatively peaceable civilization in which human sacrifice was unknown. Researchers now believe that the Ciudadela was built by an all-powerful, probably despotic ruler seeking to shift the city's center from the Pyramid of the Sun to this new memorial to his own magnificence.

In the last century of this era, Teotihuacan's rulers expanded their realm east and west into the states of Hidalgo and Morelos and dispatched military expeditions that reached as far south as Central America. They probably conquered the great city of Kaminaljuyú (on the outskirts of Guatemala City), and they forged ties to Tikal in the Petén jungle lasting 200 years. In addition to their forms of religious and artistic expression, the Teotihuacanos exported obsidian, cloth, and ceramics. In return, they received many important ritual products, such as feathers, jade, shells, and cacao beans.

The 300 years after A.D. 300 were remarkable for their stability and prosperity. No great new structures were built, and artisans began only two huge monolithic sculptures, to the Water Goddess and the Rain God. The other arts flourished: mural painting reached a new height, covering nearly every available wall in the ceremonial areas, and new stucco facades were added to the bases of the Pyramid of the Sun and the Temple of Quetzalcoatl.

The greatest change was in living quarters. The old chaotic conglomerations of dwellings were replaced by planned apartment compounds that filled nearly every available space of the city's grid. Housing between 50 and 100 people probably related by kinship units, nearly 2,000 of these compounds were built. The compound residents were not only tied by blood and marriage but by occupation and place of origin. Merchants lived in one, craftsmen in another, soldiers in a third. Archaeologists have found evidence that a few compounds were occupied by foreigners from Oaxaca and Veracruz. Many of Teotihuacan's compounds were obviously poor, but others, such as Atetelco and Tepantitla, were luxurious, with elaborate mural paintings and elegant ceremonial spaces. At its height, the city may have been home to 200,000 people, nearly all living in these compounds.

The lack of grandiose architectural schemes and the emphasis on civic life has led researchers to theorize that during the Teotihuacan III Phase the city was ruled not by one all-powerful ruler but by a group of more pacific governors. The cult of Teotihuacan continued, but the emphasis was on stability and the regular cycles of existence rather than reaching some new and more grandiose level. During this period, the land controlled by Teotihuacan reached its greatest extent, probably about 26,000 square kilometers (the size of Sicily), although many more far-flung regions no doubt sent tribute.

Around A.D. 600, Teotihuacan began to slide into a decline. No new buildings were built; no new frescoes decorated the walls. Apartment complexes were slowly abandoned, and those residents who stayed allowed the structures to fall apart. There is evidence that Teotihuacano society became polarized between the rich and powerful and the very poor. No one knows the reasons behind this decline, but researchers believe the possible causes were mismanagement, the breakdown of the trade and tribute system, health crises caused by overcrowding, and a series of particularly dry years that worsened the valley's always tenuous agriculture.

Archaeologists believe that around A.D. 725, Teotihuacan was plundered and burned. They do not know if this was caused by an internal rebellion or an external attack, but the level of destruction was remarkable. It was as if they wanted to demolish not only the city but every trace of the cult of Teotihuacan. Every building along the main ritual axis and nearly every temple in the city was burned and, if possible, razed. The altars were destroyed, and every idol was smashed. Thousands were killed; their skeletons were trapped beneath the rubble. Those who survived this holocaust gradually drifted away from the city, and a new, less culturally advanced people entered the valley and began to camp out in the ruins. The greatness of Teotihuacan would now live only in memory.

The residential zones of Teotihuacan had largely been spared the conflagration, and they were occupied by a group belonging to what archaeologists call the Coyotlatelco culture, possibly originating in the arid areas of northern Mexico. The city's population by this time (post-A.D. 750) had shrunk to a little more than 30,000. By A.D. 850, these new residents had also disappeared and were replaced by less numerous and even poorer peoples. Teotihuacan never was totally abandoned, but its subsequent inhabitants were doing little more than camping out in the ruins.

Meanwhile, the Valley of Mexico's center of power was shifting, first to the Toltec capital of Tula and then to the Aztecs' Tenochtitlan. These new civilizations could not ignore the massive ruins nearby, and, lacking historical data, they devised their own myths to account for them. They were built by the Toltecs' own ancestors, said one story; another stated that a race of giants had erected the pyramids. By the end of the Aztec era, the official account was that the gods themselves had built Teotihuacan. The cave under the Pyramid of the Sun was the emerging place of the sun, the moon, the stars, and humanity itself. Thus the era which the Aztecs (and ourselves) live in, the era of the Fifth Sun, had begun here, the starting point of all calendars. They named the pyramids after the Sun and the Moon and called the main avenue the Street of the Dead, because they thought rulers were buried in its temples.

Teotihuacan became a pilgrimage center for Aztec priests, who came to worship the massive idols still standing at the pyramid summits. Aztec architects and craftsmen copied Teotihuacan architecture and mural painting in the construction of their own capital of Tenochtitlan. Many Teotihuacan artifacts have also been found in Aztec offering caches, such as the ones buried in the Great Temple. The excavation of Teotihuacan had begun.

ARCHAEOLOGICAL   RECORD

By the time of the Conquest, the pyramids had been in ruins for centuries and were overgrown with maguey, cactus, and mesquite. The conquistadors, offspring of medieval Spain, cared little for the history of the defeated peoples. Teotihuacan was built by giants, they believed, but what was important was to destroy those idols still worshipped by the local tribes. Relying on native accounts, the priest Juan de Torquemada wrote that Teotihuacan was a Toltec city built at the same time as Tula. This misconception lasted until the first stratigraphic excavations in the early 20th century. It was not until the late 17th century that a Spaniard, Don Carlos de Sigüenza y Góngara, was curious enough about the pyramids to attempt to find out what was inside. He, like all who followed, found nothing more than stone.

By the early 19th century, objects from Mesoamerica began to appear in European museums, exciting the interest of the adventurer/collectors of that era. They ventured to Teotihuacan and found a site literally covered with obsidian chips and potsherds and seeded with thousands of figurines and larger stone and ceramic pieces. In his archaeological travelogue, *Anahuac* (1861), the Englishman Sir Edward Tylor described the pothunting riches and theorized that Teotihuacan had been built by a despotic ruler overseeing a population of slaves. In separate excavations in the 1880s, Désiré Charnay and Leopoldo Batres discovered rich burials and offering caches that to them strongly resembled objects found at Tula. Batres believed that the Teotihuacanos abstained from human sacrifice, offering to the gods only flowers, seeds, fruits, and birds.

Batres, a self-taught archaeologist, is one of the more controversial figures of early Mesoamerican archaeology. On the one hand, he was the first to get large-scale support for research from the Mexican government. He was also a pioneer of the practice of excavation, then restoration, that continues to this day. On the other hand, he dynamited the top level of the Pyramid of the Sun to facilitate a 1910 reconstruction. His reconstruction shaved off the outer layers of the south, east, and north sides of the pyramid, exposing retention walls that Batres believed were actually a fifth terrace. That terrace still stands today, giving the pyramid a fifth level when experts believe there were originally only four.

During the following decade, the new technique of stratigraphic archaeology—based on the idea that you could tell an object's age by the geological layer in which it was found—was used at Teotihuacan for the first time. The watershed 1917–22 work of Manuel Gamio proved that the city was far older than previously thought and probably predated Tula. Research continued on the ceramic sequences during subsequent decades, and archaeologists also began to extend their excavations from the ceremonial center to the outlying apartment complexes. For the first time, they began to realize how vast the city really was. Concurrent excavations in other parts of Mexico established many links between other pre-Columbian peoples and Teotihuacan. The city was no longer an offshoot of Tula but the center of its own, perhaps greater, civilization.

In 1960, a new era of Teotihuacan excavation began, first with a massive Mexican government-funded project centered around the Street of the Dead. Under Jorge Acosta and, later, Ignacio Bernal, all the temples lining this street were cleared and restored. This project's most spectacular discoveries were the carved reliefs and vivid mural paintings of the Palace of the Quetzal Butterfly.

Serpent head emerges from a circle of plumes at Teotihuacan's Temple of the Feathered Serpent.

DANIELLE GUSTAFSON

At the same time, René Millon began the massive Teotihuacan Mapping Project that identified the location and possible age of every structure on this 20-square-kilometer site. When this information was assembled, researchers could see for the first time the vast extent of the city and the complexity of its urban planning. The thousands of little squares on Millon's map also highlighted the importance of the apartment compounds to the ancient city. Combined with other work on settlement patterns in the Basin of Mexico, they could follow the rise and fall of Teotihuacan and its relationship to its closest neighbors.

The next archaeological watershed was the 1971 discovery of the cave beneath the Pyramid of the Sun. With this, the focus returned to the difficult task of recreating Teotihuacan's religion without the help of surviving sources or a written language. Much of this work has been done by art historians interpreting the many mural paintings and stone sculptures.

Recently, excavations have been performed at the apartment compounds, where archaeologists have been able to recreate the daily life of the Teotihuacanos, and at the Ciudadela. Between 1980 and 1986, a series of excavations around the Temple of Quetzalcoatl unearthed the remains of more than 100 sacrificial victims, finally putting to lie Leopoldo Batres's theory about this nonbloodthirsty civilization. The Teotihuacan Mega-Project of the 1990s paid for much reconstruction, a new museum, and excavations around the Pyramid of the Sun's base. At the same time, Linda Manzanilla directed the exploration of the old *tezontle* (volcanic stone) mines immediately east of the Pyramid of the Sun. Here, dozens of burials of post-Teotihuacano residents, including members of the Coyotlatelco culture, have been found. Nearly every worker on this project came down with respiratory ailments caused by dust and, some say, by the spirits disturbed by the intrusion.

Stratigraphic excavation is an archaeological practice based on the theory that you can tell the relative age of a buried object from the geologic layer in which it lies.

Beginning in 1998, the Pyramid of the Moon Project, a joint program of INAH and Arizona State University, began to explore the interior of Teotihuacan's second-largest pyramid. Among the exciting finds were two tombs containing human sacrifices and a large number of offerings. Archaeologists Saburo Sugiyama and Ruben Cabrera also were able to work out the seven-stage construction sequence of the massive pyramid.

Despite more than a century of archaeological research, there is still a need for large-scale excavations in nearly every area of the site. They are our only hope for answering the many mysteries of Teotihuacan.

TOURING THE SITE

The site of Teotihuacan is oriented along the north-south axis of the Street of the Dead; originally it spread an equal distance to the east and west. The ruins are bordered by a roughly oval ring road that connects with the Mexico City highway to the southwest and the Tulancingo road to the north. At present, there are three entrances to the site: two on the west side and one on the east. This tour will begin at the East Entrance.

East Entrance: The Pyramid of the Sun

Just southeast of the looming Pyramid of the Sun, you'll find the parking lot for the east entrance. The old, multistory building across the ring road is headquarters for many of the archaeologists working at the site. Looking north, you will see numerous depressions immediately east of the pyramid. These are the remains of the old *tezontle* (a volcanic stone) mines where the Teotihuacanos quarried the city's building materials. After the fall of Teotihuacan, the mines were used as homes by the members of the Coyotlatelco culture, Toltecs, and Aztecs and also as burial sites. Archaeologists in the ongoing project here have found many ceramic pieces that suggest that the mines were also a center of the cult of Tlaloc, the Rain God.

From the parking lot, a path leads down to the new museum. Turn west and walk along the south base of the Pyramid of the Sun. The pyramid is square, and at ground level each side measures 221 meters to a side. The lower level of the base was once sheathed in a stucco facade, now destroyed. The rest of the pyramid had a simple stone facing that was probably plastered and painted red. It must have been an impressive sight at sunset.

Atop the rise to the south stands the ruined Priest's House, made up of about a dozen rooms connected to a central patio. Leopoldo Batres excavated this structure in the early 1900s and found skeletons of men, women, and children with bead necklaces buried beneath the floors. Continuing on the path along the pyramid's base, you come to the Plaza of the Sun, used as a ritual space, in front of the pyramid's main, west face. A square ritual platform occupies the center of the

view of the Palace of the Sun from the Pyramid of the Sun

DANIELLE GUSTAFSON

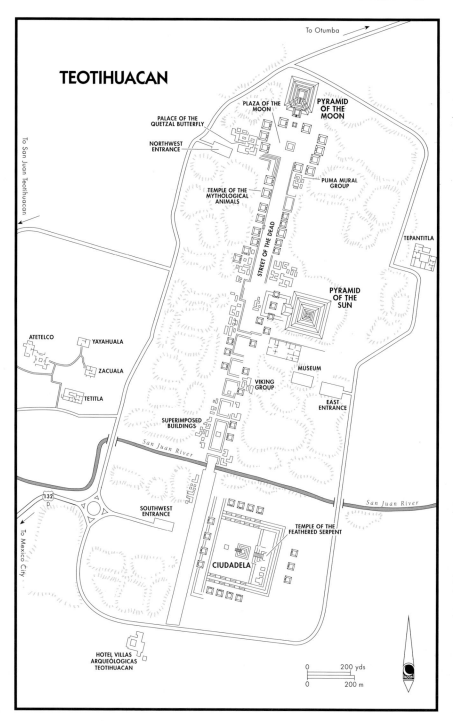

TEOTIHUACAN

To Otumba

To San Juan Teotihuacan

PLAZA OF THE
MOON

PYRAMID
OF THE
MOON

PALACE OF THE
QUETZAL BUTTERFLY

NORTHWEST
ENTRANCE

PUMA MURAL
GROUP

TEMPLE OF THE
MYTHOLOGICAL
ANIMALS

STREET OF THE DEAD

TEPANTITLA

PYRAMID
OF THE
SUN

ATETELCO   YAYAHUALA

ZACUALA

MUSEUM

TETITLA

VIKING
GROUP

EAST
ENTRANCE

SUPERIMPOSED
BUILDINGS

San Juan River

132
D

SOUTHWEST
ENTRANCE

San Juan River

To Mexico City

TEMPLE OF THE
FEATHERED SERPENT

CIUDADELA

HOTEL VILLAS
ARQUEÓLOGICAS
TEOTIHUACAN

0   200 yds

0   200 m

MooN

plaza, and it is bordered on the north, south, and west with a platform wall that separated it from the rest of Teotihuacan. Just to the north of this plaza stands the remains of the Palace of the Sun; many murals were found here, but they were removed for preservation and restoration and are not available for viewing.

The pyramid's great staircase begins at the stepped Plataforma Adosada (Semidetached Platform) jutting from the lower level. Offering caches have been found buried within the platform. At the base of the platform's western face, you see two doors, both entrances to tunnels, one man-made, the other the product of a volcanic eruption. The topmost door opens into a man-made tunnel dug in 1933 and connecting with a 1922 tunnel penetrating the pyramid from the opposite side. Within, archaeologists found stone, fill, and the buried original pyramid built during the Teotihuacan I era (100 B.C.–A.D. 150). Although archaeologists believe the pyramid contains a royal burial, no tombs or other interior rooms have ever been discovered.

The lower door is the entrance to the 98-meter-long volcanic tube that was a highly important ritual space for the Teotihuacanos. Discovered by archaeologists in 1971, this cave was altered by the Teotihuacanos to make it more sinuous and difficult to enter. Numerous artificial narrowings would have forced the faithful, probably only high-ranking priests, to alternately walk, stoop, and crawl. Once archaeologists removed the tons of fill that packed the tunnel, they found only traces of earlier rituals, mainly charcoal, fish bones, and shell fragments. Around the time of the Ciudadela construction, the cave was sealed shut, perhaps because the ruler replaced it with his own cult. The cave was subsequently looted, perhaps as long ago as the 4th century A.D. Entry to the cave is forbidden; the only key is held by Eduardo Matos Moctezuma, the site's head archaeologist.

Steps lead up the platform's south side to the main staircase climbing 64 meters to the pyramid's summit. There is no hurry. Five terraces on the way up provide good places to rest and catch your breath. The number of steps and terraces probably had religious significance, but at this point researchers do not know what it was. At each terrace's corner, archaeologists discovered ritual burials of children around six years of age and probably the victims of human sacrifice. Researchers believe that the Pyramid of the Sun was dedicated to the Great Goddess and possibly the Rain God, but as yet no definitive proof has been found.

At the top, you find a smooth, slightly rounded platform with a cooling breeze and an excellent view. This platform originally held a temple with a five-meter-tall stone idol. The latter was still standing in the 16th century but was probably destroyed by the Spanish. The vista gives you an excellent overview of the site and the surrounding towns, all of which are built on the ruins of Teotihuacan apartment compounds. On April 29 and August 12, the sun sets in the west directly opposite the pyramid and in a direct sight line from the volcanic tube below. August 12 is the date for the beginning of the present age (the Aztec era of the Fifth Sun) in 3114 B.C.

Carefully descending the pyramid, you next walk west across the plaza and over the platform to the Street of the Dead. The small platform immediately west of the staircase was built by the Aztecs for their worship at Teotihuacan. Across the street, a path leads to the parking area at the site's west-side Puerto Dos (Door Two). Turn left on the Street of the Dead, which, over the distance of 1.6 kilometers, drops to the Río San Juan and the Ciudadela.

This section of the Street of the Dead is divided into five rectangular plazas separated by platform walls. Either side of this avenue is lined with elaborate temple complexes that were not tombs for the dead but ritual spaces and dwelling places for the elite. All of these structures were built during the Teotihuacan II period (A.D. 150–300), i.e., later than the temples lining the northern half of the avenue. In the hot sun, it is probably easier to walk along the temple walls at the sides of the avenue than up and down all the staircases. This part of the tour will head down the east side of the avenue to the Viking Group, and then cross to the west side to visit two temple complexes before reaching the Río San Juan.

Just after the third platform wall, you come to the Viking Group (named after the foundation that financed the excavation) on the east side. This is a palace group comprising rooms, courtyards, and shrines built around an open central courtyard. Remnants of red frescoes are on the walls at the palace's northwest corner (right next to the platform wall). Under metal lids in one of the patios you will find the Viking Group's most remarkable feature: the remains of mica tiles that originally covered many square meters of the patio floor. This relatively fragile flooring obviously had some ritual purpose, as yet unknown. If the metal panels are closed, there should be a guardian around to open them.

South of the Viking Group stands the yet-to-be-restored Street of the Dead Complex. One of the largest building groups in Teotihuacan, this complex is surrounded by the remains of a two-meter wall. Inside are numerous rooms around a central plaza bordered by three temples.

From the south end of the Viking Group, cross the Street of the Dead on the fourth platform wall to the West Plaza Group. At this writing, this palace is being restored. The main entrance from the avenue leads you to a series of ruined rooms with the remains of columns before emerging into an open patio with a shrine in the center. At the north and south sides of the patio stand two small temples; to the west, you see a third temple decorated with painted stucco serpent and jaguar heads. You can see within the third temple the remnants of an earlier structure.

The next group on this side of the Street of the Dead is the Superimposed Buildings Complex, immediately south of the West Plaza Group. A sign marks the entrance to the Plaza of the Superimposed Temples, named for the earlier temples found underneath during excavations. Under protective roofs, you see the remains of a small *talud-tablero* temple with green, red, and white geometric frescoes. From here you take a right on a walkway through a series of rooms and down some stairs to the Subterranean Buildings, actually an earlier stage of the complex's construction. The red frescoed walls give you a good idea of the site's original decoration.

Immediately to the south of this group stands the Northwest Complex, a relatively small group with the remains of two temples. Continuing south on the

Street of the Dead, you quickly come to the Río San Juan—little more than a swampy trickle in the dry season—across which you see the massive complex of the Ciudadela. This tour returns to the parking lot behind the Pyramid of the Sun; you could also jump ahead to the Ciudadela section of this chapter.

Returning to the ring road northbound, just beyond the Pyramid of the Sun you come to another, little-used parking lot and an old site entrance. Fifty meters east of the ring road here, outside the site proper, stands Tepantitla, discovered in 1942 and one of the most sumptuously decorated apartment complexes yet found. Like many other Teotihuacan building complexes, this is a collection of rooms built around a central patio between A.D. 600 and 750, near the end of Teotihuacan's glory, probably as priestly housing.

You enter at the complex's southwest side and walk into the central, slightly sunken patio. The corner rooms are covered with modern roofs to protect the magnificent murals within. In Tepantitla's northeast corner, you find the room containing the famous "Tlalocan" mural. The archaeologist Alfonso Caso gave it this name because he associated the main figures with Tlaloc and the scenes below with Tlalocan, the mythic paradise presided over by the Rain God. More recently, the central figures have been identified as the Great Goddess, one of Teotihuacan's central deities.

The mural is painted around a central door; originally, the designs covered the entire room from floor to ceiling. On the upper level on either side of the door, you see fragmentary murals of the goddess herself with a spectacular headdress and symbolic drops of rain falling from her hands. To the lower right is "Tlalocan," depicted as a joyful place where little monkeylike human figures cavort and dance with branches in their hands. Fish, other animals, and plants abound, leading some to say that this is a water paradise and the little humans are actually swimming. To the lower left of the door, more little men play a ballgame that appears unrelated to the famous Mesoamerican ballgame. A reproduction of this mural is in Mexico City's Museo Nacional de Antropología. The room just beyond the Tlalocan mural contains frescoes of elaborately dressed priests "sowing" (the "flowers" in their hands may actually be representations of speech) in a procession along a red background.

Immediately south of these rooms stands a low temple-platform at the east side of the central patio. The rooms at the southeast corner of the complex contain the "Red Tlalocs," two faded figures now identified as the Great Goddess against a red background. These murals were the first discovered at Tepantitla. Diagonally across the courtyard, in the northwest corner rooms you find a fragmentary mural depicting the Sun as a circle with symbols inside and rays radiating outward.

Northwest Entrance: The Pyramid of the Moon

Continue north on the ring road around the top of the site, looping behind the Pyramid of the Moon, and enter the northwestern parking lot. The path between the parking area and the site is lined with souvenir shops. The government plans to move them to a shopping complex outside the site on the other side of the ring road.

Just before the entrance to the Plaza of the Moon, a sign points down a set of stairs to the Palace of the Jaguars. This is another complex of rooms and temples around a large central patio. The rooms at the north side of the patio are decorated with murals depicting plumed jaguars blowing a wind instrument made from a conch shell. The border above the jaguars is lined with alternating god-masks (perhaps the Rain God) and plumed year-symbols. Penetrating farther into the complex, you come to a room adorned with more jaguar murals. These display the famous net-jaguar, whose body is so stylized that it appears constructed from the loose meshes of a net. A symbolic roar plumes from its mouth.

Signs now point you from the central patio into the Palace of the Plumed Conches, which lies directly beneath the Palace of the Quetzal Butterfly. Built between A.D. 100 and 200, this complex was later filled with rubble to provide a base for the newer palace above. Inside you find a temple decorated with stone reliefs of conch shells fringed with feathers. Traces of red and green paint may be seen. Columns on either side of the temple are faced with reliefs of four-petaled flowers. The temple sits on a platform whose front is painted with frescoes of green parrot-type birds spouting stylized water from their mouths onto corn plants.

Chalchihuites is the Nahuatl word for "precious stones"; these were usually jade or green stone inlays on temples.

Returning to the path into the Plaza of the Moon, go down the steps to the plaza and take an immediate left up another set of stairs to the Palace of the Quetzal Butterfly. (The temple to the right has been reconstructed with seats for what is at the moment a defunct sound and light show.) Discovered in 1962, the palace follows the patio-surrounded-by-rooms model of most other Teotihuacan building complexes. You enter the palace and step into a columned room whose walls are painted with blue, red, and white frescoes of geometrical designs.

A door then leads down to the columned patio that gives the palace its name. (High-heeled shoes are forbidden here to preserve what remains of the red-painted plaster floor.) Each of the eight square freestanding columns and four corner columns is decorated with stone reliefs of a hybrid quetzal bird/butterfly bearing traces of the original paint. The face of each column holds the frontal view of this animal, while the side depicts its profile. The rest of each column is carved with at least five different symbols, including representations of water and eyes.

This patio was discovered in ruins, but enough remained to reconstruct it from floor to ceiling. You can see that many of the quetzal/butterfly panels are reproductions. The courtyard border above the columns is painted with white geometrical designs on a red background. Along the roof stand 16 freestanding plaques, one over each column and corner, in the form of the Teotihuacan year sign—a hieroglyphic date. The remains of more geometrical frescoes cover the slanted *tablero* base of the walls inside the colonnade.

In front of the Palace of the Quetzal Butterfly extends the Plaza of the Moon containing a square ceremonial platform in the center. To the east and west stand six, semirestored, stepped temple-platforms, three to a side and almost identical.

Two more temple-platforms flank the north side of the plaza. Between these temples lies the low Building of the Altars, in which researchers found 10 small altars whose ritual use is unknown. Behind the Pyramid of the Moon, you can see the notched summit of the Cerro Gordo hill, with which the entire city plan is aligned.

Like the Pyramid of the Sun, the Pyramid of the Moon is climbed by first ascending a semidetached platform. The recent Pyramid of the Moon Project tunneled into the pyramid along the north-south and east-west axes and discovered that the structure was built in seven stages. The first three stages are enclosed in the platform jutting from the pyramid's front. Then they expanded to the north and built the final four stages, each one larger than the last. At the completion of each construction sequence, the Teotihuacanos buried elaborate offerings containing sacrificed humans and animals as well as precious objects. The two offerings discovered during the recent excavations were unearthed along the north-south axis running through the center of the building (and in line with the Street of the Dead).

On top of the first staircase, 17 meters from the ground, you find a broad landing. Then you climb two more sets of stairs on the pyramid itself and reach the summit at a height of 46 meters. This is little more than a mound of rubble that has been glued together with concrete. The jutting rocks provide a few seats for the weary.

However, the summit does have an outstanding view down the Street of the Dead. To the north, east, and west, you can see numerous unexcavated ruins, mostly apartment complexes, half-overgrown with maguey and nopal cactus. About half a kilometer due east of here stands the Barrio of the Looted Murals, an apartment complex plundered earlier in the 20th century. Now it is mostly overgrown holes. Many mural fragments from this area were bought by an American collector and eventually ended up in the collection of the de Young Museum, part of the Fine Arts Museums of San Francisco and closed for renovation until 2005.

The Street of the Dead begins just south of the Plaza of the Moon. On the west side, a few steps along its length, stands the Temple of Agriculture. Behind the main temple-platform of this group, you find a triptych of large murals that give the complex its name. These murals depict conch shells, flowers, fruit branches, and water—hence agriculture—but unfortunately are in very bad shape. The complex also contains a copy of a mural showing two priests carrying braziers.

Immediately to the south stands the Temple of the Mythological Animals, whose entrance is at the back. You enter a room covered with frescoes portraying once brightly colored animals, mainly jaguars and other felines and feathered serpents. Some are fighting and even devouring one another. The blue background divided by wavy red and white lines probably represents waters.

The next group on this side of the street is the Plaza of the Columns, a relatively sprawling complex of five temples—three big and two small—built around a wide plaza. Across the Street of the Dead lies the Puma Mural Group, whose name comes from a large and bright fresco of a yellow puma with long and sharp claws. The blue, red, and white diagonal-lined background may again be water, and the line of red circles within green circles along the borders represents *chalchihuites* or precious stones. To the south, you once again come to the outbuildings along the north face of the Pyramid of the Sun.

Southwest Entrance: The Ciudadela

Returning now to the oval road around the site, proceed to the entrance at its southwestern edge. The parking lot here sits in the middle of the Great Compound, a vast plaza thought to be Teotihuacan's marketplace. The ancient city's second most important street (after the Street of the Dead) originally bisected the compound and became the central east-west axis along which many of the apartment complexes were built. At the east end of the parking lot stands the recently closed third museum, which is slated to be torn down. At this writing, its restaurant and bathrooms are still open.

Beyond the museum lies the Street of the Dead and, across the way, the Ciudadela (Citadel), Teotihuacan's largest unified architectural complex. The Ciudadela's outer edge is an enormous quadrangular platform whose sides are 390 meters long. It was almost certainly constructed to protect the ceremonies within from the gaze of the general citizenry. You climb the central stairs on the western side and on top find two of the 15 smaller temples that ring the platform (four each on the west, north, and south; three on the east). From here you look down into the Ciudadela's vast interior plaza, estimated to be able to hold upward of 30,000 people.

After descending into the plaza, head east past the square ceremonial platform in its center. Just beyond, on the south side of the plaza, stands a roof covering the Superimposed Shrines. Underneath you will see some poorly preserved geometric murals and the remains of seven small temple-shrines, one built over another.

Continuing east, the path takes you to the Ciudadela's most spectacular structure, the Temple of the Feathered Serpent. This is actually two temples, one half-superimposed on the other. First you see the later semidetached platform, actually a four-tiered *talud-tablero* pyramid with the remains of red frescoes along the base. It was built on top of the west face of the original and larger Temple of the Feathered Serpent, a pyramid dating to A.D. 150–200. This act may have been a political statement: the power that built the temple and fostered the cult of the Feathered Serpent had been overthrown.

You reach this spectacular building via a walkway at the south side of the buildings. The eastern half of the semidetached platform has been removed and the remnants constructed into a viewing platform. Directly opposite stands the Temple of the Feathered Serpent's best-preserved side. Here you see the remnants of what was originally a seven-tiered facade that wrapped around the entire building.

This *talud-tablero* facade, all cut and painted stone, represents the Feathered Serpent, one of Teotihuacan's most important deities, with flowing bodies ending in rattles and heads protruding from the facades. The conch shells nestled between the coils of the serpent bodies may indicate water. The serpent heads emerge from a circle of plumes; these are thought to represent mirror borders.

Mirrors and caves were closely linked in pre-Columbian religion; researchers believe this detail symbolizes the emergence or birth of the Feathered Serpent from a primal cave, i.e., the cave beneath the Pyramid of the Sun. Traces of red paint can be seen in the gaping mouths.

The serpent heads alternate with what archaeologists believe are not heads but headdresses, with an upper jaw of teeth, goggle eyes, and mosaic for skin. These may represent the War Serpent, an aspect of the Feathered Serpent or maybe the Teotihuacan Rain God (Tlaloc). Feathered serpent heads surrounded by plumes also emerge from the stone facing on the side of the central staircase. Below the heads, the *talud* panels are carved with more undulating serpent bodies.

After leaving the viewing area at the temple's north side, you can see behind the temple a large ruined residential complex, now off-limits to visitors because of excavations. The most impressive find of these excavations has been numerous human sacrifices, at least 120 so far, found at cardinal points around, within, and below the Temple of the Feathered Serpent. Each of the groups of victims, male and female, were of the same age and died at the same time. One of these was a tomb of 18 skeletons, all young adult males with their hands tied behind their backs. They were buried with many ritual objects, including elaborate necklaces made from shell carved in the form of human and animal teeth (you can see two of them in the site museum). Archaeologists believe these were captive warriors, sacrificed during the days of Teotihuacan's explosive growth (A.D. 150–300) to ensure their control of the population.

The Apartment Complexes

The best-preserved Teotihuacan apartment complexes lie just west of the ring road about 400 meters north of the southwest entrance. Outside the official site boundaries, this area encompasses numerous campesino houses and small plots of farmland on the eastern border of the town of San Juan Teotihuacan. A number of access roads reach the apartment complexes, but the quickest begins at the parking lot of the La Casa del Cubito restaurant just north of the Río San Juan riverbed.

Walk about 200 meters west on this dirt road, and on the right you will see the walls of Tetitla, one of the most elaborate apartment complexes yet excavated. The entrance is in the northwest corner. Like all apartment complexes, this is a walled quadrangle enclosing numerous rooms grouped around interior patios. The central patio contains a shrine built like a Teotihuacan temple in miniature. Beneath the floors of this compound, archaeologists have found burials and rich offering caches containing elaborate incense burners (some are on display in the museum).

The murals, more than 120 in all, are the high point. Here you see the Teotihuacan Rain God (Tlaloc), the God of Death, the Mother Goddess, and the Feathered Serpent. Around the doorway to the east of the central patio is a mural with six plumed felines, perhaps pumas, resting on low tables with speech symbols (growls?) issuing from their mouths. The most vivid and frightening murals represent white birds of prey, possibly owls, with their wings spread on a red background and blood dripping from their mouths.

From the entrance to Tetitla, a road curves west and a bit north to the Atetelco apartment complex. This compound follows the same model as the rest: a walled quadrangle encompassing two patios surrounded by rooms. In the central patio stands another miniature temple shrine, heavily reconstructed, with some traces of geometric designs visible on the original fragments. This is surrounded by four small temple-platforms with a few faded murals visible.

In the northwest corner of the complex lies the smaller White Patio surrounded by three smaller temples or shrines. Once again, the murals, painted along the shrine walls, are the most striking feature. An artist has reconstructed these murals in schematic form using the extant mural fragments as a guide. In the south portico you see rows of warrior figures dressed in the skins of dogs. Between them is a mesh of feathered bands with shields containing descending dog heads at their juncture. To the east, the murals depict eagle warriors between more interlaced bands. At the base of both the south and east murals, the panels are decorated with large, stylized canines wearing headdresses. The north building displays priests dressed as the Rain God (Tlaloc) or eagle warriors. The feathered bands again meet at shields with stylized birds in the middle. Below, the panels depict side views of the Rain God. On the west side of the patio stands a doorway whose lintel is decorated with a painting of a canine god, perhaps Xolotl, with deformed toes.

Tetitla and Atetelco are the two best-preserved apartment complexes. Due east from Atetelco, another dirt road takes you past two more in a good state of preservation but far fewer murals. About 200 meters east, you come to Yayahuala, another square compound surrounded by a ditch with patios and

Teotihuacan—the view south down Street of the Dead

DANIELLE GUSTAFSON

MESOAMERICAN ARCHITECTURE

The region we know as Mesoamerica is in part defined by its architecture, a collection of building types and techniques that are unique to its pre-Columbian cultures. The Olmecs, Maya, Aztecs, and other groups built structures, from peasant huts to complex cities, that responded to the climate (steamy jungles and cool, semiarid valleys) and the frequently earthquake-prone geology of their homelands. At the same time, their buildings reflected and often symbolized the religious and social systems around which they organized their lives. With so much of Mesoamerican culture destroyed by the Spanish invaders, one of the best ways we have for tracing its history and development is through its architecture. Here are six of the most important motifs:

1. **Pyramids.** The massive pyramids at sites such as Teotihuacan and Chichén Itzá are some of the most recognizable symbols of ancient Mexico. The first pyramids were probably simple mounds of fill and clay formed to resemble mountains, perhaps volcanoes. They developed into elaborate visual metaphors for the cultures' religious and political systems. The Temple of the Inscriptions at Palenque shows the principal attributes of the Mesoamerican pyramid: a flight of steps up the front, the structure rising in tiers (nine, symbolizing the levels of the Underworld), and an ornate temple on top. All these elements were a backdrop, like a theatrical stage set, for the elaborate ceremonies that occurred here.

Temple of Inscriptions, Palenque

2. **Ballcourts.** The ballgame was nearly ubiquitous in Mesoamerica.

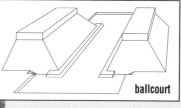

ballcourt

DANIELLE GUSTAFSON

ruined walls. All the murals have been removed to Mexico City. One hundred meters due south (Tetitla is visible just beyond) stands Zacuala, containing a palace complex on the north side, a slightly raised temple on the east, and a wide patio just outside the walls to the south. Around this patio, you see a few fragments of geometric red and white frescoes under a roof. The rest of the murals are in Mexico City. From Zacuala, you can return via Tetitla or go back to Yayahuala and turn right (east) to emerge at the ring road about a few hundred meters north of the restaurant.

Further apartment complexes under excavation lie due south in an area known as La Ventilla to the west of the ring road between Puerta Uno and the Villa Arqueológica entrance. Some of these sites were discovered during the construction, now halted, of a mini-mall for artisans. You can see the excavations from the road but are not allowed to enter them.

Courts designed for its play have been found in sites dating to 1400–1250 B.C. and all the way up to Aztec Tenochtitlan. The basic shape of the ballcourt was simple: a flat strip of ground—the playing field—between two parallel walls sloping inward. Over the centuries, they became more complex, culminating in the famous I-shaped ballcourt at Chichén Itzá, whose walls are covered with remarkable reliefs.

3. **The *talud-tablero*.** First seen at Teotihuacan, the *talud-tablero* building style was used to build palaces, temples, and other structures that rose in tiers. The sloping *taludes* alternated with vertical *tableros,* which were rectangular panels (often deco-

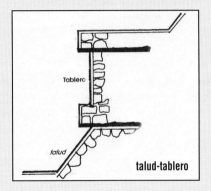

talud-tablero

rated with paintings or reliefs) surrounded by frames. The apogee of this style is the intricate Pyramid of the Niches at El Tajín.

4. **Residential compounds with courtyards.** Another of Teotihuacan's numerous architectural innovations was the palace or housing complex built around an interior courtyard. Often entered through only one doorway, these compounds housed the kinship groups that were the basic building blocks of many pre-Columbian political systems.

5. **Corbel vaults.** Most Mesoamerican ceremonial buildings were massive structures constructed of stone facings over rock and gravel fill that weighed many tons. To keep their ceilings from collapsing, the Maya developed the corbel vault, which was made from two masonry walls built up toward each other and then joined at the (narrow) top by a single capstone.

6. **Colonnaded palaces.** Mesoamerican elites always lived apart from their subjects. In the Maya region and elsewhere, they lived atop tiered temple-platforms in palaces fronted with lines of columns.

TULA

INTRODUCTION

Tula lies just outside the Valley of Mexico. It was the home of the Toltecs, one of central Mexico's most important peoples. Much of this city was destroyed by fire, but you can still clamber over the pyramids and ballcourts of the ancient ceremonial center. The iconic images of Tula are the massive black stone Atlantean (Atlaslike) warriors; you can also see other examples of the Toltec

TULA

How to get there: The ruins of Tula stand just east of the gritty town of Tula de Allende in southwestern Hidalgo. To reach them from Mexico City, head north on Highway 57 toward Querétaro and take the Tula de Allende exit just before the toll plaza about 15 kilometers north of the Mexico City/State of Mexico border. From here, it is 35 kilometers to Tula de Allende; signs will point you to the ruins. Buses to Tula depart hourly from the Terminal del Norte (Autobuses del Norte Metro station).

Hours: 1000–1800.

Admission fee: 30 pesos.

How long to tour: Three hours.

Recommended gear: Hats, sunblock, bottled water.

Museum: The Tula museum contains a good exhibition on Toltec history, including the great trek south, Tula's brief florescence, and its influence on Chichén Itzá. The displays contain numerous examples of Toltec pottery and sculpture. Of particular note are the stone standard-bearer and little Atlantean figures, both with traces of paint, and the well-preserved *chac mool.* Many of the best Toltec pieces, however, are in the Toltec Room of the Mexico City Museo Nacional de Antropología.

Food and accomodations: Downtown Tula possesses some basic restaurants and the **Hotel Sharon,** Callejon de La Cruz no. 1, tel. 773/2-0976, with 120 rooms and the cream of the crop with accommodations for up to 425 pesos, while the **Restaurant Los Fresnitos,** three kilometers east of the ruins (toward the refinery), is highly recommended for regional specialties such as maguey worms and chicken roasted in maguey leaves. Lunch for two will run you about 255 pesos.

mastery of the sculptor's art, including elaborate bas-reliefs, *chac mools,* and serpent columns.

Some visitors to Tula come away disappointed; the setting is barren and the edifices lack the grandeur and complexity of Teotihuacan or the Great Temple. Once you learn Tula's long history, however, and reflect on the controversies that have swirled around the site for the last century, you begin to understand why Tula is one of the most intriguing ancient cities of central Mexico.

Between the fall of Teotihuacan and the rise of the Aztecs, the Toltecs were the major civilization controlling central Mexico. According to native oral and written historical accounts, they came from the north, built a glittering city, and created many of the traditions that researchers consider hallmarks of Mesoamerican civilization, including the calendar system and worship of the Feathered Serpent god, Quetzalcoatl. For the cultures that came after, the Toltecs were the exemplary society, the one that all who followed sought to emulate.

"The Toltecs were wise," said one native account. "Their works were all good, all perfect, all wonderful, all marvelous, their houses beautiful, tiled in mosaics, smoothed, stuccoed, very marvelous."

Archaeologists doubt that the Toltecs invented the calendar and the worship of Quetzalcoatl. They do believe, however, that the Toltecs were a pivotal civilization, one that combined their own northern traditions with the customs and beliefs of the central Mexico region and produced a synthesis that strongly influenced every Mesoamerican society that followed.

HISTORY

Although at least six native accounts mention aspects of Tula's history, they do not exactly come up to modern standards of historiography. It is unclear which centuries the dates refer to, and the line between the mythic and the historic is often blurred. This account will rely mainly on the archaeological record, referring to the native histories only where experts believe the facts in the ground agree with the stories in the manuscripts.

Tula's site, a ridge at the confluence of the Tula and Rosas rivers, was not settled until late, about A.D. 700. Although the land was richer than it is today—oak and pine covered the hills and game and edible plants abounded—this area was never a prime spot for human habitation. Until the early Classic era, the region was home to only a few small agricultural hamlets. Between A.D. 300 and 600, the nearby town of Chingú was the regional center, covering more than 250 hectares with irrigated farm plots and modest civic-religious plazas. Chingú, which possessed a valuable lime mine, and the other area settlements were firmly in the orbit of Teotihuacan, lying just over the hills to the southeast.

Chingú was abandoned at the same time as Teotihuacan. As at Teotihuacan, the Tula region was overrun by seminomadic people from the north called the Coyotlatelcos by archaeologists. Around A.D. 700, they built a settlement at the Tula Chico (Little Tula) part of the site containing two ceremonial centers and four square kilometers of houses and terraced fields.

While the Coyotlatelcos built the first Tula, two peoples were making a decades- or perhaps centuries-long journey toward the same site. Led by their legendary ruler Mixcoatl, the Tolteca-Chichimecas came from the northwest, perhaps from the Zacatecas region. They were another seminomadic tribe of hunters and warriors who carried with them the cult of the fierce god Tezcatlipoca, the "smoking mirror," and a devotion to the custom of human sacrifice. From the Gulf Coast to the east came the Nonoalco, a group renowned for their learning and veneration of Quetzalcoatl, the Feathered Serpent. Among their ranks were probably priests, artisans, and learned people from Teotihuacan or other abandoned Classic-era cities.

The two groups became one, the Toltecs, "the people of artifice," and made

The reclining figure of a ***chac mool*** is found at sites from Yucatan to the Valley of Pátzcuaro. The Aztecs used the bowl on the chest to hold the hearts of sacrificial victims. The sculptures may have acted as intercessors between the gods and the earthly world.

BOB RACE

their capital first at Colhuacan in the southern Valley of Mexico. Here, the great Toltec leader 1 Reed Topiltzin Quetzalcoatl was born in the early 10th century. He led the Toltecs first to Tulancingo and then, in A.D. 950–980, to Tula, which lies about 125 kilometers due east.

At around this time, Tula Chico's (Little Tula's) ceremonial center was abandoned, although the surrounding residential quarter remained inhabited. Myths tell of an epic battle between followers of Quetzalcoatl and Tezcatlipoca, possibly over the issue of human sacrifice. Archaeologists believe that this quarter may have been destroyed during the battle and never rebuilt.

The two centuries between A.D. 950 and 1150, called the Tollan phase, were Tula's golden era, the height of Toltec power. The city's center became Tula Grande (Big Tula) about one kilometer north of Tula Chico. Here they built a ceremonial complex that included two pyramids, ballcourts, a skull rack, and an extensive columned "palace." The buildings were painted, usually red, and adorned with bas-reliefs and elaborate sculptural groups.

The size of Tula at its peak—around A.D. 1100—is debated, but it may have covered 13 square kilometers and contained as many as 60,000 inhabitants, making it the largest city in the Western Hemisphere at the time. The nearby Valley of Mexico began to fill with people as Tula's success brought groups from the margins, particularly the north, to live in the Toltec center.

The roots of the Toltec success were agriculture—farmers dammed the two rivers and built extensive irrigation canals—and trade. Tula controlled the mother lode of green obsidian in nearby Pachuca, Hidalgo, and at least 40 percent of the population was engaged in the production of obsidian blades and points. The Toltecs traded obsidian and other manufactured goods for ritual goods (feathers, jade, turquoise), textiles, pottery, and foodstuffs from throughout Mesoamerica.

The center for their business was Tula's bustling marketplace, from which long-distance merchants invaded the farthest corners of their world. Toltec trade routes ran west into Michoacan and Jalisco and east to the Gulf of Mexico. To the south they reached Yucatan, and to the north they may have penetrated as far as present-day New Mexico. With the Toltecs traveled their customs and beliefs, extending their reach far beyond the bounds of their empire.

Almost as soon as it began, the Toltec world collapsed. Everyone agrees that by A.D. 1200 Tula was in ruins; how it happened is hotly debated. Native accounts tell the story of the battle between followers of Tezcatlipoca and Quetzalcoatl leading to Topiltzin Quetzalcoatl's flight and the city's abandonment. The archaeological record shows that between A.D. 1150 and 1200 the ceremonial center of Tula Grande was burned and destroyed.

One reconstruction of events says that the precipitating event was an attack from the north around A.D. 1120; northern immigrants already in Tula also turned on their hosts. At the same time a conflict erupted between followers of Quetzalcoatl and Tezcatlipoca, perhaps instigated by Cholula, the other regional power. Topiltzin Quetzalcoatl fled, and, led by the ruler Huemac, the remaining

Tezcatlipoca-affiliated Tulans abandoned the city, which by A.D. 1179 lay in ruins. Huemac moved to Chapultepec (now in Mexico City) and committed suicide, while his followers scattered, carrying with them memories of the glorious Toltec past.

Tula was gone but not forgotten. The Toltecs who settled in the Valley of Mexico declared that only those of Toltec descent—or married to a Toltec—could become rulers. When another group of Chichimeca nomads entered the Valley of Mexico and began to claw their way to power, they had to intermarry with local Toltec lineages to prove their worth. After the Aztecs subjugated central Mexico in the 15th century, they returned to Tula to conduct rituals, place offerings, and strip the ruined city of everything sacred and beautiful they could find, including sculptures, jewelry, and ceramics. Many of these are probably still buried beneath the streets of downtown Mexico City. Their obvious lust for every Toltec object they could carry away is an argument against those archaeologists who say that Tula could not be Tollan because the artwork is too crude and unfinished to belong in the city of legend.

Gradually, Aztecs began to settle permanently in Tula. By the Spanish Conquest, the site was home to a bustling city of 20,000. The Spanish tore down the Aztec temples and used the stones to build an imposing church, now in the center of Tula town. Legend has it that in the 1540s native priests heard that the Spanish planned to destroy the sculpture of the Aztec god Huitzilopochtli that had stood on top of the Great Temple. Instead, they stole it and buried the idol somewhere in the hills around Tula. Fittingly, their most important god had returned to the place from which much of their civilization had sprung.

ARCHAEOLOGICAL RECORD

The Aztecs were the first to excavate Tula. They stripped the main buildings of sculptures and reliefs—Pyramid C was thoroughly ransacked—and took all the pottery, obsidian, and jewelry that was strewn over the site. Many Toltec objects have been discovered in excavations of Tenochtitlan, including large sculptures placed in temples and small figurines buried in Great Temple offering caches.

After the Spanish Conquest, the town of Tula gradually slid into the fringes of colonial life. The only people who visited the site were farmers eking out an existence from its arid soil and occasionally unearthing a pre-Hispanic object. The locals called it Cerro del Tesoro (Hill of the Treasure).

In 1880, the French explorer Désiré Charnay visited the ruins. After his reading of native accounts, he believed that all Mesoamerican pre-Aztec cultures were Toltec and the center of this great unifying civilization was Tula (he did not think any of the ancient cities predated A.D. 700). He romanticized the Toltecs as a meek, peacable, and beauty-loving people: "The religion of the Toltecs was mild like their disposition; no human blood stained their altars." Toltec life was "a perpetual spring," in contrast to the bloody, bellicose Aztecs who followed.

Tula's Burnt Palace, with reconstructed colonnades

When he visited the town, it had shrunk to fewer than 2,000 inhabitants, mostly Indians. The ruins had been ransacked by treasure-seekers and builders looking for bricks. He immediately began work in the Tula Grande area, digging three structures that are possibly the first residences (as opposed to temples) scientifically excavated in the New World. He carefully mapped them and published engravings of the numerous large stone sculptures and ceramic pots discovered during his work.

During the 1930s, scholars returned to the Tula-Tollan problem. The historian Wigoberto Jiménez Moreno studied native accounts and early maps and from the similarities between the map names and the tales decided that Tula was Tollan. This led to Tula's major excavation, beginning in 1940 under the leadership of Jorge Acosta.

Most of what archaeologists know about Tula comes from Acosta's 13 field seasons during the subsequent two decades. Although he did excavate the circular pyramid at El Corral (near Tula Chico), the center of his work was Tula Grande. He discovered the massive Atlantean columns, the Serpent Wall, the ballcourts, and the Aztec offerings. He established Tula's chronology compared to those of Teotihuacan and Tenochtitlan,

Tula in Yucatan

For archaeologists, the great mystery about Tula involves its relationship with Chichén Itzá, the ancient city built hundreds of kilometers away on the Yucatan Peninsula. One view holds that a group of warriors, perhaps led by Quetzalcoatl, sailed east to Yucatan and founded Chichén Itzá, while others say that Tula was built by invaders from Yucatan. This puzzle can be solved only by a comprehensive excavation of the Yucatan site.

TULA AS TOLLAN

Aztec historical accounts contained numerous references to a great but destroyed city called Tollan, where a king named Quetzalcoatl reigned and art and culture reached their heights. After centuries of searching for Tollan, in the 1930s the historian Wigoberto Jiménez Moreno identified the ruins of Tula as the ancient city. Although most archaeologists have accepted this designation, a few have begun to raise doubts—they see few signs of superlative culture and craftsmanship in the archaeological finds. Some believe that Teotihuacan might have been the real Tollan. The main problem is that the Aztecs looted Tula and transported all the fine objects to Tenochtitlan, so we may never truly know.

and he worked out a basic Toltec mythology centering around the cult of Quetzalcoatl in his guise as Tlahuizcalpantecuhtli, the Morning Star. His greatest achievement was his work on Pyramid B, which he excavated and restored.

In 1968, INAH's Proyecto Tula began work to fill out Acosta's research. Led by Eduardo Matos Moctezuma, the researchers mapped the site and the surrounding region, studied the native accounts, and compiled the post-Conquest history of the town. They also restored Ballcourt 2, excavated the residential complex at Dainí, two kilometers north of Tula Grande, and dug test pits at Tula Chico.

Two years later, Proyecto Tula was joined by a University of Missouri team under Richard A. Diehl. Tula's population was one of the major puzzles they hoped to solve. To get a better idea of the ancient city's density, they excavated domestic zones around Tula Chico and El Corral. When a massive irrigation project was planned for the low-lying regions of the site, they performed an emergency excavation at the "Canal Locality" to salvage what they could before it was inundated. They also discovered and dug a massive obsidian pit, which was one of the many proofs of the mineral's importance for Tula's economy.

The most recent Tula excavation occurred at the site of the present museum halfway between Tula Grande and Tula Chico. In 1980 and '81, an INAH team dug the residential complex here (you can see the dwelling foundations as you exit the museum into the site) and discovered numerous burials, almost all curled in fetal positions, some with simple pottery offerings.

This small Toltec Atlantean (Atlas-like) figure probably held up an altar, but now may be found in the Tula museum.

DANIELLE GUSTAFSON

Today, as at almost all other Mesoamerican sites, much archaeological work remains to be done.

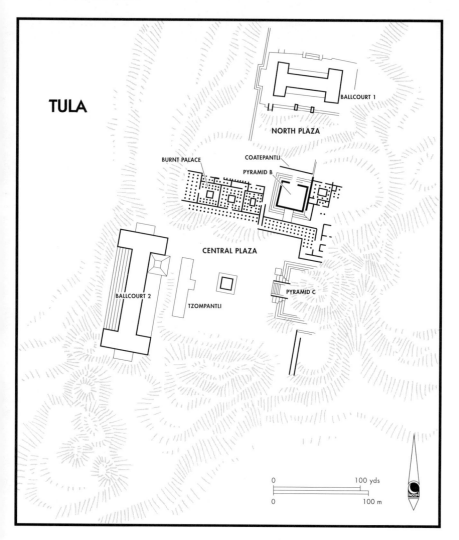

TULA

BALLCOURT 1

NORTH PLAZA

BURNT PALACE

COATEPANTLI

PYRAMID B

CENTRAL PLAZA

BALLCOURT 2

TZOMPANTLI

PYRAMID C

0   100 yds

0   100 m

T O U R I N G   T H E   S I T E

You enter the site through the museum (dedicated to Jorge Acosta) just west of the main parking lot. Around the building, you can see the foundations of the residential complex excavated in the early 1980s.

From the museum it is about a half-kilometer shadeless walk to the Tula Grande part of the site. The ancient city covered as much as 13 square kilometers of land, including nearly all the area traversed by the path, which was a residential district (as yet unexcavated). The ridge on which Tula stands runs on a rough north-south axis except for the southern tip—the site of Tula Grande—which curves slightly to the west. The early ceremonial center at Tula Chico was aligned just to the west of due north, while Tula Grande tilted an equal distance to the east.

You approach Tula Grande, the heart of the great Tollan-phase (A.D. 950–1150) Toltec capital, from the northwest. The path enters the North Plaza, and on your right you see Ballcourt 1, a low raised platform with the sunken court in the center. The I-shaped playing surface measures 67 meters by 12 meters and was built in three successive stages. The two later playing floors were covered with red or blue painted plaster, and decorative plaques (later removed by the Aztecs) lined the court walls. Beyond the north and west sides of this structure, the hillside drops off, exposing the sides of the enormous platform on which Tula Grande is built.

On the south side of the plaza rises Pyramid B (also called Building B), Tula's most famous edifice. As you approach this temple-platform, the first structure you encounter is the Coatepantli, or Serpent Wall, protected by a corrugated metal roof. Measuring 40 meters in length by 2.2 meters in height, the Coatepantli is a freestanding wall decorated with some of Tula's most intriguing and grotesque sculptures.

Along the top of the wall runs a line of masonry cut-outs that produces a vaguely undulating pattern. Both sides of the wall are adorned with three levels of friezes. The top and bottom reliefs replicate a running stepped pattern that was originally painted red. Between, the unique center frieze depicts a line of feathered rattlesnakes with enlarged heads and short bodies engulfing the skull and neck of a skeleton. The body of the latter appears to be still attached, because a leg with some flesh still attached to the knee straddles the snake's back. The snakes on the right and left sides are pointed toward the center; unfortunately that part of the wall was destroyed, so researchers do not know if there was some central image they were aiming at. Four standard-bearer sculptures found on the ground here may have originally been placed atop the wall. Jorge Acosta believed that the serpent relief represented the myth of Quetzalcoatl in his guise as the Venus, the Morning Star (Tlahuizcalpantecuhtli), a role the god assumed after being burned on a pyre.

Immediately behind the Coatepantli stands Pyramid B itself. This is a square platform measuring 38 meters to a side and 10 meters high. The building rises in five tiers, and archaeologists believe that it was constructed in three stages.

Pyramid B, stucco relief of skull emerging from serpent's mouth

Most of what you see now is Stage II, because, except for the north side, almost all of the Stage III temple was removed by the Aztecs. They also dug a large trench into the north side of the structure in order to remove the massive sculptures from the top. Jorge Acosta found many sculpture fragments in the trench, including the massive warrior columns.

The Toltecs reused many of the tablets that decorated the Stage II facade on the Stage III structure. You can see many of them on the north and east sides of the building immediately behind the Coatepantli. Along the top of the facade runs a line of coyotes with lolling tongues; below, the panels show birds of prey (eagles or buzzards) devouring hearts with blood dripping down. Next comes a line of pumas, and the lowest level of reliefs returns to birds eating hearts. All of these animals almost certainly represented orders of Toltec warriors (much like the divisions of the Aztec military, which followed a knight-like order).

Interspersed among the animals are panels showing a goggle-eyed face staring out the gaping mouth of a feathered monster with crouching paws on either side. Acosta believed that once again this was Tlahuizcalpantecuhtli (Quetzalcoatl as the Morning Star being devoured by a serpent), the deity to whom the pyramid was dedicated. Almost abutting the pyramid's east face is Building 1, also known as the Palace of Quetzalcoatl. The best way to view this complex is from the top of Pyramid B, rather than from ground level.

An **atlatl** is a weapon made from a handle that acts as a lever, increasing the throwing length of the arm and propelling a short spear or dart at high speeds.

Your tour continues by retracing your steps along the base of Pyramid B until you reach the main staircase on the south side. The path skirts the Burnt Palace and enters a colonnade facing the Central Plaza. Near the base of the steps you see a black *chac mool* missing its head. Four square columns flank the bottom of the staircase. As you ascend, you see on either side stones jutting from the unfinished pyramid facade; these served as supports for the decorative panels.

On top of Pyramid B, you first come to the remains of two round columns. These were carved to resemble the body of a serpent with a scaled belly and a feathered back. Each column section fit into the next with a plug-and-socket connection. As at Chichén Itzá, the columns were built with the serpent's head at the base and its rattle at the top. They flanked the entrance to the now-disappeared main temple.

The next row of sculptures are Tula's most famous icons, four massive Atlantean (Atlaslike) warrior columns. The one on the left is a copy (the original is in the Mexico City Museo Nacional de Antropología) while the rest are largely authentic. Made in four sections, the columns represent standing warriors with ornamental headdresses, butterfly-shaped breastplates, large belts, and leg wrappings. Ornamental stones were probably placed in their eye sockets. Pressed close to their sides, their arms grasp an atlatl (throwing spear) on one side and an incense bag on the other. These columns supported the roof of the outer temple room.

Where the inner room was you see only four square pillars carved with reliefs of four warriors—each probably representing a military order—alternating with panels showing bundles of wrapped spears or darts.

From the east side of the pyramid, you have a good view of Building 1. This was a raised platform measuring 60 by 40 meters that was built in at least seven stages. On top of the platform are the remains of one large patio surrounded by rooms and a few side rooms and corridors along the south side. This structure was evidently occupied by people who could afford to redecorate frequently—the floor of one room had 24 separate layers.

On the west side of Pyramid B, you can overlook the Burnt Palace, also called Building 3, a series of three large colonnaded halls that are this tour's next stop. When you descend the pyramid's staircase, you will stand among the long colonnade that runs along the platform on the north side of the Plaza Central and connects Pyramid B with the Burnt Palace.

Turn right and walk west along the columns. Almost touching the west face of Pyramid B, the Burnt Palace is a complex of three large halls and six small rooms, the whole surrounded by colonnades. Jorge Acosta named it the Burnt Palace because he found traces of destruction by fire—charred roof timbers—perhaps from the final conflagration that destroyed the city. He also discovered evidence, such as piles of pottery fragments, that suggested that the palace was sacked immediately after the fire. Scholars originally thought this complex was a royal palace, but now most believe that it acted as a council chamber for the Toltec state.

The three main halls are roughly square, and each contains 28 or 32 columns built around a sunken central patio. The columns supported flat roofs made from wood beams, poles, river pebbles, and plaster. The walls were lined with low benches, and each hall contained one or two small altars.

You first come to Hall 1, whose entrance is in the passage between the palace and Pyramid B. Numerous stone and ceramic fragments were discovered here, including a broken *chac mool*. A large cache of pottery was found beneath the floors.

The central Hall 2, which has square rather than round columns, is more interesting. Under protective roofs on the north and south walls, you can see well-preserved stone reliefs along the base of the benches. The tablets depict processions of men, probably warrior-rulers, below a narrow frieze of serpents on a blue and red background. Beneath the floor, Acosta found a number of offering caches containing jade, shells, beads, and mosaic mirrors. In this hall, he also found a perfectly preserved *chac mool* (in the National Museum of Anthropology) that has become one of the iconic sculptures of Mesoamerica; a replica replaces it.

Continuing west, you come to Hall 3, which replicates the layout of Hall 1 but is in worse condition. Behind these three halls lie the six smaller rooms numbered 1 through 6. Most had three or four columns supporting the rooms, and remnants of friezes were found in one. They acted either as storerooms or as spaces for private functions. Another colonnade abuts the north side of the palace and connects it with the North Plaza.

Graphic evidence shows Aztec occupation in the Burnt Palace after the fall of the Toltecs: garbage pits filled with Aztec ritual pottery (incense burners decorated with skulls, etc.) and at least one Aztec tomb.

Steps on the south side of the Burnt Palace lead down to the Central Plaza, the heart of Tula Grande. In the center stands the square Adoratorio (Temple) measuring 8.5 meters to a side. With four staircases ascending its single tier, it strongly resembles the Eagle Platform at Chichén Itzá, which was also excavated and restored by Acosta. Within, he found two Aztec offering caches (pottery vessels and figurines) and a fragment of a *chac mool.*

The west side of the plaza is dominated by Ballcourt 2, which was excavated by INAH's Proyecto Tula. On the right front you see the remnants of a *tzompantli,* or skull platform; the sides are decorated with stone reliefs of skull racks. Similar platforms were found at Chichén Itzá and Tenochtitlan. The ballcourt is about one-third larger than Ballcourt 1 but was far more damaged. From the top, you can see to the south and west the mounds of a number of unexcavated temples and the residential complexes excavated by Charnay more than a century ago.

If you cut back across the plaza, on the east side you will find the ruins of Pyramid C, the largest and most damaged structure in Tula. Its entire west face, including the main staircase, was destroyed by a gigantic pit dug by Aztec-era treasure seekers. Buried in and around the structure, Acosta found numerous Aztec offerings, including pottery, shells, flint blades, and jade. On the ground in front you see a large circular stone resembling a millstone whose function is unknown.

The pyramid originally had five tiers, possibly built in three phases, but only the first three tiers of the west facade have been reconstructed. You can climb a rough path to the summit and have a good view of the warriors atop Pyramid C. From here, you also have a good view of the Tula region. The large hill to the west is Cerro Magoni, site of pre-Toltec and Toltec settlements. To the north you see the Endo reservoir, and to the east lies the El Salitre swamp, around which were Toltec residential districts and obisidian workshops. Beyond loom the tanks of a large Pemex oil refinery. The bustling, dusty town of Tula de Allende lies just south and west.

The last sight on our tour of Tula is a small altar under a corrugated roof at the beginning of the colonnade between Pyramids C and B. Here you see another bench with a fragment of a relief depicting two ritually dressed men under an undulating serpent border.

TENAYUCA

INTRODUCTION

Situated in an obscure northern suburb of Mexico City, Tenayuca is the best-preserved Aztec temple still standing. Tenayuca is renowned for its serpent symbolism; the ceremonial precinct is surrounded by hundreds of stone reptiles,

TENAYUCA

How to get there: Tenayuca's pyramid stands on the northern fringes of Mexico City. The easiest way to reach the site is to take a taxi from the Terminal del Norte (Autobuses del Norte Metro station). By car—and with an excellent map—head all the way north on Eje Central (Av. Lázaro Cárdenas) and veer left on Acueducto Tenayuca, continuing about 15 blocks until you turn right on Av. Pirámides. The ruins lie about two blocks north.

Hours: Daily 1000–1700.

Admission fee: 17 pesos.

How long to tour: One hour.

Recommended gear: Hats.

Museum: Just inside the entrance to the site stands a small museum with good exhibits and a number of the stone sculptures that were found during the excavation in the late 1920s.

and more serpent heads jut from the pyramid wall. If you want to experience the ambience of the pre-Hispanic Valley of Mexico far from the hue and cry of tourists, go to Tenayuca.

Tenayuca's roots lie in the pre-Aztec period. Shortly after the fall of Tula (shortly before A.D. 1200), a chieftain named Xolotl led his tribe into the valley from the north. They subjugated a number of the area tribes and settled in Tenayuca. Xolotl's descendants erected the early stages of the pyramid on this site. After the Aztecs rose to power, they continued its expansion, building it into one of the more impressive structures in the valley. Archaeologists believe that this pyramid was the model for all the Aztec temples that followed, including Tenochtitlan's Great Temple. Tenayuca was forgotten by the Spaniards after the Conquest; this neglect preserved the pyramid's ruins until they were excavated early in the 20th century.

HISTORY

Lying on the shores of Lake Texcoco, Tenayuca was occupied as early as the Middle Preclassic era (1200–400 B.C.) and later became an outpost of Teotihuacan. According to native accounts, around the time of Tula's destruction a northern tribe called the Chichimeca assembled near the mythical gathering point of Chicomoztoc. They were led by their chieftain Xolotl, who took them first to the ruins of Tula and then into the Valley of Mexico. Here they subjugated the nearby tribes and made their capital at Tenayuca. Archaeologists believe Xolotl actually ruled between A.D. 1250 and 1270, well after Tula's fall. This was probably the time they succeeded in stabilizing their relatively modest domain (not the entirety of Toltec lands, as their histories claimed).

Like all the tribes who settled in the valley at this time, the Chichimeca wrapped themselves in Toltec culture, learning to speak Nahuatl—the language of the the valley and spoken by many groups—and depend on agriculture instead of hunting and gathering. They also attempted to expand their tribute network through warfare. Unfortunately, there was too much competition; a number of other northern tribes were settling in the region at the same time, including the Tepanecs at Atzcapotzalco and the Acolhuas at Coatlinchan. They all were warrior tribes of about the same strength; consequently alliances through trade and marriage were more popular than war.

Around A.D. 1300, another band of nomads entered the valley. Calling themselves the Mexica, they stopped in Tenayuca, where they saw the imposing double pyramid surrounded by a wall of almost 150 serpents. When the Mexica founded their own city in Tenochtitlan, they evidently used Tenayuca pyramid as the model for their own Great Temple.

In the early 14th century A.D., the fourth Chichimeca ruler, Quinatzin, moved his capital from Tenayuca to Texcoco across the lake. Tenayuca diminished in size and importance. When the rising Tepanecs of nearby Azcapotzalco decided to expand their domain, Tenayuca was one of their first targets. Around A.D. 1370, they hired a mercenary army from Tenochtitlan and Tlatelolco, and shortly after Tenayuca was part of the Tepanec empire. The youthful Tepanec prince Tezozomoc became Tenayuca's ruler, the first step to a rule that would last a half century and dominate the entire valley.

Tepanec control lasted until A.D. 1426 (the year after Tezozomoc's death), when the Aztec-led Triple Alliance defeated Azcapotzalco, beginning almost a century of Aztec power in the Valley of Mexico. During this era, Tenayuca remained a secondary town. As a religious center, however, it continued to be important, perhaps because the Aztecs considered the Chichimeca honored predecessors of their rule. The temple was consecrated to Huitzilopochtli and Tlaloc, the principal Aztec deities, and every 52 years (the main Aztec religious cycle), the structure was enlarged, making it one of the largest buildings in the valley.

In 1521, the Spaniards passed through Tenayuca on their final campaign against the Aztecs. The conquistador Bernál Díaz wrote: "Then we went on to Tenayuca, a large town, which was also deserted and which we called the city of snakes, on account of the three snakes they kept in their temple and worshipped as gods."

After the Conquest, Franciscan monks destroyed the idols in the temple and used some of the stones to build the neighboring chapel. Tenayuca dwindled and eventually was engulfed by nearby Tlanepantla. Today, Tenayuca is a poor suburb of Mexico City lying just below Cerro Tenayo to the north.

ARCHAEOLOGICAL RECORD

Tenayuca's temple was never torn down, so its presence was never forgotten. Leopoldo Batres scouted it as an archaeological site in 1898. Between 1925 and

1929, teams from the Dirección de Arqueología, a predecessor of INAH, excavated and restored the site. Their results were issued in a lavishly illustrated 1935 volume that remains a model for archaeological reports.

TOURING THE SITE

The site fills the plaza in the heart of Tenayuca, a dilapidated neighborhood that at least has the distinction of age compared to the surrounding district. The pyramid rests on a massive base lined on the north, south, and east with almost 150 stone serpents facing outward. This is the famous Coatepantli, or Wall of Serpents, that impressed the Aztecs. Their heads are carved stone, while their coiled bodies are constructed of rock and mortar. Traces of paint remain on the heads; each line of serpents was painted differently, apparently to reflect their orientation toward the directions. More serpent heads jut from the pyramid walls above; decorative elements, they also held up the structure's facing.

Walk now to the west side of the pyramid where the main staircases descend. Like almost all the later Aztec temples, Tenayuca's structure is divided in two. The north and

The Coatepantli, or "Wall of Serpents," runs along the base of Tenayuca's main pyramid.

south halves of the pyramid are reached by separate staircases. On top stood two temples; during the Aztec era, the southern one was dedicated to Huitzilopochtli, their main deity, while the north temple was devoted to the pan-Mesoamerican Rain God Tlaloc. It is not known if the early Chichimeca stages of the pyramid had different gods.

The staircase in front of you represents the seventh and last stage of the pyramid's construction. From the earliest phase, the temple was always bipartite, rising in four steps to two separate temples on top. The current base is roughly square, 60 meters to a side, and the structure rises about 17 meters to the platform on which the original temples stood. Like the Great Temple of Tenochtitlan, Tenayuca's pyramid was expanded every 52 years to mark the beginning of a new religious cycle. As you walk up the steps, you will notice that some of the stones are carved with glyphs; these represent dates, warrior shields, precious stones, and solar disks among other symbols. Archaeologists have not been able to arrange these symbols into a coherent order or text. At the top of the steps, you look down into a well that drops to where the fifth-stage staircase begins its ascent. Signs forbid you from climbing to the top of the temple.

Descending back to the base, you see at the southwest corner of the pyramid a small altar projecting from the wall. The sides are decorated with stone skulls, and the interior walls originally contained murals of skulls and crossed bones. This altar was a *tzompantli* or "skull rack" on which the Aztecs displayed the skulls of sacrificial victims. More of the skulls are exhibited in the site museum.

Further altars of serpents stand on the north and south side of the pyramid just beyond the platform. Larger than those along the wall, these are also coiled; their stone heads have turned-back snouts topped with elaborate crests. These represent Xiuhcoatl, the fiery serpent who was used by Huitzilopochtli to slay his sister Coyolxauhqui (see the Great Temple section below). Just to the east of each serpent stands a small rectangular platform.

As you walk along the pyramid's south side, you can see an indentation where archaeologists uncovered a serpent from an earlier stage of the structure. The base of the pyramid is also penetrated by tunnels on the south, east, and north sides. These were made during the excavations to analyze the construction of the temple and search for tombs. None of the latter were ever found.

After visiting the pyramid, it is interesting to stop by the neighboring chapel of San Bartolo. This 16th-century structure was constructed with Aztec stones; many carvings are still visible in the walls.

As long as you're this far north, continue north on Av. Pirámide to see the pyramid at the nearby site of **Santa Cecilia Acatitlán**. To travel from the La Raza Metro Station to Tenayuca, take one of the small vans marked "Pirámide."

THE GREAT TEMPLE

INTRODUCTION

In the heart of Mexico City, the ruins of the Great Temple provide a fascinating window into a Mesoamerican civilization at its height. This Aztec pyramid was discovered by chance in 1978, and subsequent excavations unearthed a number of spectacular finds, such as the massive Coyolxauhqui stone and the life-size ceramic Eagle Warrior statues. Most of these artifacts are beautifully displayed in the museum (one of Mexico's best) immediately behind the ruins. Scholarly

DESIGN MOTIFS OF ANCIENT MEXICO

THE GREAT TEMPLE

How to get there: The Great Temple ruins lie just northeast of the Zócalo along Calle Argentina between Calles Moneda and Justo Sierra. The easiest way to reach them is to take the Metro to the Zócalo station and walk north about 100 meters.

Hours: Daily 0900–1700.

Admission fee: 30 pesos.

How long to tour: Two hours.

Museum: The site museum is one of the best archaeological museums in Mexico. Its focal points are a huge diorama recreating ancient Tenochtitlan and the original Coyolxauhqui Stone that lay at the foot of the temple's Huitzilopochtli side. The exhibitions display an unparalleled collection of artifacts found in the excavations. These include full-size ceramic eagle warriors and an amazing assemblage of objects that were buried in the temple's numerous offering caches. One of these offerings was a jaguar skeleton whose jaws held a crystal ball; and other caches held objects from throughout Mesoamerica and plant and animal remains taken from the furthest reaches of the Aztec empire. The museum also contains a large and scary display on human sacrifice.

analysis of the excavations has provided a wealth of clues about Aztec religious and political life. Among these was definitive proof that this structure was the holiest place in the Aztec world, literally the center of their Universe—the placement of the Coyolxauhqui stone; all of Tenochitlan's roads converging on this one central point; and the presence of the most important shrine to the primary gods of Huitzilopochtli and Tlaloc.

At first glance, the Great Temple ruins are a jumble of disparate architectural elements—stairs going nowhere and unconnected walls. The Spaniards razed the top half of this Aztec holy place immediately after the Conquest and built houses on the foundations. What you see is almost all the stages of building construction exposed at once, like an onion sliced in half showing all its layers. Once you walk through the site and see the excellent reconstructions in the museum, you can begin to imagine how this temple had such a hold on the beliefs and daily lives of the Aztecs.

HISTORY

The story of the Aztecs is wrapped in myth and legend. As they rose to power in the Valley of Mexico, they rewrote their history to justify their dominion over others. They had not always been so successful.

According to myth, they began as a very small and very poor tribe, living on an island named Aztlan (Land of White Herons) in a lagoon somewhere on the farthest margins of the Toltec empire. Aztlan's site is unknown, but it may have been Mexcaltitlan near the Nayarit coast or a highland lake in Guanajuato

THE AZTEC ROYAL SUCCESSION

The following is a list of the *tlatoani,* or rulers of Tenochitlan from its A.D. 1325 founding (date not certain) to the Spanish Conquest, accompanied by the dates of their reign.

1325 (1345?)–1372 Tenoch	1469–1481 Axayacatl
1372–1390 Acamapichtli	1481–1486 Tizoc
1390–1417 Huitzilihuit	1486–1502 Ahuizotl
1417–1427 Chimalpopoca	1502–1520 Motecuhzoma Xocoyotzin (Motecuhzoma II)
1427–1440 Itzcoatl	
1440–1469 Motecuhzoma Ihuilcamina (Motecuhzoma I)	1521 Cuauhtemoc—his reign lasted less than 90 days

or Michoacan. Around A.D. 1000, the Aztecs (People of Aztlan) abandoned their home on orders from Huitzilopochtli (Hummingbird on the Left), their fierce tribal god. Huitzilopochtli was originally a historical person, a great chieftain who was later deified. On the journey, Huitzilopochtli renamed them the Mexica, perhaps after a group that joined the Aztecs on their trek. He promised his people that they would eventually conquer "all the peoples in the Universe."

(The Mexica were not renamed "Aztecs" until centuries after the Spanish Conquest. For simplicity's sake, I will continue to call them Aztecs.)

The next 350 years are the story of the Aztecs' epic struggle to find a new home, a new identity as an agricultural people (as opposed to hunter-gatherers), and power and wealth. Their first stop was Chicomoztoc, site of a womblike cave with seven rooms. According to the origin legends of many Valley of Mexico tribes, this was their ancestral birthplace, and here too the Aztecs were reborn, symbolically giving themselves the same lineage as those more established tribes.

The Aztecs stopped at resting places for years, sometimes decades. At one of these, Huitzilopochtli's sister Malinalxochitl rebelled against her brother's rule and split off from the tribe, taking a group of followers southward to found the town of Malinalco. Tribal squabbles at another stop, Coatepec, threatened Huitzilopochtli's very existence and afterward became one of the core myths of the Aztec religion.

For some years, they had been settled at Coatepec, a hill somewhere north of Mexico City, when Huitzilopochtli told his people it was time to move on. Another tribal dispute began, pitting the chief against the breakaway group led by his sister. In the myth, another of Huitzilopochtli's sisters, Coyolxauhqui, learns that her mother, Coatlicue, has become pregnant from a magic ball of feathers that fell from the sky. She rounds up her 400 brothers and they storm the hill, killing their mother for shaming them. Inside Coatlicue, however, is the baby Huitzilopochtli already fully dressed for battle. Reborn as the Sun God and wielding the "Fire Serpent," he slays his sister and defeats his 400 brothers. Coyolxauhqui's body rolls down the hill, breaking into pieces before coming to rest at the base. From this juncture, Huitzilopochtli as the Aztec tribal god embodies the most powerful force of nature, and female sacrifice becomes a crucial rite to ensure crop fertility and a bounteous harvest. This myth is enshrined in stone on the south half of the Great Temple.

The Aztecs arrived in Tula around A.D. 1165, perhaps taking part in the Toltec empire's fall. From then on, the Aztecs deified their predecessors, identifying themselves whenever possible with Toltec achievements. From here they moved into the Valley of Mexico, as the poorest and most recent of the valley's many new arrivals.

Their first years were difficult. Their relatives the Malinalcans had poisoned the local chieftains against them, and they were constantly harassed and evicted. Eventually, they begged the Toltec-descended leader of Culhuacan for protection and a bit of land. He gave them part of the lava field near Cuicuilco and, to everyone's surprise, they thrived, living off snakes and other local fauna and working as mercenaries.

They may have been poor, but they were not meek. They avidly intermarried with the local Toltec lineages and eventually reached such a status that they felt they could ask the Culhua for an aristocratic bride. A local chief agreed and gave his beautiful daughter to be the bride of their ruler. The Culhua did not know that she was to be bride of their god, not their chief. When the princess's father arrived for the celebration, a priest was dancing in the skin of his daughter. She had been sacrificed to Huitzilopochtli. Outraged, the Culhua killed all the Aztecs they could and drove the rest into the marshy swamps of Lake Texcoco.

Wet, hungry, bleeding from wounds, and shivering from cold, the night that followed was the Aztecs' darkest hour. Their god did not desert them, however. His priests reminded them that the heart of one of their enemies had been thrown into the swamp and that Huitzilopochtli had told them that on the spot

THE PHASES OF TENOCHTITLAN

As the all-important center of Aztec life, the history of Tenochtitlan is lengthy and typically portrayed in phases tied to times of major construction on the temple.

First Phase—No longer visible because of decay from the rising water table. It was probably a crude temple made from reeds and mud begun in either A.D. 1325 or 1345, when the Aztecs founded their city.

Second Phase—Date glyph found for A.D. 1390; this phase became the prototype for the sub-

sequent five stages as the subsequent stages all looked like this phase, only bigger.

Third Phase—Rapid expansion took place in the vicinity of A.D. 1431.

Fourth Phase—Accurate dating is uncertain.

Fifth Phase—Contained no date glyph and was ravaged by the Conquest.

Sixth Phase—Contained no date glyph and was also mostly destroyed by the Spanish.

Seventh Phase—Approximately A.D. 1510–1521.

it fell would be an eagle sitting on a nopal cactus. There, the Aztecs would found a city from which they would conquer the Universe. The next morning, they saw the eagle and cactus (also the symbol of modern Mexico) just as the god had said. They immediately began construction of a crude reed shelter that was the first phase of the Great Temple. They named their city Tenochtitlan, Place of Rock and Cactus. The year was A.D. 1325.

Along with the jaguar warriors, **eagle warriors** were an elite military and religious group who fought battles and took part in ceremonies honoring the Sun God.

Forced into another difficult habitat—this time a swampy island in the middle of a lake—the Aztecs once again flourished. They lived off birds, fish, frogs, and other wildlife and began to construct *chinampas*, the "floating gardens" on which many lake-dwellers grew grains and vegetables. The women paddled their canoes to surrounding towns to sell produce and animals, beginning a trade network that would eventually run to the ends of Mesoamerica.

The Aztec chieftain who helped found their city and led it for the first 25 years was Tenoch, who was given the title *tlatoani,* or speaker. Under him, the Aztecs undoubtedly expanded and improved their principal temple and added an adjacent shrine to the Rain God Tlaloc, their other main deity.

The Aztecs assiduously formed new alliances with the more powerful peoples who lived around the Valley of Mexico's lakes. After Tenoch died, they asked for and received a Culhua nobleman named Acamapichtli as their new *tlatoani,* once again giving them the important Toltec cultural connection.

In addition to the Culhua, the other power in the valley was the Tepanecs, who made their capital in Atzcapotzalco. From A.D. 1371 to 1426, the Tepanecs were ruled by the brilliant Tezozomoc, a Machiavellian leader who built the largest state in the valley since Teotihuacan. Tezozomoc hired the Aztecs as a mercenary army, sending them on campaigns throughout the valley and to conquer regions immediately outside, including Cuernavaca and Toluca. Ever the warriors, the Aztecs performed so well that they became important tribute-gatherers, fielding an army that almost equaled the Tepanecs.

The Great Temple's second stage was built during this period of rapid Aztec growth. Archaeologists found the date-glyph for the year A.D. 1390 on the structure. This temple provided the model for the five stages that followed, most obviously the divisions between the north—Tlaloc—and south—Huitzilopochtli—halves of the temple. In front of the Tlaloc shrine, archaeologists found a brightly painted *chac mool* that was obviously a copy of those found in Tula, only less well-made. The Huitzilopochtli side was the site of the Stone of Sacrifice, a bare stone with a rounded top. The sacrificial victims were bent backward to give the priests easier access to their hearts. The Spanish saw a similar stone atop the last stage temple.

The Aztecs' fortunes changed dramatically with the death of Tezozomoc. He was succeeded by his unpopular and politically inept son Maxtla. The Tepanec victories had given them many enemies, and the Aztecs saw a chance to defeat the Tepanec by forming alliances with the most powerful of these enemies. In 1426, the Triple Alliance of Tenochtitlan, Texcoco, and Tlacopan (later called Tacuba) besieged Atzcapotzalco. After 114 days, they broke the Tepanec defenses and captured their leader. Maxtla was seized and ritually sacrificed, his blood scattered in the four directions of the compass. Tenochtitlan was now the dominant partner in an alliance that would rule central Mexico for almost a century.

The new *tlatoani* was Itzcoatl, a powerful Aztec warrior, who governed with the aid of Tlacaelel, his brother and the power behind the throne for the next five decades. The Great Temple was once again expanded, possibly in A.D. 1431. This third-stage temple added flights of steep stairways and the standard-bearer sculptures you see today.

Itzcoatl was succeeded by Motecuhzoma I, under whom Tlacaelel rewrote Aztec history to justify their dominance. They were now the true heirs of the Toltecs, living at the center of the Universe and given the divine tasks of making day follow night and bringing the rains. To do this, they needed captives, so Tlacaelel began the tradition of "Flowery Wars" against Tlaxcala and Huexotzingo. These were ritual battles fought solely to provide victims for sacrifice to the gods. The center for these religious tasks was the Great Temple.

This stage temple, which had a date glyph for A.D. 1454, was the richest found by archaeologists. The sides were decorated with undulating stone serpents, frogs, and large braziers. The massive platform on which the temple now rests was added, and the Coyolxauhqui stone was placed in front of the steps on the Huitzilopochtli side. Dozens of offerings were buried at this time, including one on the Tlaloc side containing the bones of 42 children, almost certainly sacrificial victims.

Motecuhzoma I was succeeded by Tizoc, considered the least distinguished of the rulers. His reign cut short when he died by poisoning, he was succeeded by his brother Axayacatl and then Ahuizotl, two empire-builders who extended the Aztec dominion near and far. They took over Tlatelolco—the neighboring market center that around A.D. 1340 had been founded by a Mexica splinter group—and captured lands in every direction, including some as far away as Guatemala. The only groups they failed to subdue were the Tarascans in Michoacan and the Tlaxcalans just to the west.

In 1487, Ahuizotl decided to glorify the Aztec achievement and mark a crucial date in their religious calendar by holding a massive dedication ceremony for an expanded Great Temple. Captives from the many Aztec wars were brought to Tenochtitlan by the thousands, and rulers of the Aztec tribute states were obligated to attend. How many captives were actually sacrificed is fiercely debated by Mesoamerica experts.

Native accounts say that 80,400 captives were executed over four days. Ahuizotl began the sacrifices; blood was soon running down the Great Temple in streams and congealing in the city streets. Some experts say this number is an exaggeration, perhaps invented by the Spanish to justify their conquest. They point out that the priests would have had to sacrifice 14 captives a minute day and night to kill them all in four days' time—a near impossibility. And then what would they do with the bodies? Nevertheless, that an enormous sacrifice did take place is confirmed by a number of native accounts and it is hard to deny that human sacrifice was the most important rite in the Aztec religion.

Archaeologists are not sure which stage of the temple was the one glorified at this ceremony. Neither the fifth nor the sixth stages contained date glyphs. From the fifth stage, only a platform remains from the ravages of the Conquest. The sixth stage was also largely destroyed by the Spanish; only three stone serpent heads have been found. Immediately north of the Great Temple, however, researchers discovered three shrines, including a skull rack, and the Eagle Precinct. The latter was a sacred place for the eagle warriors; inside were murals depicting costumed men ready for battle and two amazing life-size ceramic sculptures of warriors in full eagle regalia. They are on display in the site museum.

Ahuizotl was succeeded by Motecuhzoma II, also known as Motecuhzoma Xocoyotzin, the last Aztec *tlatoani*. Despite Spanish claims to the contrary, Motecuhzoma was the warrior his predecessors were. He continued the expansion of the Aztec empire, ordering expeditions in Oaxaca and against his perennial enemy, Tlaxcala. The latter failed, embittering the Tlaxcalans to such an extent that they would ally themselves with anybody to bring down the Aztecs.

Motecuhzoma was also deeply religious, spending much of his time in the Sacred Precinct built around the Great Temple. The Aztecs put great faith in omens, and Motecuhzoma's reign began with some considered particularly inauspicious, including a comet and a fire in the Great Temple. When Cortés landed with his troops in Veracruz in 1519, rumors spread that he was Topiltzin Quetzalcoatl, the Toltec ruler returned to reconquer his empire. Motecuhzoma certainly took these claims into account, but, contrary to Spanish accounts, he was not paralyzed by fear. His envoys offered the Spanish food of the gods—meals sprinkled with the blood of sacrificial victims—and food of men—tortillas, corn, and turkey. The Spanish ate the food of men; they were mere mortals and would be dealt with as such.

The conquistadors marched toward Tenochtitlan from the Gulf Coast, making allies with Aztec enemies along the way, most notably the Tlaxcalans. Despite Aztec delaying tactics, the Spanish entered their capital, where they were welcomed until Motecuhzoma could find a way to dispatch them. They were housed in the palace of Axayacatl, Motecuhzoma's father, just outside the Sacred Precinct and literally in the shadow of the Great Temple.

Tensions quickly rose. Using the pretext of the killing of six Spaniards by Aztec subjects on the coast, Cortés took the poorly guarded Motecuhzoma hostage. Cortés demanded that an altar to the Virgin Mary be placed atop the Great Temple and then insisted that the idols of Tlaloc and Huitzilopochtli be removed. He showed his abhorrence of the pagan faith by striking the latter god's beaten gold mask with a crowbar.

Before the Aztecs could respond, Cortés was forced to run back to the coast to counter the expedition of his Spanish rival Pánfilio Narváez. He left 80 men guarding Motecuhzoma. The nervous Spaniards watched as Aztec priests enacted a ceremony in a nearby courtyard. Suddenly, they panicked, rushing on the defenseless Aztecs and slaughtering them. When Cortés returned victorious and with many fresh soldiers who had been convinced of their share in the potential loot, both Aztec and Spaniard knew that it was time for a showdown.

As the Aztec attack began, Motecuhzoma was sent up on a rooftop to plead for peace. He was met by a shower of stones and throwing darts, struck, and fatally wounded. The Aztec forces climbed the Great Temple and rained projectiles down on the Spaniards. Cortés led his troops on a counterattack, charging with them up the temple's steps and hacking at the defenders. When they reached the top, they seized the idols, which had been replaced during his absence, and hurled them down the steps. Then they set fire to the shrines atop the holiest Aztec site.

Despite their victory, the Spaniards' position was untenable. They had to flee, which they did under cover of night, carrying their gold and vulnerable to Aztec snipers. Dozens were killed or drowned by greed as their loot pulled them down when they tried to swim across the canals. Nevertheless, Cortés and the bulk of his force survived. Their Tlaxcalan allies took them in and treated their wounds. The Spanish began to plan the end of Tenochtitlan.

Residents of the Valley of Mexico constructed *chinampas*, tiny blocks of arable land, from brush and mud in the shallows of the great lakes.

In the summer of 1521, the Spanish and their Indian allies began to lay siege to the Aztec's island capital. The attackers were systematic and ruthless. Starvation and disease laid waste to the residents of Tenochtitlan, and the Spanish slowly closed the noose. This was total war, with immense slaughter of both warriors and women and children and the burning and razing of the enemy city. The conquistadors captured Tenochtitlan and advanced on Tlatelolco, the last Aztec stand (see Tlatelolco section following). On August 13, 1521, the last Aztec ruler, Cuauhtemoc, was captured while trying to escape. The last great Mesoamerican civilization was ended; the era of the New World had begun.

What parts of the Aztec city they did not destroy in battle, the Spaniards pulled down during the subsequent decades. It can be assumed that the Great Temple was a particular target of Spanish revenge. What was not pulled down in anger was razed as part of a religious crusade. The Inquisition, targeted at heretic faiths, was then gathering steam in Spain, and Catholic priests took special joy in eliminating every last remnant of Mesoamerican religions. In 1531, Bishop Zumarraga announced that he had destroyed 5,000 temples and 20,000 idols. The preferred building material for Catholic churches was the stone from Aztec temples.

The land where the temple had stood was given to a conquistador named Ávila. He built a mansion here, which was inherited by his two sons. They rebelled against the Spanish Crown, refusing to pay taxes, and in 1566 they were executed for treason. The mansion was razed and the site strewn with salt so that nothing would grow. Afterward, it became a garbage dump. Buildings were eventually erected here, and the site's last secular occupant was the Porrua and Sons bookstore (now relocated just to the north).

ARCHAEOLOGICAL RECORD

What was left of the Aztec capital was buried under Mexico City. A 17th-century archbishop named Palafox made it his task to find all the fragments of Aztec sculptures and reliefs lying around the city and bury them so they would not influence impressionable (probably native) minds. Any discussion of the Aztecs, except to condemn them, was forbidden. The Aztec empire was gone and almost forgotten.

In 1790, the residents of Mexico City were suddenly reminded of the past beneath their feet. The viceroy ordered the resurfacing of the Zócalo, the main square and heart of the city. During the excavation, the workers unearthed two monumental sculptures, the Sun Stone and the Coatlicue sculpture, that were so massive and finely made that the local scholarly community could not ignore them. They were described in a short book by Antonio de León y Gama that emphasized the excellence of the sculptures' aesthetic qualities. Copies of the book made their way across the Atlantic, arousing the interest of European intellectuals.

Stimulated by this discovery, in 1794 a Spanish priest named Fray Servando Teresa de Mier gave a sermon in honor of the Virgin of Guadalupe lamenting the destruction of Aztec relics and stating the radical idea that the Aztec religion deserved respect and study, not condemnation. Further, he said that the Quetzalcoatl known from the Toltec myths was actually St. Thomas, a 10th-century holy man come to evangelize the Americas. Unfortunately for Fray Servando, the Inquisition was still very much active; he was tried and persecuted. Nevertheless, Mexican scholars remembered his defense of the Indian religion.

In 1802, the German explorer Alexander von Humboldt arrived in Mexico City to see the Coatlicue sculpture described in de León's book. He discovered that it had been moved to the university, where the rector had buried it in an underground corridor—local Indians had begun making pilgrimages to it and leaving offerings (meanwhile, the Sun Stone was stored in a building next to the Metropolitan Cathedral). Humboldt received permission to disinter it and described the stone in one of his widely published travel books. He also wrote sympathetically about the Indians' plight under Spanish rule.

the fearsome face of an Aztec god

DANIELLE GUSTAFSON

Interest in Tenochtitlan took off at the end of the 19th century. Scholars knew that the main Aztec religious structure, the Great Temple, lay somewhere north of the Zócalo and perhaps slightly to the east. The archaeologist Leopoldo Batres was certain it was buried under the Metropolitan Cathedral. He eagerly followed the course of a 1900 sewer excavation under the cathedral, hoping at

MOTECUHZOMA'S MEAL

It is a measure of Cortés and his men's innate arrogance and surety of their religion that they were not humbled by the Aztec capital of Tenochtitlan. What they experienced was a city that was far larger, more beautiful, and more sophisticated than anything they knew in Spain. Not least of the wonders was the food. Here is Bernal Díaz del Castillo's description of one of Motecuhzoma's daily meals: For his meals his cooks had more than thirty styles of dishes made according to their fashion and usage; and they put them on small low clay braziers so that they would not get cold. They cooked more than three hundred dishes of the food which Motecuhzoma was going to eat, and more than a thousand more for the men of the guard. . . . I heard it said that they cooked the meat of young boys for him; and as they had so many different dishes of so many different things, we could not see if it was human flesh or something else, because every day they cooked him fowl, wattled fowl, pheasants, native partridges, quail, domestic and wild ducks, deer, peccary, reedbirds and doves and hares and rabbits, and many other birds and things that are native to this country, that are so numerous I could never finish naming them, and so will leave them. I know that after our captain reprimanded him for sacrificing and eating human flesh, from that time forward he gave orders that that sort of food not be cooked for him. Enough of this, let us return to the manner that they served him during his meal, and it was thus: if it was cold they made him a fire of glowing coals, which did not smoke; and the odor of the bark of which they made those coals was most fragrant; and so that they did not give him more heat than he wished they put in front of him a screen worked in gold, depicting idols. He sat on a low, richly worked soft seat, and the table was also low, and made in the same manner as the seat, and there they put tablecloths of white fabric, and some rather large handkerchiefs of the same, and four very beautiful and clean women gave him water for his hands out of a kind of deep acquamanile, which they call jicales, and to catch the water they put down a kind of plate, and gave him the towels, and two other women brought him the tortillas; and when he began to eat they put in front of him a thing like a door of wood all painted up with gold so that he could not be seen eating; and the four women stood aside, and there came to his side four great lords and elders, who stood, and from time to time Motecuhzoma chatted with them and asked them questions, and as a great favor gave each of those old men a dish of what he had been eating. . . . They served him on Cholula pottery, some red and some black. While he was eating it was unthinkable that there be any disturbance or loud speech among his guard, who were in rooms near that of Motecuhzoma. They brought him fruit of every sort available in that country, but he ate very little of it, and from time to time they brought him some cups of fine gold, with a certain drink made of cacao, which they said was for success with women; and then we thought no more about it; but I saw that they brought more than 50 great jars of prepared good cacao with its foam, and he drank of that; and the women served him drink very respectfully, and sometimes at meal times there were very ugly hunchbacked Indians, who were very short of body and deformed, and some of them told ribald stories; and there were others who must have been jesters, who made witty remarks, and others who sang and danced, because Motecuhzoma was very fond of pleasures and songs, and he ordered the leftovers and jars of cacao given to them. The same four women removed the tablecloths and returned with water for his hands, which they did with much reverence. Motecuhzoma spoke to those four old noblemen of worthwhile things, and they took their leave with great respect, and he rested.

every moment to see temple walls. Unfortunately, he neglected to look behind him, because the sewer cut right through the southern half of the temple as it passed under Calle Guatemala.

In 1913, Manuel Gamio discovered the southwest corner of the Great Temple during a building demolition, and two decades later Emilio Cuevas found a stairway leading up to the building's platform. Unfortunately, they did not identify their finds as part of the temple. Subsequent excavations included digs along Calles Cuba and Argentina and work during the 1966 subway excavation. In 1974, a dig in a patio of the National Palace unearthed remains of Cortés's palace and of a circular Aztec temple. The Great Temple remained on the missing list.

In 1977, INAH organized the Museum of Tenochtitlan project to find and excavate the Great Temple. Their work progessed slowly until early on the morning of February 21, 1978, when an electrical company lineman unearthed the Coyolxauhqui stone. Head archaeologist Eduardo Matos Moctezuma immediately recognized it as one of the most important sculptures of the Great Temple. The full excavation began a month later.

The dig lasted two years and unearthed six of the seven stages of the temples and numerous priceless objects, many of which were found in the more than 100 offering caches discovered within the structure. The excavation was followed by restoration work and the construction of the museum at the back of the site.

These excavations proved what archaeologists had long theorized. The Great Temple was the axis around which rotated all phases of Aztec life—religion, politics, war, and agriculture. Not only did the building mark the Aztec empire's founding, it acted as the center of the cults of their two most important gods, Tlaloc and Huitzilopochtli, respectively the god of rain and agriculture and the tribal god of war and power. Each half of the temple represented a hill crucial to the two gods: Tlaloc's home and the site where Huitzilopochtli slew his evil sister, Coyolxauhqui. The entire empire became involved in ceremonies taking place at the Great Temple. Wars were begun to seize captives for sacrifice, and every sector of society had to provide ritual goods and participants for the ceremonies.

The Great Temple's symbolic content went even further: it was the geographic center of the Universe. The four directions began at this point, radiating first through a ceremonial precinct filled with temples built in alignment with the Great Temple and then extending to all parts of their empire and beyond to the boundaries of the world. The structure also connected the celestial spheres with the Underworld. The temple platform represented the level of earth, while the tiers of the temple represented the 13 divine levels above. Below, the temple was a sort of umbilical cord connecting to the nine levels of the Underworld. It was only through ceremonies enacted atop the Great Temple that the Universe was able to continue, that made day follow night and caused the precious rains to fall on the crops.

In the late 1980s, two more stone monument sculptures were found just outside the perimeter of the site. One was a great carved eagle with a hole in its back for sacrificial hearts; the other was the cylindrical Motecuhzoma I stone whose sides were engraved with a relief showing the ruler's victories. Since then, no great Aztec ruins or objects have been unearthed from downtown Mexico City. They are still there, however, waiting some stroke of luck to bring them to light.

TOURING THE SITE

You enter the site through a colonial building opposite the east side of the Metropolitan Cathedral. (The little plaza in front contains a pool with a replica of the Aztec capital.) At the ticket office, you can hire the services of an official guide; there is also a good bookstore here. Make your purchases now, because the site exit is beside the museum.

Beyond the entrance, a doorway opens onto a platform overlooking the southern perimeter of the ruins. Here you have one of the best views of the Great Temple's structure and the various layers of construction. The latest stages are the outermost; the earliest viewable stage—II—is protected by the large roof in the middle. Unfortunately, no trace of the first stage temple remains. Lower-level excavations beneath the water table were hampered by water leaching into the pits. The walkway railing holds descriptive plaques at important viewing points; unfortunately, they are so corroded by the city's smog as to be unreadable.

You face the southern walls of the Great Temple. This half was dedicated to Huitzilopochtli (Hummingbird on the Left), the Aztecs' main deity, while the northern half was reserved for the cult of the Rain God Tlaloc. Small stone serpent heads jut from the walls at intervals. To your right, you see two stone braziers adorned with bows flanking a large serpent head sitting atop the Stage IV temple platform. Due east (right) of the viewing platform stands the Red Temple, a small structure dating to the Stage VI era. It is built in the style of and painted with references to Teotihuacan, the major pilgrimage destination for the Aztec rulers. The Red Temple faces east, the opposite of the Great Temple.

You descend the stairs and walk north, crossing into the boundaries of the Great Temple. On your right is an undulating stone serpent, and large serpent heads emerge from the sides of the staircases. Although serpents most often represent Quetzalcoatl, the Feathered Serpent god, here they are Xiuhcoatl, the fire serpent associated with Huitzilopochtli (the serpents on the north side are Tlaloc's and may signify lightning). This level of the temple platform was built during Stage IVb, when many of the most elaborate sculptures were added to the temple.

The walkway comes to a stone platform. On the wall abutting the street, a plaque commemorates the Ávila brothers who in 1566 were executed for treason, after which their house was destroyed and the ground covered with salt. This spot was the intersection of Calles Argentina (now the pedestrian zone

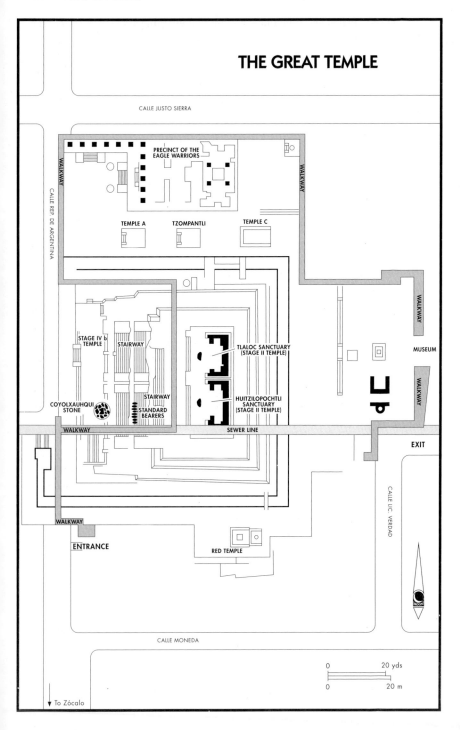

THE GREAT TEMPLE

CALLE JUSTO SIERRA

CALLE REP. DE ARGENTINA

WALKWAY

PRECINCT OF THE
EAGLE WARRIORS

TEMPLE A   TZOMPANTLI   TEMPLE C

WALKWAY

WALKWAY

STAGE IV b
TEMPLE

STAIRWAY

TLALOC SANCTUARY
(STAGE II TEMPLE)

MUSEUM

COYOLXAUHQUI
STONE

STAIRWAY

STANDARD
BEARERS

HUITZILOPOCHTLI
SANCTUARY
(STAGE II TEMPLE)

WALKWAY

WALKWAY   SEWER LINE

EXIT

WALKWAY

ENTRANCE

RED TEMPLE

CALLE LIC. VERDAD

CALLE MONEDA

0   20 yds

0   20 m

↓ To Zócalo

above) and Guatemala. If you take a right, you enter the 1900 brick sewer pipe that ran under Calle Guatemala.

In a few steps, you see on the left a replica of the famous circular Coyolxauhqui stone (the original is the centerpiece of the site museum) lying at the exact spot it was discovered in 1978. The stone depicts the broken body of the goddess Coyolxauhqui after she was hurled from Coatepec hill, here represented by the Huitzilopochtli side of the temple. The stone was found bearing traces of blue and red paint; the sculpture must have originally been quite electric. Just east of it, archaeologists discovered a large offering cache containing a greenstone engraving of Mayahuel, the pulque goddess, and numerous ceramic vessels.

Continuing east along the sewer line, you pass through the Stages IV and III staircases of the Huitzilopochtli temple. On your left, you see four replicas of stone standard-bearer sculptures with little wells in their chests. Archaeologists believe these represent either the dead brothers of Coyolxauhqui or sacrificial victims with holes in their hearts. Their right hands originally held wooden poles, hence the "standard-bearer" name.

The sewer line continues, boring right through the heart of the temple (it is amazing that the workers never realized what they were digging through). You take a left into the Stage II temple, the best preserved of all the levels. A huge roof protects its summit. The right half of the temple was consecrated to Huitzilopochtli. At the top of his staircase, a stone is carved with the date-glyph 2-Rabbit, possibly A.D. 1390. Beyond, you see the god's sacrificial stone with its curved top. Victims were bent backward over the stone, exposing their chests to the priest's razor-sharp obsidian knife. Behind stands the remain of Huitzilopochtli's shrine, the small temple that housed his idol. The Spanish claimed that the temple-top reeked of blood, which lay in clotted pools about the shrine. Huitzilopochtli's idol is rumored to be hidden in a cave in the hills near Tula.

To your left stands Tlaloc's temple, representing Tonacatepetl, the divine mountain of corn that is the base of all human nourishment. Atop the platform sits a brightly painted *chac mool*. The sculpture, bearing a receptacle of sacrificial hearts on its stomach, is executed in the style of Tula, only with far less artistry. The shrine walls behind are painted with dimly visible murals. They contain Tlaloc motifs—thick, gogglelike circles—and a human figure in an elaborate costume.

The walkway continues north and ascends a staircase. To your right, you see two more Stage IV braziers flanking a serpent head; these are dedicated to Tlaloc and are a counterpoint to the Huitzilopochtli braziers you saw on the south side. The path now turns west (left) toward the street. To your left, you see remains of colored marble flooring; a small chamber originally rose here. Beyond, the Stage IVb platform is base to another stone serpent undulating toward a pair of stone frogs identified with Tlaloc. Many rich offering caches were found at the base of the staircase on the east side of this platform.

Take a right down the steps. On your right opens the long Stage VI patio running all the way to the east perimeter of the ruins. The south side contains a line of three small structures, Temples A, B, and C. The nearest, Temple A, is a simple unadorned platform; the other two are more interesting, but you need to walk around the walls to get a better view.

The north side of the patio is dominated by the Precinct of the Eagle Warriors. From this vantage point, you can see the steps flanked by stone eagle heads descending into the patio. The eagle warriors were members of an aristocratic military order whose power is shown by their shrine's closeness to the Great Temple. If you walk around the corner to the site's northern border, you can look into their structure. Here archaeologists found the life-size ceramic sculptures of the warriors in their eagle costumes (now in the museum). The walls are lined with elaborate carved and painted banquettes. The scenes—a procession of warriors and priests below a running border of plumed serpents—show clear Tula influence. The red ochre paint still burns brightly.

Just beyond this structure, you have a good view of Temple B, better known as the *tzompantli* or skull rack. This platform was decorated with stone skulls (see them inside the museum entrance) and was the base for a wooden rack that held hundreds, perhaps thousands, of skulls of sacrificial victims. Found nearby, some of them are on display in the museum with holes in the foreheads for the wooden bars on which they were displayed.

At the end of this leg of the walkway, you can see Temple C, also known as the North Red Temple. Like the one on the south side of the site, this was built and decorated in Teotihuacan style and faces east. Closer to the walkway, you see a patch of wooden stakes; the Aztecs stuck these in the muddy ground to keep the building foundations from sinking.

The walkway now winds around to the museum entrance. In the ruins below the entrance, you can see the remains of a Spanish fountain, colonial columns, and more foundation stakes. The museum is a must. It contains some of the greatest sculptures and ceramics found in Mexico, and the exhibition on the offering caches alone is worth the price of admission. The displays bring to life the power, complexity, and strangeness of Aztec culture.

Just south of the museum lies the site exit, which brings you to either Calle Carmen or Calle Moneda on the north side of the Presidential Palace.

TLATELOLCO

INTRODUCTION

Since the discovery of the Great Temple, Tlatelolco has been overshadowed by the wonders of Tenochtitlan. Tlatelolco was a clear second in pre-Hispanic days as well; Tenochtitlan controlled Aztec religious life, and its warrior-rulers won the most glorious victories in battle. Nevertheless, without Tlatelolco, a separate city-state that lay just over two kilometers (a mile) from the Great Temple, the

TLATELOLCO

How to get there: Tlatelolco's ruins lie amid the apartment towers of the Tlatelolco housing development. To reach them, take the Metro to the Tlatelolco station and head east between the high-rises to the site. By car or bus, you head north on Eje Central; they lie just to the right between Av. R. Flores Magon and Av. M. González.

Hours: Daily 0700–1800
Admission fee: Free.
How long to tour: One hour.
Recommended gear: Hats.

Aztec empire would not have been able to spread its tentacles to the farthest borders of Mesoamerica.

Tlatelolco was famous throughout pre-Columbian Mexico for its enormous market, perhaps the largest in the Western Hemisphere until that time. The market was the focal point for a vast trade network whose routes spread as far as Yucatan, Guatemala, and the Pacific Ocean. The trade ties that Tlatelolco forged were crucial in building and sustaining the system of tribute that supported the courts and temples of Tenochtitlan.

Tlatelolco is far less visited than the Great Temple. The site was excavated and restored decades ago, and the finds were modest compared to Tenochtitlan's great religious sculptures. However, those interested in the Aztecs and their relation with modern Mexico should definitely visit this site. Tlatelolco has been the setting of three tragic events in Mexican history. The Aztecs made their last stand against the Spanish here; overrun, they surrendered on August 13, 1521. Four centuries later, just before the opening of the 1968 Olympics, the Mexican military opened fire on a student gathering in a Tlatelolco plaza; hundreds were massacred. Then, in September of 1985, an earthquake rocked Mexico City; flimsily constructed Tlatelolco apartment buildings collapsed like accordions, with great loss of life.

Tlatelolco is now formally known as the Plaza de las Tres Culturas. The modern tower of the Secretary of Foreign Relations overlooks the Convent of Santiago Tlatelolco, which in turn stands over (and is constructed with stones from) the Aztec ruins. Each culture gained power from defeating the earlier one; what they did not do, unfortunately, was learn from their predecessors' mistakes.

HISTORY

History is written by the victors, and this was especially true with the Aztecs. Much of what researchers know about Tlatelolco's history was written by Tenochtecas; they demean Tlatelolco and glorify Tenochtitlan. Consequently, there are many unknowns about the relationship between the two neighboring cities. There are hints that in the early days Tlatelolco was the more important of the two and perhaps even received tribute from Tenochtitlan. It is also unclear when Tenochtitlan actually took over its neighbor. Until new historical information is uncovered, however, anthropologists must grudgingly accept the official Tenochca accounts.

The site of Tlatelolco was originally a muddy island in the middle of the shallow lakes that filled the Valley of Mexico. Some evidence exists of pre-Aztec occupation, probably by people who harvested the lakes' rich plant and animal life. About A.D. 1344, in the second decade after the founding of Tenochtitlan, a group of Aztecs split off from the main tribe and settled on the island that would become Tlatelolco. There was only a limited amount of land on Tenochtitlan's island; dissatisfied with the division of property, a group decided to found a separate community.

The Tlatelolcans were still Aztec, however, in both ideology and practice. Their founding myth closely paralleled Tenochtitlan's: a whirlwind had led them to an island with a sandy mound; on it they found a round shield, an arrow, and an eagle—strongly reminiscent of Tenochtitlan's cactus, eagle, and snake. Like the Tenochteca, they petitioned a local power—in their case, Tezozomoc of Atzcapotzalco—for a ruler who would link them to the post-Toltec central Mexican dynasties. He gave them his son, Cuacuapitzahuac, who was also kin to Tenochtitlan's dynastic clan.

Under their new ruler, Tlatelolco became part of the Valley of Mexico's intricate network of tribute relationships, giving them both responsibility—honoring Tezozomoc through gifts of both staples and luxury goods—and opportunity.

Like many Aztec temples, Tlatelolco's Great Temple is bipartite, i.e. built in northern and southern halves. The southern portion is devoted to Huitzilopochtli, the sun and war god, while the northern half represents Tlaloc, the rain god.

DANIELLE GUSTAFSON

With the Tenochtecas, the Tlatelolcans found work fighting as mercenaries for Tezozomoc against his rivals, first Culhuacan and later Tenayuca. Eventually, the Tlatelolcans would move up to fighting on their own account. By the mid-15th century A.D., they had their own tribute network of secondary towns in the Valley of Mexico.

Tenochtitlan always dominated its smaller sibling; its warriors won the bigger victories, and its priests controlled the all-important religious sphere. The Tlatelolcans had to find their own specialty to succeed. Cuacuapitzahuac pointed them in the right direction—trade. He established the first large-scale market and began the Tlatelolcan tradition of *pochtecas*, or long-range merchants, who spread first through the valley and then to the farthest reaches of Mesoamerica. By A.D. 1390, the name "Tlatelolcan" was already synonymous with "merchant." Three decades later they controlled the long-distance trade in luxury goods such as quetzal feathers and turquoise that were essential to Aztec religious and aristocratic life. During the Triple Alliance war, Tlatelolco used its trade ties to muster support for the Aztec cause. By the time the Aztecs achieved victory, they already had allies throughout central Mexico.

The 50 years following the Aztecs' A.D. 1426 victory over the Tepanecs were a golden age for Tlatelolco. The Aztec empire spread throughout central Mexico behind the twin spearheads of Tenochtitlan warriors and Tlatelolco merchants. Tlatelolcan *pochtecas* learned the language and customs of foreign tribes and often acted as spies and emissaries for the Aztec cause, collecting strategic information on the enemy ahead of the Aztec army. Once the foreigners were subjugated, the Tlatelolcans established the trade routes back to the Valley of Mexico. As the conquering state, the Aztecs dictated the terms of trade and often forced subject states to trade valuable commodities for gaudy "luxury goods"—the pre-Columbian equivalent of necklaces of bright beads. The Aztec empire grew in great leaps.

Back in Tlatelolco, Cuacuapitzahuac's son Tlacateotl had moved the market into spacious quarters near the main ceremonial precinct. This became the hub of the trade network, perhaps the largest market of pre-Columbian America. Every fifth day, as many as 60,000 crowded into the market square. The stalls resembled those that crowd Mexican streets today, with mats covered by fabric shades to protect from sun and rain. The vendors sold an incredible variety of wares, including slaves, gold, edible dogs, shoes, chile peppers, skins, pottery, turkeys, tobacco, canoes, decorative feathers, squashes, seeds, and so on. The main units of currency were cacao beans and mantles of cotton cloth; they also used strips of copper and quills filled with gold dust. When market-goers disagreed, they could take their arguments to a court of justice right on the premises and plead their cases. Punishments were onerous; stealing brought a mandatory death sentence.

In A.D. 1473, Tlatelolco's idyll ended. Axayacatl, Tenochtitlan's ruler, decided that Moquihuix of Tlatelolco was plotting against him. Some anthropologists believe that Tenochtitlan already controlled Tlatelolco and Moquihuix was

FIVE SUNS: AN AZTEC LAMENT

This Aztec-era cosmological account describes the five eras—"suns"—in which humanity has lived. Each era ended with disaster—the Aztecs were particularly sensitive to the fragility of the cosmological balance—and they expected the same of the current, fifth-sun era.

Thus it is told, it is said:
there have already been four manifestations
and this one is the fifth age.

So the old ones knew this,
that in the year 1-Rabbit
heaven and earth were founded.
And they knew this,
that when heaven and earth were founded
there had already been four kinds of men,
four kinds of manifestations.
Also they knew that each of these
had existed in a Sun, an age.

And they said of the first men,
their god made them, fashioned them of ashes.
This they attributed to the god Quetzalcoatl,
whose sign is 7-Wind,
he made them, he invented them.
The first Sun or age which was founded,
its sign was 4-Water,
it was called the Sun of Water.
Then it happened
that water carried away everything.
The people were changed into fish.

Then the Second Sun or age was founded.
Its sign was 4-Tiger.
It was called the Sun of Tiger.
Then it happened that the sky was crushed,
the Sun did not follow its course.
When the Sun arrived at midday,
immediately it was night
and when it became dark,
tigers ate the people.
In this Sun giants lived.
The old one said
the giants greeted each other thus:
"Do not fall down," for whoever falls,
he falls forever.

Then the third Sun was founded.
Its sign was 4-Rain-of-Fire.
It happened then that fire rained down,

those who lived there were burned.
And then sand rained down.
And they say that then
it rained down the little stones we see,
that the tezontle stone boiled
and the big rocks became red.

Its sign was 4-Wind,
when the fourth Sun was founded.
It was called the Sun of Wind.
Then everything was carried away by the wind.
People were turned into monkeys.
They were scattered over the mountains,
and the monkey-men lived there.

The fifth Sun,
4-Movement its sign.
It is called the Sun of Movement
because it moves, follows its course.
And the old ones go about saying,
now there will be earthquakes,
there will be hunger
and thus we will perish.
In the year 13-Reed,
they say it came into existence,
the sun which now exists was born.
That was when there was light,
when dawn came,
the Sun of Movement which now exists.
4-Movement is its sign.
This is the fifth Sun which was founded,
in it there will be earthquakes,
in it there will be hunger.

This Sun, its name 4-Movement,
this is our Sun,
in which we now live,
and this is its sign,
where the Sun fell in fire
on the divine hearth,
there in Teotihuacan.
Also this was the Sun
of our prince of Tula,
of Quetzalcoatl.

—From the *Anales de Cuauhtitlán*,
translated by Grace Lobanov and Miguel León-Portilla

planning to oust them. According to Aztec histories, the two cities' excuses for war were among the most mundane: Tlatelolco maidens had yielded to the blandishments of Tenochtitlan swains; afterward, they complained to their mothers, who went to Moquihuix and demanded revenge. In turn, Moquihuix was married to Axayacatl's sister, a skinny shrew whom Moquihuix neglected; she went to Axayacatl and demanded revenge.

The native histories continue with the story of perhaps the most bizarre military campaign in human history. When Moquihuix heard that Axayacatl's army was massing for an attack, he tried to repel them with a unique force. The first line of the Tlatelolco force was a squadron of naked women; they squeezed their breasts to squirt milk at the advancing foe. Behind came a brigade of naked boys adorned only with feathers. For a moment, the Tenochteca warriors were baffled; they regained their wits, however, and their commanders ordered the Tlatelolco force imprisoned. The army then charged into Tlatelolco and cornered Tlatelolco's leaders atop their main pyramid. Moquihuix and his favorite dwarf were hurled down the steps to their deaths.

Tlatelolco became a ward of Tenochtitlan administered by a Tenochteca military governor. Tlatelolcans' trade continued, but they lost almost all the rights of an independent city-state, including the power to collect tribute and perform important religious ceremonies. In war, they were demoted to the role of porters. The Tlatelolco dynasty disappeared. They were also forced to pay elaborate tribute to Tenochtitlan; their obligations, including numerous luxury ceremonial goods, were illustrated in the *Codex Mendoza,* the great book of Aztec culture and history written shortly after the Conquest.

The Tlatelolcans did not lose their separate identity and almost certainly resented Tenochteca rule. In 1519, however, when a band of motley Spanish conquistadors arrived backed by an army of Indians sick of Aztec rule, the Tlatelolcans were clearly on the side of Tenochtitlan. Motecuhzoma took the Spaniards to visit the Tlatelolco market. One of the conquistadors, Bernal Díaz, later wrote: ". . . we were astounded at the great number of people and good quantities of merchandise, and at the orderliness and good arrangements that prevailed, for we had never seen such a thing before." The Spaniards were taken to the top of Tlatelolco's pyramid, from which they had a view over the entire city and the surrounding lake: "We saw [pyramids] and shrines in these cities that looked like gleaming white towers and castles: a marvelous sight."

Two years later, the conquistadors returned at the head of a larger army. They besieged Tenochtitlan; the Aztecs fought for their lives, but it was not enough. The Aztec force was pushed back from Tenochtitlan to Tlatelolco. There, they were either killed or forced into the lake, and Tlatelolco's pyramid was set ablaze. Cuauhtemoc, the last Aztec ruler, tried to flee in a canoe, but he was captured, bringing an end to the century-old Aztec empire.

After the Conquest, the Spaniards tore down Tlatelolco's pyramid and used its stones to build the church of Santiago Tlatelolco and the neighboring Franciscan convent, called the Imperial College of the Holy Cross. The latter became a school for the sons of the Aztec aristocracy to convert them to Catholicism and train them in the rules of the Spanish system. The convent also became a center for the study of native cultures; here the priest Bernardo de Sahagún wrote his *History of the Things of New Spain,* the seminal work on Aztec culture.

Tlatelolco's market gradually dwindled as the Zócalo became the focal point of trade. For a while, neighborhood artisans flourished by manufacturing fake Aztec pots and selling them to the early Spanish settlers as souvenirs—the start of a long history of Mesoamerican fakes. Nevertheless, the neighborhood slowly slid into poverty. By the early 20th century, it was home to sprawling train yards and a few factories and poor slums. The convent now acted as a military prison.

In the late 1950s and early '60s, ambitious city planners decided to revitalize Tlatelolco. The neighborhood's slums and factories were torn down and replaced by modern apartment buildings situated among green spaces and parking lots. The modernist tower of the Secretary of Foreign Relations was placed on top of some of the lesser Aztec ruins, and at least one temple was destroyed to make way for a widened avenue. They restored the Catholic church and converted the convent into an archive of diplomatic history. The area was dubbed the Plaza of the Three Cultures to celebrate the melding of pre-Hispanic, colonial, and modern Mexico.

Since the 1968 student massacre, however, the area has existed as a blot on Mexican history, not one of its shining achievements. The zone's reputation was further injured during the 1985 earthquake. The builders had cheated on the construction materials, and some of the modernist skyscrapers collapsed with great loss of life. Today, the name Tlatelolco is associated with tragedy, both ancient and modern.

ARCHAEOLOGICAL RECORD

Tlatelolco has been known as an archaeological site at least since the early 19th century. When cholera epidemics led the church sextons to dig new grave pits, they found ceramic artifacts and skeletons with flattened skulls and filed teeth. Slightly more scientific excavations were performed in 1862 and during the 1890s, when President Porfirio Díaz ordered historians to dig up ancient treasures for display at an exposition in Madrid.

The site's major excavation began in 1944 under the guidance of Pablo Martínez del Río from INAH and Robert H. Barlow, a brilliant bohemian from California who believed himself the reincarnation of an Aztec priest. For the rest of the 1940s, they excavated and restored the bulk of Tlatelolco's ceremonial center and opened test pits in the nearby neighborhood. What you see of Tlatelolco now is almost all their work. They published numerous interim reports and ethnohistorical studies in INAH's *Memorias* quarterly but unfortunately never published a final report.

INAH archaeologists have performed two major studies since then, first in the early 1960s and most recently between 1987 and 1989 as part of the Great Temple Project. The latter excavation unearthed a rare Aztec mural on Temple M and numerous offerings, including skeletons of sacrificial victims, among them infants. To date, very little of either study has been published, and most of the artifacts rest in the INAH storerooms.

TOURING THE SITE

You can enter the site from numerous points, but this tour will begin from the entrance on Eje Central just north of the Secretary of Foreign Relations tower.

From street level, you have a good view over the ruins. The parallels with the Great Temple site are immediately evident: you see a west-facing temple split in two with separate staircases for the north and south halves; in front stand the staircases that represent the temple's later stages of construction. To the north and south of the temple lie plazas around which stand numerous smaller temple platforms and altars. Tenochtitlan's ceremonial precinct was obviously a model for Tlatelolco.

Great Temple with Church of Santiago Tlatelolco behind

Below and to the right of the entrance viewing platform stands Temple R, a semicircular structure dedicated to Ehecatl, the god of winds. It probably was topped with a conical thatched roof representing the cave from which the winds were believed to emerge. Descend the steps and on the right you see a glass case covering two skeletons called "The Lovers" because they are male and female and lying side by side. They were probably sacrificial victims.

Just east stands Temple M, also known as the Calendar Temple. Around the temple is a running line of reliefs carved with glyphs. Thirteen glyphs outlined with traces of white paint appear on three sides of the temple, representing the first three 13-day segments of the Aztec calendar. In 1989, archaeologists uncovered a mural showing the

gods Oxomoco and Cipactonal (also known as the Primordial Pair) who invented the calendar; it has been removed.

The walkway continues past Temple M on the right. On the left stands
Tlatelolco's Great Temple, a near-replica of Tenochtitlan's. This was built in as
many as eleven separate stages, three marked by the large freestanding staircases. In the center, you find the Stage II Great Temple, which is relatively intact.
As in Tenochtitlan, the south half was dedicated to Huitzilopochtli, the main
Aztec deity, while the north half was dedicated to the Rain God Tlaloc. The
shrines on top were destroyed, and almost no monumental sculpture has been
found. Archaeologists believe that the final phase of this temple was taller than
the one in Tenochtitlan. Motecuhzoma may have taken the Spaniards to the top
because of the better view.

To the right of the walkway lies the complex of buildings known as Temple
W or the Palace. This was a series of small rooms built around a patio; archaeologists surmise that this was a noble dwelling. Attached to the Palace are a series of small altars and temple. Standing at the Palace's northeast corner, the
tallest of these is Building L, which is built in the Teotihuacan style *(talud-
tablero)* of the Red Temple next to Tenochtitlan's Great Temple. Its facade was
covered with murals, largely geometric designs, now removed.

At the back of the Great Temple, the walkway takes a left to the patio in front
of the Church of Santiago Tlatelolco, which was begun almost immediately
after the Conquest. Here, the great 16th-century priest, Bernardo de Sahagún,
taught the sons of Aztec nobles and compiled his monumental work, the *History of the Things of New Spain*. Although the church was reconstructed during
the 17th and 18th centuries, its walls still contain many stones from Tlatelolco's
Great Temple. The interior is worth a brief visit; unfortunately the decor was
stripped during the 19th century. The conch-shaped baptisimal font saw the
baptism of Juan Diego, the Indian who was given the miraculous cloth bearing
the image of the Virgin of Guadalupe, Mexico's patroness. Translated, the
plaque opposite the church entrance reads:

> *On August 13, 1521, heroically defended by Cuauhtemoc, Tlatelolco fell
> into the power of Hernán Cortés. This was neither victory nor defeat; it
> was the sad birth of the mestizo nation that is the Mexico of today.*

Now walk along the north side of the church to the modern plaza just behind.
This was the site of the pre-Olympics student massacre; a plaque gives the date:
October 2, 1968. This lies at the east end of a long Aztec plaza that stretches all
the way to the Eje Central avenue. From here, an Aztec causeway headed north
across the lake to the holy hill of Tepeyac, now the site of the Basilica of the
Virgin of Guadalupe.

A walkway heads along the wall marking the site's north boundary back to Eje
Central. In the Aztec plaza stand a number of small square and circular platforms
and altars. The first is the round Altar B, and just south of it stands the square
Temple A, also called the *tzompantli* (skull rack) because the skulls of decapitated

SPARE THE ROD AND SPOIL THE CHILD

The Spanish conquistadors described the Aztecs as savage pagans. After the Conquest, they soon discovered that these "savages" actually had a strict code of behavior, as demonstrated by these panels from the *Codex Mendoza*, in which illustrations by Aztec artists have been annotated by Spanish priests.

In the top panels, a father teaches his son how to use a fishing net, while a mother teaches her daughter to spin. In the bottom panels, both parents warn their children against being deceitful and threaten to punish them with maguey thorns. The dots represent the age of the children, while their food ration is represented as 1.5 tortillas.

CODEX MENDOZA

victims were found in it. Immediately north of the Great Temple stand two large platforms, Temples J and I respectively, each with twin staircases facing south.

The walkway returns to Eje Central; to return to the street, you have to walk through the tunnel under the avenue and emerge on the other side. From the sidewalk in front of the Great Temple, you can see just below you a small altar and part of a circular platform. In 1960, a temple dedicated to Quetzalcoatl was removed from beneath your feet to make way for the street.

The dedicated will want to make one more stop in Tlatelolco. From behind the church, follow the "Mural Siquieros" signs about 200 meters due east to the Museo Tecpan. This is a 16th-century convent that was built on the ruins of a palace *(tecpan)* belonging to Cuauhtemoc, the last Aztec ruler. The interior contains the 20th-century three-dimensional mural by David Alfaro Siquieros called *Cuauhtemoc against the Myth*. Among other things, it depicts Aztecs battling a mounted Spaniard; mostly what you see are the horse's hooves.

SANTA CECILIA ACATITLÁN

INTRODUCTION

The tiny Aztec site of Santa Cecilia Acatitlán is recommended only for the zealous: it is of minor importance and is nearly impossible to find. The site's great attraction is that archaeologists reconstructed it to look as much as possible like a complete Aztec temple. It also lies in a pleasant, tree-filled area of the valley (not far from Tenayuca) and contains a small but good museum of Aztec sculpture.

HISTORY

Acatitlán does not appear in any native histories or post-Conquest accounts of the Aztecs. Catholic priests knew about the temple—they built a chapel using its stones to counter its influence—but the ruins remained unexplored until the early part of the 20th century.

ARCHAEOLOGICAL RECORD

Acatitlan was first excavated in 1922 by a team from the Dirección de Arqueología. In 1961, an INAH project under Eduardo Pareyón Moreno completed the

SANTA CECILIA ACATITLÁN

How to get there: Finding this tiny site is not easy. The best method is to head north from Tenayuca on Av. Pirámide, turn left on Av. San Rafael and take the second right on Calle Pirámide de Tula. It lies behind the colonial-era chapel in the old town of Santa Cecilia.

Hours: 1000–1700, closed Monday.

Admission: 17 pesos.

How long to tour: 45 minutes.

Museum: Housed near the entrance, the site museum is in a modest 19th-century house. It contains Aztec sculpture from Tenayuca, downtown Mexico City, and Acatitlan. The last pieces are relatively simple and crudely executed—a measure of this site's low status.

DANIELLE GUSTAFSON

Santa Cecilia Acatitlán's pyramid and temple

excavation and restored the temple to its current state. The site museum was also opened at this time and named after Eusebio Hurtado Dávalos, INAH's director in the early 1960s.

TOURING THE SITE

You enter the site through a gate and face the temple. This rests on a large stone platform with a small plaza in front. Like most Aztec pyramids, this structure is bipartite, facing west with separate staircases for the north and south halves. The great difference between this and other Aztec pyramids is that the south, or Huitzilopochtli, half is far larger and more elaborate than the neighboring Tlaloc side. The north half is short and bare, while the taller south side is topped with a temple. Flanked by two large stone braziers, this is a reconstruction of a simple Aztec temple. It contains one door opening into a simple chamber below a relatively elaborate roof. The front roof facade would have been painted with a mural, probably symbolic designs rather than a figurative scene.

VALLEY OF PUEBLA

Cholula's unreconstructed Great Pyramid, with a Catholic shrine on top, rises over the town.

RICHARD A. DIEHL

The Valley of Puebla rivals the neighboring Valley of Mexico for the antiquity of its human settlements. Although the valley's pre-Hispanic cities never built empires that rivaled Teotihuacan or Tenochtitlan, centers such as Cholula were among the most populous in Classic-era central Mexico. Cholula's Great Pyramid was the largest structure ever built north of the Maya region, while the mural painters at Cacaxtla produced some of the finest Mesoamerican artwork yet discovered. These cities thrived off both agriculture and trade. The valley contains some of the best soil in central Mexico; at the same time, its location on the main route between the Valley of Mexico and the Gulf made it an important stop on the Mesoamerican trade network. In the end, however, the Cholulans suffered for their position: hundreds were slaughtered by conquistadors marching from Veracruz to Tenochtitlan.

Lying just to the east of the Valley of Mexico, the Valley of Puebla is easily accessible by cars and buses on Highway 150.

THE LAND

The Valley of Puebla, comprising parts of the states of Puebla and Tlaxcala, lies just east of the Valley of Mexico. The Popocatépetl and Iztaccíhuatl volcanoes form its western boundaries, while on the east it runs all the way to the Pico de Orizaba, the highest point in Mexico. Its northern border is Tlaxcala's La Malinche volcano; it spreads south to the far border of the Río Atoyac's valley.

The Valley of Puebla is technically an alluvial plain formed by the drainage systems of the Ríos Atoyac and Nexapa, both flowing into the Río Balsas. The region is blessed by rich soils fed year-round by runoff from the snow-capped volcanoes; some of that water is harbored in the region's many lakes. The land is also known

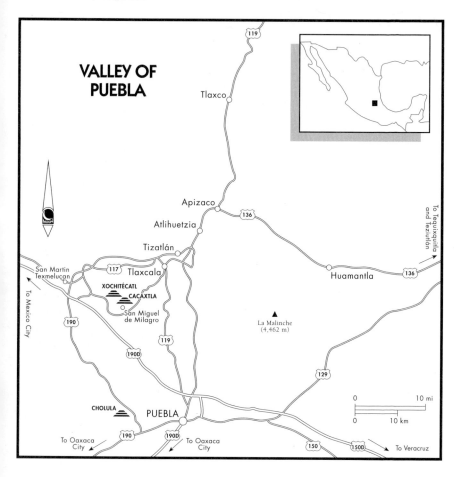

for its deposits of clay, which were used to manufacture some of Mesoamerica's finest pottery—the last Aztec emperor dined off only Cholula plates. Today, the city of Puebla is still renowned for its ceramic and tile industries.

The Valley of Puebla's location is one of the most advantageous in Mexico. From here, you can easily reach the Gulf Coast, Oaxaca, and the Valley of Morelos, and you can bypass the volcanoes and enter into the Valley of Mexico via Teotihuacan to the north. This setting was the key to the early establishment and nearly continuous expansion of human settlement in the valley.

Climate

Most of the Valley of Puebla lies at between 2,000 and 2,500 meters, slightly lower than Mexico City. The climate is nearly the same as the Valley of Mexico—temperate and semihumid—only with slightly more rainfall. The rainy season runs from June through September, and there is little year-to-year variation in rainfall. The great Popocatépetl and Iztaccíhuatl volcanoes cast a long shad-

CITY OF PUEBLA

The city of Puebla contains many hotels and the excellent **Museo Amparo,** Calle 2 Sur 708, tel. 22/46-4646, with good regional archaeological exhibits. Housed in a colonial mansion, three blocks south off the *zócalo,* the collection offers state-of-the-art headsets for a small additional charge, which provide a wealth of background information. Open daily except Wednesday 1000–1700; free on Monday.

ow over the western part of the valley; Cholula and the city of Puebla can seem quite cold and clammy. Popocatépetl has also become significantly more active in recent years, and seismologists now have full-time monitoring stations on its slopes. The prevailing winds are usually to the east; eruptions sometimes cover Cholula and the surrounding area with a fine coating of ash.

Flora and Fauna

The Valley of Puebla was originally covered with pine-oak forests teeming with deer, mountain lions, wild turkeys, rabbits, and other wildlife. Human habitation has changed all that, however. Since well before the arrival of the conquistadors, the valley's flora has been shaped by agriculture. The forests were chopped down and replaced by fields of maize, chile, amaranth, squash, maguey, and the other Mesoamerican staples. Today, many of these fields—particularly around Puebla—are being replaced by enormous factories.

HISTORY

Humans were drawn to the Valley of Puebla perhaps as early as the Upper Pleistocene—21,000 years ago. A center of these early hunters was Valsequillo, now inundated by a reservoir south of Puebla city. The river here attracted herds of now-extinct mammals, including mammoths, horses, antelopes, and camels, whose bones have been found along with chipped stones that some archaeologists believe are the product of human labor.

The evidence of human occupation becomes clearer when you jump ahead to around 7000 B.C. In the Valley of Puebla, hunter-gatherers made seasonal settlements in caves and rock shelters in the Valsequillo region and along the Río Atoyac. Here archaeologists discovered stone scrapers, grinding stones, and points for spears and arrows. They hunted now-extinct horses and antelope as well as rabbits and gophers, but also subsisted on wild fruits and grasses.

Just southeast of the Valley of Puebla lies the Tehuacan Valley, which leads down into Oaxaca. Here, the archaeologist Richard S. MacNeish found evidence of the earliest domestication of plants—the origins of New World agriculture. The inhabitants lived in small bands that traveled a set route between two or three caves or shelters depending on the season and whether they were hunting

CENTRAL MEXICAN GODS

It would take a book much fatter than this to describe all the major and minor deities of every Mesoamerican culture. Like many polytheistic peoples, the Zapotecs, Maya, and other groups had a vast pantheon of gods representing nearly every concept of both the natural and spiritual worlds. Their major gods could also have many lesser manifestations associated with different forces of nature and specific calendar dates. To make matters more complicated, they frequently merged with other gods to produce distinct deities. The following is a list of some of the deities worshipped by the Aztecs and others across Late Post-Classic central Mexico at the time of the Conquest.

1. **Chalchiuhtlicue** (She of the Jade Skirt). The goddess of lakes and streams, Chalchiuhtlicue is depicted with a stream issuing from beneath her skirt. In some representations, male and female infants are shown floating down the stream, obviously linking the goddess with the act of childbirth.

2. **Cinteotl.** The Maize God, Cinteotl is usually shown holding corncobs or with them issuing from his headdress. Cinteotl presided over the staple crop of Mesoamerica with a female consort known in the Valley of Mexico as Chicomecoatl.

3. **Huehuecoyotl** (Old Coyote). The god of music, dance, and sexuality, Huehuecoyotl was the patron deity of artists and craftsmen. Unfortunately, men and women born during his calendar period were prone to sexual overindulgence.

4. **Mayahuel.** She was the goddess of the maguey, the spiny plant that thrived in the Central Mexican highlands. The maguey had hundreds of uses, from building material to source of the sap that produced the alcoholic pulque drink. Sometimes described as "the woman of 400 breasts," Mayahuel was also associated with fertility.

5. **Mictlantecuhtli.** With his gaping skull from which protruded a red tongue, Mictlantecuhtli was the Central Mexican death god. He reigned over Mictlan, the Underworld, with his consort Mictecacihuatl.

ILLUSTRATIONS: CODEX BORGIA

or collecting plant food. The latter was a variety of wild fruits, amaranth, chile, and—most important—maize, which became the Mesoamerican staff of life. As they learned how to plant the seeds and improved their methods of cultivation, they gradually became more sedentary, founding the first year-round settlements by about 4000 B.C.

These developments spread to the Valley of Puebla. In 2000 B.C., residents were settled into a number of small farming communities where they grew corn, beans, squash, chile, amaranth, and avocados—all enduring staples of rural Mexican life. A millennium later, these settlements had grown to as large as 200 dwellings and possessed small ritual centers with raised stucco-covered ceremonial platforms. They produced beautiful ceramics, including braziers and

6. **Ehecatl-Quetzalcoatl.** The "plumed serpent," the god Quetzalcoatl was found in almost all Mesoamerican cultures from Teotihuacan on. In his guise as the duck-billed Ehecatl-Quetzalcoatl, he became the Wind God, the one who brought the precious rains, and was worshipped throughout central Mexico at the time of the Conquest.

7. **Tezcatlipoca** (Smoking Mirror). Tezcatlipoca was the archsorcerer, god of warriors and rulers, and often considered the supreme god of the Central Mexican pantheon. He was often depicted battling another powerful god, Quetzalcoatl, their cosmic conflict representing the opposition between earth and wind. In his manifestation as Red Tezcatlipoca, he is also associated with the hunt god Mixcoatl.

8. **Tlaloc.** Rain was the most important natural force in Mesoamerica; without it there would have been no life. Pre-Hispanic artwork is filled with representations of the Rain Gods, either the Maya Chac or, here, the goggle-eyed Tlaloc. The Aztecs thought Tlaloc was so crucial that he shared the top of their bifurcat-ed pyramids with Huitzilopochtli, their tribal deity.

9. **Xipe Totec** (The Flayed God). Xipe Totec is shown as a man wearing the skin of a sacrificial victim. To invoke the help of this deity, Aztec warriors wore the flayed skins of their prisoners of war during a 20-day series of ritual events, probably associated with the beginning of the agricultural cycle.

10. **Xochiquetzal** (Flower Quetzal). Associated with youth, sexual pleasure, and flowers, Xochiquetzal was the goddess of young motherhood, pregnancy, and childbirth. She was also the patroness of skilled artists, who celebrated her festival by presenting a young woman in the goddess's guise. Priests then sacrificed and flayed the impersonator, and one donned her skin and mimicked sitting at a loom and weaving while the artists danced around him.

pots in the shape of animals. The archaeological evidence also contains hints of trade with other parts of Mesoamerica.

The largest of these settlements was Tlalancaleca in Tlaxcala, which some archaeologists see as a precursor to Cuicuilco over in the Valley of Mexico. Its residents constructed agricultural terraces fed by irrigation canals, built platforms using *talud-tablero* architecture and worshipped a number of recognizable gods, including Tlaloc and Huehueteotl (the fire god seen at Cuicuilco). At its height in 400 B.C., Tlalancaleca covered 65 hectares and controlled the entire valley, with trade ties to the Gulf, Oaxaca, and West Mexico. Three hundred years later, it was supplanted by a settlement that would grow to become one of the largest in central Mexico—Cholula.

CHOLULA

INTRODUCTION

When Cortés's army arrived in Cholula, they found a city with 365 temples, one for every day of the year. Cholula was one of the largest and oldest cities in central Mexico; its Temple of Quetzalcoatl drew pilgrims from throughout Mesoamerica. In revenge for a failed attack on the conquistadors, the Spanish razed Cholula's temples and replaced them with dozens of churches. Luckily, they ignored a nearby mound that they took for a hill; it turned out to be the Great Pyramid, one of the largest structures built in Mesoamerica—it dwarfs the Egyptian pyramids in volume. Archaeologists have barely scratched the surface of this massive edifice. Nevertheless, you can penetrate the pyramid via a series of tunnels and view a number of still mysterious altars discovered around its perimeter. Cholula's many churches are also worth a visit; feast days accompanied by the boom of rockets are held almost daily.

HISTORY

There are many gaps in Cholula's chronology. The Spanish destroyed most of the city; the modern town rests on the ancient foundations, making it difficult to excavate. The Great Pyramid is so large that its complete exploration is nearly impossible; there is almost certainly important evidence hidden inside its bulk.

The area we know as modern Cholula was first settled by 1700 B.C.; at one point it was actually two separate villages, but these eventually merged into one. By 400 B.C., when Tlalancaleca was the dominant force in the valley, Cholula covered 65 hectares and was growing rapidly. Three hundred years later it occupied two square kilometers and had eclipsed Tlalancaleca for regional control. The Cholulans soon began the construction of the Great Pyramid, which, like Teotihuacan's Pyramid of the Sun, was built over a spring that may have originated in a cave.

Through the Classic era (A.D. 150–600), Cholula rose with Teotihuacan. There is evidence of Teotihuacan influence in some of the architecture but not enough for archaeologists to believe that Cholula's powerful neighbor ever held sway here. The center of Cholula was the Great Pyramid, which rose in four major stages to become the largest structure in central Mexico. It was so large that the Aztecs and other Postclassic peoples believed early Cholula had been built by a race of giants.

The Great Pyramid was the center of a ceremonial precinct surrounded by residences and markets. At its height around A.D. 600, Cholula covered 13 square kilometers and had as many as 80,000 inhabitants. Because of the ar-

CHOLULA

How to get there: The great pyramid of Cholula stands in the middle of the town of the same name 10 kilometers west of Puebla (numerous buses and vans ply this route).

Hours: Daily 1000–1700.

Admission fee: Free.

How long to tour: Two hours.

Recommended gear: Hats, sunblock, bottled water, hiking boots.

Museum: Opposite the pyramid and the entrance to the site stands the small site museum (closed Monday) whose highlight is a cutaway model reconstructing the original pyramid. Free.

Food and accommodations: The excellent though pricey **Hotel Villa Arqueológica Cholula,** Av. 2 Poniente 601, tel. 22/47-1966, fax 47-1508, just south of the ruins, is a good base for your explorations of the region. Amenities include a/c, tennis courts, swimming pool, a library, and a restaurant.

chaeological problems mentioned above, very little is known about life during Classic-era Cholula.

Archaeologists debate what happened in Cholula during the period that followed. Excavations suggest that the city was partially abandoned; some researchers believe that the population had shrunk to only 1,000 in A.D. 800. A century before, the Gulf Coast Maya traders known as the Olmeca-Xicallanca had entered the region and built well-defended settlements at Cacaxtla and at Xochicalco in the Valley of Morelos to the northwest. In the 1970s, many archaeologists decided that Cacaxtla's rise—and possibly a volcanic eruption—had forced the Cholulans to flee their city. Now, however, some are saying that Cholula was not so completely abandoned—the Olmeca-Xicallanca did settle here and build the last stage of the Great Pyramid. A Maya occupation has also been confirmed by ethnohistorical accounts.

The Olmeca-Xicallanca abandoned their central Mexican strongholds during the Early Postclassic (A.D. 900–1200). At Cholula, their place was taken by Tolteca-Chichimeca groups cut adrift by the fall of the Toltec empire. They moved Cholula's center away from the Great Pyramid and constructed a second enormous temple—said to be larger than Tenochtitlan's Great

**Doña Marina, Cortés's mistress/translator
—from the Codex Florentino, circa 1540**

Temple and dedicated to Quetzalcoatl—which today lies at the heart of the modern town.

Cholula once again grew rapidly to cover eight square kilometers and hold 30,000–50,000 inhabitants. Its success was spurred by trade and by pilgrims from throughout the region coming to worship Quetzalcoatl. Cholula was a center of the *pochteca,* the long-distance trading clans (Quetzalcoatl was their patron deity) who traveled to the far corners of Mesoamerica exchanging fine central Mexican ritual objects—ceramics, jade work, textiles, obsidian knives—for cacao beans and the raw materials to make those objects. Cholula did not dominate the valley—it had to share its power with Tlaxcala and Huejotzingo—but it was strong enough to resist the rapidly growing Aztec empire.

In 1519, Cholula was the site of one of the most notorious events in Mexican history. Fresh from defeating the Tlaxcalans and making them his allies, Cortés and his army marched into Cholula. The Aztecs had convinced the Cholulans to greet the Spaniards as honored guests—for a while. However, an informer told La Malinche, Cortés's native translator, of Aztec and Cholulan plans to ambush the Spaniards in the main square where the surrounding streets were so narrow that escape would be impossible. Instead, the conquistadors trapped dozens, perhaps hundreds, of Cholulan nobles in the square.

Cortés harangued them for their treachery; the Spaniards had come in good faith, and the Cholulans had planned to murder them. The conquistador Bernal Díaz wrote: "... They were planning to kill us and eat our flesh, and had already prepared the pots with salt and peppers and tomatoes." Cortés ordered "a musket to be fired, which was the signal we had agreed on; and they received a blow they will remember forever, for we killed many of them, and the promises of their false idols were of no avail." The consequences of this act continue to reverberate in modern Mexico. Motecuhzoma II, the Aztec emperor, who had planned the ambush, then felt forced to invite the conquistadors into Tenochtitlan.

After the Conquest, one of the first places the Spaniards returned to was Cholula, the center of the pagan cult of Quetzalcoatl. They razed his temple and vowed to replace the 365 smaller shrines they had counted with 365 churches. Their destruction succeeded more than their creation: the temples were all destroyed, but only a few dozen churches were built. Cholula's Iglesia de San Gabriel in the center of town now rests on the Temple of Quetzalcoatl's foundations.

The vengeful Spaniards did not at first realize, however, that the hill looming over the center of town was actually a man-made construction—the Great Pyramid. In 1533, the Franciscan priest Toribio de Motolinía climbed to the summit and discovered "idols" and offerings. When they realized that worship of the pagan gods continued here—the hill was dedicated to the god Chiconauquiahuitl—they erected first a chapel and then, in the late 19th century, the church of Nuestro Santuario de los Remedios.

ARCHAEOLOGICAL RECORD

Cholula's Great Pyramid ensured that the site has never been forgotten. Sixteenth-century Spanish priests such as Diego Durán described the structure and the religious practices that took place on its summit. When the era of the explorer-travelers began with Guillermo Dupaix in the late 18th century, Cholula was one of the must-sees on the route. Numerous 19th-century and early 20th-century archaeologists collected artifacts here, including Désiré Charnay, Adolph Bandelier, and Eduard Seler.

The era of comprehensive excavations began in 1931 with a project led by Ignacio Marquina. The center of the investigation was the Great Pyramid, and the main technique was tunneling. They had decided this would be the best way to unlock the chronology of the structure's construction and also to discover if any treasure-filled tombs lay within. Pits were dug around the pyramid's base, but the main effort went into the tunnels. By 1956, more than eight kilometers of tunnels had been constructed, with few results except preliminary observations on the construction stages.

In 1966, INAH began the ambitious Proyecto Cholula, designed to do for the Valley of Puebla what the large-scale Teotihuacan project did for that area. The project leader, Miguel Messmacher, was fired after less than a year and replaced by Ignacio Marquina. The bulk of the excavations occurred on the southern side of the pyramid, where they unearthed and restored a large ceremonial complex and residential areas in the fields beyond. The excavations unfortunately ended after less than two years; INAH did, however, publish a comprehensive report.

Since then, the Cholula area has been the site of only a few small projects, including excavations by Sergio Suárez Cruz in the ceremonial complex and stratigraphic studies on the nearby campus of the University of the Americas. A huge amount of research remains to be done.

Cholula

RICHARD A. DIEHL

TOURING THE SITE

The Great Pyramid is the center of the Cholula archaeological zone. Pre-Hispanic residents called it Tlachihualtepetl, or "man-made mountain." The structure measures roughly 400 meters on a side and is oriented to the north-northwest, aiming at the setting sun on the summer solstice. A spring rises from beneath the pyramid—probably the reason it was located here—and it may have also covered a cave. A chamber that may have simulated an artificial cave has been found in the center of the pyramid.

The site entrance lies on the road running along the pyramid's north face. You can park on the shoulder and pay your admission at the little guardhouse. A small doorway leads into the pyramid's network of tunnels; you will be offered the services of a Spanish-speaking guide.

The tunnel leads straight to the pyramid's center; incandescent bulbs illuminate the way. The outermost layer, the Postclassic Stage 4, was probably never completed. It is quickly followed by Stage 3 (Classic era) and then a series of layers representing additions to the Stage 2 temple, also dating to the Classic. Finally you come to the Stage 1 Preclassic temple built around a rubble core. Each stage of the temple was faced with stucco-covered stone; the fill for all but the earliest stages was adobe bricks. Atop the Stage 1 structure, archaeologists found the remains of a square temple. The facade was decorated with murals depicting human skulls with insect-like bodies.

As you walk through the tunnels, you can see side tunnels leading up and down and ancient drainage pipes. At the center, you are shunted around some corners before turning left toward the light of day shining from the pyramid's east doorway. You exit by the side of the Sanatorio de Guadalupe (a hospital); turn right and head south along the east face of the structure. A path leads up the pyramid to the church on top. Turn right (west) again at the corner of the pyramid to enter the ceremonial precinct where most of the excavations have been conducted.

You see a complicated series of structures attached to the south side of the pyramid; these represent more than a thousand years of construction during Stages 2, 3, and 4. Unfortunately, the lack of descriptive labels makes this assemblage of platforms, facades, and staircases very confusing for visitors.

You first come to Structure 5, a *talud-tablero* facade dating to Stage 3 that originally held a mural depicting a feathered serpent. Partially covering this is Structure 6, a platform, in front of which lies a sunken patio whose floor is constructed of large mosaic flagstones. This patio was originally much larger than the small segment that you see. Next you come to Structure 4, a platform that lies on the east side of the famous Patio of the Altars.

The patio lies in front of a staircase in the center of the pyramid's southern face. Here archaeologists discovered a series of large carved stone reliefs and sculptures; these probably date to the Classic era but their exact symbolism and ritual use is

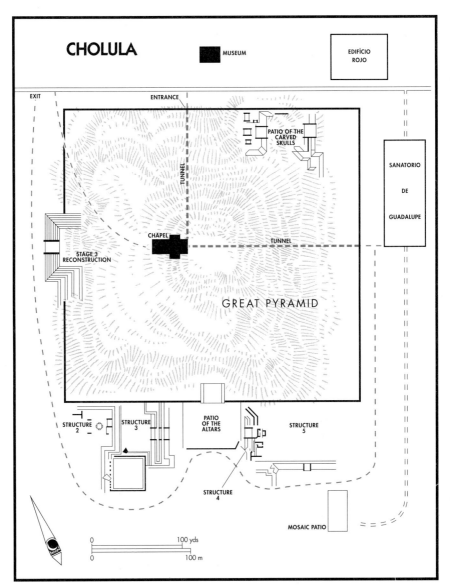

unknown. But first, on the side of Structure 4, you come to Altar 1, a rectangular stela framed with a running scroll pattern; it rests on a pedestal whose sides are carved with the same pattern. Next you see a large round stone carved in the shape of a head but with far less skill than the Olmec colossal heads. This is followed by a reclining stone figure (little more than a blob) and a basalt obelisk.

A platform next to the central staircase holds Altar 3, with a peaked top above another running curve design framing a blank center. On the west side of the plaza lies Altar 2, a 10-ton stone whose sides are decorated with the same scroll pattern and also two serpents. On the north side of the plaza, you see a pit in which archaeologists found the Aztec Altar, a small pyramid-shaped structure dating to the Early Postclassic. A protective glass covers some of the ceramic offerings found in the altar.

Altar 2 abuts Structure 3, which is a mirror of Structure 4. Structure 3's facade is painted with the famous *Bebedores* (Drinkers) mural depicting about 100 figures—all males dressed only in loincloths—drinking from ceramic vases and bowls. Most researchers assume they were drinking pulque, the fermented juice of the maguey plant, but others believe the drink could have been a hallucinogenic concoction brewed from mushrooms or the peyote cactus. In any case, the scene almost certainly represents a ceremony of ritual drunkenness. A corrugated roof protects part of the mural, but unfortunately visitors are not allowed close enough to view it. It has severely decomposed since being exposed to light and air.

At the southwest corner of the pyramid stands Structure 2, another platform. The top may have been a residential complex surrounding a series of small patios. You can look down into a deep trench between the path and the reconstructions to see the original base of the platforms. A burial was found here rich with greenstone beads and shell ornaments; from the skull deformation, archaeologists believe the deceased may have been an Olmeca-Xicallanca merchant.

The path continues around the corner to the west side of the pyramid. Here you see another tunnel entrance and the heavily reconstructed stairway and facade belonging to the pyramid's Stage 3. These stairways face the railroad tracks and, in the town just beyond, the Cerro Cocoyo, a large archaeological mound that has never been excavated.

Just north of the stairway, a hole in the fence is the site exit. From here, you can take the main causeway up to the church atop the pyramid; the view of the surrounding valley and the volcanoes to the west is excellent.

After exiting the site, you see the remains of the pyramid facade and another tunnel entrance on the northwest corner of the structure. There remain two other areas not on the official tour but still worth visiting. Just beyond the main tunnel entrance, on the northeast corner of the pyramid stands the Patio of the Carved Skulls. This was an elite residential complex in the midst of which archaeologists

found a small pyramid-shaped altar decorated with plaster skulls. Beneath it was the burial of a man and woman accompanied by Early Postclassic-era offerings. Across the road from the patio stands the Edificio Rojo (Red Building), a large rectangular platform dating to the Classic era. It was attached to the pyramid during Stage 4 construction.

Aztec relief of crouching dog, Anthropology Museum, Mexico City

XOCHITÉCATL

INTRODUCTION

Standing on a hilltop less than two kilometers west of Cacaxtla, the fortified city of Xochitécatl was the central Mexican counterpart to that satellite of the Maya world. The relationship between the two settlements has never been explored. Xochitécatl may have been the ritual center for the central Mexican farmers and laborers who supported Cacaxtla's Mayanized elites. Xochitécatl is also far older than its neighbor; its structures include a unique circular temple whose ritual use has yet to be explained. Xochitécatl's ceremonial center is compact, and you can easily clamber over the main sights in an hour.

HISTORY

Xochitécatl was founded around 300 B.C. at the beginning of the Late Preclassic. During this era, the first stages of the settlement's main structures were completed, including the Pyramid of the Flowers, the Serpent Building, and the Spiral Building. From A.D. 150 to 600, Xochitécatl's population shrunk and no new ceremonial platforms were constructed. This downturn coincided with the florescence of the great city of Cholula in the valley below.

In the 7th century, Cholula began its decline, and the Olmeca-Xicallanca arrived in the area to begin construction of Cacaxtla's great edifice. Xochitécatl's fortunes rebounded; the Olmeca-Xicallanca added new stages to the old temples, and built the platform called the Building of the Volcanoes at the foot of the Pyramid of the Flowers. Excavations from this era contain a trove of luxury objects from throughout Mesoamerica, another sign of Xochitécatl's good fortune.

After Cacaxtla's abandonment, however, Xochitécatl again waned. Desultory occupation continued until the Conquest, when the site was abandoned for good.

ARCHAEOLOGICAL RECORD

Pedro Armillas mapped Xochitécatl and the surrounding sites in 1941. During the late '60s, a German-led project under Bodo Spranz conducted some preliminary excavations at the site and produced a rough chronology. Xochitécatl was named one of the Salinas administration's Archaeological Special Projects in the early 1990s; the expedition was led by INAH's Mari Carmen Serra Puche (also then director of the Mexico City Museo Nacional de Antropología) and

CACAXTLA

How to get there: The adjacent sites of Cacaxtla and Xochitécatl are actually in the state of Tlaxcala just north of the Puebla border. The easiest way to reach them is by car from the San Martín Texmelucan exit off Highway 150; from here, follow the signs 12.5 kilometers east to the hillside sites.

Hours: Daily 0900–1800.

Admission: 20 pesos for each site.

How long to tour: Two hours for Cacaxtla; one hour for Xochitécatl.

Recommended gear: Hats, sunblock, sturdy shoes or sneakers.

Museums: A tourist complex (museum, gift shop, and restaurant) stands at Cacaxtla's site entrance. The museum features a broken life-size ceramic figure of a striding man and some stucco ornaments shaped like corncobs and flowers. (You can rent the services of an official guide, both English- and Spanish-speaking, for a small charge in the tourist complex.)

Xochitécatl's small site museum contains many interesting mold-made figurines. Some are articulated, and others represent women giving birth to baby figurines through holes in their stomachs.

XOCHITÉCATL

Ludwig Beutelspacher Baigts. The site was excavated and the main structures were restored. The project report has yet to be published.

TOURING THE SITE

The road up to Xochitécatl stops at a parking area just below the hilltop. At the top of the walkway, the path takes you to the right and the Serpent Building. The main staircase of this rectangular temple-platform (73 by 58 meters at the base) faces north, but you take a separate ramp up to the top level. In a trench running through the center of the floor here, you find a stone basin containing a broken stone serpent's head, thus the name of the structure. The label claims that the basin was used in "water rites" but does not say what these were. Stone sculptures of a jaguar and a person were also discovered here, all dating to the Late Preclassic.

The Serpent Building faces a ceremonial plaza on which stands the low platform called the Building of the Volcanoes, dating to around A.D. 750—far later than the other structures. The reason behind its naming is not stated.

The path proceeds east to Xochitécatl's largest building, the Pyramid of the Flowers, measuring roughly 144 by 115 meters and rising to a height of 30 meters. Another Late Preclassic structure, this bears many similarities to Teotihuacan's Pyramid of the Moon. The Pyramid was built in eight tiers of stone faced with flat rock and stucco. A platform about halfway up the west side is the site of two more stone basins called Monoliths 1 and 2; sculptures were found in the first. The pyramid also hid the burials of 30 people, mostly child sacrifices, and further stone monuments. The summit holds broken columns and lintels, all that remains of a temple. From here, you have an excellent view of Cacaxtla to the east and the volcanoes to the west. You can see how this location overlooking the Valley of Puebla would have such strategic value.

The last structure lies across the ceremonial plaza to the west. The unique Late Preclassic Spiral Building measures 50 meters in diameter and 16 meters tall. Apparently, no staircase took the Xochitécatlans up to the summit; instead there were 13 circular tiers that the inhabitants must have had to climb like giant steps. You can ascend a metal staircase—almost a ladder—to the summit, where you find a modern Christian cross. Other central Mexican circular temples were dedicated to the Wind God; it is not known if this had the same use. The 13 tiers also may have been associated with a calendar system.

CACAXTLA

INTRODUCTION

Cacaxtla, a hilltop site in southern Tlaxcala, is home to the most dramatic and best-preserved murals yet found in Mexico. Interestingly, these are not the product of long-established central Mexicans but, from their style and subject matter, were obviously created by Maya or Maya-influenced groups, most likely the Olmeca-Xicallanca. The largest murals depict grisly battle scenes with warriors slaughtering defeated enemies; other paintings feature amazingly lifelike plants and animals and fantastical blue dancers dressed in skirts. Cacaxtla is easily accessible from the Mexico City-Puebla Highway (150) and is rapidly becoming the most-visited central Mexican site outside the Valley of Mexico.

HISTORY

Only Cacaxtla's ceremonial center has been excavated; archaeologists have yet to perform comprehensive stratigraphic studies that should establish a firm chronology for the site.

It is not known when Cacaxtla was first settled; the neighboring fortified settlement of Xochitécatl was first settled in the Early Preclassic. Xochitécatl was occupied into the Postclassic; until more excavations are performed, researchers cannot say how the two cities interrelated. There is also evidence of connections to a number of other nearby sites—ruined temple-platforms, altars, and residential areas dot the hillsides. These may have comprised some larger regional political entity; much more research is needed.

Most archaeologists date Cacaxtla's apogee from A.D. 650 to 900, roughly the same epoch as Xochicalco in the nearby Valley of Morelos. Like the latter site, it was constructed as a hilltop fortress surrounded by defensive terraces and moats. Also like Xochicalco, Cacaxtla was evidently a city built on trade, warfare, and tribute—themes they celebrated in its murals.

According to carbon 14 studies, the battle mural in Building B was executed shortly after A.D. 650, while the Building A murals were painted about a century later. Beginning about A.D. 850, Cacaxtla was gradually abandoned. The Cacaxtlans may have planned to return: they carefully buried the murals in a protective layer of fine sand before filling in the rooms with dirt and rocks. No evidence for substantive later settlement has been found.

ARCHAEOLOGICAL RECORD

In the late 16th century, the Spanish historian Diego Muñoz Camargo described a ruined hilltop fortress that natives called Cacaxtla (place of the *cacaxtli,* or merchant's backpack). Local informants told him that this had been the seat of the Olmeca-Xicallanca, a tribe from the Gulf Coast.

The site was then forgotten, covered over by centuries of erosion, until 1940 when Pedro Armillas explored the mounds and decided that this was the Cacaxtla mentioned in Muñoz's text. The site was surveyed a number of times during the following decades, but no official excavations took place until 1975. On September 13th of that year, local pothunters tunneled into the mound and discovered first an elaborate carved lintel, part of which they destroyed, and then a stunningly colored mural—a treasure trove. Fortunately, it was too big and too attached to a wall. Stung by conscience, they informed a local schoolteacher, who took the news to the authorities.

INAH's Puebla-Tlaxcala regional center was called in to protect and restore the murals. Over the next four years, Diana López de Molina and Daniel Molina Feal excavated the central part of the Cacaxtla edifice, called the Gran Basamento (Great Foundation). They not only unearthed the rest of the mural on the portico of Building A, but discovered the great battle scene in Building B.

In 1985 and 1986, INAH excavations resumed under first Andrés Santana and Rosalba Delgadillo and then Pedro Ortega and Lino Espinosa. Digging around the perimeter of the foundations, they exposed further murals in the Temple of Venus and the amazing merchant scene at the side of the Red Temple staircase. Since then, the only discoveries have been made by workers digging supports for the roof cables; in the late 1980s, they found more mural fragments and the life-size ceramic sculpture of a striding man now in the site museum.

TOURING THE SITE

The site lies in the first set of hills rising to the north of the broad plain that is home to the cities of Puebla and Cholula. From this strategic location, Cacaxtla's rulers could control much of the valley. You walk almost a kilometer west along the side of a ridge, past small mounds and one rebuilt temple platform, before reaching the main part of the site. This lies on a hilltop protected from the elements by a massive metal roof resembling an aircraft hanger.

Cacaxtla originally stood among fields and mud and thatched roof huts. The main edifice rose above these commoners' dwellings in great tiers that doubled as fortifications. The flat-roofed complex was constructed of adobe and mud faced with white lime stucco that must have gleamed in the midday sun. Columned porticos gazed out in the four cardinal directions. Inside, the walls were painted with a riot of brightly colored murals, many of them depicting scenes of bloodshed.

You climb a flight of wooden stairs up to the Great Foundation. On the right a door leads to a beehive-shaped chamber built into the platform base; this was a storage bin for grain, probably corn. You enter the structure through the Room of the Columns; two circular pillars rise from the floor. The main complex consists of a series of larger or smaller patios and plazas, many with altars, surrounded by rooms that acted as residences, civic-ceremonial spaces, and storage areas.

We will take the walkway to the left (south) and save the most spectacular sights for last. This section is called the Palace after the cluster of rooms that may have been living quarters. The walkway takes you by the Patio of the Rhombuses, so-called for the designs that flank the doors, and out into the Patio of the Altars with a square, sunken altar in the center. The next room complex is Building F on the edifice's south end. From here you can look down

CACAXTLA

JAGUAR WARRIOR
BUILDING A
BIRD WARRIOR
BATTLE MURAL
NORTH PLAZA
ACCESS
ROOM OF COLUMNS
THE LATTICE
PATIO OF THE RHOMBUSES
THE PALACE
RED TEMPLE
PATIO OF THE ALTARS
THE STAIRWAY
GROUP 2
TEMPLE OF VENUS
BUILDING F

0   20 yds
0   20 m

on the *talud* walls that cover the foundations; these were made with volcanic tuff faced with basalt and whitened with lime stucco. On the ridge to the south stand three unexcavated temple-platforms around a little plaza.

The walkway now leads west up stairs to the largely unexplored section called Group 2 (the completely excavated complex is Group 1). On the west side of this, archaeologists discovered the Temple of Venus (also called the Star Chamber) containing two rectangular columns decorated with murals. Each depicts eerie-looking blue figures who are apparently dancing. They wear what appear to be skirts and stand on a wavy water motif with representations of water-related animals below. The borders are adorned with half stars that represent the planet Venus. From their dress, researchers believe the broken-off figure on the left (south) is a female, while the one on the right—masked and possessing a large scorpion tail behind, wings on the arms, and jaguar paws—is male. Captives may have been held in this room, waiting for the right alignment of Venus to signal the hour of their sacrifice.

The path continues north; on your right you see a stairway heading down amid a blaze of bright paint. This is the Red Temple, so-called for the red surrounding the entrance. Unfortunately, you can only see one part of the room's murals, but this is an amazing part. It depicts the Maya god L, the god of merchants, as an old man leaning forward on his cane while behind him his merchant's backpack is propped up by a staff. Strapped to the pack are such precious wares as quetzal plumes, a turtle shell, and an elaborate headdress.

The merchant god stands on a feathered serpent border that ends in a great quetzal feather plume in the upper right. Below this are pictures of plants, birds, and shells. In front of the god rises a cacao tree, the trade of whose fruit was the major reason the Maya entered central Mexico. To the left, you see a cornstalk whose fruit is not cobs but little human heads, perhaps representing the Maize God. Further cornstalks

Cacaxtla mural of Bird Warrior

C. EARLE SMITH JR.

and cacao trees rise from the side of the staircase, while a large blue toad rests on what appears to be running water containing more animal and Venus star symbols. The painting depicts the sources of Cacaxtla's wealth: water, fertile land, and trade.

A similar mural showing a captive warrior in full battle dress covers the wall opposite—unfortunately, it is out of sight—and a bench on the floor is painted with life-size renderings of gaunt captives—the victims kept here until the Venus signs were in the right position for sacrifice.

The path continues up the west side of the edifice passing La Celosía (The Lattice), a small room with a stucco grid, perhaps replicating reeds, at the entrance. You then descend some stairs and walk along the side of the North Plaza. On your right a pillar contains the remains of a stucco relief with plants growing around the figure's feet. Along the north wall of this plaza you have a panoramic view of a savage slaughter.

This is the famous Battle Mural, depicting the bloody conflict of the Jaguar and Eagle Warriors at the moment the battle turned the Eagle Warriors' way and they began to butcher their opponents. Stone lances pierce the Jaguar Warriors' stomachs sending forth streams of blood; mouths grimace in agony. The art historian Mary Miller believes the scene depicts an actual battle between a Maya group—the Jaguar Warriors with their Maya noses and flattened foreheads—and the more Mexicanized Eagle Warriors.

Scattered throughout the scene are a wide variety of symbolic elements, including date glyphs and owls, the birds of war. Interestingly, these do not include the long hieroglyphic texts found in nearly every piece of Classic Maya monumental art. Some researchers believe the Cacaxtlans painted purely pictorial scenes because they were trying to reach a central Mexican audience that could not read Maya writing.

The structure above the mural is Building B, a long structure with a row of columns in front. At the far end of the murals, a stairway ascends to Building A, the site where those pothunters made their discovery back in 1975. Two columns flanking a doorway are decorated

> The Evening "Star," **Venus** is one of the brightest objects in the sky. Most Mesoamerican religions anthropomorphized Venus as a male god of warfare, danger, and drought. Mesoamerican astronomers accurately tracked the planet's course, and its phases determined the dates of many important festivals, including sacrifices.

with intensely colored, highly complex murals. They depict a Jaguar Warrior (left) and a Bird Warrior (right) clutching in their arms ceremonial bars. The Jaguar Warrior stands on a jaguar whose serpentlike body becomes the border; his ceremonial bar consists of bundled lances dripping raindrops, the sign of fertility. The Bird Warrior's bar has a stylized monster face on the end; his skin is painted black, and he stands on a feathered serpent whose body also becomes the mural's border. A quetzal bird flies to his right. Both outside borders contain the same water animals you saw in the Temple of Venus and Red Temple murals.

The other symbolic elements include date glyphs and the Venus half stars. The bird and the jaguar may have represented Cacaxtla's main warrior castes; their blood fertilized the soil and allowed the crops to grow.

The walkway next takes you behind Building B past the Sunken Patio and Platform Y to the northwest corner of the edifice. At the end of the path, you look down and see the Conejeros, or Rabbit Hutches, a room filled with little pens, perhaps for keeping animals. You now return to the main entrance and exit this complex.

You are not allowed to stray off the path and walk around the perimeter of the site. If you look at the southeast side of the structure, you can see some of the eight construction stages and get an idea of the incredible labor—all human—that built this massive edifice.

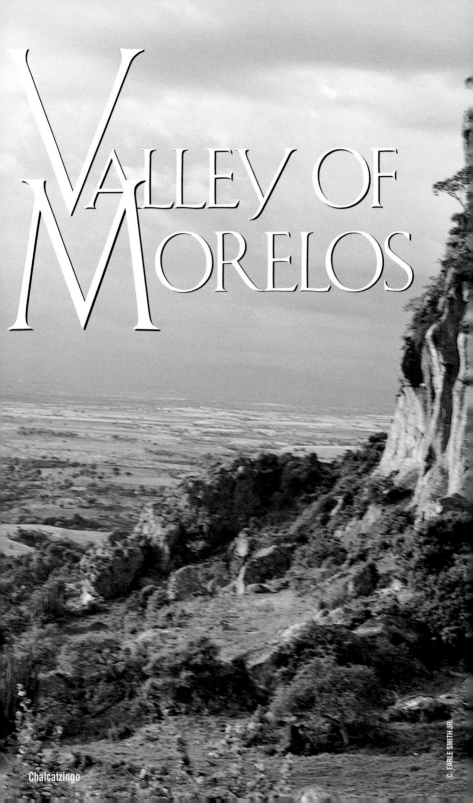

Valley of Morelos

Chalcatzingo

L ying due south over the mountains from Mexico City, the Valley of Morelos has been a retreat for city-dwellers ever since Aztec times. Nineteenth-century tourist brochures called it the "Land of the Eternal Spring," where it is neither too hot nor too cold, where the rain falls gently, and where there are abundant springs for bathing. Today, most cars and buses use Highway 95 from Mexico City. Unchecked development, particularly around Cuernavaca, has paved over many of Morelos's natural attractions. Nevertheless, there are still many spots out in the country where you can see what drew the Aztec emperors here.

For the last 500 years, Morelos has been famous for its resorts—the privileged escapes of people such as Cortés and Motecuhzoma II. Before the Aztecs captured the region, however, the Valley of Morelos was an important agricultural center. The early residents grew the staples of maize and other grains, beans, and fruit, and were also important suppliers of cotton, which was woven into cloth and used as currency. Morelos was also a gateway between the Valley of Mexico and lands to the west and south. Some of the groups that came to power here originated very, very far away.

THE LAND

The Valley of Morelos would be better called the Valleys of Morelos. The region lies immediately south of the Sierra de Ajusco, the southern border of the Valley of Mexico that was formed by a volcanic eruption around A.D. 100. The volcanic ash spilled down the mountainsides, forming long fan-shaped plains that run all the way to the Río Balsas in Guerrero. Between the plains run snow- and spring-fed rivers that divide the Valley of Morelos into a series of valleys, all running from north to south and ending at the Río Balsas, which

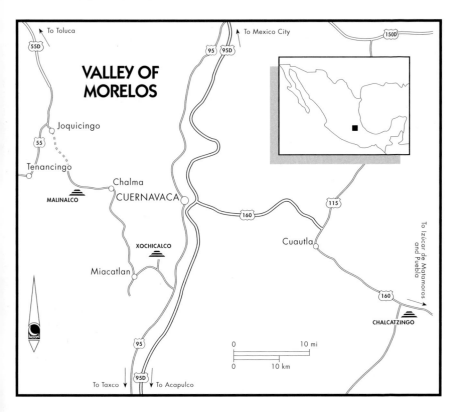

empties into the Pacific. Most of Morelos's rivers empty into the Río Amacuzac, which runs along the state's southern borders before flowing into the Balsas.

The northernmost part of the valley lies in the pine-covered heights of the Sierra de Ajusco. This quickly drops to a gentler incline between 1,000 and 1,500 meters, at which altitude most of the State of Morelos lies. Here you find good soils and abundant springs, many of them thermal, to water the crops. At the lowest altitudes of the state—the southern border—you are in the hot, dry *tierra caliente,* home to cacti and snakes.

Climate

Altitude is the primary determiner of climate in the Valley of Morelos. The north lies in the cold, dry zone of the Valley of Mexico; the summer rainy season brings fog and drizzle. The middle regions have long been famous for the lack of temperature fluctuation over the seasons; it rarely wavers from an average of 59–68°F. The winters are generally dry, while in summer-time rain showers occur most afternoons. In the lower altitudes along the southern border, the climate is warm and semiarid nearly year-round, with marginal rainfall.

CUERNAVACA HOTELS

For archaeological explorations, the best place to base yourself is the rapidly growing city of Cuernavaca. Among its moderately priced hotels, the best is the family-oriented **Hotel Papagayo**, tel. 73/14-1711, at Motolinea 13, or the small **Posada de Xochiquetzal**, tel. 73/18-5767, at Leyva 200. Both have pools.

The valley's river systems are also important climatic factors: the broader the river valley, the moister the atmosphere. Western Morelos is comparatively wet and lush, while the eastern borders are dry. There, the rivers have cut deep gorges, so much of the surrounding landscape is water-starved and the few population centers cluster around springs. Certain protected river valleys foster small areas of tropical climate with warm, humid air and lush vegetation.

Flora and Fauna

Like the climate, the Valley of Morelos's flora and fauna depend on the altitude. The mountains are covered with pine forests grading into oak at lower elevations. These forests were once home to abundant wildlife such as bear, mountain lion, deer, fox, squirrel, and rabbit; today only the last two are found in abundance.

Below 1,500 meters, you find oaks, mimosas, *ahuehuetes* (a Mexican conifer), acacias, and, near water, willows. As the land drops into the semiarid region, many varieties of cactus appear, including nopales, as well as agaves and scrub oaks. The dry hills are home to many snakes and lizards, most famously the iguana, which is the specialty of many roadside restaurants south of Cuernavaca.

HISTORY

Morelos has been occupied at least since the Early Preclassic (1800–1200 B.C.). There is some evidence that Archaic-era hunters chased mammoths and other now-extinct mammals in the region. Agriculturists settled across the valley around 1500 B.C. and built a series of small and medium-sized villages that show loose trade links to Tlatilco in the Valley of Mexico. At these sites, archaeologists have also found ceramics, jade, and carved stones all in the distinct style of the Olmecs, whose homeland lay hundreds of kilometers away along the Gulf Coast. The most famous of these is the ceramic head of a baby found by George Vaillant at Gualupita, now part of Cuernavaca.

Archaeologists believe that Olmec "missionaries" may have carried the objects into the region as part of expeditions that combined trade and proselytizing. They must have been successful, because they founded the Olmec outpost of

CUERNAVACA MUSEUM

On the central Plaza de Armas, Cuernavaca's **Museo Cuauhnahuac** is Cortés's old palace, built on the ruins of an Aztec residence in 1522. Its exhibitions contain a number of locally found pre-Columbian sculptures as well as a Diego Rivera mural on the second floor. It's open Tues.–Sun. 0900–1900.

Chalcatzingo that soon became the largest settlement in the valley. Its influence was felt throughout central Mexico, and, even after its collapse, it probably influenced later cultures such as existed at Teotihuacan and Monte Albán.

CHALCATZINGO

INTRODUCTION

Although it lies slightly off the tourist track, the unique site of Chalcatzingo is worth a visit. It is the only major Olmec site found so far in central Mexico. Its numerous rock carvings have provided crucial clues to the structure and iconography of the mysterious Olmec religion. Chalcatzingo's setting is a natural amphitheater formed by two towers of rock rising from the middle of a semiarid plain. As you clamber around the boulders, you can understand why the Olmecs built their outpost here and why, long after the Olmecs disappeared, the striking backdrop remained a pilgrimage destination well into the Aztec era.

CHALCATZINGO

How to get there: The ruins of Chalcatzingo do not appear on every map. From Cuernavaca, head east through Cuautla and then continue 20 kilometers toward Izúcar de Matamoros before turning south on the Jonacatepec road. About two kilometers to the south, a dirt road runs east to two large rock towers, at the base of which you find the village and site of Chalcatzingo. The road—more like a track—from the village up to the ruins is heavily potholed.

Hours: Tues.–Wed. 1000–1700, Thurs.–Sun. 0900–1800, closed Monday.

Admission fee: 10 pesos.

How long to tour: Two hours.

Recommended gear: Hats, sunblock, bottled water, hiking boots.

HISTORY

The earliest settlers were probably drawn to this site above the gorge of the Río Amatzinac for a combination of symbolic and practical reasons. Called the Cerro Chalcatzingo and the Cerro Delgado, the twin towers of rock rising 300 meters from the valley floor provided a natural religious focus. Archaeologists believe that Cerro Chalcatzingo also contained a cave in which the priest-rulers performed rituals. Hills were associated with divinities in all Mesoamerican religions, and caves were thought to be entrances to the Underworld. Among the rocks grew numerous plants with medicinal and sacred uses, and nearby the settlers found sources of clay and iron ore, both profitable items of trade. Most important, the soil was good and springs flowed from the rock towers to the river below. With sources of both spiritual and physical sustenance, Chalcatzingo could not fail to attract human settlement.

The earliest era of Chalcatzingo occupation, called the Amate phase, dates from between 1500 and 1100 B.C. During this time, more than a dozen Early Preclassic villages arose in the Valley of Morelos. Through their ceramics, particularly the "pretty lady" figurines, they all show the influence of Tlatilco lying just over the mountains in the Valley of Mexico. Tlatilco, in turn, was influenced by a more distant culture, the Olmecs, who would later center their attentions on Chalcatzingo. During the Early Preclassic, the only feature to differentiate the latter site from its neighbors was a long platform mound that is the first permanent ceremonial construction yet found in the valley.

During the next 400 years at Chalcatzingo, called the Barranca phase, its residents built elaborate agricultural terraces and irrigation systems around the bases of the two rock towers. Most people lived and worked on their farming plots; the area called Terrace I was developing into a ceremonial precinct with platform mounds and possibly a ballcourt. The ceramics still show the influence of the Valley of Mexico, but there is also an intrusion of gray ware from Oaxaca and Puebla—the first signs of a trade route skirting the Valley of Mexico to the south and reaching toward the Gulf Coast.

Chalcatzingo reached its apogee, the Cantera phase, between 700 and 500 B.C. It was a major regional center, by far the largest of the almost 50 towns and villages in the Valley of Morelos, and it was perhaps the largest settlement in central Mexico. The exact size of the population is subject to debate, but most estimates run 600–1,000 people. The ceremonial area doubled in size, and the farming and residential areas spread into the valley. Most of Chalcatzingo's amazing rock carvings date to this era. Archaeologists believe that they illustrate the reigning politico-religious cult wherein the ruler is elevated to the level of a divinity and interacts with gods.

These carvings and other artifacts show the obvious stylistic influence of the Olmec civilization then flourishing at sites such as La Venta and Tres Zapotes on the Gulf Coast. At the same time, Chalcatzingo's residents used the same

Barranca-style ceramics as the occupants of the other valley settlements. It is still a subject of debate, but the current belief is that Chalcatzingo was basically central Mexican in culture although controlled by the Gulf Coast Olmecs (perhaps after intermarrying with the Chalcatzingo ruling clan). The Olmecs used the site as a trading center where they could exchange central Mexican raw materials—iron ore, clay, obsidian, greenstone—for finished Olmec goods, such as figurines and polished stone mirrors. Chalcatzingo was perfectly situated to act as a gateway between central Mexico and the Gulf.

Chalcatzingo declined after 500 B.C. for unknown reasons. At the same time, western and central Mexican settlements such as Monte Albán and Cuicuilco began their expansion into regional powers. Chalcatzingo never recovered, although the Teotihuacanos built several small temples and a ballcourt here. They also painted crude pictographs (hands, geometric designs) on many cliff faces, particularly on the Cerro Delgado. The caves near the top of this hill were used as homes in both the Classic and Postclassic eras.

Like most Mesoamerican civilizations, these later residents continued the worship of their predecessors' gods. This practice endured into the early Aztec era, when they constructed steps leading up to Monument 2 and placed large braziers on either side of the carving. At this time, the main population center was the agricultural settlement of Tetla a half kilometer east of the site. After the Conquest, Chalcatzingo was forgotten, and erosion and rock slides covered up its monuments.

ARCHAEOLOGICAL RECORD

A farming village called Chalcatzingo was founded just northwest of the twin hills. The villagers tilled the soil at the base of the cliffs; they knew that some of the boulders scattered about were covered with mysterious carvings but paid them no mind—they were part of the landscape. In 1932, a torrential rainstorm shook them out of their indifference. The flood of water caused rock slides and washed the earth away from the boulders. When the villagers returned to their fields the next morning, they made a startling discovery: the rains had uncovered more carved stones, some with large and intricate designs.

The most impressive of these depicted a seated personage surrounded by what appeared to be a giant mouth. The villagers named it El Rey—"The King" (now called Monument 1)—and word of the discovery eventually reached Mexico City. In 1934, Eulalia Guzmán, a government archaeologist, visited Chalcatzingo (at this time called Cerro Cantera) and studied El Rey and the other carvings and theorized that they might be Teotihuacano or even Olmec.

The first excavations began in 1952 under INAH's Román Piña Chan. He dug 11 test pits at Chalcatzingo as part of his exploration of Morelos Formative-era sites. He decided that "Archaic Olmecs" had lived here and dated the carvings to

500–200 B.C. During this time, widespread looting occurred at the site, and many pieces ended up in foreign collections.

Chalcatzingo's major excavation occurred from 1972 to 1974, under David C. Grove of the University of Illinois and the Morelos-Guerrero regional center for INAH. The expedition mapped the site and excavated the Central Plaza, the residential areas, and all known major structures. They also explored the surrounding region and discovered further carvings and numerous pictographs dating to the Late Classic. Their work helped revise the Formative-era chronology of central Mexico and replaced Piña Chan's chronology with one that established a much earlier occupation of the site.

Since 1976, when Grove's expedition returned to dig test pits in order to verify their chronology, work at Chalcatzingo has been minimal.

TOURING THE SITE

The road from Chalcatzingo town ends at a rough parking lot next to the site's Central Plaza. This tour will return to the plaza after a hike around Chalcatzingo's most notable rock carvings. Facing you are the two rock towers, both approximately 300 meters tall, which provide a natural amphitheater for the settlement. On your right is the larger Cerro Chalcatzingo, while on the left stands the Cerro Delgado, covered with slightly more vegetation.

A path from the entry leads up the hill past two small platform mounds and the site office toward the base of the Cerro Chalcatzingo. The base is circled by a layer of talus, or rock and boulder debris, which has fallen off the hill. After about a half-kilometer hike, you come to a straw shelter over the face of a boulder. It protects Chalcatzingo's Monument 1, the site's most famous artifact, also known as El Rey.

This bas-relief carving depicts not a king but a female ruler seated within a stylized cave shaped like a monster's mouth (caves and snakelike monsters were associated with most Mesoamerican religions). Stylized puffs of smoke curl from the cave's mouth, while exclamation-point-shaped raindrops fall from clouds overhead. The ruler wears an elaborate headdress and holds in her arms the lazy-S cloud symbol; another cloud symbol forms her throne. Tufts of vegetation grow from the top of the monster-cave.

Archaeologists believe the relief depicts a shaman-ruler engaged in a rite to produce rain (they totally reject the spaceship theory found in books such as *Chariots of the Gods* by Erich von Däniken). It is rumored that the entrance to a cave, perhaps the same one depicted in the carving, lies beneath the stone, but no one has attempted to find it. The stone lies beside the main drainage channel off Cerro Chalcatzingo beginning at a large cleft in the cliff face that also may have mystical significance.

To the left, another thatched roof covers a boulder on which you find Monuments 6 and 7. On the right side of this boulder, Monument 6 depicts a striking-

CHALCATZINGO

MONUMENT 22

MONUMENT 21

TERRACE 15
MAIN PLAZA

MONUMENT 27
TERRACE 6

Cerro
Delgado

ROAD

PARKING
AREA

PLATFORM
MOUND

TERRACE 1

0   50 yds

0   50 m

Path

Path

MooN

Path

MONUMENT 13

MONUMENT 2

Path

Path

MONUMENT 1

Cerro Chalcatzingo

ly realistic squash plant with seven leaves and four flowers emerging from a vine that ends in a curling tendril. Continuing left, you come to a heavily eroded carving, Monument 7, that archaeologists believe represents an animal crouching atop a scroll.

Further reliefs are found on the rock face to the left of the boulder. The first is Monument 8, portraying another animal crouching on a lazy-S symbol while a bifurcated scroll emerges from his mouth and ends just below a sinuous cloud from which two raindrops fall. Next you come to Monument 11, one more crouching animal below a raindrop-shedding cloud.

From this vantage point, you have an excellent view of the Valley of Morelos rising to the still-active Popocatépetl Volcano to the north. If you descend a few steps, a path heads to the right along the base of the cliff, descending first and then ascending to another boulder assemblage. A sign points right to Monument 2, also known as the Procession of the Warriors. These reliefs are difficult to view or photograph because they are carved on one wall of a narrow crevice. The scene shows a row of four people, three walking and one seated. Two of the walkers bear long staffs or paddles that some call ritual objects and others believe are weapons. The walkers wear masks and headdresses, while the seated person has the mask on the back of his head and wears a horned headdress above.

To the left, a straw roof covers the recently discovered Monument 31, depicting a large reclining feline crouching on and digging its claws into a prone human. Above floats another lazy-S cloud motif. A large stone to the left displays Monument 3, another feline sitting beneath some sort of plant, perhaps a cactus. The cavities on the left side of the boulder are probably artificial, possibly caused by rituals performed here.

Continuing left, you come to a wide slab of rock carved with Monument 4, which shows two snarling felines, possibly jaguars, with two helpless humans in their claws. The felines are decorated with various symbolic elements whose interpretation remains vague. The scene appears to be on its side, leading archaeologists to believe that the boulder was tipped over from its original position.

About a dozen paces to the left, another boulder has been carved with Monument 5. This shows a large crocodile-like creature either swallowing or regurgitating a human. The monster is covered with scales or feathers and its long bifurcated tongue extends past the human. The thematic similarities in Monuments 31, 3, 4—animals attacking humans—with those of Monument 5 have led archaeologists to believe they were carved at the same time.

A path leads down the hill to Monument 13 under another thatched roof. This depicts a baby-headed personage in profile seated within a monster mouth facing outward. It appears to be an into-the-cave frontal view of the same scene as Monument 1; it even has the tufts of vegetation sprouting from the monster mouth.

This tour now heads due north along the base of the Cerro Delgado to a corrugated metal roof beside the remains of a low platform mound. The roof shelters Monument 27, a cracked reddish stone on whose bottom half you see the legs of a walking figure. It appears to hold a scepter and is either dressed in an animal skin or carries the dead animal, possibly a deer. Beyond, another roof covers Monument 25, a round altar carved around the sides with an undulating line motif. These monuments lie on the easternmost border of Cantera-phase Chalcatzingo's residential and civic-political ward.

You next cross a little gully (the hills' main drainage channel) to the heart of the Olmec settlement. You enter a large plaza—little more than a broad cleared space—with structures to the north and south. The north complex, just below the level of the plaza, is made up of two platform mounds. The first you approach contains a sunken patio with A-shaped wall niches and, under a thatch roof, the carved altar known as Monument 22. This unique construction is built from several stone slabs carved with the eyes and mouth of a earth-monster. Altars at other Olmec sites such as La Venta had niches in the front with seated figures of rulers leaning out of them; the style of Monument 22 has no known antecedents in the Olmec world. Beneath the altar, archaeologists found several burials rich with offerings—obviously people of rank.

Return to the main plaza, where a corrugated roof to the right covers Monument 21, a stela depicting a standing woman facing a column carved with symbolic motifs of unknown meaning. The woman and column stand on top of the face of another earth-monster, leading archaeologists to believe that the relief depicts the raising of the World Tree, which was the primordial act in a number of Mesoamerican religions.

Finally, you head south across the plaza to the center of the ancient settlement. The south end of the plaza is bordered by the remains of a ballcourt. Immediately beyond rises the site's main platform mound, the largest construction at Chalcatzingo, measuring approximately 110 by 60 meters. On the platform's west end sits a circular pyramid dating to the Classic era. This structure is about 35 meters wide and nine meters high. Another small pyramid from the Classic era (both may have been built by Teotihuacanos) lies just southwest.

If you want to explore further, more but inferior stone monuments lie on the peripheries of the site. You can also climb the dusty, difficult paths to the tops of the two hills. Monument 10, depicting a human head, lies on the summit of Cerro Chalcatzingo, while the caves of Cerro Delgado possess numerous large but crude pictographic paintings dating to the post-Olmec era.

XOCHICALCO

INTRODUCTION

The hilltop city of Xochicalco, The Place of the House of Flowers, was the largest settlement in pre-Columbian Morelos. Its beautifully reconstructed Temple of the Feathered Serpent—the centerpiece of the Xochicalco acropolis—is one of the masterworks of Mesoamerican architecture. You can easily spend hours clambering over the densely clustered ruins. The other sights include an amazing underground solar observatory, numerous tunnels, ballcourts, and a network of raised causeways. The latter were part of Xochicalco's elaborate system of fortifications. The city was built in the troubled centuries after the collapse of Teotihuacan. Many of the militaristic aspects of Xochicalco's organization you find reflected in later civilizations such as the Toltecs and the Aztecs.

HISTORY

Xochicalco has one of the shortest historical records of any major Mesoamerican site. The city was founded around A.D. 650 by the Olmeca-Xicallanca, a

XOCHICALCO

How to get there: Xochicalco lies within easy striking distance from Cuernavaca. Head south on Highway 95 about 25 kilometers until you see the sign for the ruins turnoff heading west. After seven kilometers (just before the Laguna del Rodeo on your left), the road up to the site passes on the east side of Xochicalco's hill; you can see the remains of ancient terraces that give the city its wedding cake–shaped appearance. The parking lot lies in the saddle between the Cerro Xochicalco and the Cerro de la Bodega just to the east.

Hours: Daily 1000–1700.

Admission fee: 20 pesos.

How long to tour: Three hours.

Recommended gear: Hats, sunblock, bottled water, sturdy shoes or sneakers.

Museum: Just before arriving at the site parking lot, you see on the right the new site museum housed in a large green building. Inside you find good exhibitions on the area's history and a number of interesting objects, including stelae and paving stones carved with animal motifs, found during excavations.

group of Maya (not Olmec) traders whose homeland was the Gulf Coast of Campeche. Slightly later, they established the settlement of Cacaxtla in the nearby Valley of Puebla.

The Olmeca-Xicallanca incursion in central Mexico took place during the era of Teotihuacan's decline and partial destruction. Indeed, their entry into the region may have precipitated the downfall of the great Valley of Mexico city. When the Olmeca-Xicallanca first arrived, they competed for and eventually took over the Teotihuacanos' extensive routes trading obsidian, feathers, cacao, greenstone, and cotton. Trade and the linked activity of gathering tribute after military victories were Xochicalco's lifeblood; in the surrounding semiarid countryside grew precious cotton but not enough food to support a community this size.

RICHARD A. DIEHL

royal relief on the Temple of the Feathered Serpent

Like Chalcatzingo for the Olmecs, Xochicalco gave the Olmeca-Xicallanca a strategic position along the main trade routes between the Valley of Mexico and Oaxaca, the Valley of Puebla and, beyond, the Gulf Coast and the Maya region. This trade did not come easily. Mesoamerica's Late Classic era (A.D. 600–900) was a troubled one; Teotihuacan's collapse had led to unrest, warfare, and the entry of nomadic tribes from the north. The Xochicalcans felt compelled to build their city on a hilltop surrounded by an elaborate series of fortifications and accessible only via heavily guarded causeways. This is a radical departure from the sprawling, open design of cities such as Teotihuacan. They also constructed smaller fortified settlements on nearby hilltops. It is not known if Xochicalco was ever attacked; perhaps the sight of the defenses was enough to repel invaders.

The Olmeca-Xicallanca also carried their culture into the Valley of Morelos. The reliefs that cover the Temple of the Feathered Serpent are in pure Maya style; they depict Maya gods, deified rulers, and tribute coming from defeated cities. Xochicalco's I-shaped ballcourts are a Maya innovation and were probably the first in central Mexico. They were later copied by the Toltecs and Aztecs. The Olmeca-Xicallanca also brought the first commemorative stelae and a writing system using glyphs that have yet to be deciphered.

Xochicalco's apogee lasted from A.D. 700 to 900. The city at its height contained 10,000 to 15,000 inhabitants. This does not include the surrounding settlements, whose ties to Xochicalco are thought to have been loose except during warfare. Xochicalco had trade and/or tribute ties throughout Mesoamerica, including to the Valley of Mexico, Puebla, Oaxaca, Guerrero, Veracruz, Hidalgo, Michoacan, and the Maya south. Then it suddenly ended.

Around A.D. 900, Xochicalco was mysteriously burned and abandoned, perhaps after an internal revolt. Unlike most other major central Mexican sites, the buildings were never reoccupied. The agricultural possibilities of the region may have been too sparse to support a community on farming alone.

ARCHAEOLOGICAL RECORD

Despite its abandonment, Xochicalco was one of the few Mesoamerican sites that was never forgotten, even after the Conquest. It was too close to Cuernavaca, the favorite vacation spot of both the Aztec and the Spanish rulers, to ever disappear.

In his great 16th-century work, the *History of the Things of New Spain*, Bernardo Sahagún mentioned Xochicalco along with Tula and Teotihuacan as noteworthy ancient sites. Scholarly interest in pre-Columbian cultures resumed in the late 18th century. In 1777 and 1784, a priest named José Antonio de Alzate visited Xochicalco to determine whether the ruins reflected "the black and vile colours in which they are usually depicted by Foreign Authors." It seems that European philosophers had declared the Native Americans base and evil savages in contrast to the brilliant and enlightened civilizations of the Old World. Alzate's 1791 book describing his visit contained copious if inaccurate illustrations and began a spate of visitors to Xochicalco.

During the 19th century, Xochicalco seems to have been on the route of nearly every explorer and adventurer to pass through Mexico; the most illustrious tourist was the Empress Carlota during her husband Maximilian's brief and disastrous reign in the 1860s. Among the earliest visitors was Guillermo Dupaix, who had been commissioned by Charles IV of Spain to document the ancient sites of his New World empire. Dupaix's famous work described dozens of Mesoamerican sites from the Valley of Mexico to Yucatan and spurred much European scholarly interest in pre-Columbian Mexico.

stone sculpture in the form of an axe-shaped parrot head from Xochicalco

The era of the amateurs came to an end in 1909 with the arrival of Leopoldo Batres. Fresh from his excavations at Teotihuacan and Monte Albán, he began at the Temple of the Feathered Serpent. His excellent reconstruction of this temple made it clear that Xochicalco was the product of Maya rather than Teotihuacano or Toltec civilization. Unfortunately, the 1910 outbreak of the Mexican Revolution stopped his excavations, and for the next eight years the site was used as an encampment by both Zapatista and federal soldiers.

A **glyph** is a character or letter in a writing system based on a mixture of phonetic and pictographic elements, such as that used by the ancient Maya.

Work at Xochicalco resumed in the 1920s with a mapping project and then Alfonso Caso's 1929 discovery of Ballcourt 1. In 1934, Eduardo Noguera of the Institute of Anthropology (later INAH) began almost three decades of excavations and reconstructions at the site. Xochicalco's ritual center, the Acropolis, was explored and rebuilt, and the first accurate site maps were produced. Noguera was succeeded in the 1960s first by César Sáenz and later Pedro Armillas and Jaime Litvak King. During the latter project, excavations spread to the lower terraces of Xochicalco's hill. In 1969 and 1970, Sáenz returned to dig Buildings B and E.

Since then, most of the excavations have focused on Xochicalco's defensive perimeter and on the fortified settlements atop the nearby hills. In 1978, the University of Kentucky's Kenneth Hirth led a mapping project to identify all the settlements, structures, and ancient roadways in the Xochicalco region. In 1984 and 1986, Norberto González Crespo of Morelos INAH directed excavations on the site's causeways and network of fortified ditches and ramparts. The early

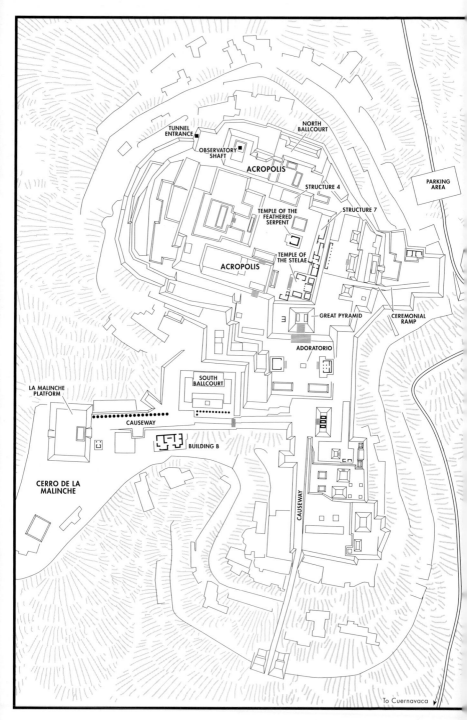

TUNNEL
ENTRANCE

NORTH
BALLCOURT

OBSERVATORY
SHAFT

ACROPOLIS

PARKING
AREA

STRUCTURE 4

TEMPLE OF THE
FEATHERED
SERPENT

STRUCTURE 7

ACROPOLIS

TEMPLE OF
THE STELAE

GREAT PYRAMID

CEREMONIAL
RAMP

ADORATORIO

LA MALINCHE
PLATFORM

SOUTH
BALLCOURT

CAUSEWAY

BUILDING B

CERRO DE LA
MALINCHE

CAUSEWAY

To Cuernavaca

CERRO COATZIN

CAUSEWAY

MUSEUM

XOCHICALCO

MOON

```
0                150 yds
0                150 m
```

1990s Proyecto Xochicalco under González Crespo concentrated on restoring the remainder of Xochicalco's central temples and residences and on constructing an elaborate site museum.

TOURING THE SITE

A path and stairway lead from the parking area up to the north side of the ruins. You enter the main plaza of Xochicalco's Acropolis, the cluster of civic-religious structures at the summit of the hill. In front of you stands the ornate Temple of the Feathered Serpent, one of the masterworks of Mesoamerican architecture. You see Leopoldo Batres's 1909 reconstruction. The design is eccentric *talud-tablero,* with a uniquely tall slanting *talud* topped by a relatively short *tablero.* The structure was built in three stages, each a larger copy of the first. All four sides of the temple are adorned with bas-reliefs carved in the style of the Classic Maya.

Until recently, archaeologists believed the panels told of a new fire ceremony marking the start of a new 52-year calendar round; the participants were priest-astronomers from around Mesoamerica. Now, however, the pacific star-gazers have been replaced by fierce warriors. Spurred by the reinterpretations of Mesoamerican and particularly Maya societies, researchers now say the reliefs glorify rulers, warriors, and their system of conquest and tribute.

The bottom *talud* panel depicts a large feathered serpent winding along the side of the temple. In the niches formed by the serpent's coils sits a

Maya ruler wearing an elaborate headdress. A glyph bears his name, 9 Wind, which also happens to be the birthday of the Feathered Serpent god Quetzalcoatl; the ruler is obviously associated with the powerful god. The *tablero* above is divided into panels showing seated men with large, handled jars facing large mouths that appear poised to eat quadripartite circles. Archaeologists believe this is a record of the cities and towns conquered by the Xochicalcans and the tribute received from them. Further feathered serpents flank the main staircase. On top stand the remains of a masonry temple. This too is decorated with reliefs, showing 12 seated warriors in profile wearing battle gear and carrying shields and darts. The Xochicalcans obviously spent more time preparing for battle than gazing at the stars.

The Temple of the Feathered Serpent is flanked to the north by a second temple platform the same size but far less elaborate. Facing the steps across the plaza to the west stands a complex of temples and rooms that probably included elite residences and civic-ceremonial spaces. This is the site's highest point, with an excellent view down the hillside to the south. Further residential complexes flank the plaza on the north (Structure 4) and east sides (Structures 6 and 7). The latter two buildings contain banquettes placed with niches below that probably held offerings.

Just south of Structure 6 at the southeast corner of the plaza stands the Temple of the Stelae, also called Structure A. Atop this platform, you find a courtyard with rooms to the sides and back. In the early 1960s, archaeologists found three rectangular stelae interred beneath the floor. The originals are in Mexico City's Museo Nacional de Antropología; their inscriptions have not been translated but probably relate to rulers, dates, and places (not deities as previously thought).

To the right of this temple's main staircase, four walls enclose the plaza-level Room of the Offerings. Archaeologists found buried beneath the floor a number of stone and ceramic offerings and a skeleton flexed in fetal position. Many of the offerings were associated with the Mesoamerican ballgame, including two stone belts and a *hacha* ballgame marker. A square glyph stone marked the burial; it is not known if the dead person was a sacrificial victim (killed after a ballgame?) or a Xochicalco aristocrat.

Behind this temple, you find another of Xochicalco's unique constructions: a ramp (probably ceremonial) paved with 252 stones carved with animal designs—birds, snakes, butterflies, and various mammals. A canopy protects the stones, making them somewhat hard to see or photograph. You can reach this ramp from a staircase just south of the Room of the Offerings or from the northeast corner of the main plaza. Just east of the ramp lies the East Ballcourt, a small I-shaped structure next to which archaeologists found another stone carved with date glyphs. One of the latter displayed a remarkably lifelike head of a rabbit. The ballcourt apparently contained only one ring—perhaps it was too small for two—carved with bats and macaws.

From here, you walk down to a lower level plaza in the center of which stands the Adoratorio; this is a low platform topped by a tall, roughly finished stela on which you see two carved glyphs, again probably representing dates. The east and west sides of the plaza are respectively flanked by Structures C and D, both nearly matching temple platforms with patios and interior rooms. On the north side stands the Great Pyramid, also called Structure E, the tallest building at Xochicalco.

The plaza also acts as terminus for a causeway that heads due south down into the valley. This was probably the main road into Xochicalco; it was guarded by walls and a fortified gate about halfway down the hill.

A path continues down the hillside to a zone that has been only partially excavated and restored. The first structure is the South Ballcourt, the largest at the site. Archaeologists believe that it was this I-shaped court that the Toltecs and Aztecs used as the model for their own. The sides are adorned with two intricately carved ballcourt rings. Another causeway heads west from the ballcourt. On the left (south) side, you see a series of buildings, the largest of which is the warrenlike residential complex of Building B. The causeway ends about 200 meters west of the ballcourt at the Cerro de la Malinche, actually just a ridge of Cerro Xochicalco. Here you find a wide but unexcavated temple platform.

Below drop the terraced ridges on which the lower-status Xochicalcans built their homes and engaged in small-scale farming. The terrace walls also doubled as defensive rings that protected the city from attack. These areas have barely been explored. The circular lake in the valley below is the Laguna del Rodeo, so named for the horse races that are occasionally held along its shores.

For the last part of the tour, return to the north side of the main plaza. A path leads down the hill and along the north side of the Acropolis. On your right is the North Ballcourt with the two rings lying on the ground in the center. Above, one of the terraces contains a room that was the steam bath where the players purified themselves.

The path continues around the hillside to a small plaza at the entrance to a tunnel. Cerro Xochicalco is perforated with 32 caves; unlike at Chalcatzingo, where the caves had primarily ritual use, these caves were mainly used as storage areas. The entrance is open 1100–1400; a guide will give you a short tour (Spanish only).

The high point of this tour is a visit to the underground Solar Observatory, a stucco-lined room containing an altar. A narrow light shaft perforates the ceiling and exits on the northwest side of the Acropolis. The light that falls through this shaft possesses an eerie glowing quality. This effect is caused by its shape, formed by small stones in a twisting hexagonal pattern. The guides like to show how shadows cast in this light—they use visitors' hands as models—have light inside the shadow as well as outside.

The Xochicalcans may or may not have cared about this trick of light. Far more important was the room's use as a solar observatory. When the sun passes through its zenith, a shaft of noontime sunlight blazes down through this hole.

At this latitude, this happens twice a year on May 14 and 15 and July 28 and 29. The dates of the sun's zenith were imporant in Maya ritual calendars.

This ends the official tour, although there is much more to Xochicalco. The west side of the Acropolis was probably a necropolis; archaeologists found many burials here. Unfortunately, walking along this hillside is made difficult by loose rubble. You can also take a path—the remains of an ancient causeway—up the Cerro de la Bodega just east of the parking lot and see the remains of the wide but low platform there. The surrounding hills are dotted with temples and fortifications that have been explored but not yet excavated.

MALINALCO

INTRODUCTION

Carved from the living rock of a mountainside, the ruins of Malinalco cling to a narrow terrace that overlooks some of central Mexico's most spectacular scenery, which resembles a Chinese brush painting. Malinalco is technically within the State of Mexico. The valley belongs to the Valley of Morelos's drainage system, however, and is easily reached from Cuernavaca and Xochicalco.

Malinalco's temple complex was built by the last Aztec emperors; the ornate structures were used for secret rituals by high-status warrior castes or perhaps even by the emperors themselves. The buildings' highly symbolic layout and decoration are some of our most intriguing clues to Aztec religio-political practices.

HISTORY

Malinalco has been occupied on and off since the Archaic era (pre-1800 B.C.). It lies in the well-protected valley of the Río Malinalco, which eventually flows into the Río Balsas. The climate is temperate almost year-round and produces abundant summer rains; rich crops of staples such as maize, as well as cotton and fruits, were grown along the valley floor. The settlements were established on the cliffs above, easily defended from raiders.

The earliest part of Malinalco was built on the hilltop 215 meters above the valley floor. Here archaeologists found small temple platforms and altars dating to the end of the Classic era. Among the objects were lidded stone offering caches that resembled those discovered at Xochicalco.

During the Early Postclassic, Malinalco was settled by the Matlazlincans, a people who occupied this mountainous border territory between the Valleys of

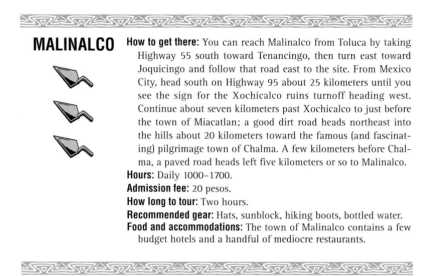

MALINALCO

How to get there: You can reach Malinalco from Toluca by taking Highway 55 south toward Tenancingo, then turn east toward Joquicingo and follow that road east to the site. From Mexico City, head south on Highway 95 about 25 kilometers until you see the sign for the Xochicalco ruins turnoff heading west. Continue about seven kilometers past Xochicalco to just before the town of Miacatlan; a good dirt road heads northeast into the hills about 20 kilometers toward the famous (and fascinating) pilgrimage town of Chalma. A few kilometers before Chalma, a paved road heads left five kilometers or so to Malinalco.

Hours: Daily 1000–1700.

Admission fee: 20 pesos.

How long to tour: Two hours.

Recommended gear: Hats, sunblock, hiking boots, bottled water.

Food and accommodations: The town of Malinalco contains a few budget hotels and a handful of mediocre restaurants.

Morelos and Toluca. They may have been part of Tula's tribute network, and they were certainly vassals of the post-Toltec Culhuas of the Valley of Mexico.

The Malinalco of this era also features in the Aztec origin myths. As the wandering tribe approached the Valley of Mexico, Huitzilopochtli quarreled with his troublesome sister Malinalxochitl. Enraged, Huitzilopochtli and the main body of the Mexica decamped in the middle of the night, leaving Malinalxochitl and her followers asleep. The latter group wandered south and eventually settled at Malinalco, according to myth. Years later, a Malinalco chief named Copil encouraged the Valley of Mexico's established tribes to throw out the Mexica newcomers. Copil was killed in battle, and his heart was torn out and tossed onto the island where Tenochtitlan was later founded.

In A.D. 1476, the Malinalcans were conquered by the army of the Aztec emperor Axayacatl. Ten to 15 years later, the emperor Ahuizotl ordered Tenochtitlan's guild of stonemasons to begin construction of a temple complex at Malinalco. According to Aztec records, much of the labor used was forced; those who refused to go were thrown in jail. The construction proceeded sporadically during the next decade and may have continued through the arrival of the Spaniards—Malinalco's Building 6 was never completed. In 1520, the distraction of Cortés's invading army halted all work at the site.

After the Conquest, the Cuernavacans—allies of Cortés—accused Malinalco of attacking them. Cortés sent a lieutenant, Andrés de Tapía, with 90 soldiers to crush the rebels; after the Malinalcans' defeat, the temple complex was abandoned. In 1537, Augustinian monks arrived in the valley and began the construction of their beautiful convent using stones from the Aztec temples.

ARCHAEOLOGICAL RECORD

The ruins of Malinalco were never forgotten, although rubble filled the temples (protecting the sculptures from priests and treasure hunters). The site was described by a number of archaeologists in the early 1900s. During this era, locals discovered an elaborate and perfectly preserved wooden drum at the site (now in Mexico City's Anthropological Museum). Formal excavations began in 1935 under José García Payón of the Dirección de Monumentos Prehispánicos. All the site's major structures were excavated and restored by García Payón in the next decade. During the late 1980s, an INAH expedition did work on the early temple complex on the hilltop above, but results have yet to be published.

García Payón believed that Malinalco's Aztec temple complex was built as a center for the ritual activities of the Jaguar and Eagle Warriors, two of Tenochtitlan's most elite military castes. These warriors were described by a number of post-Conquest ethnohistorical documents, and a ritual precinct dedicated to them was found next to the Great Temple in Mexico City. More recently, however, archaeologists such as Richard Townsend have theorized that the temples, particularly Building 1, were constructed as symbolic caves where the Aztec rulers, possibly including the emperor, could hold council while ritually connecting themselves with the deities. In doing this, they also symbolically asserted their dominion over this part of their empire.

TOURING THE SITE

The entrance to the ruins lies a few blocks west (uphill) of Malinalco town's main square. A small site museum stands at the end of the road; from here you take a path that zigzags a little more than a kilometer up the hillside to the ruins.

You enter the site on the southwest corner of the terrace that holds the main temple complex. The terrace is slightly more than 100 meters above the valley floor; the view is tremendous. Immediately on your right stands Building 6; never completed, it appears to have been planned as a small circular temple attached to a rectangular platform.

Next, on your left, you come to Malinalco's most famous structure—the astonishing Building 1. This was entirely (even the sculptures) carved from the solid rock of the hillside; on either side you see drainage channels to divert rainfall from the temple. Building 1 was originally covered with brightly painted stucco. The main staircase—13 steps—was flanked by large carved jaguar sculptures, while a third carving, now badly eroded, arose from the middle of the steps.

Atop the steps stands the main temple, now covered with a conical thatched roof that probably resembles the original. On either side stand further sculp-

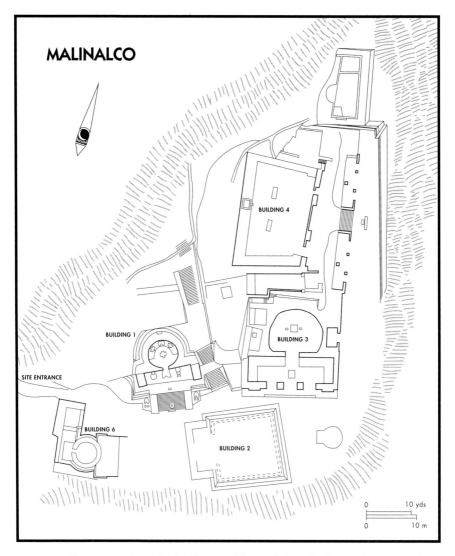

MALINALCO

BUILDING 4

BUILDING 1

BUILDING 3

SITE ENTRANCE

BUILDING 6

BUILDING 2

0   10 yds

0   10 m

tures. The one on the right—badly eroded but called an Eagle Warrior by García Payón—sits on a carved serpent. The left-hand sculpture is in a worse state of repair; García Payón believed it to be a Jaguar Warrior seated atop a drum draped with a jaguar skin, but this is very hard to see.

The temple doorway is far clearer; it is carved in the shape of a giant serpent's mouth. On either side you see eyes and great fangs, while the serpent's forked tongue acts as a welcome mat in front of the door. This figure undoubtedly represents the earth-monster—you also see it at Chalcatzingo—the symbolic entrance to the cave in which the major deities, including the sun, were born.

Inside the entrance you find a stunning circular chamber hewn from solid rock. This was carved by hand using simple stone tools—an immensely time-consuming effort. The back half of the chamber is ringed by a low semicircular bench on which are carved three sculptures. These represent a jaguar in the center and eagles on either side; according to García Payón, these were skins symbolizing the two warrior orders, while Richard Townsend believes they represent the entire animal in the form of ritual thrones. A third eagle is carved from the stone in the center of the floor. Behind its tail lies a circular hole that was originally lidded and contained offerings.

Opposite this temple stands Building 2, a simple raised platform facing west whose stones were plundered for the Augustinian convent in town. It is a good site for taking photos of both the temple and the valley below. Next you come to Building 3, immediately to the right of Building 1. This was also carved from solid rock. A step takes you up between two column bases to a rectangular antechamber. In the middle of the floor lies a sunken altar bearing traces of fire damage. A bench runs along the walls; the walls above were originally covered with murals. A fragment of a painting depicting a warrior procession has been removed. A door leads back to a second circular chamber with another square sunken altar. García Payón believed this temple was dedicated to the deification of dead warriors.

In front of this temple stands Building 5, a small circular platform facing west that was badly damaged. Our tour now continues left around Building 3's corner to Building 4. This you reach by ascending a short flight of stairs. The entrance originally lay between two large rectangular pillars, but this was later blocked, and the entries became two small doors on either side. Inside you find a 14- by 20-meter hall with a bench running along three walls. In the center of the bench lies another sunken altar. In the middle of the room are the bases of two columns that originally held up wooden beams supporting a solid roof made completely from rubble.

Building 4 stands at the northern limit of Malinalco's ceremonial complex. On the slopes below, you can see remains of further structures and more of the old drainage channels. A path leads to the older settlement atop the hill; this is technically not open to the public.

Malinalco's Building 1

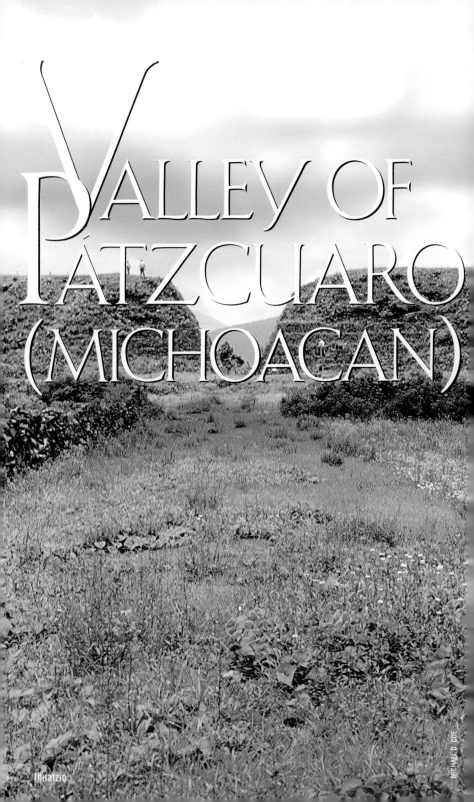

Valley of Pátzcuaro (Michoacan)

Ihuatzio

bout 40 kilometers west of Morelia, the pine-covered highlands of
Michoacan are one of the most scenic regions of Mexico. They are
also home to one of Mesoamerica's most interesting and—despite
years of archaeological research—mysterious civilizations, the
Tarascans. The center of their domain was the Valley of
Pátzcuaro and a line of settlements strung around the beautiful lake at its heart.
At the time of the Spanish Conquest, the Tarascans were the second-most pow-
erful empire in Mesoamerica. Their traditions live on in the customs of many
Lake Pátzcuaro–area residents.

THE LAND

Like most Mesoamerican civilizations, the Tarascans were defined by their geography. From the north the Central Plateau sweeps down, ending at the Río
Santiago-Lerma basin. The Sierra Madre mountains on the plateau's western
side were the main trade route between North America and Mesomerica, and
Tarascan territory lay at the route's southern end.

The Michoacan Highlands begin just south of the Río Lerma and continue to
the Río Balsas basin about 200 kilometers to the south. In between lies the Neo-
volcanic axis, a band of volcanoes and high-altitude valleys that runs from the
Pacific eastward through the Valley of Mexico all the way to the Gulf Coast.

In Michoacan, the effect of this volcanic and seismic activity is particularly
evident. From the air, it looks like a choppy green sea, with volcanoes and cinder cones—many of them active—scattered here and there apparently at random.
The most recent major eruption was Paricutín in 1943; earthquakes are common. For its pre-Columbian inhabitants, this terrain was both a blessing and a
curse: it was easy to defend from foreign invaders, and isolation fostered cultural unity. Unfortunately, water drained quickly through the porous volcanic

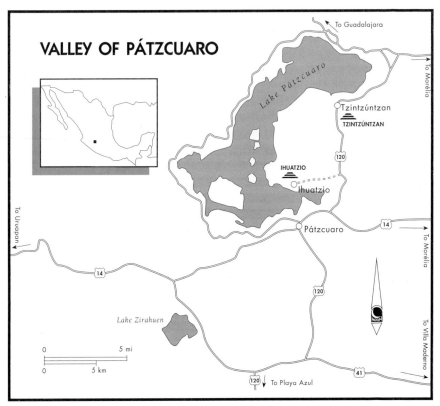

VALLEY OF PÁTZCUARO

To Guadalajara

Lake Pátzcuaro

Tzintzúntzan

TZINTZÚNTZAN

To Morelia

IHUATZIO

Ihuatzio

120

Pátzcuaro

14

To Morelia

14

To Uruapan

120

Lake Zirahuen

To Villa Moderno

0   5 mi

0   5 km

120   To Playa Azul

41

soil, so there were few streams or ponds; supplies of water were always limited. Water became the key to the development of Tarascan civilization.

Climate

Central Michoacan is the wettest place in the Mexican Highlands. More than 80 percent of the rain falls during the June to September wet season, while the winter months are cool and dry with occasional frosts. Archaeologists believe the climate was not very different during the Tarascan heyday of the 14th and 15th centuries.

Flora and Fauna

After the arid Valley of Mexico, the green lushness of the Michoacan Highlands can be a shock. The mountains are covered with pines and firs, while at lower levels you see oaks, scrub oaks, and alders. The lakeshore is

wild peccary

BOB RACE

MORELIA MUSEUM

The **Museo Regional de Michoacán** at Allende 305 in Morelia has a Tarascan exhibit. It is a modest but good exhibition of pre-Columbian history and some interesting artifacts. One section is a library, which includes children's books. Open Tues.–Sun. 0900–1900; admission 38 pesos.

thick with reeds. The animal life includes deer, rabbits, squirrels, foxes, and a wide variety of birds, including many species of ducks. The shallow Lake Pátzcuaro teems with native whitefish and with newly introduced black bass. As recently as the 19th century, the hills also were home to peccaries, wolves, wild turkeys, pumas, and jaguars, but these have been hunted out. All of these animals provided food, clothing, and ritual objects for the Tarascans.

HISTORY

Michoacan has been overlooked by Mesoamerican archaeologists. The few excavations that have been performed give us only a rough idea of when humans first arrived and how their cultures progressed. Until recently, the accepted theory has been that pre-Tarascan Michoacan cultures were small and fragmented, barely contacting each other, let alone the rest of Mesoamerica. It was thought that compared to the better-known pre-Columbian cultures, the Tarascans were uncultured barbarians outside the main Mesoamerican traditions. Recent studies have shown, however, that the region was far more sophisticated than many archaeologists believed. If the Spaniards had never arrived, the Tarascans may have been poised to become the dominant power of central Mexico.

The earliest Michoacanos were Archaic-era hunters who chased mammoth and bison around Lake Chapala and other bodies of water. The oldest agricultural settlement yet found is the Early Preclassic (1500–1200 B.C.) village at El Opeño near Zamora. Here archaeologists found "shaft-tombs" (underground tombs reached by a vertical tunnel) containing offerings of ceramic pots and figurines. The tomb style and offerings were obviously related to settlements in the nearby state of Colima that represent the early horizon of Western Mexico's rich Tomb Culture villages.

During the Late Preclassic (400 B.C.–A.D. 150), the dominant culture centered around Chupicuaro next to Lake Cuitzeo on the Michoacan-Guanajuato border. This large village is best-known for its highly stylized ceramics. Archaeologists unearthed more than 400 burials accompanied by beautiful, brightly painted pots and figurines of naked women, probably deities. The dead were interred with their dogs, which act as guides to the Underworld in many Mesoamerican religions.

HOW TO RAZE A VILLAGE

War and destruction were an integral part of Mesoamerican life and politics. This Tarascan account relates the method for obliterating an enemy village and killing its weakest inhabitants—a tactic not unknown in the 20th century.

When a village is to be destroyed, the Cazonci sends throughout the province for wood for the temples, and all the chiefs, with the people from their villages, come and make a broad road as far as the place where they are to encamp. All the lords and their people from Mechuacán travel this road, while the people of the villages arrive at the place where the maps of the enemy village have been traced [on the ground]. They array all the squadrons, and the more principal gods take positions on the road that goes straight to the village that is to be destroyed. All the other nations with their gods surround the entire village, and at a certain signal, all attack as one, setting fire to the village and sacking it with all its subjects. They take all the people, men, women, children, and babies in their cradles, count them, and separate all the aged, the babies, and those wounded by arrows, and they sacrifice them, as has been told. They place guards on all the roads and trails, and right there they take from the people all the gold, silver, rich feathers, and precious stones that they captured in the raid and all the spoils. They do not allow them to keep any of the blankets, copper, ornaments of gold and silver, jewels, or feathers. They destroy the village and are pleased with their success.

—from *The Chronicles of Michoacán,* translated and edited by Eugene R. Craine and Reginald C. Reindorp

So far, archaeologists have found no Mesoamerican cultures whose objects appear to be precursors to Chupicuaro's distinctive pottery. After Chupicuaro died out, none of their artistic traits seem to have been picked up by other cultures. This apparent alienation from the rest of Mesoamerica has led many archaeologists to surmise that Chupicuaro and other West Mexican cultures took their main traits from outside Mesoamerica. Because of a number of stylistic and technological parallels (shaft-tombs, metallurgy, textiles), the seagoing cultures of South America's Pacific Coast are the prime candidates as origin points.

Archaeologists long believed that the region missed the great Classic-era florescence of both Teotihuacan and the Maya region. In recent decades, however, they have discovered signs of strong Teotihuacan influence at the sites of El Otero, Tres Cerritos, and Tingambato 1. The latter site a few kilometers west of Lake Pátzcuaro contains ballcourts, plazas, and a central plaza in obvious Teotihuacan style dating to the Late Classic era (A.D. 650–900).

The first evidence of a sophisticated yet homegrown Classic-era culture in southern Jalisco and northern Michoacan was discovered during the recent excavation of Teuchitlan, a large settlement in the shadow of Jalisco's Tequila volcano. Unlike the vast majority of Mesoamerican communities, this was designed in a circular pattern (as opposed to a rectilinear grid). The ceremonial center was a conical pyramid surrounded by a circular plaza. This in turn was bordered by a series of raised platforms, either dwellings or religio-political spaces, under which were tombs. The town closely resembled the ceramic sculptures of little towns that are often found among Western Mexico shaft-tomb offerings. The formality of its proportions shows that the settlement's design was obviously planned beforehand.

Teuchitlan appears to have been the center of a distinct culture that flourished A.D. 200–800. Smaller Teuchitlan-style settlements have been found throughout southern highland Jalisco and into northern Michoacan. These sites also contain evidence of links to the rest of Mesoamerica: ballcourts and mortuary offerings depicting volador dancers (see El Tajín in Coast of Veracruz chapter).

At the end of the Classic era, Western Mexico saw another intrusion of what may be South American influence. Inca-style structures were built in coastal Guerrero, and new, more advanced textile and metalworking techniques appeared in the region. Once again, the vehicle for this influence is thought to be seagoing canoes, perhaps originating from Ecuador. South American contact could also help answer one of the great questions of Michoacan archaeology: what was the origin of the Tarascans, the group that came to dominate the region? Their language, Purépecha, is related to none in Mesoamerica but seems to have roots in Quechua, one of the most widespread South American tongues.

Before the Tarascan ascendancy, there is a gap in the Postclassic archaeological record of Michoacan. Once again, the sites are small and relatively isolated, with only weak contacts with the rest of Mesoamerica. The inhabitants of Apatzingan in the *tierra caliente* worked copper and constructed temples in the shape of *yácatas,* the keyhole-shaped platform style later used by the Tarascans. Those sites farther east showed greater influence from central Mexico. At Cojumatla southeast of Lake Chapala, they traded along the routes of the Toltecs and Mixtec-Puebla culture. The residents of Postclassic Michoacan had one particularly marketable skill: metallurgy. Their metal (copper, gold, or silver) beads, buttons, rattles, and blades became a precious commodity in the growing markets of Mesoamerica.

Between A.D. 1000 and 1200, the focus turned to the center of Michoacan, particularly to the lush shores of Lake Pátzcuaro. The local Purépecha-speakers were joined by migrants from the north, including Nahuas and a group of Chichimecs who called themselves the Wakúsecha, the Eagles. Each group brought with it its patron deities and distinct styles of ceramics and metalwork. Through a combination of force, cajolery, and intermarriage with local elites, the new arrivals competed with the more established lakeshore residents for power and tribute. The winner would build the foundation of the Tarascan dynasty whose empire even the mighty Aztecs could not defeat.

TZINTZÚNTZAN

INTRODUCTION

Set on a ridge overlooking scenic Lake Pátzcuaro, Tzintzúntzan is the most impressive site in Western Mexico. The dimensions of its main ceremonial center are eye-popping. We can only marvel at how a culture that used neither wheel nor draft animal constructed the Great Platform measuring 400 by 180 meters. A visit to Tzintzúntzan is also a testament to the muteness of the ruins. The excavations performed so far have revealed only a limited amount of information about Tarascan history and culture. Thankfully, archaeologists have been able to fill in some of the blanks with the great, post-Conquest Tarascan history, *The Chronicles of Michoacan.* Many of the traditions illustrated in that manuscript can still be seen in practice today: witness the island residents fishing for whitefish with butterfly-shaped nets from canoes.

HISTORY

Excavations have yet to probe the earliest layers of Tzintzúntzan's stratigraphy. Consequently, archaeologists do not know much about the site's early history, except that it was occupied at least from A.D. 1000 on. The early inhabitants likely spoke a version of Purépecha, the main language of central Michoacan, and worshipped the cult of Xaratanga, the goddess of the moon and fertility.

The group that came to dominate the region, the Wacúsecha, originated in the mountains to the northeast, perhaps in Guanajuato or Querétaro. Although they probably also were Purépecha-speakers, they were not agriculturists and fishermen like the early lake-dwellers but nomadic hunter-gatherers. They lived off deer and rabbit and collected wild fruits and vegetables. To the fish-eaters around the lake, the Wacúsecha lifestyle was that of barbarians.

When they entered Pátzcuaro's valley, the Wacúsecha carried with them the idol of their patron deity, Curiacueri, the god of hunting, fire, warfare, and the sun. As for the Aztecs upon entering the Valley of Mexico, it took generations for the Wacúsecha to find a place for themselves on the crowded lakeshore. The older tribes, worshippers of Xaratanga or the Rain Goddess Cuerauaperi, sneered at the recent arrivals and insulted their god. Friction turned to conflict, and at one point the locals massacred a group of Wacúsecha elders.

During the first half of the 14th century A.D., salvation came in the person of Tariacuri, a Wacúsecha prince who became the *cazonci,* the representative of Curiacueri and thus the ruler of his people. The Wacúsecha were living in three

TZINTZÚNTZAN

How to get there: To reach Tzintzúntzan's ruins from Pátzcuaro, head east about five kilometers on the Morelia road and then turn north on the road heading along the west shore of the lake. After about 10 kilometers, you see the enormous platform rising on the hillside to your right.

Hours: Daily 0900–1800.

Admission fee: 14 pesos.

How long to tour: One hour.

Recommended gear: Hats, sunblock, bottled water.

Food and accommodations: Served by a number of bus companies and a train line that runs to Mexico City, the town of Pátzcuaro is a popular tourist destination with many budget and moderately priced hotels. Among the best is the **Hotel Los Escudos,** tel. 434/2-0138, on the Plaza Grande at Portal 73, 30 rooms with TV. Many of the restaurants down by the lake specialize in local whitefish, the main protein source of the ancient Tarascans.

lakeshore settlements: Pátzcuaro, Ihuatzio, and Tzintzúntzan. Around A.D. 1325, particularly heavy rains flooded their fields, leaving them close to starvation. Rather than retreat, they banded together and attacked the other lakeshore towns; victorious, they demanded tribute of food. Tariacuri justified his attack by pointing to their neighbors' treatment of Curiacueri; they had defied the divine order and had to be punished. From this new state encompassing the entire valley of Pátzcuaro, Tariacuri built the foundations of the Tarascan empire.

One of Tariacuri's first tasks was to build a state religion that would unify the various ethnic groups under his control. Curiacueri, the Wacúsecha patron god, was symbolically married to the goddess Xaratanga, the principal deity of the older valley groups. Their mother became Cuerauaperi, the other important regional goddess. As the Tarascans' state evolved, their religion changed as well. By the mid-15th century A.D., their goals had become aggressively expansionist and their culture one of the most militaristic in Mesoamerica. Curiacueri, the war god, was elevated, while the worship of the more benevolent goddesses was downplayed.

The Wacúsecha remained the aristocratic lineage that produced the empire's rulers. The new state, however, encompassed a number of different tribes and so the larger group was renamed the Purépecha (the Aztecs called them the "Michoaque"–the source for "Michoacan"–and named Curiacueri "Taras," whence the Lake Pátzcuaro natives' current name). Their daily lives also reflected a mix of Wacúsecha and lake-dweller cultures. Although the men all carried bows and arrows and glorified hunting, the staple foods were fish, maize, and amaranth. Warfare was exalted, yet their real economic strength came from native crafts such as weaving, feather work, carpentry, wood and stone carving, and, particularly, metallurgy. Tarascan metalwork, including bells, tweezers, needles, axes, and figurines, generally of copper, was coveted throughout Mesoamerica and provided the backbone of the trade economy.

The Tarascans were avid consumers of their own crafts. They manufactured copper pincers to depilate their skins, and in their ears and lips they wore large, delicately carved obsidian spools, some of the finest found in Mesoamerica. The men's customary dress was long, sleeveless shirts, and they also shaved their heads—giving them a distinct and warlike look compared to neighboring tribes.

On Tariacuri's death, he decreed that power would be shared between the three main Tarascan cities of Pátzcuaro, Ihuatzio, and Tzintzúntzan. In reality, Pátzcuaro was at first the dominant partner, followed by Ihuatzio. By A.D. 1450, Tzintzúntzan, with a population of 25,000–35,000, had emerged as the Tarascan power, and it remained the empire's capital until the Spanish Conquest.

Lake Pátzcuaro was the center of a Tarascan empire that by A.D. 1500 had encompassed almost all of the present state of Michoacan and included 91 separate settlements along the densely populated lakeshore. The Tarascan strategy for expansion was distinctly different from nearly all other Mesoamerican states, which, in addition to warfare, used alliances by intermarriage and trade to increase their empires. The Tarascans relied solely on military power. After defeating their enemies, they placed military governors and Tarascan garrisons in their main towns and then looked onward for their next target. They also believed in strong borders. Unlike all other Mesoamerican empires, whose limits were always vague, the Tarascan lands were clearly delineated and guarded by sentries of heavily protected hilltop forts. They were so successful that archaeologists believe that if the Spanish had not intervened the next rulers of central Mexico would have been the Tarascans.

Because of the rapid expansion of both empires, a conflict between the Aztecs and the Tarascans was inevitable. In 1478, the Aztec emperor Axayacatl advanced on the Tarascan border with a force of 24,000 Aztecs and their allies. They captured a border post but learned that a Tarascan force of 40,000 was preparing to attack the following day. That night, Axayacatl wanted to back out, but his commanders advised him to fight rather than being shamed by retreat. When daylight came, the Tarascans inflicted on the Aztecs their greatest pre-Conquest defeat. Their allies were destroyed, and Axayacatl and 200 Aztecs barely escaped with their lives.

In the decades that followed, Axayacatl's successors made numerous gestures for peace with the Tarascans, but these were rebuffed, at first violently. Between A.D. 1490 and 1495, the Aztec ruler Ahuizotl captured most of what is now Guerrero immediately south of the Tarascan empire. Perhaps as a sign of respect for this new Aztec threat, Tarascan leaders did attend the coronation of Motecuhzoma II in A.D. 1502. Nevertheless, at the time of Cortés's arrival in Mexico the Tarascans remained the greatest threat to the Aztec empire.

In 1520, the Aztecs sent two delegations to the Tarascan ruler asking for troops to help fight the Spanish; they were rejected both times. Meanwhile, European diseases such as smallpox were running rampant through the region, killing aristocrats and commoners alike. The Spaniards arrived in the Lake Pátzcuaro region in 1522; first came a conquistador searching for food supplies and then an embassy from Cortés bearing gifts for the *cazonci*.

They were followed by the conquistador Cristóbal de Olíd at the head of 270 Spanish troops and a small army of Indian allies. The last Tarascan ruler decided to retreat rather than meet the Spaniard. Olíd occupied Tzintzúntzan and sacked the temples of gold and other precious objects. After he left, the *cazonci* traveled to the Valley of Mexico, where he met Cortés and gave him homage. From this point onward, the Tarascans—much weakened by epidemics of European diseases—were effectively Spanish subjects. The first Franciscan priests arrived in 1527.

Three years later, the Tarascan region was invaded by the avaricious conquistador Nuño de Guzmán fleeing with a medium-sized army from a royal tribunal. He captured the last *cazonci*, demanding gold and other tribute. When the treasures did not appear, he had the Tarascan tortured and burned at the stake for "treason." Guzmán then headed north to Sinaloa, killing and pillaging all the way. The Tarascan settlements were either burned or abandoned by Indians fleeing the depradations of the conquistadors who were left to rule the region.

News of Guzmán's exploits led to an outcry in Mexico City and Spain. The conquistador was eventually shipped home in disgrace, and Don Vasco de Quiroga came to Michoacan to pacify the rebellious Indian population and right the wrongs. He succeeded so well that he was named bishop of the Pátzcuaro region, making his base first in Tzintzúntzan and then in Pátzcuaro, which became the main town of the valley. By the end of his life, Quiroga was much beloved by the native tribes, and his ashes are buried in Pátzcuaro's Basilica de la Virgen de Salud (which is built on a Tarascan temple foundation).

ARCHAEOLOGICAL RECORD

As in almost every other major site in central Mexico, parts of Tzintzúntzan were destroyed by the Spanish priests who arrived in the 16th century. In 1852, a priest who was an amateur archaeologist tore down most of Yácata 5 in a misguided attempt to excavate it. Charles Harford, a British explorer, burrowed into Yácata 2 in search of buried treasure. He uncovered perfectly cut facing stones but little else. The last 19th-century excavations were performed (but never published) by Dr. Nicolás León, an expert on the Tarascans from the Museo Regional de Michoacán.

The modern era of Tarascan archaeology began in 1930, when Alfonso Caso and Eduardo Noguera from the Museo Nacional de Antropología in Mexico City surveyed Michoacan's sites. They explored Tzintzúntzan but thought it too damaged by agriculture and inept earlier excavations to begin work. Caso and Jorge Acosta returned in 1937 to begin two years of mapping, cleaning, and the excavations of Yácata 5, Buildings A and B, and a number of burials. In 1940, the project was taken over by Daniel Rubin de la Borbolla, who over six years performed the largest excavation of Tzintzúntzan to date. Almost all the work you see today dates to this era, including the restoration of the Great Platform, Building B, and Yácatas 1 and 5.

There have been further expeditions by INAH in 1962 and by Román Piña Chan of the Escuela Nacional de Antropología in 1962, 1964, and 1968 (all as yet unpublished). In 1977 and 1978, Rubén Cabrera Castro of INAH returned to excavate on the Great Platform and reconstruct Yácatas 2, 3, and 4. The most recent INAH project began in 1992 under Efraín Cárdenas.

Despite all these projects, archaeologists have barely scraped the surface at Tzintzúntzan. Among the many topics that still need study are the complete sequence of occupation, the construction history of the Great Platform, and the size and extent of the settlement.

TOURING THE SITE

Tzintzúntzan, which means Place of Hummingbirds, occupies a ridge overlooking the town of Tzintzúntzan's red roofs and the northeast corner of Lake Pátzcuaro. The site is worth visiting just for the setting and the fresh breeze blowing through the trees.

Just beyond the parking lot stands a small museum containing exhibits on Tarascan history and a few artifacts. Beyond, you walk up to the northeast corner of the Great Platform, the Tarascan settlement's ceremonial center. This enormous structure measures 400 by 180 meters and is built of stone over a

MICHAEL D. COE

Tzintzúntzan yácata

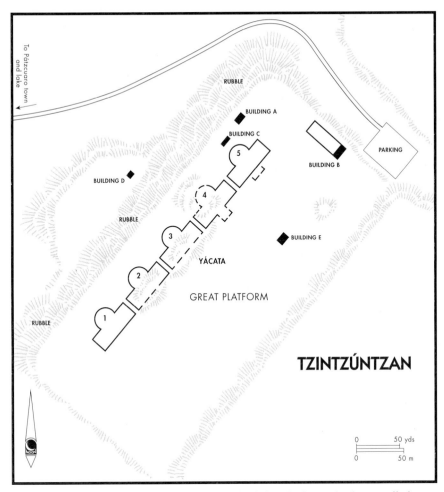

To Pátzcuaro town and lake

RUBBLE

BUILDING A

BUILDING C

5

BUILDING D

BUILDING B

PARKING

4

RUBBLE

3

BUILDING E

2

YÁCATA

GREAT PLATFORM

1

RUBBLE

RUBBLE

TZINTZÚNTZAN

0   50 yds
0   50 m

rubble fill. What is presumably the front of the platform—the long wall that overlooks the town—faces the northwest; it is not known if the alignment has astronomical significance.

Exiting through the museum's back door, the first structure you encounter is Building B, also called the Palace. These are rectangular foundations enclosing a series of rooms built around patios. Buried beneath the floors were hundreds of human bones; it is not known if these were Tarascans or the bones of their enemies. One of the patios contains the remains of an altar surrounded by the remains of circular columns.

If you continue west to the northwest corner of the Great Platform, you have an excellent view of Tzintzúntzan town and the lake beyond. Looking down, you will be impressed by the platform's tremendous size: the wall drops three to seven meters to ground level and runs the 400-meter length of the structure. To your left, you can see the remains of a large ramp leading up to the center of the platform. This was the main access to Lake Pátzcuaro. Farther on, a gap in the wall shows where archaeologists excavated to an earlier stage of the platform's construction.

The west side of the platform is lined with five *yácatas*, the signature buildings of Tarascan culture. These are keyhole-shaped temple platforms composed of attached circular and rectangular structures. Those at Tzintzúntzan are built in eight tiers, with the circular side facing west and, opposite, staircases descending the rectangular side onto the Great Platform's plaza. The five were built with only a narrow gap separating one from another and are thought to be dedicated to the Tarascan patron deity, Curiacueri, and his four brothers. The *yácatas* acted as bases for wooden temples holding idols of the gods; they probably also doubled as tombs for Tarascan rulers, although none have been discovered so far.

The first *yácata*, number five, and the last, number one, are in the best state of reconstruction. Like most central Mexican temples, the *yácatas* were built in stages; they diverge from their Toltec and Aztec counterparts in their facing—finely fitted slabs of basalt called *janamus* that closely resemble the temple sheathing at South American sites such as Machu Picchu. Between *yácata* five and the edge of the platform lie the remains of two small structures, Buildings A and C, the latter perhaps an altar and the former dating to the early Spanish era.

At the end of the line of *yácatas*, you come to the south side of the Great Platform. This has been converted to Tzintzúntzan town's soccer field. West of the *yácatas*, their staircases face a large plaza now occupied by a grove of sweet-smelling trees. There is not much to see here except the obsidian chips strewn about the ground—the Tarascans were masters of obsidian carving—and some rubble, perhaps of dwellings, along the plaza's west side. The only structure in the plaza is Building E opposite *yácata* four; this L-shaped structure may have been a storehouse for ritual goods.

The **yácata** are the signature buildings of Tarascan culture composed of attached circular and rectangular structures forming a roughly keyhole-shaped temple.

The Great Platform was the center of Tzintzúntzan. The rest of the settlement was spread out among the hills and along the lakeshore. Like Teotihuacan, Tzintzúntzan was divided into wards, perhaps as many as 15, each with a particular specialty, such as obsidian-carving or fishing. The Tarascan dwellings were made of wood and straw, so scant traces remain of them. Serious excavations have yet to be performed in the residential areas.

The adventurous can continue their tour by hiking about 300 meters up the hill east of the platform to two unexcavated rectangular temple platforms. Smaller structures and the ruins of a Spanish chapel are scattered about the hillside to the south.

IHUATZIO

INTRODUCTION

Ihuatzio was the Tarascan capital after Pátzcuaro and before Tzintzúntzan. Halfway between those two towns, it lies on a peninsula jutting into the western side of Lake Pátzcuaro. Although the site is sprawling—more than 120 acres—only a fraction has been excavated and opened to the public. The most unusual features of the site are the interconnected raised platforms that may have been used as causeways. Ihuatzio is off the main tourist route—a week may go by without a visitor—and is recommended for anyone who likes to bushwhack.

HISTORY

Until more excavation is performed, it is difficult to say very much about Ihuatzio's past. Archaeologists assume that it was occupied before the Tarascan ascendancy. After the death of Tariacuri, the great Tarascan ruler, power was divided between Pátzcuaro, Ihuatzio, and Tzintzúntzan. Under Hiriapan, Tariacuri's nephew, Ihuatzio rose to become the dominant city of the trio and the base from which the Tarascans set forth to conquer neighboring lands. Ihuatzio's power waned after Hiriapan's death, and by the Spanish Conquest it was a mere satellite of Tzintzúntzan. During the colonial era, the ruins were abandoned to farmers.

A **surface study** is the initial archaeological research of a site that includes mapping and gathering artifacts but no excavations beneath the earth's surface.

ARCHAEOLOGICAL RECORD

The most persistent excavators of Ihuatzio have been the pothunters who have looted many of the site's tombs. Locals have also removed many of the stones for use as building material. In 1931, Alfonso Caso and Eduardo Noguera mapped the site and performed a surface study. Caso returned in 1937 and 1938 to complete the map and clear and restore Structures 1 and 2. Among his discoveries were skeletons interred between these two temples and a *chac mool* carved in a distinct, angular style with a slash across its cheeks. Caso believed that the *chac mool* and a stone table or throne carved in the form of a coyote (discovered earlier) were evidence of Toltec influence. No significant work has been performed at the site since Caso's two seasons.

IHUATZIO

How to get there: Ihuatzio lies halfway between Tzintzúntzan and the Morelia road. Take the paved and then dirt road five kilometers west to the impoverished town of Ihuatzio. At the west end of the new plaza a very poor dirt road heads right about one kilometer to the ruins.

Hours: Daily 1000–1800.

Admission fee: 14 pesos (bring exact change).

How long to tour: 45 minutes.

Recommended gear: Hats, sunblock, bottled water.

TOURING THE SITE

Ihuatzio lies among fields that use the old Tarascan walls as boundaries. After entering the gate, you emerge into a large rectangular plaza called the Parade Ground. The walls to the left and right are actually long, five-meter-high platforms with staircases leading up them. Archaeologists believe the flattened tops of the platforms are ritual causeways connecting to other parts of the site.

At the west end of the plaza stand the twin Structures 1 and 2. These square tiered pyramids have staircases facing east; because of their loose stones, they are unclimbable. You

Ihuatzio

can see remains of the fitted basalt slabs that sheathed the structures. Some of these slabs were found carved with circles, spirals, and other symbols. Through the narrow path between the pyramids, you can see the giant statue of José María Morelos on the Janitzio Island in the middle of Lake Pátzcuaro.

If you climb to the top of the causeway at the southwest side of the plaza, you can see to the south three unexcavated *yácatas*—essentially mounds—standing in the middle of another, larger plaza, now a field. The sides of this plaza are lined with more interconnected causeway platforms. Beyond the *yácatas* at the south end of this plaza lies a circular mound, also unexcavated, dubbed the Observatory.

More mounds and causeways can be seen to the west and north. If you walk over to the north side of the Parade Ground, beyond the north causeway you can see a unique curved causeway that may have been used as a battlement. Technically, you are not supposed to leave the Parade Ground part of the site; security is generally sparse.

MICHAEL D. COE

THE NORTH

ruins of Paquimé

T he arid expanses of northern Mexico have always been a frontier, although not so sharply delineated as today. This region encompasses the states that border the U.S., including Baja California, Sonora, Chihuahua, Coahuila, Nuevo Leon, and Tamaulipas, as well as Durango and Zacatecas just to the south. The lack of water obliged the pre-Columbian inhabitants to live a simple, nomadic existence. While they were "primitive" by our standards, they were also tough; their culture survived until the 19th century in some of the more remote areas. What sets them apart from the rest of Mexico's indigenous groups is that they were more closely linked with the cultures of the American Southwest than with Mesoamerica. The most developed of them provided a bridge, a trading link between North and South. For the archaeological tourist, the pickings are slim; these cultures left few remains spread very far apart. However, there are a few sites, such as Paquimé (also known as Casas Grandes), whose uniqueness and fascinating history make them well worth a detour.

THE LAND

Between the Pacific and the Gulf of Mexico, rugged mountains and broad, dry plains comprise most of northern Mexico's terrain. The main geological features are two mountain ranges, the Sierra Madres Occidental and Oriental, in the west and east, which enclose a high plateau called the Central Mesa. This plateau runs all the way from the Bajio region of central Mexico north to the high plains of West Texas and New Mexico. Aridity was the only barrier to commerce between North and South here, and most developed cultures of northern Mexico arose along the western side of the plateau. East of the Sierra Madre Oriental, the land slopes into the lush Gulf coastal plain of Tamaulipas. On the other side of the 3,000-meter peaks of the Sierra Madre Occidental lie the hills and deserts of Sonora, which borders the Gulf of California. Beyond is the 950-kilometer-long Baja peninsula, a strip of rock and sand that provided few footholds for its indigenous inhabitants.

Climate

The north receives the least rain of anywhere in Mexico; it is also the region of the greatest temperature extremes. Sonora's Altar Desert goes from 120°F in summer to freezing in winter and receives only a trace of rain. Central Chihuahua is slightly wetter, but the temperatures are often over 100°F in the hot months and can drop to 15°F in winter. The wettest regions are the higher elevations of the western Sierra and the Tamaulipas coast. The rest of the area is divided between desert in most of Baja, Sonora, and eastern Chihuahua and semiarid steppe in the rest. What there is of rain falls May to October; the dry season is usually completely so. However, yearly variation is great, and there are summer droughts and winter rains and snowfalls.

Flora and Fauna

Northern Mexico's plant life is mostly a variation on the themes of scrub desert and grassland. The only anomaly is the dry evergreen forest in the upper elevations of the Sierras and Baja California. There are some patches of completely barren desert in Sonora and Chihuahua, but the rest is home to at least some flora. Scrub bushes, particularly acacia, mesquite, and creosote, are common, as are cacti, including agave, organ pipe, and prickly pear. Much of the Central Mesa is covered with dry grasses; the monotony is occasionally broken by tall cottonwoods and walnut trees along riverbanks. The Baja deserts preserve a number of unique species, such as the whiplike cirio plant and the elephant tree with its engorged trunk. The North's limited vegetation is a by-product of poor soils. The only region with a rich enough topsoil to support a dense human population and intensive agriculture are the grasslands of northwestern Chihuahua, which lie along the main pre-Columbian trading routes.

Northern Mexico is also a frontier for animal life, representing the northern and southern limits of many North American and Mesoamerican species. The large mammals found there are white-tailed and mule deer, bears, mountain lions, peccaries, pronghorn antelopes, and desert bighorn sheep. Also native to the area are smaller species such as armadillo, prairie dog, rabbit, squirrel, dog, and fox. Where there is water there is bird life, including duck, goose, wild turkey, quail, and partridge. Water also attracts turtles, frogs, and insects, all of which were part of the indigenous diet. Snakes and lizards are also common. Along the coasts, the sea provided most of the food in the form of the lowly mollusk, such as clams. The Gulfs of California and Mexico are also rich in fish life, but, despite these abundant resources, the pre-Columbian tribes were apparently not very efficient fishermen—archaeologists have found huge middens of mollusk shells but few fish bones.

HISTORY

Ten thousand years ago, at the end of the Ice Age, northern Mexico was a much cooler and wetter place. The lush vegetation fed large, now-extinct mammals, such as mammoths, horses, camels, and sloths, as well as bison, which had migrated south to avoid the glaciers covering much of North America. In their wake followed paleo-Indians, early hunters armed with spears and darts. Archaeologists have found a number of sites in Tamaulipas, Chihuahua, and Baja California with skeletal remains of mammoth and bison kills. Scattered among the bones were Clovis and Folsom points, as well as stone scrapers and knives for butchering the animals. Similar Clovis-type points have been found from Alaska to Panama. Paleoarchaeologists have interpreted these findings to mean that the early hunters belonged to one, widespread culture with minimal cultural differences.

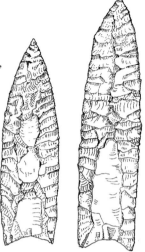

Clovis points

By 7000 B.C., a drastic climatic change was in the works. World temperatures rose, the glaciers receded, and northern Mexico became hotter and drier. The large mammals died off, perhaps because of the combined effects of the changed ecology and overhunting. The North's inhabitants were forced to supplement their diet with vegetal matter, mainly mesquite, pumpkin and sunflower seeds, and grasses. As the peoples' diet changed, so did their technology. They still used the hunting points, but they also needed needed flat stones called *manos* to grind seeds and baskets for gathering plants. A large variety of fiber products began to be produced, made mostly from agave cacti, including mats, sandals, and nets. Rabbits, deer, birds, and reptiles were the main game—a far cry from giant mammoths!—which they killed with traps or atlatls, a throwing stick used to hurl darts with surprising force. Despite these advances, there was rarely enough food. Settlements of more than 100 people were unknown, and these bands still had to migrate, but probably in a set pattern between winter, summer, and fall camps. Their homes were usually caves and rock shelters, although they occasionally built domed brush shelters in the open near watercourses.

Between 7000 and 3000 B.C., this transition from hunters to hunter-gatherers, from nomads to seminomads, was replicated across Mexico. Unlike in central and southern Mexico, however, this was not accompanied by the rise of early agriculture centering on the cultivation of maize. The soils of northern Mexico were too poor for corn; the Archaic stage never left. There were enough

LOUISE FOOTE

advances, such as the addition of beans and squash to the diet and the emergence of shamanistic religions, for researchers to decide that these peoples merited a change of name to Desert Culture. However, the basic cultural patterns for most of the region remained unchanged until the arrival of the Europeans.

During the Postclassic era (A.D. 900–1521), the civilizations of central Mexico called the Desert Culture peoples the Chichimecs, or People of the Dog (not an

THE TARAHUMARA

It is hard to imagine a more rugged homeland than the canyon country between the high plains of Northern Mexico and the steamy Pacific Coast. Here the Tarahumara Indians have carved out a self-sufficient world largely untouched by modernity. The first Europeans to come to this part of western Chihuahua were gold-hungry Spaniards followed closely by Jesuit priests seeking converts. They found the Tarahumara, a shy, gentle people who they forced into towns and used as slave labor in mines. In the 18th century, after the mines ran out and the Jesuits were expelled from Mexico, the white men left the Tarahumara alone. Protected by their nearly inaccessible territory, they were largely forgotten by the outside world until the construction of the Copper Canyon railroad in the mid-20th century. In the intervening centuries, they had reverted to their traditional ways, augmented only by a thin veneer of Catholicism and a few European inventions such as the plow and the violin.

The Tarahumara, who call themselves the Rarámuri, do not live in towns. Arable land is so sparse that it is more convenient for each family to live in a *rancho* (a one- or two-room, earth-floor house) that could be hours from the nearest neighbor. The men spend their days tilling the fields; the women take care of the home, make the meals—usually a corn flour gruel—and tend the children and the chickens, goats, and sheep. Despite the families' isolation, the Tarahumara often meet their neighbors at communal events. The most common of these are the *tesguinadas,* corn

beer parties, usually held when somebody needs help clearing a field or building a house. After the work is done, everybody must get drunk. Somebody plays a violin, others dance or wrestle; by the end of the party there have been a few fights and most of the guests are either asleep in the house or in the cornfield outside. The *tesguinadas* are an outlet for all the frustrations of living in this harsh, parsimonious environment.

The Tarahumara are best known for their speed and endurance as runners. This skill has been developed by necessity; lacking horses, they frequently have to race over the hills after stray livestock. They stage regular footraces in which the contestants must run as far as 100 miles over 20 hours, all the while kicking a wooden ball ahead of them. The audience wagers heavily on the outcome, sometimes the bulk of their worldly possessions. Tarahumara runners have had some success in marathons but have been hampered by the fact that they prefer to run barefoot or with simple sandals— not the best footwear for urban pavement.

The Tarahumara have long tried to keep the outside world at a distance. They call the mestizos who populate the nearby towns the *chavóchis,* the "bearded ones," and consider them evil and aggressive. Though lumber companies, Protestant evangelists, tourists, and drug traffickers are all encroaching on their way of life, the Tarahumara still have two great advantages: their extreme environment and the fierce independence that makes them perfectly suited to that terrain.

epithet). When drought hit the north, the Uto-Aztecan speaking Chichimecs would raid their richer neighbors to the south, the northernmost outposts of Mesoamerica. The more ambitious of them migrated permanently to central Mexico. Many of the most celebrated civilizations, including the Toltecs and Aztecs, claimed Chichimec ancestry. Little is known about the groups that remained in the north. The Desert Culture tribes of Tamaulipas, Nuevo Leon, and Coahuila fiercely resisted the Spaniards and were obliterated with such a vengeance that it is not even known what language they spoke. The peoples of Sonora had a close association with the Hohokam Culture of Arizona, whose ceramics are found throughout the region. In the northwest of the state, Las Trincheras was a fortified hilltop town built on terraces; a similar system is used by the Tarahumara of the Chihuahua Sierra for agriculture today.

The only anomalies within the Desert Culture were the groups that lived along the thin strip of land on the eastern side of the Sierra Madre Occidental that ran from southern Zacatecas all the way up to northwestern Chihuahua. This strip was covered with grassland and a layer of relatively rich topsoil, perfect for intensive agriculture. At the same time, it received more rain than the deserts to the east and had fewer natural barriers than the mountains on the west—it was the perfect trading route between central Mexico and the American Southwest.

Up until the last few centuries B.C., this region's tribes resembled the rest of the Desert Culture peoples, with perhaps a greater reliance on simple agriculture. Then, in Durango and Zacatecas, the Preclassic Mesomerican traits of maize and bean farming, ceramics, and platform architecture began to slowly trickle in. A few centuries later, the first great Classic central Mexican civilization, the Teotihuacano, began to develop in the Valley of Mexico. At the same time, around A.D. 200, a fortified town showing far greater development than anything else in northern Mexico was built on the Durango-Zacatecas border. It was called Alta Vista and within a century strong Teotihuacano influences showed themselves there. The center was a ceremonial courtyard lined with masonry columns, and archaeologists also found evidence of the Mesoamerican cults of the Feathered Serpent and the Rain God Tlaloc. Why would the Teotihuacanos venture into the dangerous north? The surrounding hills are filled with ancient mines that produced malachite, cinnabar, rock crystal, hematite, and other stones necessary for Teotihuacano ritual objects. Turquoise from the American Southwest was also found during excavations. Alta Vista was abandoned and burned around A.D. 500. Nevertheless, Mesoamerican traditions were continued by a number of nearby population centers.

One of these is La Quemada, 160 kilometers to the southeast and 32 kilometers south of Zacatecas. Built on a strategic hilltop overlooking the north-south trading route, this fortified town was surrounded by massive masonry walls and connected to nearby settlements by 13 stone roadways. This evidence suggests that La Quemada was built to protect the northern frontier of Mesoamerica from Chichimec invaders. The occupation of La Quemada has never been properly worked out, because the site was thoroughly looted and burned, perhaps by Chichimecs, in the early part of the millennium. It certainly postdated Alta Vista, and its zenith was probably around A.D. 900–1000. After its abandonment, the northern limit of Mesoamerica slipped back to the south.

The trade routes continued, however, and central Mexico's influence continued to flow north. It was felt most strongly at the site of Paquimé, hundreds of kilometers north of La Quemada. Its residents were not Mesoamericans but part of the Mogollon Culture of New Mexico.

PAQUIMÉ

INTRODUCTION

The grass- and scrub-covered Casas Grandes Valley lies in the northwest corner of Chihuahua. Eight hundred years ago, a rise above the valley's seasonal stream was home to the bustling center of Paquimé. This was the principal trading center of northern Mexico; from here, Mesoamerican goods such as tropical birds headed north, while rarities from the American Southwest, including turquoise, traveled south. Paquimé's unique mixture of Mesoamerican and Southwestern influences can be seen in the stepped platforms and pueblo-style

PAQUIMÉ

How to get there: Set in the middle of Chihuahua's rolling plains, the ruins of Paquimé lie just south of the town of Nuevo Casas Grandes. By car or bus, you can reach it in three to four hours from Ciudad Juárez or the city of Chihuahua. There is also a very slow train that runs this route. The ruins lie six kilometers to the south of town (local buses run here).

Hours: Daily 0800–1700.

Admission fee: 20 pesos.

How long to tour: Two hours.

Recommended gear: Hats, sunblock, sturdy shoes or sneakers.

Museum: The excellent Museum of the Cultures of the North at the site entrance covers pre-Hispanic cultures from Baja California to Tamaulipas. The high points of its exhibition are the many boldly patterned Paquimé ceramics.

Food and accommodations: For archaeological tourists, the best nearby hotel is the **Hotel Paquimé**, tel. 164/4-13-20, fax 4-06-58, at Av. Juárez 401 in Nuevo Casas Grandes, with phones, TV, a/c, and heat. Its founder, one of the original excavators of the Paquimé ruins, built a small museum of artifacts on the premises.

adobe apartment buildings. After a two-century efflorescence, the city entered a period of degeneracy and decline and then was destroyed by fire and abandoned around A.D. 1350—the lessons of its history can be illuminating. The site lies 8.4 kilometers southeast of the farming center of Nuevo Casas Grandes, which is easily reachable by car or bus from Ciudad Juárez and Chihuahua.

HISTORY

The Casas Grandes Valley was home to human settlement as far back as the early hunters. By A.D. 200, small agricultural villages were scattered throughout the valley. Ceramics appeared and the houses began to be built in a rectangular shape with adobe walls. The dead were buried beneath their floors with elaborate ceramic offerings; many of these were beautiful Mimbres-style pots from southern New Mexico. The central ceremonial space strongly resembled the Great Kivas (large circular adobe structures) of the Southwest, and the main foods were corn and beans grown in the surrounding irrigated fields. From this evidence, it is clear that early Paquimé fell within the realm of New Mexico's Mogollon Culture.

Around A.D. 1060, Paquimé's size and culture changed dramatically. Obviously following a master plan, its builders laid out an urban complex of ceremonial spaces, residential areas, markets, and storehouses. The ceremonial spaces were distinctly Mesoamerican, including an I-shaped ballcourt, a circular platform temple, and a cross-shaped platform oriented to the four directions. Other Mesoamerican traits found here were copper bells and the cult of the Feathered Serpent.

CURTIS SCHAAFSMA

Paquimé

These signs—and the abandonment of the kivas—suggest that Paquimé came under the control of religious/political emissaries from central Mexico who taught them their customs and reorganized their economy as a trading center. Mesoamerica's main power during this era was the Toltecs, who were in the midst of their expansionary Tollan Period (A.D. 900–1150). The Toltecs' foreign agents were the *pochtecas,* or long-distance traders, and it was likely a group of these who initiated the transformation of Paquimé.

Within 50 years, Paquimé covered 125 acres and was home to more than 5,000 inhabitants. Its influence was felt throughout the region. After A.D. 1100, the Mesoamerican ballgame, Feathered Serpent cult, and other traits began to appear across the Southwest. Paquimé ceramics have been discovered as far north as Mesa Verde in Colorado (and as far south as Teotihuacan in the Valley of Mexico).

This expansive phase lasted until A.D. 1261, when something went wrong at Paquimé. No one knows if it was an internal revolt or an external attack, but the city suddenly entered a period of decline. The ceremonial spaces were turned into residential areas made of poorly built houses; the Mesoamerican idols were destroyed; and the once elegant apartment houses became slum dwellings subdivided into warrens of tiny rooms. The outlying villages were also burned, perhaps after an attack by a foreign tribe.

Finally, in A.D. 1350 the history of Paquimé ended in a violent conflagration. This fire caught many by surprise; archaeologists have found their skeletons pinned beneath collapsed walls. The city was abandoned, and the peoples of northern Mexico returned to their Desert Culture ways.

The first European to visit Paquimé may have been Alfaro Nuñez Cabeza de Vaca on his epic wandering between Florida and the Pacific in the 1530s. Francisco de Ibarra entered Chihuahua in 1564; his account mentions a rude tribe living among ruins thought to be Paquimé. The Indians called the ruins "Paquimé" and said that its former inhabitants had been defeated by a tribe from across the sierra.

The few Spaniards who settled in the valley were ousted in the 1680s by Apache bands coming from the north and killing both whites and native Indians. They closed the region for two centuries, and only a few foolhardy travelers sent back reports on Paquimé. After the brutal repression of the Apaches in the late 19th century, settlers began to return, including American Mormons escaping the antipolygamy laws of 1882. Their descendants still keep up the custom in the town of Juárez a few kilometers to the west.

ARCHAEOLOGICAL RECORD

The first professional anthropologist to visit the area was Adolph Bandelier in 1885. His report drew the interest of Carl Lumholtz, who during the 1890s performed excavations at Paquimé. The fine ceramics he found stimulated much archaeological and looter interest. The ruins were the site of a bloody 1911 Mexican Revolutionary battle between federal troops and the rebel army of Francisco I. Madero, and many fallen soldiers are apparently buried on the grounds.

The only full-scale excavation at Paquimé was performed between 1958 and 1961 by Charles DiPeso of the University of Texas. He published his results in a massive, eight-volume report in 1974. Since then, the only work performed at the site has been the restoration of the slowly crumbling adobe walls. In the early 1990s, the Museum of the Cultures of the North was built at the entrance.

TOURING THE SITE

You enter the site from the northwest. Take the path branching to the left. On your right, you see the classic, I-shaped Mesoamerican ballcourt with low platforms forming its north and south sides. This construction is one of the strongest signs of Mesoamerican influence at Paquimé.

The walkway heads east (downhill); to the left, a path branches off to the remains of a residential quarter. Many flexed skeletons accompanied by burial offerings were discovered beneath these floors. Nearby are four stone-lined pits. Charred maguey hearts were found at the bottom, and researchers believe that they were used to produce an alcoholic beverage in a process similar to that which makes tequila.

Return to the main path, and the next structure east of the ballcourt is the Mound of the Offerings. This irregularly shaped platform held five tiny rooms beneath which archaeologists found an elaborate offering, including a miniature red stone altar and necklaces with human bone ornaments. Just beyond lies a wide, stone-lined pit that was connected to Paquimé's hydraulic system and probably acted as a reservoir.

The wide stone plaza to the east was the site's largest ceremonial space and acted as a divider between the civic-religious and the residential quarters. Across this plaza stands the site's most unusual structure, a cross-shaped platform standing about a meter high. Its arms point in the four directions at four small circular platforms standing just beyond. This structure certainly had a ceremonial function, perhaps associated with the seasonal cycles.

The path continues to the east side of the site. Here, a hodgepodge of worn adobe walls are all that remain of the extensive residential complexes. Since their unearthing in the late 1950s, many of the walls have been slowly melting from occasional rains and human contact. To keep them from crumbling further, please do not walk on them.

Directly opposite the cross-shaped platform, the first walls you encounter along the path belong to a group of one-story structures built around a patio. Many of the residential patios served as communal hearths; numerous manos and metates— the two stone parts of the pan-Mesoamerican corn-grinding apparatus—were

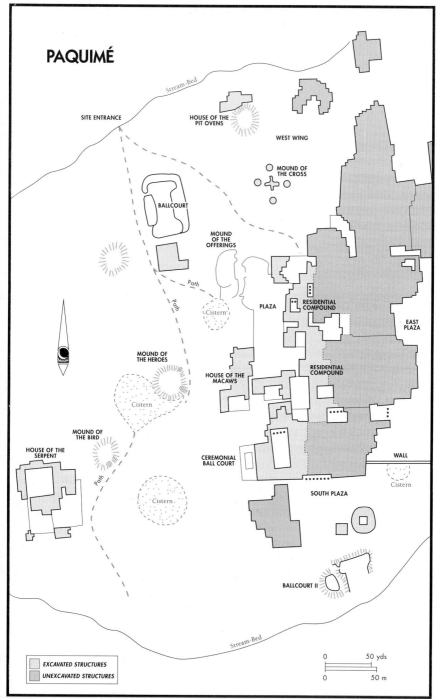

PAQUIMÉ

Stream-Bed

SITE ENTRANCE

HOUSE OF THE
PIT OVENS

WEST WING

MOUND OF
THE CROSS

BALLCOURT

MOUND
OF THE
OFFERINGS

Path

PLAZA

RESIDENTIAL
COMPOUND

EAST
PLAZA

Cistern

MOON

MOUND OF
THE HEROES

HOUSE OF THE
MACAWS

RESIDENTIAL
COMPOUND

Cistern

Path

MOUND OF
THE BIRD

HOUSE OF THE
SERPENT

CEREMONIAL
BALL COURT

WALL

Cistern

Path

Cistern

SOUTH PLAZA

BALLCOURT II

Stream-Bed

| | EXCAVATED STRUCTURES |
| | UNEXCAVATED STRUCTURES |

0   50 yds

0   50 m

found here. You can also see the distinctive T-shaped doorways with wooden lintels. These tiny portals may have had a defensive function, because only one person—stooping—can fit through at a time.

The path turns south around a corner and, after another patio, takes you to a three-story apartment complex. To support these heights, the walls were as thick as 1.3 meters at the base and tapered up to less than half that width. You can see the wooden beams that supported the upper floors and the tiny rooms that acted as sleeping lofts. In the winter, the rooms were heated by braziers set into wall niches. The mazelike interiors must have been quite gloomy, because the only windows are narrow slits (also for defense).

The path heads up a small hill by the side of the tallest—five stories!—apartment building. You can peer down into the interior from the top. Not all these rooms were living spaces; archaeologists also found rooms for grinding seed and storage areas for shells, feathers, and turquoise. Beneath the basement lie the remains of Paquimé's hydraulic system. Stairways lead to underground handmade caverns used as baths and steam rooms.

On the other side of the hill, the last building complex abuts a patio that was used to store tropical birds. You can still see the remains of cages along one of the walls. Excavators found the skeletons of more than 100 parrots and macaws—all residents of tropical jungles far to the south—among the debris.

Our tour now returns to the ceremonial quarter. As you walk along the south side of the archaeological zone, the first structure you reach is the Mound of the Revolutionaries. This circular, stepped platform is the largest ceremonial edifice at Paquimé. It received its name from a 1911 Mexican Revolutionary battle fought here between federal troops and the rebel army of Francisco I. Madero. Legend has it that the Maderistas discovered a fabulous treasure while digging this mass grave.

To the west, the next structure is a low platform supposedly built in the form of a flying bird. In the southwestern corner of the site stands another building complex that researchers believed acted as a guard post. Hidden in the scrub-covered arroyo to the west lies a sinuous 97-meter-long mound that represents the Feathered Serpent.

ERIN DWYER

pottery from the Casas Grandes Area

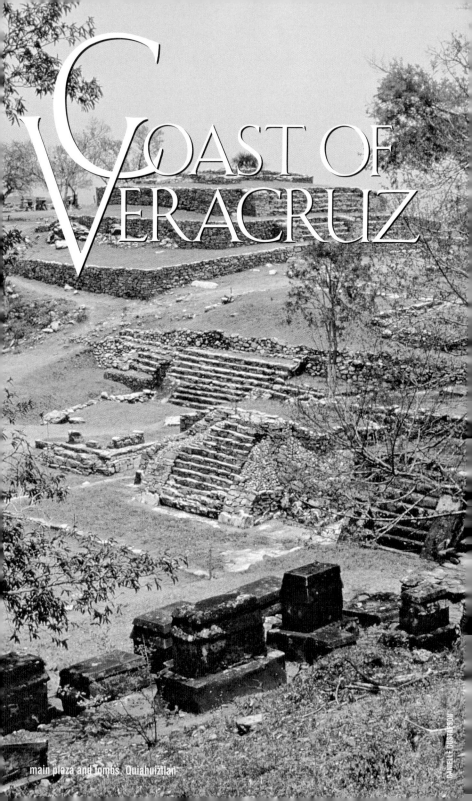

Coast of Veracruz

main plaza and tombs, Quiahuiztlan

M ost travelers pass through Veracruz on their way between Mexico City and Yucatan. The ruins are not bunched in any one area but strung along the coast; the city of Veracruz is the best base for exploration.

Running from near the Texas border to the steamy river deltas of the south, the coast of Veracruz was home to some of the earliest and most important Mesoamerican cultures. Their development was spurred by the region's rich flora and fauna—what you could not pick off the trees, you could catch in the rivers. Out of this abundance grew the Olmecs, Mexico's first civilization, who built large ceremonial centers adorned with massive stone monuments (including colossal heads) when the rest of Mesoamericans were living in simple villages. They were followed by Classic-era civilizations such as that found in El Tajín, lying in the foothills of northern Veracruz. El Tajín's dense, elaborate urban center rotated around the Mesoamerican ballgame; 17 courts have been found so far, many decorated with reliefs depicting the rituals surrounding the game. El Tajín was succeeded by coastal centers such as Zempoala, where Cortés found his first allies and began his expedition to conquer the Aztec empire.

THE LAND

The coast of Veracruz is defined by the waters of the Gulf of Mexico to the east and the Sierra Madre Oriental mountain chain to the west. Between them lies the 50- to 100-kilometer-wide strip of flat coastal plain and foothills in which the Olmec and Classic-era Veracruz civilizations flourished. This strip continues all the way to Yucatan and, via the Isthmus of Tehuantepec, to the Pacific Coast; it provided a crucial pathway between the Maya region and the cultures of central and northern Mexico.

The Sierra Madre Oriental peters out in southeast Veracruz at the Isthmus of Tehuantepec, the narrowest point in Mexico between the Pacific and the Gulf of Mexico. Southern Veracruz consists of flat, steamy plains (now mostly cleared for cattle pasture) with meandering rivers and large coastal lagoons. The only anomaly in this landscape is the sudden intrusion of the Tuxtlas, a small volcanic range rising to 1,400 meters on the coast between the Río Papaloapan and Río Coatzacoalcos. The Olmecs came to this region of narrow valleys, lakes, and rich soils to find the giant pieces of basalt from which they carved their monuments.

Climate

From sea level to an altitude of 500 meters, coastal Veracruz is *tierra caliente* (hot land), enjoying a hot and humid tropical climate almost year-round. The Sierra Madre Oriental acts as a buffer to the moist air from the Gulf; rain is possible in any month. The formal rainy season runs from June to October, when

JALAPA MUSEUM

The region's best archaeological museum is housed in the state capital of Jalapa. The beautiful and relatively new **Museo de Antropología** (built in 1986) contains a wealth of important artifacts, including colossal heads from San Lorenzo and early Maya stelae. North of downtown on Av. Jalapa, the L-shaped structure is surrounded by botanical gardens. It's open Tues.–Sun. 0900–1700.

heavy downpours flood fields and rivers overflow. Days of soaking rain are also common during the winter Nortes (Northerns), the cold and windy storms from North America. From July through early November, coastal Veracruz is a frequent target of hurricanes, many of which have inflicted heavy damage over the centuries.

Flora and Fauna

Coastal Veracruz's humid climate and rich, deep soils produce a lush vegetation. Coconut palms (an early colonial import from Africa) line most of the coast, while the seaside lagoons and protected estuaries are bordered by dense thickets of mangrove. In the inland forests and jungles—now almost all cut down for cattle ranches or, in the hills, slash-and-burn agriculture—you find a wide variety of economically important plants, including mahogany, rubber, copal, and cedar trees, as well as cacao, mamey, and zapote. The products of the cacao (chocolate) and rubber trees were particularly important to pre-Columbian cultures. An indigenous orchid produces pods whose flavor is now found across the globe—vanilla.

The animal life found along the coast includes many pan-Mesoamerican species, including deer, turkey, peccary, and dog. Migrating birds also stop here, and the year-round birdlife includes a number of species of duck. Early cultures received much of their protein from water-borne foods. Turtles, catfish, and shark were all part of their diet; the favorite finned food, however, was snook, a popular game fish that lives in lagoons and rivers. Archaeologists believe that, for the Olmecs at least, the flesh of sacrificed captives was another important source of protein.

H I S T O R Y

A complete chronology for the cultures of coastal Veracruz awaits much more research. Unexcavated mounds dot the region like mosquito bites, explored only by pothunters. Of those sites that have been dug, only a handful of results have been published and even fewer as final reports.

The earliest settlement yet found in Veracruz lies near Santa Luisa, a small town on the mouth of the Río Tecolutla (not far from El Tajín). At the deepest levels, archaeologists found the remains of mastodons, giant sloths, and horses dating to 12,000–10,000 B.C. No sign of human presence appears until about 5600 B.C. Hunter-gatherers set a temporary camp here and left obsidian scrapers and points among other debris. These early Veracruzans lived from hunting, fishing, and collecting tubers and other plant foods.

Formal agriculture came late to the residents of this region: the rivers and es-

THE BALLGAME: PLAYING FOR KEEPS

The residents of Mesoamerica were likely as obsessed with sports as we are. Researchers call their favorite pastime the "ballgame." However, this refers not to one game but to a number of games that evolved over time and had different meanings in different cultures. Versions of these ballgames have been found throughout the New World and on many Caribbean islands; some are still played today in rural parts of Oaxaca and northwestern Mexico. In Mesoamerica, playing the ballgame appears to have been the obsession of every adolescent and adult male from the ruler on down. Part of the yearly tribute demanded by the Aztecs from their Gulf Coast vassal states was 16,000 rubber balls!

The Mesoamerican form of the ballgame was invented either by the Gulf Coast Olmec or on the Soconusco Plain of southeastern Chiapas. Ancient rubber balls have been found at the Olmec site of El Manatí in lowland Veracruz, and archaeologists have found the remains of what appear to be ballcourts at the Preclassic sites of San Lorenzo and La Venta. The oldest complete ballcourt yet discovered, however, is the one recently unearthed at the Soconusco site of Paso de la Amada, dating to 1400 B.C. The general form of the ballcourt was a rectangular floor, often of masonry, which was bordered along the long sides by sloped or vertical walls. The courts were divided into two main types, central Mexican and Maya. The former were I-shaped with walls at the far ends, while the latter were also I-shaped but without walls. The central Mexican ballcourts had stone rings set into the center of the side walls (one of the many signs of central Mexican

influence at Chichén Itzá is the rings on the main ballcourt). The Maya walls were bare or used other forms of "goals," such as the sculptures of bound captives found at Toniná. Archaeologists believe that most of the ballcourts known today were elite playing fields reserved for the aristocracy; the commoners played their games on rough, "sand lot" courts whose existence has been erased by the passage of time.

The most common Mesoamerican versions of the ballgame were played by two teams of one to 11 players wearing thick pads around the waist. No copies of the rules have been found, but the object of the contest seems to have been to hit a solid rubber ball weighing as much as 2.5 kilograms through the stone rings. The ball, which could kill a man, could be struck only with the hips, buttocks, or knees—the Aztec name for the game was *ulamaliztli*, the "hip-ballgame." The games were accompanied by vigorous wagering; the stakes could be money, valuables, or even human lives. Early Spanish eyewitnesses report spectators fleeing at the end of a game to avoid the victor collecting his winnings: their clothes.

For many Mesoamericans, the game was probably primarily a sport. As the players ascended in status, however, the ballgame took on important religious and political meanings. The game was used to resolve disputes and as a means for people to assert their social or political status. When Nezahualpilli told Motecuhzoma II that three comets presaged the end of his empire, the Aztec ruler did not believe him. They played the ballgame to test the prophecy's truth; Motecuhzoma lost. In Yaxchilan, numerous lintels depict rulers

tuaries were such a rich source of protein that they were not forced to turn to seasonal crops for sustenance. By 1700 B.C., however, at least some of the pillars of the Mesoamerican diet—chiles, beans, and tomatillos—had reached the area. As the settlements grew, they had to increasingly rely on the agricultural staples, which eventually also included maize. Santa Luisa was the site of a small village whose inhabitants produced simple ceramics. Around 1150 B.C., those

and rulers-to-be playing the ballgame as a way of affirming their right to power.

The ballgame furthered the dynastic strategies of Mesoamerican rulers because it connected them to the gods, who were, not coincidentally, also ballplayers. The ballcourt was associated with the Underworld, and the movement of the ball represented the sun passing from day to night and back to day. In the Popul Vuh, the Maya mythic account, the Hero Twins Hunahpu and Xbalanque defeat the Lords of the Underworld in a series of ballgames and rescue their father, the Maize God, thus bringing good crops back to earth. Round stones placed in the floors of Maya ballcourts are marked with a quatrefoil cartouche that symbolizes the entrance to the Underworld.

After a battle, captives were often taken to the ballcourt to play against their captors; after their defeat (it is unclear if they were ever allowed to win) they were decapitated. The blood spouting from their necks was the ritual fertilizer for good crops. In some ceremonies, the decapitated head was used in place of the ball. Ballcourt reliefs at El Tajín and Chichén Itzá depict the decapitation ceremonies and the blood turning into vines or huge vats of pulque. The Maya also trussed captives into the shape of a ball and rolled them down the temple steps to their deaths. The famous hieroglyphic staircase at Yaxchilan contains depictions of this ceremony. Like most Mesoamerican sacrifices, this ritual had its good and bad sides: the captive died a horrible death, but on the other hand he became a god.

In the modern world, games such as football, soccer, and baseball are often used as metaphors

Elaborately carved stone *palmas* were attached to the stone yoke worn around a player's waist during pre- and post-ballgame ceremonies.

for our societies. Researchers believe that the residents of Mesoamerica found a metaphor for their own world view in the ballgame. Despite their expertise at play, there was something uncontrollable, even random, about the movement of the ball. The outcome of this instability was frequently horrible—death—but there was nothing one could do but give in to the mysterious laws of the gods.

ceramics showed the sudden influence of the Olmecs, Mesoamerica's first civilization, which had sprung up just to the south.

The Olmec heartland occupies the steamy lowlands of southern Veracruz and western Tabasco. Around 1700 B.C., migrants (perhaps from the Pacific Coast of Chiapas) built a village at San Lorenzo on the banks of the Río Coatzacoalcos. Within 200 years, this had become the first great Olmec center. The inhabitants built a massive platform from clay and earth—there were no sources of construction stone in the region—as their ceremonial center, including one of the earliest ballcourts found in Mesoamerica. From the nearby Sierra de los Tuxtlas, they quarried chunks of basalt weighing many tons, dragged and floated them to San Lorenzo, and carved them into massive stone monuments. Among the numerous sculptures found here are huge altars with rulers sitting in niches in their sides and many of the famous Olmec colossal heads. These depict flat-faced rulers wearing protective headgear for the ballgame; they may have been deified dead rulers. (Archaeologists discount the theory that the heads show African origins; from the epicanthic fold of the eyelid and other attributes, they look far more Native American than African.)

Around 900 B.C., San Lorenzo was abandoned and its monuments were defaced and ritually buried. By this time, Olmec culture had begun its spread out of the heartland. Their distinctive "jaguar baby" figurines and carved jade pieces have been found not only in central Mexico (Tlatilco) but south and west (Oaxaca and Guerrero) and as far away as Copán in Honduras. Of the numerous Olmec centers that arose to take San Lorenzo's place, the largest in the Olmec heartland was La Venta, lying just east of Veracruz in the state of Tabasco.

Well worth a visit, La Venta lies on an island in the swamps running along the east bank of the Río Tonalá. The ceremonial center is built around an enormous clay pyramid, at the time one of the largest structures in Mesoamerica. Among the remarkable artworks found here are more colossal heads, three mosaic floors in the form of jaguar masks, and a tomb constructed of basalt pillars. Perhaps the most famous discovery is Offering 4, consisting of 16 jade and serpentine figures arranged in a circle (now in Mexico City's Museo Nacional de Antropología). Many of La Venta's stone sculptures can be seen in the Parque Museo La Venta in Villahermosa, Tabasco.

At its height, La Venta had a population of 18,000 and a system of agricultural terraces built along the banks of the river. About 400–300 B.C., this city, too, reached a mysterious and violent end. Many sculptures were ritually defaced and buried, and the site was abandoned. La Venta's successor as center of the Olmec world appears to have been Tres Zapotes, lying just beyond the Sierra de los Tuxtlas 120 kilometers to the west.

TRES ZAPOTES

INTRODUCTION

Colossal heads—those portraits of Olmec rulers carved from enormous boulders—first appeared to the modern world at Tres Zapotes in 1869. Since then, archaeologists have discovered numerous large monuments at the site, as well as a stela bearing one of the earliest Long Count dates found in Mesoamerica. Unfortunately, this relatively obscure part of Veracruz has languished since the last excavations 60 years ago. The site itself is a set of grass-covered mounds in the middle of a pasture, while the impoverished town of Tres Zapotes contains a small site museum housing a number of stone monuments.

HISTORY

The first settlement at Tres Zapotes dates to the Early Preclassic era. The site became a center of the Olmec culture at the end of La Venta's occupation, probably around 300 B.C., and remained so for the next three centuries. The inhabitants manufactured stone monuments, including the largest colossal head yet found, from basalt quarried in the Sierra de los Tuxtlas just to the east and produced thousands of Olmec-style ceramics.

One of the most remarkable finds from this era is Stela C (now in Mexico City's Museo Nacional de Antropología), which bears on its back a Long Count date that in our calendar translates to September 3, 32 B.C. This is only four years later than the earliest Long Count date yet found, December 8, 36 B.C., from Chiapa de Corzo in Chiapas. The Olmecs thus could have been the inventors

TRES ZAPOTES

How to get there: The easiest way to reach this half-forgotten town is from Santiago Tuxtla on the western edge of the Sierra de los Tuxtlas. From the main square, a road heads southwest into the lowlands. After about five kilometers, a semipaved and heavily potholed road turns west to the town of Tres Zapotes.

Hours: Daily 0900–1700.

Admission fee: Free.

How long to tour: One hour.

Recommended gear: Hats, sunblock, bottled water, sturdy shoes or sneakers.

Museum: A small site museum is in Tres Zapotes town.

of the Long Count calendar system, which was later used by the Maya and most other Mesoamerican cultures. (The Zapotecs of Oaxaca had their own, earlier calendar system not based on the Long Count.)

Until more excavations are performed, it will remain unclear when the Olmec influence disappeared from Tres Zapotes. From the deliberate mutilation of some of the monuments, archaeologists surmise that the end of this era came suddenly. By A.D. 300, the site was distinctly smaller and showed evidence of ties to Teotihuacan and the nearby Early Classic (A.D. 150–600) Veracruz site of Cerro de las Mesas. Tres Zapotes rebounded between A.D. 600 and 900 to its period of greatest population. The inhabitants built numerous mounds and, like the people of El Tajín to the north, were assiduous contestants of the Mesoamerican ballgame.

The last period of Tres Zapotes's occupation was the Early Postclassic (A.D. 900–1200) when the ceramic styles were distinctly different from previous eras. The site was related to such coastal centers such as the Isla de Sacrificios (an island just off the city of Veracruz) and may have been influenced by the Toltec civilization then flourishing in central Mexico.

ARCHAEOLOGICAL RECORD

During the 19th century, the Tres Zapotes area was owned by the Hueyapan sugarcane plantation. In 1858, a plantation worker discovered the first colossal head—Monument A—and a decade later José María Melgar y Serrano published an account of the find. His article noted the "Ethiopian" features of the head

DANIELLE GUSTAFSON

Pyramid mound at Tres Zapotes

and suggested this showed that ancient Africans had come to the New World and formed the basis of at least some of the Mesoamerican civilizations. (Although this theory still has its adherents, nearly every Mesoamerican archaeologist believes it highly unlikely.) Melgar's article brought an expedition from Mexico City to Tres Zapotes to collect objects for the 1892 Madrid exposition.

The first excavations at Tres Zapotes were performed between 1938 and 1940 by the great Olmecologist Matthew Stirling and his team from the Bureau of American Ethnology. With financing from the National Geographic Society, they excavated the major mounds at the site and unearthed numerous basalt monuments. The team also dug numerous stratigraphic pits that helped establish a chronology for the site (and for southern Veracruz in general).

In the late 1960s, Robert J. Squier led an excavation at La Cobata a few kilometers from Tres Zapotes. His most notable find was the largest colossal head ever found; unfortunately it was crudely sculpted, making it also the ugliest colossal head. It now reclines under a gazebo in the main square of Santiago Tuxtla. No results of this expedition were ever published. The only Tres Zapotes project since then was a small Mexican expedition under Ponciano Ortiz Ceballos that discovered signs of pre-Olmec occupation at the site. Although the interest of the archaeological community has strayed, farmers continue to discover stone monuments in their fields.

Over the years, that first colossal head, Monument A, sometimes called the "Hueyapan Head," has remained a focus of interest. Two attempts were made to move it to Mexico City, in 1897 and 1922, but the head was too heavy and both attempts failed; it now rests in the museum in Tres Zapotes town.

TOURING THE SITE

Tres Zapotes lies in the watershed of the Río San Juan just west of the Sierra de los Tuxtlas. In 1939, it took seven hours (if you were lucky) to reach the site by boat and horseback from the nearest road.

A good place to begin your tour is at the small site museum (open 0900–1700, free) at the west end of Tres Zapotes town and then head out to the mounds north of town. The museum guardian can tell you how to reach the site itself. At the museum you'll find Monument A, the first colossal head ever found, as well as three worn stelae and a number of other carved monuments, some massive. These include two tenons, carved stone pillars that transform into human or animal forms at one end; these would have acted something like horizontal beams in the structure of a temple.

Nearly 200 mounds dot the landscape north of town. The easiest to visit is Mound Group 3, just west of the road two kilometers north of town. Here you find one large mound and four smaller ones in the middle of a cow pasture. There is not much to see except for potsherds and occasional obsidian fragments scattered over the ground. Visitors are frequently joined by an archaeology enthusiast from town who will explain (in Spanish) his theory of the ruins and attempt to sell pieces of ancient pots. Due south one kilometer stands Mound Group 2, and the smaller Mound Group 1 lies to the southwest. Stone monuments have been found throughout the site.

EL TAJÍN

INTRODUCTION

After the disappearance of the Olmecs, the coastal plains saw the rise of the Classic Veracruz civilization (many call it Totonac, after the current native inhabitants of the region, but no proof exists of a direct tie between them and the ancient tribes). El Tajín was the Classic-era metropolis of this region, the largest city in northeastern Mexico between the fall of Teotihuacan and the rise of Zempoala. Crammed into a valley in the lower foothills of the Sierra Madre Oriental, El Tajín contained dozens of elaborate temples, including the unique Temple of the Niches built with one recess for every day of the solar year. It is also home to an unprecedented number of ballcourts—17 have been discovered so far. The ballgame was at the center of the city's ritual life; the finest of the site's many stone reliefs depict rulers involved in the stages of the game rituals.

A visit to these steamy ruins can take the best part of the day. You can also watch the Totonac dancers at the site entrance perform the Dance of the *Voladores* (Flying Men); hanging by their feet from a rope, they spin down from the top of a pole and alight just before crashing into the ground.

EL TAJÍN

How to get there: The sprawling ruins of El Tajín fill a valley about 22 kilometers east-southeast of Poza Rica (known as an oil-refining city). The easiest way to reach the site is via the road heading eight kilometers southeast from the town of Papantla.

Hours: Daily 0900–1700.

Admission fee: 30 pesos.

How long to tour: Three hours.

Recommended gear: Hats, sunblock, sturdy shoes or sneakers, bottled water, rain gear during rainy season.

Museum: A small but good museum is at the site entrance.

Food and accommodations: The most popular base for visiting the ruins of El Tajín is the large town of Papantla. The best hotel is the **Hotel Premier**, Juan Enríquez 103, tel. 784/2-2600. You'll find a restaurant and snack bar at the site entrance.

HISTORY

Despite the decades of excavations at the site, there remain large gaps in El Tajín's chronology. The city's builders excavated much of the soil around the ceremonial center to use as fill, thereby erasing any usable stratigraphy. A better understanding of the area's chronology awaits careful exploration of the numerous surrounding sites.

Archaeologists believe El Tajín became a regional center by about A.D. 100; there is not yet any evidence for substantial earlier occupation. Excavations at nearby sites such as Santa Luisa show that the region's Preclassic inhabitants were more closely related to the Huastecs of northern Veracruz than to the current Totonacs (probably Postclassic arrivals) who call the area home.

El Tajín's earliest center was probably around the Arroyo Group at the southern end of the site (near the entrance). From A.D. 300 to 600, the building program gradually crept north to the head of the valley and up the ridges to the west. The substructures for the Pyramid of the Niches and the Tajín Chico area were built at this time. These ambitious early building complexes were all well-planned. As the city became more crowded, however, a crucial problem emerged. The possibilities for expansion were limited; later buildings—such as those around the South Ballcourt—are shoe-horned in, destroying the beauties of the earlier architecture.

El Tajín reached its height between A.D. 900 and 1100. During the 10th century, its ruler was 13 Rabbit, who we see on a series of reliefs carved on the columns found in the Building of the Columns. These carvings depict him participating in the ritual human sacrifices that reaffirmed his right to rulership. Human sacrifice and the closely related Mesoamerican ballgame were at the

El Tajín's famous Pyramid of the Niches, with one recess for every day of the year.

DANIELLE GUSTAFSON

core of El Tajín's ritual life. As well as the 17 ballcourts at the site, archaeologists have found numerous objects, such as *yugos, palmas,* and *hachas* that were used to mark stages in the game and the surrounding ceremonies. Some of the courts may have been for practice, but the elaborately decorated South and North Ballcourts were devoted to high-status rituals.

Early Postclassic El Tajín covered 500 hectares and held a population in the tens of thousands; its empire extended for hundreds of kilometers along the Veracruz coast. By A.D. 1150, however, the culture had collapsed and the city was almost totally abandoned. The exact cause for this cataclysm is unknown. Archaeologists now believe that a major catalyst was environmental degradation; El Tajín and the surrounding region had passed the upper limit on human habitation. The soil could not support this multitude, and a few bad harvests led to upheaval and the end of the system that attached the population to these lands.

During the Late Postclassic (A.D. 1200–1520), a new people moved into the vacuum caused by the abandonment of El Tajín. These were the Totonacs,

THE TOTONACS

The waves of heat rising from the green jungle dance with the simple melody of a flute and drum. The music comes from atop a pole nearly 100 feet tall, where you see five men dressed in bright red and white and festooned with ribbons. On the very top stands the musician, who at the same time performs death-defying leaps and steps on a space barely large enough for his feet. On a square frame just below sit four men with their waists wrapped by thick ropes. When the song ends, without fanfare they tumble over backward into space. The frame begins to turn, the ropes unwind from the pole, and the men fly in ever-widening circles, past green hills and a narrow valley packed with pyramids and temples, headfirst to earth. Just before it seems that they will surely crash, they perform neat somersaults and land on their feet.

The Dance of the Voladores (Flying Men), the best-known ritual of the Totonac Indians of northern Veracruz, is performed daily at the ruins of El Tajín. It is part a commercial entertainment for tourists and part a political statement, an affirmation of the Totonacs' spiritual ownership of these ruins. (Archaeologists believe the ancient city was actually built by another people, con-

tradicting the Totonacs' oral history.) The real Totonac life, however, takes place in the fields and dense green forests of the surrounding hills. The region's lush environment and frequent rainfalls allow for an existence that takes full advantage of nature's bounty.

As with most other Mexican Indian groups, life revolves around the growing of maize using the milpa system of agriculture. A plot of jungle is hacked down with machetes; the deadwood is burned; and on the resulting field, or milpa, the Totonacs sow corn and squash and beans with sharp planting sticks. After a few years, the corn has used up the soil's nutrients and the field is allowed to revert to jungle. During this fallow period, the Totonacs plant vanilla orchards among the remaining trees and harvest the long pods to make into vanilla extract. In the lowlands, they plant sugarcane, another cash crop. Even in the simplest Totonac house, a *casa de palma* made of a thatched roof and bamboo or sapling walls, there is a richness reflective of the environment. The neatly swept yard contains pens for domestic animals (chickens, pigs, etc.) and a wide variety of vegetation, including shade trees, fruit trees, and all kinds of flowering plants.

who may have been Chichimec nomads from the arid plateaus to the north-west. They settled around El Tajín but not in the ceremonial center proper; this they used as a necropolis, burying their dead among the temples of a disappeared people.

During these centuries, the coast of Veracruz was invaded by a number of central Mexican armies, including the Toltecs and the Aztecs. By the end of the 15th century, most of the Totonac centers along the central Veracruz coast were paying tribute to Tenochtitlan.

ARCHAEOLOGICAL RECORD

In March of 1785, a local official named Diego Ruíz stumbled into an obscure part of north-central Veracruz while searching for an illegal tobacco field (its cultivation was a royal monopoly). Instead of contraband, he found the miraculously well-preserved Pyramid of the Niches, which the local Totonac Indians had apparently been hiding from the Spanish authorities. His drawing of the pyramid was published in a Mexico City newspaper and later reprinted in the Jesuit priest Pedro Marquez's 1804 work on Mexican antiquities.

The news brought a slew of 19th-century explorers, most notably Karl Nebel, who published some dramatic lithographs of the pyramid and a description of the site. They were followed by more scientific investigators in the late 19th and early 20th centuries. Eduard Seler and Teobert Maler both did extensive explorations of El Tajín, which they published with copious illustrations.

In 1924, the Mexican government granted the first funds for El Tajín's restoration. After a few years of studies, the project, led by Agustín García Vega, performed the first restoration of the Pyramid of the Niches and began a four-year series of excavations in 1934. As they cleared the site, they finally began to realize the extent of the ancient city.

In 1939, José García Payón took the helm of the project, beginning a 39-year career centered around El Tajín. He led the excavations of many major buildings, extending the work to Tajín Chico during the 1950s, and oversaw much consolidation and restoration. After the discovery of oil just to the west, Pemex, the Mexican oil company, built the first roads into the area, and the era of mass tourism began.

This era of excavations ended in 1963. During the late 1960s and 1970s, most of the work performed at the site was maintenance. The most important archaeological program was Paula and Ray Krotser's project to produce the first complete map of the site and excavate stratigraphic pits that would help clarify El Tajín's murky chronology.

In 1984, INAH and the Veracruz government initiated the ongoing Proyecto Tajín to explore and restore the remainder of the site. The project has been led by Jürgen Brüggemann, under whom dozens of buildings have been consolidated and restored, including most in the Arroyo Group and Tajín Chico. In the early 1990s, they opened an elaborate new site museum financed by Pemex. Work continues at this writing, most notably the restoration of the murals in Tajín Chico's Building I. As always, however, many questions remain to be answered.

TOURING THE SITE

At the north end of the parking lot stands a building complex housing shops, a cafeteria, a museum, and the site entrance. The museum is worth a visit; it contains some explanatory displays about the site and a few interesting objects, such as ceramic feet that were the base of some sculpture. The most important pieces here are the stone column reliefs that depict 13 Rabbit, the 10th-century ruler of El Tajín, engaged in ritual sacrifice.

Most of the ruins are oriented along the north-south axis of a narrow valley. You are entering via what was probably the main route into El Tajín from the coast. Heading north from the entrance, the main path enters the Arroyo Group, a large plaza flanked on four sides by large, relatively crudely constructed temples. (Be warned that the climbing of almost all temples is forbidden.) Unlike the rest of the urban area, no later temple was added to the center of the plaza. Archaeologists believe this open space, occupying the city's entrance, was El Tajín's main marketplace. On the north side of the plaza stands Building 16, which displays the first of many rows of niches that you will see at the site. An unrestored ballcourt lies just beyond the plaza's southwestern corner.

The path exits the plaza's northeastern corner and passes between Ballcourts 13/14 on the left and 17/27 on the right (they are given dual numbers from the names of the structures that flank them). Like most—but not all—of El Tajín's courts, these are I-shaped with closed ends. A simple stone mosaic along the interior facade forms crosses that some archaeologists believe are associated with the Venus cult.

From here, a path branches left into the site's Central Zone. In the last centuries of El Tajín's existence as an urban area, the city builders apparently had to throw out their carefully planned arrangement of plazas and temples because of overcrowding. They needed more temples, so they simply built them in the middle of plazas, crowding them among the older structures. In the Central Zone, you find well over a dozen large and small structures, including some of El Tajín's most important ritual areas.

The path enters the South Ballcourt, which runs east-west between Building 6 to the south and, opposite, the large platform of Building 5. Unlike the other ballcourts, this is one long straight court with no walls at the two ends and straight rather than sloping interior walls. Its walls are decorated with six relief panels that are crucial to our understanding of the rituals surrounding the Mesoamerican ballgame.

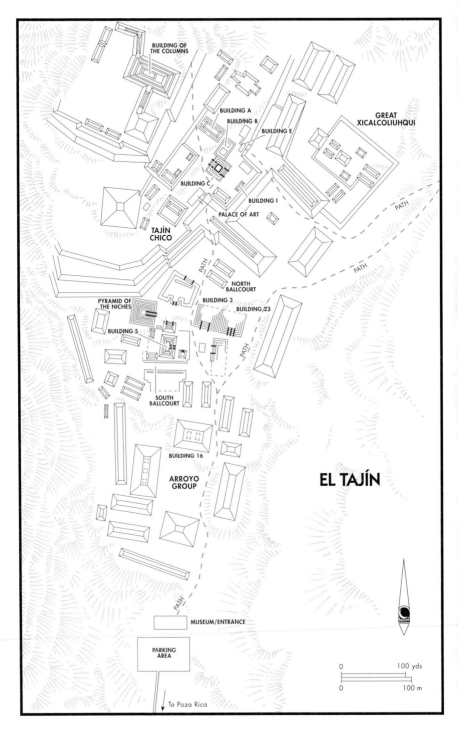

BUILDING OF
THE COLUMNS

BUILDING A

BUILDING B

BUILDING E

GREAT
XICALCOLIUHQUI

BUILDING C

BUILDING I

PALACE OF ART

PATH

TAJÍN
CHICO

PATH

PATH

NORTH
BALLCOURT

PYRAMID OF
THE NICHES

BUILDING 3

BUILDING 23

BUILDING 5

PATH

SOUTH
BALLCOURT

BUILDING 16

ARROYO
GROUP

EL TAJÍN

PATH

MUSEUM/ENTRANCE

PARKING
AREA

MooN

0   100 yds

0   100 m

To Poza Rica

According to S. Jeffrey K. Wilkerson, these panels form a sort of cartoon strip which should be read in a particular order: southeast, southwest, northwest, northeast, north central, south central. The first panel on the left, or southeast, corner of the wall shows a ballplayer donning his ritual clothing much like a warrior preparing for battle. On the right, you see the death deity arising from a pot; he is repeated in the next three scenes. At the far end— southwest—the relief depicts a player reclining on a bed with an eagle dancing in front of him while musicians play rattles and drums. The northwest corner panel opposite brings us to the ballcourt; wearing ballgame belts, the two players face each other with speech scrolls emerging from their mouths, and two men costumed as gods (the one on the left is the Tajín Rain God) stand or kneel on the walls. The panel at the northeast corner shows the finish to a game: one player is held by his arms while the other drives a flint knife into his chest; the Tajín Rain God sits on the right.

The central two panels take us into the Underworld. On the north side, the dead player stands in front of the seated Rain God (the Wind God sits behind) and points down to a vat of sacred pulque. To the left and right, the scene is flanked by stylized lunar glyphs, femurs, and Venus glyphs, while above flies a bifurcated

pulque god. Finally, the south central panel shows the successful culmination of the ritual. The Rain God replenishes the vat of pulque by driving a perforator through his penis, sending drops into the vat. The gods of the wind and the moon float above, and the scene is again framed by the pulque god on top and the lunar, femur, and Venus symbols on the side. The taking of the ballplayer's life has once again replenished nature's store.

Return now to the ballcourt's east side and the front of the large platform immediately to the north. Five structures of varying sizes occupy the top of the platform; the largest is the central Building 5. This two-stage temple is constructed from a low *talud* topped with a row of niches where the *tablero* would be and then a long *talud* rising to the top. Just above the first tier, the base of the central staircase is the site of a V-shaped

The relief shows the rain god perforating his penis, sending drops of blood into a vat of *pulque* (a fermented drink) below.

sculpted column depicting a seated figure with a skull for a head. This may represent the temple's deity or, as some archaeologists say, the patron deity of El Tajín. Unfortunately, you are not allowed to get close enough to see it clearly.

The building faces east over a small plaza containing a raised altar. On the plaza's east side stands Building 15, a long platform with two staircases going up. The north side of this structure almost touches the twin Buildings 3 (left) and 23 (right). The former is an early seven-level pyramid that was originally painted blue; the latter is one of the last built at El Tajín, rising in five tiers unadorned with niches.

The west side of Building 3 faces yet another small plaza. On the far side stands the famous Pyramid of the Niches, also called Building 1, El Tajín's most famous (and first discovered) building. Although it looks relatively simple, this elegant building is a complex construction of thousands of stone blocks fitted into each other like pieces of a jigsaw puzzle. The structure rises 20 meters in seven tiers, with a broad staircase ascending its eastern face. The staircase is bordered by a step-and-fret motif, perhaps representing lightning, and six benches containing three niches each jut from the steps at intervals.

The tiers rise in *talud-tablero* form, with each *tablero* composed of dozens of square niches numbering 365 in all. These undoubtedly represent the days of the solar year. El Tajín's inhabitants may have originally placed offerings in the niches; it may even have acted like a giant calendar. The pyramid's exterior was painted red, while the niches were colored black to heighten the dramatic effect. The interior has been only partially explored; the structure was built on another, far simpler temple that was constructed during the first phase of the urban center. Various sculptures, including a large portrait of a royal figure, were found at the foot of the stairs. The holes in the square blocks along the base held poles that were probably adorned with ritual banners.

Just south of the pyramid stands a low platform running east-west, probably a residential complex. A large thatched roof covers a series of small rooms. Around the base of the outer wall runs a long, fragmentary relief still bearing traces of red paint. Due west stands Building 12, which rises in a two-stage *talud-tablero* structure similar to Building 5. Its unique feature are its niches, which are separated from each other by freestanding columns rather than walls.

Returning to the plaza in front of the Pyramid of the Niches, you see a large, low unrestored mound along its northern border. If you take the path exiting to the right (east) of it, you will enter a larger open space in the middle of which stands the North Ballcourt. Like the South Ballcourt, the walls of this 26-meter-long court are decorated with six bas-relief panels, three each on the north and south sides. Unfortunately, they are badly worn and only partially legible; a running scroll pattern frieze connects them along the top of the wall. The northwest and the southwest panels are the clearest, respectively showing a ruler donning ritual gear and gods gathered around a vat of pulque.

West of this ballcourt lies a field of large pieces of rock and stucco, perhaps massive paving stones. From here, a path leads up a retaining wall to the terrace that contains Tajín Chico (Little Tajín). Archaeologists believe this was an elite residential area where Tajín's rulers lived and consulted in special buildings devoted to civic rituals. It also has a commanding view over the city's ceremonial center. Although this terrace uses the valley's natural contours, it is almost totally man-made, built using tons of fill from the valley floor.

On top of the wall, the path leads to the right and Building I, also called the Palace of Art, a low platform built on an east-west axis and covered with a protective thatched roof. This structure was constructed in five stages, and artworks belonging to at least two of those stages have been discovered and restored. Along the outside runs a low stucco frieze of teeth (or triangles) interspersed with columns. You are not allowed into the building, but you can see further decorations along the interior walls. Along the lower walls runs a unique stucco frieze consisting of more teeth and, above, rows of what would appear to be calabash squash on stalks. Above you see bluish frescoes of vegetation motifs. Further murals, some of which depict weird zoomorphic beings, decorate the interior walls.

A short flight of steps just to the east leads up to a small plaza at the heart of Tajín Chico. The plaza's north side is bounded by three civic structures. First you see Building C, a three-tier platform with step-and-fret motifs set into niches running along the *tableros*. A colonnaded room decorated with murals stood on top of the platform; fragments of the wood and stone roof have been found. Archaeologists believe this structure was used for audiences between El Tajín's ruler and his people. A wide staircase on Building C's west side descends into a small plaza behind the Palace of Art.

Immediately to the north—touching actually—stands Building B, a two-level elite residence. A staircase climbs into the building's interior, where you find a courtyard and the remains of six square columns. The whole was covered with a massive wood and concrete roof that must have weighed many tons. Another stair ascends to the second level and an exit to the east.

To the west of this structure you find Building A, another, more elaborate residential complex. The entrance is to the south. The stairs cut into the center through a facade built to look like a temple staircase (much like the false stairs on the Río Bec region Maya temples). The steps lead up to an interior passage that runs around the rectangular perimeter of the structure. The outer passage walls are decorated with stone mosaics, including the step-and-fret motif and a design that approaches the shape of a swastika. Murals adorned the inner walls.

From here, a path winds to the hilltop, where you find the acropolislike complex around the Building of the Columns. This was probably the palace of El Tajín's ruler. On the front of the Building of the Columns itself, archaeologists found the famous columns carved with scenes of 13 Rabbit's victories in battle. Unfortunately, at this writing tourists are prohibited from this area.

Just north of Building B stands the diminutive Building E. Inside, you find a flight of stairs that leads back down to the valley floor. You cut through a thick growth of vegetation—the teeming flora that ever threatens to engulf the ruins—

pass some uncleared mounds, and emerge at the side of a large and utterly unique stone wall. This is the Great Xicalcoliuhqui, or Great Enclosure, formed by the 360-meter-long wall running in the shape of a squared spiral that closely resembles the step-and-fret design repeated all over the site. The wall is actually a narrow platform with a *talud-tablero* exterior face and niches adorning both the *tableros* and the *taludes*. The inner plaza is uncleared; if you follow the wall around, in the center you can find two temple mounds and the remains of two ballcourts. The Great Enclosure was probably the site of ritual activities involving the ballgame. Due north at the base of Tajín Chico's terrace lies the Great Ballcourt, also uncleared, the largest court at the site.

This is the end of the official tour but not the end of the site. Mounds dot the valley to the north and the surrounding ridges. The ridge west of the Arroyo Group was an important residential area, and more ballcourts and mounds are hidden by the tangle of forest to the east of the stream running along the valley.

QUIAHUIZTLAN

DESIGN MOTIFS OF ANCIENT MEXICO

INTRODUCTION

High on a hillside terrace overlooking the Gulf of Mexico stand the ruins of Quiahuiztlan. This Totonac center is best known for its tombs, more than 70 of them, each shaped like a miniature temple. Less well-known is Quiahuiztlan's place in Mexican history: it was here that Cortés formed the pact with 20 Totonac chieftains that gave him his first native allies against the Aztec empire. This site is also a pleasant stop on the road from Veracruz to El Tajín; the view is breathtaking.

HISTORY

The earliest occupation of Quiahuiztlan may date to the Early Postclassic (A.D. 900–1200), the unsettled era when groups across Mesoamerica abandoned their comfortable valley settlements for fortified villages in the hills. Quiahuiztlan's location was nearly impregnable: it lies high on a ridge of the Cerro de los Metates with only one access up a steep slope to the west. If forced back, the inhabitants could flee to the top of the nearby Peñon de Bernal, a massive basalt plug with sheer cliffs on three sides.

Quiahuiztlan reached its peak during the Late Postclassic (A.D. 1200–1520) when the major temples of its ceremonial center were erected. Like many Totonac settlements of central Veracruz, they buried their elite dead in above-ground tombs shaped like miniature temples. Quiahuiztlan also controlled

QUIAHUIZTLAN

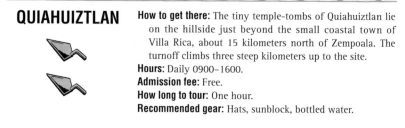

How to get there: The tiny temple-tombs of Quiahuiztlan lie on the hillside just beyond the small coastal town of Villa Rica, about 15 kilometers north of Zempoala. The turnoff climbs three steep kilometers up to the site.
Hours: Daily 0900–1600.
Admission fee: Free.
How long to tour: One hour.
Recommended gear: Hats, sunblock, bottled water.

the small protected bay four kilometers east on the Gulf. Its population probably reached the thousands, with many people living in huts dotting the hillside terraces.

In the early 16th century, Quiahuiztlan was one of the most powerful centers on the Veracruz coast. Nevertheless, like all other towns in the region, it had to pay tribute to the Aztec emperor Motecuhzoma II. When Aztec emissaries arrived, they were treated with respect, fear, and secret loathing. In 1519, the Totonacs thought they had found an answer to the Aztec demands: allying themselves with Hernán Cortés and his troop of gold-hungry soldiers.

Cortés's first landing on the Veracruz coast was the port of San Juan de Ulua next to the present city of Veracruz. Clouds of mosquitoes made that spot unhealthy, so he sent an expedition under Francisco de Montejo (later conqueror of Yucatan) to find a better harbor. Fifty-eight kilometers to the north they saw "a town which looked like a fortified port and was called Quiahuiztlan, and ... beside it was a harbour in which [they] thought their ships would be safe from northerly gales." Cortés ordered his men to pack and move north to this new location.

They chose another, closer spot instead, which they named Villa Rica de la Vera Cruz (now called La Antigua), but Cortés still wanted to visit Quiahuiztlan. On the march north, they spent the night at the Totonac center of Zempoala, where Cortés met his first ally, Xicomecoatl, the so-called "Fat Chief" of Zempoala. The troop then continued north, and the next day marched up to the fort-city. If there had been any resistance, wrote the conquistador Bernal Díaz, it would have been very hard to capture.

The Spanish visit was a complete surprise, so they were able to enter the heart of the urban area. Díaz continues:

> When we got to the top of the fortress, to the square on which their temples and great idol-houses stood, we found fifteen Indians waiting, all dressed in fine cloaks and each bearing a clay brazier full of incense. These Indians came up to Cortes, and perfumed him and all the soldiers near him. Then with deep bows they asked our pardon for not having come out to meet us, assured us that we were welcome, and asked us to rest.

The party was shortly joined by the Fat Chief, who joined the local rulers in a litany of complaints against the Aztecs. This diatribe was cut short by the arrival of five "cocksure" Aztec emissaries who ignored the Spaniards and scolded the Totonacs for entertaining the foreigners against the orders of the Aztec emperor. The Totonacs quailed in fear and hastened to gather sacrificial victims that the Aztecs could take back to Tenochtitlan. This plan was cut short when Cortés arrested and bound the emperor's emissaries. The Totonacs demanded that they be sacrificed so they would not tell their emperor, but Cortés secretly released them, telling them to inform Motecuhzoma II that he was their friend.

Finding the prisoners gone, the Totonac chiefs asked Cortés what was to be done—the Aztec armies would surely kill them all. Bernal Díaz writes:

> Cortés replied with a most cheerful smile that he and his brothers who were with him would defend them and kill anyone who tried to harm them; and the caciques [chiefs] and their villages one and all promised to stand by us, to obey any orders we might give them, and to join their forces with ours against Montezuma and all his allies.

The Spaniards and 20 Totonac chiefs signed a treaty, and the Spaniards founded a new town, also named Villa Rica de la Vera Cruz by the little bay on the Gulf. Here they built a church, a market square, houses, and a small fortress. You can still visit this town, now called just Villa Rica. From here, the conquistadors embarked on their expedition against the mighty Aztec empire.

After the Conquest, Quiahuiztlan was gradually abandoned—the diseases carried by their European allies had killed off most of the Totonacs. Its location was forgotten, and it would be centuries before anyone would again enter the ruins of Quiahuiztlan's unconquerable fortress.

ARCHAEOLOGICAL RECORD

Although Quiahuiztlan's existence was known from the accounts of the Spanish Conquest, no one bothered to look for it until the 1890s. An expedition under Don Francisco Paso y Troncoso, the first excavator of Zempoala, visited Villa Rica but failed to find the Totonac fortress. In 1943, José Luis Melgarejo published a work describing the site and tombs on the Cerro de los Metates and identifying it as the Quiahuiztlan of the historical accounts. He performed some exploratory digs at the site, as did José García Payón in the late 1940s, but the first large-scale excavation was carried out by Alfonso Medellín Zenil of Veracruz University in 1951 and 1953.

The site languished for another four decades until the 1980s, when a team from INAH and Veracruz University's Institute of Anthropology began consolidation and restoration work there. Small-scale excavations are continuing.

TOURING THE SITE

You park at the top of the steep access road and then walk up to the site. A path climbs a ridge where you find two tombs and the remains of a Totonac tank for storing water. Although their shapes are different, all Quiahuiztlan tombs follow the same pattern: they look like miniature *talud-tablero* temples with a very short flight of stairs ascending to a tiny one-room sanctuary on top. The bones—usually only the skull and the long bones of the arms and legs—were buried inside the base of the temple.

Below, the site's main terrace contains two temples—the larger is Pyramid 1 and the smaller Pyramid 2—fronting on a small plaza with an altar in the middle. This was the main ceremonial area, probably the spot where Cortés and his lieutenants were met by priests carrying incense burners. Beyond toward the edge of the terrace lies a small ballcourt and the Eastern Cemetery. This is an assemblage of 23 small tombs, most facing south or west.

As you return to the main plaza, to the west stands the Central Cemetery. You first come to a line of four tombs that are the largest and most elaborate on the site. The southernmost is Tomb 1, which is of sufficient size to actually be used as a temple; its top is decorated with a line of seven stylized merlons (an architectural form also found on the battlements of castles). A line of more than 30 smaller tombs runs along the base of the hillside. The west end of this terrace is occupied by a low platform that was probably an elite residence.

DANIELLE GUSTAFSON

Totonac tomb in the form of a miniature temple at Quiahuiztlan

Up on the hillside, you find the South Cemetery, which consists of only four tombs, including one with two small doorways into the miniature sanctuary. The surrounding slopes were occupied by terraces for humbler residences and small agricultural plots.

You can see the bumps of more Mesoamerican mounds on the surrounding hillsides. A path leads to the forbidding summit of the Peñon de Bernal; locals say it takes only 1.5 hours to climb the rock.

ZEMPOALA

INTRODUCTION

At the time of the Conquest, Zempoala (also spelled "Cempoala") was the Totonac capital and the largest city on the Gulf of Mexico, with a population perhaps reaching 30,000. The city was divided into 10 large wards separated by walls that doubled as dikes against the frequent floods of the nearby river. Zempoala was the first large Mesoamerican center visited by Europeans and the place where Cortés made his first important native ally, Xicomecoatl, better known as the "Fat Chief." Unfortunately for visitors, only a small part—the main ceremonial precinct—of the site has been restored and that work was completed (with a little too much concrete) a half-century ago. Nevertheless, it remains a place where history was made: the mingling of European and Native American that is modern Mexico could be said to have begun in Zempoala.

HISTORY

Zempoala lies on the flat coastal plain six kilometers from the Gulf and a little more than a kilometer from the banks of the Río Actopan (also called the Río Chachalacas). Here, the soils are adequate, and the river and nearby Gulf

---

ZEMPOALA

How to get there: Forty kilometers on the coastal road north of Veracruz city (Highway 180), a left turn takes you two kilometers into the town of Zempoala. The ruins lie on the far side of town; you also see mounds rising between the houses.

Hours: Tues.–Sun. 0900–1800.

Admission fee: 14 pesos.

How long to tour: 1.5 hours.

Recommended gear: Hats, sunblock.

Museum: A small, often-closed museum is near the parking area.

contain rich sources of protein in their fish and shellfish. The main danger of this region are the floods that frequently overflow the riverbanks and inundate the town.

The Zempoala area has been occupied at least since the Preclassic; early settlements were built on mounds to protect them from floods. Not much is known about the Preclassic- and Classic-era residents—occupation was probably sporadic—except that they were not the Totonacs who later built Zempoala.

The Totonacs moved onto the coastal plain during the height of the Toltec empire (A.D. 1000–1150). Archaeologists believe the Toltecs had pushed the Totonacs out of their settlements on the eastern slopes of the Sierra Madre Oriental and down to the coast. This was an opportune time for the migration, because the fall of El Tajín left a vacuum in the regional power structure.

Zempoala was founded during the 12th century and early on showed the influence of Cholula, then the dominant central Mexican city-state. A detailed chronology of Late Postclassic Zempoala awaits further exploration. It is clear, however, that over three centuries the settlement grew from a village to a city of 30,000 and gradually shook off the Cholula influence to become more purely Totonac.

In the mid-15th century, Zempoala and many other coastal Veracruz centers were attacked and defeated by the Aztec armies of Motecuhzoma I. They were assessed a heavy tribute in goods and victims for sacrifice; to guarantee their delivery, the Zempoalans were regularly visited by haughty and demanding tax collectors backed up by the all-powerful Aztec army.

By the time Cortés and his forces arrived on the Veracruz coast in 1519, the Totonacs groaned under the Aztec domination. As the Spaniards marched north from their malaria-ridden first camp at San Juan de Ulua, they heard of a town on the way named Zempoala. They sent word of their impending arrival, and they were met on the outskirts by 20 Zempoalan dignitaries. The conquistador Bernal Díaz wrote:

> . . . [They] brought us some cakes of their very finely scented rose-petals. These they presented to Cortés and the horsemen with every sign of friendliness, saying that their lord was awaiting us at our lodgings, since he was too fat and heavy to come out and receive us. Cortés thanked them, and we continued our march; and as we came among the houses we saw how large a town it was, larger than any we had yet seen, and we were full of admiration. It was so green with vegetation that it looked like a garden; and its streets were so full of men and women who had come out to see us that we gave thanks to God for the discovery of such a country.

In the center of town, they met the Fat Chief, Xicomecoatl, who fed them and gave them quarters. After the Totonac presented him numerous gifts, including gold jewelry, Cortés asked how he could repay this hospitality.

On hearing this, wrote Díaz, the fat *cacique* heaved a deep sigh and broke into bitter complaints against the great Montezuma and his governors, saying that the Mexican prince had recently brought him into subjection, had taken away all his golden jewelry, and so grievously oppressed him and his people that they could do nothing except obey him, since he was lord over many cities and countries and ruler over countless vassals and armies of warriors.

Cortés promised to consider the matter and the next day departed for Quiahuiztlan, where the Spaniards and Totonacs forged their momentous alliance against the Aztecs. After a number of adventures in which the Spaniards proved their strength and resolve, they returned to Zempoala. There, the Fat Chief offered them eight Totonac maidens, each a chief's daughter; he did this partially out of fear and partially to ensure that they did not lose the Spaniards as allies.

Cortés said he would accept them only on certain conditions: the Totonacs must destroy their pagan idols and stop the custom of human sacrifice (which Díaz claims took place daily in Zempoala). Further, the maidens must be baptized and Christianity instituted as Zempoala's official religion. The conquistadors then smashed the idols themselves, set up a Christian cross, and instructed the Totonacs in the basics of a Catholic Mass. The next day, the maidens were baptized and parceled out among the Spaniards.

The Totonacs were now bound to the Spaniards' fate. In August of 1519, Cortés and his men set out with 40 Totonac warriors and 200 porters for the Aztec capital of Tenochtitlan. During the next months, they won victory after victory through force and guile and eventually ended up in the heart of Tenochtitlan with Motecuhzoma II, the Aztec emperor, as their hostage. Meanwhile, however, Cortés's old enemy, the Cuban Governor Diego Velásquez, was plotting against him. His lieutenant, Pánfilo Narváez, landed in Zempoala and forced the Fat Chief to hand over Cortés's store of gold. Motecuhzoma heard about this dissension in the Spanish ranks and sent messengers to Narváez to encourage him.

Cortés was forced to launch an immediate counterattack. He left a small force guarding the Aztec emperor and marched with the main body of his troops toward Zempoala. Narváez and his men were camped out in Zempoala's temples. During a heavy rainstorm in the middle of the night, Cortés's force attacked using copper-tipped native lances. They put out Narváez's eye and killed five of his men. After they surrendered, almost all of Narváez's troop asked to be taken over to Cortés's side—the lure of Mesoamerican gold had inflamed them too.

According to Bernal Díaz, one of Narváez's troop had smallpox, and the disease quickly spread among the Zempoalans. After this battle, Zempoala disappeared from accounts of the Conquest. Decades later, Spanish chroniclers said that Zempoala was nearly emptied, no doubt decimated by European illnesses.

ARCHAEOLOGICAL RECORD

Zempoala's location and significance in Mexican history were never forgotten. In the late 19th century, Zempoala was the site of one of the first large-scale—if amateur—excavations in Mesoamerica. The 1891–92 expedition was led by Don Francisco del Paso y Troncoso, who had been trained as a doctor, with the assistance of two Mexican army engineers. The project, called the Scientific Exploratory Commission of Zempoala, identified and cleared all the major structures and produced a complete map of the site delineating the 10 main walled complexes. They then constructed a large wooden model of Zempoala that became part of the Mexico exhibit at the 1892 Madrid exposition. Afterward, the expedition continued working at the site until 1912.

Zempoala's major scientific excavation was led by José García Payón from 1938 through the late 1940s. The focus of his attention was the major temples in the ceremonial center, which he excavated and restored. Most of what you see at the site today is due to his work.

In 1978, INAH began the three-year Veracruz coast project under Jürgen Brüggemann. Its researches filled in many of the gaps in our knowledge about Zempoala; the studies included excavations of the city's complicated hydraulic systems, residential zones, and some of the outlying temples. Since then, no major excavations have been performed.

TOURING THE SITE

You enter the site from the south. The gate takes you into Zempoala's main ceremonial precinct, one of the 10 wards into which the city was divided. This oblong area is bordered on all four sides by a one- to two-meter-high wall that is wide enough to double as a platform. The wall's primary purpose appears to have been as a dike to protect against the frequent floods of the Río Actopan, which flows through the modern village just to the south. Underground, archaeologists found a series of aqueducts that took fresh water from the upper reaches of the river and distributed it through the city.

Take a left at the entrance and head to the Great Pyramid at the southwest corner of this quadrangle. This is a rectangular temple rising in three large tiers to a platform. Dating to the early 16th century, it is probably one of the last structures built in Zempoala. To the south is a small, square raised platform, while to the north rises the Temple of the Wind God. The shape of the latter structure—a circle attached to a rectangle—closely resembles the *yácatas* found at Tzintzúntzan and other Tarascan sites in Michoacan. A circular temple, possibly devoted to the Wind God, stood on top, and its platform was bordered with ornamental merlons (they resemble the battlements along the top of a castle).

The tiny structure immediately south of the staircase was probably a tomb in the style of Quiahuiztlan.

Just to the north of this structure, a wide staircase crosses over the precinct wall like a stile. This is the clue that led researchers to believe that the walls' primary purpose was dikes. If they were not meant to block water, the access to the precincts would have been through gates.

Next, you cut across the plaza to the Great Temple in the north center of the quadrangle. This was probably Zempoala's most important temple. It is also one of the oldest; archaeologists found three earlier construction stages under the topmost. The structure rises in 13 tiers to the large platform on top. This was the base of a long structure, now gone, with two square columns at the entrance and four rooms inside. Cortés's enemy Pánfilo Narváez made this his headquarters on the rainy night that he was blinded and defeated. From here, you have an excellent view of the ceremonial precinct and further temples in the surrounding fields. A small rectangular temple and a square altar occupy the plaza in front of the Great Temple's staircase.

Immediately east of the Great Temple stands the structure called the Temple of the Chimneys. A long, low, L-shaped platform extends from this building to the north and south. In front of the temple's main staircase lies a rectangular platform with the remains of four columns inside a ruined structure. These columns had wooden centers; when the wood deteriorated, the stone columns resembled chimneys, from which the complex takes its name. Atop the staircase, you find the remains of a two-room temple. In the plaza just southwest of the Temple of the Chimneys lies a unique altarlike enclosure bordered by a low wall with merlons running along the top; its use is unknown. Inside, archaeologists found the remains of a tomb and stone sculptures in the shape of dogs.

DANIELLE GUSTAFSON

ceremonial altars in Zempoala's main plaza

These are the major sights of the ceremonial precinct. Beyond this area, however, are dozens of temples. Paths into the sugarcane fields to the north and east lead into secondary precincts containing numerous structures, some of which have been restored. The so-called Temple of Charity standing about 200 meters to the east is a two-tier structure decorated with fragments of stucco reliefs. It is named for the hundreds of stucco skulls that once adorned the facade of a small structure at the base of the temple's staircase—archaeologists believe this complex was dedicated to the god of death.

More, largely unexcavated, mounds lie among the houses of Zempoala town. Some of the humbler structures here are built in the same style—thatched roof and wood and adobe walls—as the residences of the pre-Hispanic proletariat.

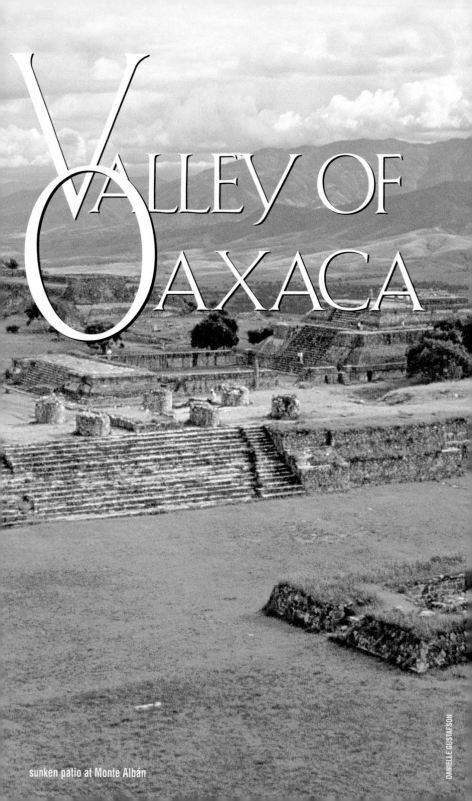

Valley of Oaxaca

sunken patio at Monte Albán

D ry and relatively isolated from the rest of Mexico by mountainous terrain, the Valley of Oaxaca has produced one of Mesoamerica's earliest civilizations: the Zapotecs. This group developed possibly the first calendar and writing systems and built complex urban areas when most Mesoamericans were living in villages. During the Postclassic era, the Zapotecs were joined in the valley by the Mixtecs, who built elaborate fortified settlements in the valley and transcribed their history in beautiful codices.

The descendants of the Zapotecs and the Mixtecs still inhabit the valley today; their traditional ways have ensured the preservation of many pre-Hispanic practices (dances, foods)—Oaxaca is one of Mexico's richest areas for the production of folk art. The city of Oaxaca and the surrounding valley are also one of the most popular tourist destinations in interior Mexico, with excellent hotels and other services.

THE LAND

The jagged ridges of Cortés's crumpled sheet of paper are a perfect description of Oaxaca, one of Mexico's most rugged regions, with mountains rising to 3,000 meters. In the center of the state lies the Y-shaped Valley of Oaxaca at an elevation of about 1,500 meters. The valley is made of three arms: the Etla subvalley in the north, Tlacolula in the east, and, to the south, Valle Grande. The Río Atoyac flows south through the Etla and Valle Grande subvalleys and eventually empties into the Pacific. The Tlacolula subvalley is formed by the Río Salado, which meets the Atoyac just south of Oaxaca City.

Covering 2,000 square kilometers, the Valley of Oaxaca is by far the largest area of arable land in the state. The valley floor also possesses rich soil that can sustain intensive agriculture—a primary reason for the early growth of civilization

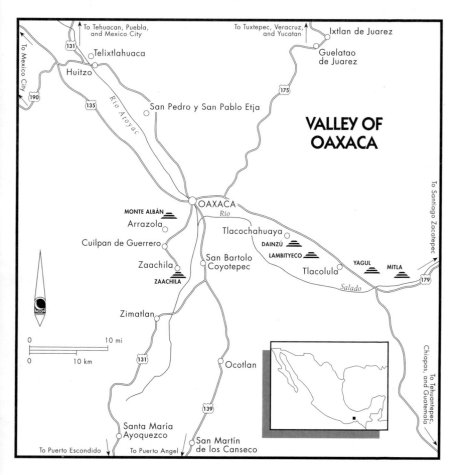

in the region. The steep walls that surround the valley also protect its inhabitants from marauding aliens—either nomads or armies from competing cultures. This combination of protection and rich resources allowed valley residents to develop an advanced civilization that shows little sign of outside influence.

In Oaxaca city, vendors in the amazing series of markets just south of the main plaza sell many pre-Columbian specialties, including grasshoppers, chocolate, and huge mounds of mole.

Climate

The Valley of Oaxaca's climate is classified as temperate but arid. Afternoon showers fall between May and September, but this is not enough to make up for the loss of moisture through evaporation that occurs during the year. From October through April the skies are generally cloudless with cool nights and warm days (hot days in April). This aridity makes terrestrial sources of water—rivers and

OAXACA HOTELS

The colonial city of Oaxaca makes a perfect base from which to explore the valley's various archaeological sites. Among its many hotels, you can stay at the moderate **Hotel Marqués del Valle,** Portal de Calveria s/n, tel. 951/6-3677, fax 6-9961, on the main plaza; credit cards accepted. Or bask in the comfort of the **Hotel Misión de Los Angeles,** on Calz. Porfirio Díaz 102 on a hill to the north of town, tel. 951/5-1500, fax 5-1680. It offers 152 rooms, several restaurants, a swimming pool, and two tennis courts; credit cards accepted.

springs—crucial for sustaining life. Luckily, the valley is blessed with at least one year-round resource: the Río Atoyac. All the earliest valley settlements are clustered along its banks.

Flora and Fauna

Oaxaca's flora depends on water. During the long dry season, the valley is dusty and brown from dry leaves and sunburnt vegetation. Part of the reason for this may be the success of the valley's human occupants. Millennia ago, they chopped down the forests of pine, oak, and madroño that filled the valley, releasing into the air all the moisture conserved by the roots.

Today the valley floor is almost all farmland; farmers grow maize, beans, squash, and agave for manufacturing mezcal. In isolated places you still may see patches of mesquite and acacia forest. The hillsides are covered with a scrub forest of thorn and cacti. As the elevation rises, the forests turn to oak, pine, manzanita, and madroño; the mountaintops are covered with pine.

The valley's earliest inhabitants were hunters who chased antelope, deer, and jackrabbits. The antelope are now confined to the High Plains of North America, but deer and rabbits may still be found along with raccoons, peccaries, opossums, lizards, quail, and doves. Almost all of these are confined to the remote hills; human habitation is too dense and too adept at hunting for them to succeed on the valley floor.

DANIELLE GUSTAFSON

Mixtec skull inlaid with turquoise and shell from Monte Albán's Tomb 8, now in the Museo Regional de Oaxaca.

HISTORY

Ten thousand years ago, small groups of hunters moved through the forests that filled the Valley of Oaxaca searching for game. Judging by the refuse piles they left, they were most successful at killing rabbits. Archaeologists found these remains and some spear points in a series of caves in the hills near Mitla and in an open air campsite down by the Río Mitla. Early hunters also foraged for fruits and berries but pickings must have been slim: none of these camps was a year-round settlement.

The first plant domesticated by the early Oaxacans was the bottle gourd, a variety of cucurbit grown to be used as utensils. New tests indicate these may have been cultivated as long ago as 8000 B.C., making them the earliest domesticated plant in Mesoamerica. By 5000–3500 B.C., the inhabitants of these sites had also begun to cultivate beans and maize. They may have learned their skills from the nearby Tehuacan Valley, where the oldest cobs of corn have been found.

Agricultural techniques grew more sophisticated over the next millennia, and the valley's human population expanded and spread out. By 2000 B.C., the Etla subvalley north of Oaxaca City had become the center of human settlement. Here the early residents found abundant water, rich soils, and a trade route north to the Tehuacan Valley. The largest village here was San José Mogote, which for the next 1,500 years was the dominant force in the valley.

In the era between 1400 and 1150 B.C., San José Mogote covered seven hectares and possessed a small ceremonial center. The latter is evidence of incipient social stratification; burials, however, were still simple, being placed beneath house floors with spartan offerings. Intensive agriculture in the region's rich soils was the main source of food, but the early residents also hunted deer and peccary. The Etla subvalley was home to eight other settlements, while Valle Grande had four and the Tlacolula region only one.

Shortly after 1150 B.C., the region's social life underwent dramatic changes. A ceremonial platform was constructed in San José Mogote, and there is evidence

OAXACA MUSEUMS

Five blocks north of the mall on Calle Macedonio Alcalá in Oaxaca, the **Museo Regional de Oaxaca**, tel. 951/6-2991, housed in the former Convent of Santo Domingo, is a must for archaeological tourists; it houses the treasures of Monte Albán's Tomb 7 and many other beautiful Zapotec and Mixtec pieces. It's open Tues.–Sun. 1000–1800. The

Museo Rufino Tamayo, Av. Morelos 503, tel. 951/6-4750, also has a good collection of pre-Columbian ceramics collected by artist Rufino Tamayo (1899–1991), known for his desire to preserve and bring Mexican art to his countrymen. It's open Monday and Wed.–Sat. 1000–1400 and 1600–1900, Sunday 1000–1500.

RUINS TOURS

Numerous downtown travel agencies organize tours to visit the surrounding ruins; try the ones in the Hotel Marqués del Valle, Portal de Calveria s/n, tel. 951/6-3677, fax 6-9961, or in the Hotel Mesón del Ángel at Mina 518, tel. 951/6-6666.

of an elite priestly class who were buried with elaborate offerings. These offerings contain symbolic markings that some archaeologists see as evidence of connection to the Olmec region of the Gulf Coast; other researchers believe the symbols are part of a homegrown religious system based on Earth and sky spirits. During the next three centuries, the number of valley settlements doubled to 40 and the population tripled to 2,000, half of it in San José Mogote. In 850 B.C., the latter settlement covered 20 hectares around a large temple-platform.

Between 850 and 600 B.C., San José Mogote began to acquire rivals, including the neighboring settlement of Huitzo and Yagul in Tlacolula and Tilcajete in Valle Grande. Archaeologists believe that this was an era of struggle in the valley. The southern end of the Etla subvalley was depopulated, perhaps to make it a buffer zone against Tlacolula and Valle Grande. Some of the new settlements such as Yagul were not valley farming villages but fortified villages up on the hillsides. At San José Mogote, archaeologists found a stone bas-relief (Monument 3) depicting a naked man sprawling in a contorted pose distinctly reminiscent of the Danzantes (Dancers) at Monte Albán. They believe that he is a captive sacrificed after the defeat of an enemy city. Between his feet is a

DANIELLE GUSTAFSON

The stone mosaics of the Column Group at Mitla are the most sophisticated found in Mesoamerica. The patterns may indicate the clan of the high priest.

calendar glyph, the earliest example of Zapotec writing and one of the earliest found in Mexico.

At its height, San José Mogote was a large village with a population of 1,000, elite residences, and a civic-religious area built on a hilltop in the center of town. By 600 B.C., this had all come crashing down: San José Mogote was abandoned for unknown reasons. Shortly thereafter, a hilltop in that no-man's-land at the south end of the Etla subvalley became the site of the region's largest and most sophisticated settlement: Monte Albán.

MONTE ALBÁN

INTRODUCTION

Monte Albán's hilltop setting strategically commands the Valley of Oaxaca. For more than a millennium, the Zapotec people ruled the entire region from this fortified city. After the Zapotec collapse, the city was used as a necropolis by Mixtec rulers; the jade and gold treasures of Tomb 7 are one of the great discoveries of Mexican archaeology. Today, Monte Albán is one of Mexico's most popular archaeological sites, drawing throngs to the ruins and the breathtaking views over the valley.

Monte Albán's importance lies not only in its beauty and endurance. It is also one of the primal sites of Mesoamerican culture, where early forms of many of its core attributes—writing systems, calendars, religious beliefs, and types of architecture—were brought to a new, higher level. Because of the site's dry climate and long record of archaeological preservation, many of these attributes are clearly visible today—a boon to both tourists and researchers.

BOB RACE

HISTORY

At the south end of the Etla subvalley stands an arid hill rising 400 meters off the valley floor. For most of the Preclassic, human habitation bypassed this hilltop in favor of settlements such as San José Mogote, built on the rich lands down by the Río Atoyac. Around A.D. 500, however, San José Mogote was abandoned, and an unknown group of Zapotecs (probably from more than one settlement) climbed to the barren hilltop and made it their capital.

Only a tiny fraction of today's site contains remnants of the Monte Albán I

MONTE ALBÁN

How to get there: These famous ruins stand on the hilltop about seven kilometers west of Oaxaca city's main plaza. The Hotel Mesón del Ángel, Mina 518, tel. 951/6-6666, runs frequent buses up to the site. You can also drive there by taking the road west across the Río Atoyac at the south end of the city and heading left at the fork.

Hours: Daily 0800-1800.

Admission fee: 20 pesos.

How long to tour: Three hours.

Recommended gear: Hats, sunblock, sturdy shoes or sneakers, bottled water.

Museum: The new museum stands just above the parking lot. Inside you find bathrooms, a gift shop, and much-needed shade. The collection includes some of the better Danzante stones, representing sacrificed captives, and a number of later stelae depicting deified rulers and other scenes accompanied by long but as-yet-untranslated hieroglyphic inscriptions.

---

era (500–100 B.C.). Although some early structures have been found beneath the North Platform, most lie at the southwest corner of the Main Plaza. Here, the east wall of Building L was faced with more than 300 bas-relief carvings known as the Danzantes (Dancers). These depict naked men in contorted postures that some see as representing dancing or swimming. Current archaeological thought, however, now believes that these sculptures show the naked, mutilated corpses of defeated enemies. Much like Monument 3 from San José Mogote, these stones boast of Monte Albán's military prowess. Glyphs on the stone give the names of the dead men; researchers assume that Monte Albán now had domination over their settlements. War and tribute were probably the basis for the Monte Albán economy, as in most other Mesoamerican urban centers.

Within a century, the population had jumped to more than 5,000, and by the end of Monte Albán I it totaled more than 17,000, a third of the valley's estimated 50,000 inhabitants. Aside from a few constructions in the ceremonial center, most Monte Albán I structures were immediately practical: terraces for houses and farming, irrigation canals and defensive walls on the hill's northwest and southeast slopes. After 100 B.C., however, Monte Albán had achieved enough stability to begin a more ambitious building program.

During the Monte Albán II era (100 B.C.–A.D. 200), the city's residents laid out the Main Plaza, which was paved with white stucco, and built early stages of the North Platform. In the center of the plaza stood a rock outcropping which became the site of Buildings G, H, I, and the arrowhead-shaped Building J. The latter structure was one of the first in Mesoamerica with a clear astronomical orientation (another sign of the Zapotecs' advanced development) and was decorated with stone plaques depicting defeated cities. Archaeologists believe many of the latter refer to cities outside the Valley of Oaxaca, reaching almost as far as the Tehuacan Valley, the Pacific Coast, and the border with Chiapas. The Zapotec state was now an empire with contacts to the rest of Mesoamerica.

Structures back at Monte Albán reflect this new status. A ballcourt and palace-type residences were built beside the Main Plaza. When they died, the Monte Albán elite were not buried in spartan tombs anymore but in elaborate multichamber mausolea decorated with murals and filled with offerings. These offerings contain ceramic evidence of trade ties with the natives of Chiapa de Corzo in Chiapas and with the rapidly growing city of Teotihuacan to the north. Monte Albán's leaders must have been content: they were rich and, because of their protected setting, they faced no outside threats. The horizon was clear for Zapotec civilization.

The next 500 years were Monte Albán's golden age. During the Monte Albán III era (A.D. 100–600), the city grew to cover 6.5 square kilometers and had a population of around 25,000. The hillside below the ceremonial center was covered with more than 2,000 terraces for houses and farm plots, and the valley below held an estimated population of 100,000. Most of the Monte Albán you see today dates from this era. The main constructions were the North and South Platforms and the line of temples and residences along the east side of the Main Plaza.

The Zapotec characteristics that had been established in earlier centuries continued, only with greater sophistication. Tombs and palaces were even more elaborate. Defeated captives remained part of the subject matter of stone sculptures; the inscriptions were far longer, however, and the carving style was more intricate and stylized. Sculptures also depicted deified rulers and historical events. Among the latter was a series of panels on the South Platform that commemorated the visit of nobles from Teotihuacan. Trade between the two cities

Monte Albán's main plaza, with arrowhead-shaped Building J, probably an observatory, in the foreground

DANIELLE GUSTAFSON

was well-established: one of Teotihuacan's wards was settled by Zapotec artisans probably from Monte Albán.

Monte Albán's heyday ended after A.D. 600 for reasons that are still unclear. Like Teotihuacan, the city was gradually abandoned during the Monte Albán IIIb-IV period (A.D. 600–1250) while other peoples moved in to fill the vacuum. This poorly defined era is the subject of intense debate; archaeologists do not even agree on its length. They do seem to agree that as Monte Albán waned, other Valley of Oaxaca Zapotec centers such as Jalieza, Zaachila, Lambityeco, and Mitla grew in power. Between A.D. 700 and 950, the Mixtecs descended from their mountainous valleys to the north and west and settled in the Etla subvalley. What had been the great Zapotec empire became a series of small states built around fortified cities.

During the Monte Albán V era (A.D. 1250–1520), the Mixtecs, who had married into the elite Zapotec lineages, controlled the remains of Monte Albán. Mixtec rulers emptied some of the old Zapotec tombs and buried their own elite in them. The famous treasures of Tomb 7 are Mixtec rather than Zapotec. Monte Albán was still occupied—its population was between 4,000 and 8,000—but the Main Plaza and the surrounding ceremonial area were totally abandoned. Some ritual practices probably continued here, however. When the Spanish built the city of Oaxaca just east of Monte Albán's hill, the hilltop was abandoned for good. Today, the slums of Oaxaca City are now climbing the east slopes of the hill. The ruins of Monte Albán have been declared a protected area to defend it against encroaching urbanization.

ARCHAEOLOGICAL RECORD

For the four centuries after the Conquest, Monte Albán competed with Mitla, supposed site of a vast treasure, for the attentions of historians and explorers. The 17th-century priest Francisco de Burgoa wrote a complete history of Oaxaca region that included a substantial section on Zapotec and Mixtec history and religion and a brief mention of Monte Albán. Guillermo Dupaix visited Monte Albán in 1806 and included paintings of the Main Plaza in his book on Mexico's antiquities. Eduard Seler, William H. Holmes, and Leopoldo Batres all explored the site but remained far more interested in Mitla.

Finally, in 1931 the great Mexican archaeologist Alfonso Caso, who had previously made a study of Zapotec sculptures, began the first of 18 seasons excavating at Monte Albán. One year later, he discovered the treasure of Tomb 7, and Monte Albán suddenly overtook Mitla as the site that captured the most scholarly interest. He was assisted by Jorge Acosta and later Ignacio Bernal, both of whom went on to become giants in the field. This team excavated the Main Plaza, discovered 172 tombs, and established the first chronology for the Valley of Oaxaca. Their work remains a benchmark of excellence in Mexican archaeology.

In 1964, Kent Flannery began the Human Ecology Project to study the development of early agriculture and village life into urban civilization. In 1971, he convinced Richard Blanton to begin the Settlement Pattern Project to determine the rise and fall of villages, towns, and cities in the valley and the surrounding region. Both these projects, which included the Monte Albán area, helped position the site in the larger context of regional and chronological development.

Smaller-scale excavations continued around Monte Albán. In 1974, Marcus Winter dug residential terraces on the hillside below. INAH excavations in 1975 and the late 1980s explored the Adoratorio on the east side of the Main Plaza and parts of the North and South Platforms.

Between 1992 and 1994, Marcus Winter directed the Monte Albán Special Project that excavated and consolidated much of the North Platform and part of the South Platform. They also rebuilt the museum and many of the structures, including tombs, on the north end of the site and around the parking lot.

As always, much work remains, especially on the South Platform. One hopes that further studies will answer the many questions, such as what happened in Postclassic Monte Albán, that are now the subject of contentious debate. Nevertheless, Monte Albán is one of the most thoroughly excavated sites in Mexico with much to offer the visitor.

TOURING THE SITE

Just beyond the parking lot, a path from the museum leads to the hilltop. On the right stands a statue of Alfonso Caso, the Mexican archaeologist who led the most important excavations of Monte Albán. The local workers frequently place a cigarette in his hand—smoking was one of his favorite pastimes. The path enters the Main Plaza from the northeast, by the side of the North Platform.

The first structure you come to is the I-shaped Main Ballcourt measuring 41 by 24 meters. This appears never to have had ballcourt rings. Atop the plaza-side sloping wall you see a stone sculpture that may represent a grasshopper. The ballcourt dates to the Monte Albán II era (100 B.C.–A.D. 200); a nearly identical court from the same period has been found at San José Mogote, leading researchers to believe that this was the standardized size for an official game.

Across the path from this structure, on the southeast corner of the North Platform you see a doorway with a carved lintel and, on the inside of the jambs, a relief depicting a figure. After the ballcourt, you arrive at Building II, a temple-platform topped with two sets of five pillars that were apparently left open to the wind. A tunnel begins on the south side of this platform and leads to the line of structures running along the center of the plaza. Priests may have used this so they could perform ritual functions without being seen.

This building faces the Main Plaza, one of the largest in Mesoamerica, measuring 300 meters by 200 meters. It was originally covered with white stucco on

DANIELLE GUSTAFSON

Monte Albán ballcourt

top of a stone slab pavement. The next structure along the east side of the plaza is Building P, another temple-platform. This faces the Adoratorio, also called the Sunken Patio, a square sunken altar that dates to the Mixtec Monte Albán V period. A burial discovered between the Adoratorio and Building P contained five adult skeletons covered with a profuse array of jewelry. The most spectacular piece in this trove was the famous bat mask pectoral piece crafted from jade (now in the Mexico City Museo Nacional de Antropología).

The adjacent structure is the Palace, also called Building S, which possesses the same type of base as the previous temple-platforms. On top, however, you find about 12 rooms built around a patio; they almost certainly formed an elite residence. Next, on the plaza's southeast corner, you come to Mound Q, an unexcavated IIIb-IV period temple-platform that had a small temple on top.

The south side of the plaza is dominated by the massive South Platform, on top of which stand two smaller pyramids. The architects of Monte Albán liked to reuse stelae and other stone pieces from earlier stages. During the IIIb-IV reconstruction of the South Platform, they placed early period III stelae on the northeast and northwest corners of the base. Stelae 1 through 4 on the northeast corner show scenes of enthroned rulers, captives, and defeated cities; on their sides—hidden—were a series of panels depicting the visit of Teotihuacan nobles to Monte Albán. Offering caches of jade and beads—the same type as found in Teotihuacan—were discovered beneath the stelae.

You reach the next level of the South Platform by ascending a 40-meter-wide staircase (Danzantes were reused to the right of the staircase). Here you find the large Mound III, which has been partially excavated, and a smaller unnamed

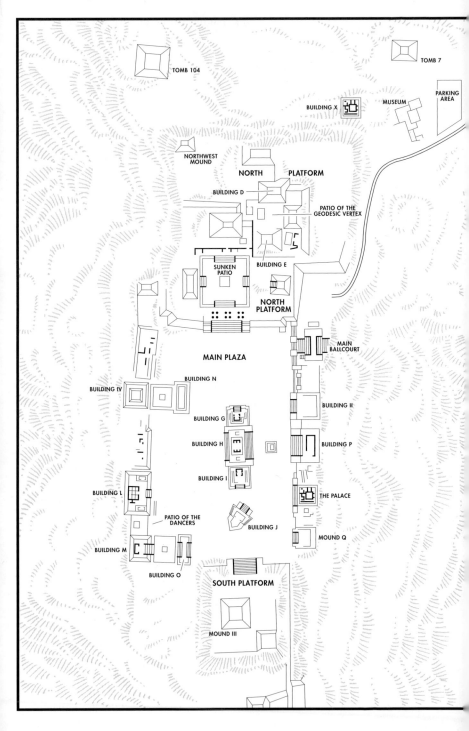

TOMB 104

TOMB 7

PARKING AREA

BUILDING X

MUSEUM

NORTHWEST MOUND

NORTH PLATFORM

BUILDING D

PATIO OF THE GEODESIC VERTEX

SUNKEN PATIO

BUILDING E

NORTH PLATFORM

MAIN PLAZA

MAIN BALLCOURT

BUILDING N

BUILDING IV

BUILDING II

BUILDING G

BUILDING H

BUILDING P

BUILDING I

BUILDING L

THE PALACE

PATIO OF THE DANCERS

BUILDING J

BUILDING M

MOUND Q

BUILDING O

SOUTH PLATFORM

MOUND III

To Oaxaca

TOMB 105

MONTE ALBÁN

0   100 yds

0   100 m

mound to the left. This is one of the best sites for views of the valley to the south and, in the opposite direction, over the Main Plaza. To the south and west of this platform stand a series of smaller mounds that are being excavated now; these include Building 7 Deer (named for a calendric glyph found here), which is a group of four buildings around a small plaza 250 meters south of the South Platform. You can also see the remains of terraces descending the ridge beyond.

On the northwest corner of the plaza stands the temple-patio-temple group known as System M. First you come to the rectangular platform of Building 0, which forms the west side of a patio containing a sunken altar. On the east side stands Building M, a larger temple-platform that had another temple on top.

Building M also forms the south wall of the Patio of the Dancers, home to Monte Albán's most famous sculptures. The west wall of this patio, which was originally buried under Building L just to the north, is one of Monte Albán's oldest structures. The wall was set with hundreds of relief panels that depict naked men in contorted postures, thus the name Danzantes (Dancers). Archaeologists now believe these represent sacrificed captives; scrolls radiating from their genital areas symbolize the flow of blood after mutilation. The reliefs were set in four layers, with the largest vertical carvings at the lowest level, followed by a row of narrow horizontal reliefs. Next come a row of smaller vertical carvings topped by the final series of horizontal reliefs. Some of the horizontal Danzantes were reused to form the steps of Building L. Many of

relief panels showing Danzantes

DANIELLE GUSTAFSON

the Danzantes here are reproductions; the originals were removed for their protection. The top of Building L, dating to period IIIb-IV, contains a small residential complex; further palace areas lie in Area L, the unexcavated mound just to the north.

This is a good time to explore the row of four structures running up the center of the plaza. They are built on a spine of rock that was apparently too difficult to demolish during the plaza's construction. The first, at the southern end of the row, is the amazing arrowhead-shaped Building J. This was the only Monte Albán structure built off the main north-south axis of the site; the main staircase faces northeast, while the point of the arrowhead faces opposite. It almost certainly has an astronomical alignment, probably with the bright star Capella. The tunnels that perforate the structure were made during excavation.

The walls around Building J's base are decorated with more than 40 period II stone reliefs that show glyphic representations of hills with a sign—a rabbit head, for example—that identifies the place (Hill of the Rabbit). Archaeologists believe each hill corresponds to a defeated settlement; some reliefs also include an inverted human head with closed eyes—the dead enemy chief. Most of these settlements likely correspond to small states in the rugged hills and valleys of the surrounding region.

North of Building J runs the complex of Buildings G, H, and I, which may have been considered one structure. It was begun in period II; what you see today dates to period IIIb-IV. The complex probably acted as a great altar, with the central Building H the focus of ritual activity and Building I to the south and the northern Building G acting as annexes. An offering cache containing shell, bone, and two mosaic masks was found buried within Building I.

From Building G now head back to the west side of the plaza. Here you find the temple-patio-temple complex called System IV, a near-exact replica of System M. Building N juts into the plaza, followed by the patio and Building IV (also called Building K) rising to the west. To the north of the patio stands a poor-quality period II stela on which you can make out some date glyphs.

Archaeologists' tunnels penetrate the north side of Building IV. Inside (bring a flashlight) you can see the large slabs that faced the earlier period II temple. A low platform that has been only partially excavated lies to the north of Building IV. The earliest section dates to period I, while the residential complex on top may be IIIb-IV.

On the north side of the Main Plaza, a wide staircase acts as the grand entrance to the North Platform, a far larger and more complicated structure than the South Platform. Another poorly preserved stela stands in the plaza at the foot of the steps. On top of the stairs, you pass through two rows of six columns and see before you the large Sunken Patio measuring 50 meters to the side. The square patio is lined with staircases on each side and an altar rises in the middle. The latest stages of many of this area's structures date to the Monte Albán V, or Mixtec, period, including the altar and Building B just to the west of the patio. Somewhat set back from the east side of the patio stands the reconstructed Building A, while Mound I-Romano occupies the north side.

Just east of the latter mound, a staircase takes you up to the Patio of the Geodesic Vertex, the second large temple grouping atop the North Platform. Atop the stairs stands a small temple containing two columns; a stela representing the "God of the Wide Beaked Bird" was found here. The temple complex here takes its name from the modern survey marker that indicated the highest point on the hill. This was the Building of the Geodesic Vertex that rises to the east of the patio. The north side of the patio is occupied by Building D, while opposite lies Building E. Halfway up Building E's staircase stands a reproduction of a stela depicting five figures, perhaps in a change of power ritual.

The north side of the North Platform is occupied by the North Mound behind Building D and, to the west, the Northwest Mound. Just beyond the latter structure at the foot of the North Platform lies another residential complex, which covers Tomb 104, one of the gems of Zapotec art. A hatchway in the middle of the patio leads you down to the tomb's antechamber. The facade over the low doorway contains a niche in which sits a ceramic sculpture probably representing the dead man dressed in the costume of a god.

Beyond the glyph-covered door stone is the main chamber of the tomb. Here the dead man lay, with another funerary sculpture at his feet and dozens of pottery vessels stashed in five niches along the walls. The walls were decorated with bright murals depicting gods and royal personages (perhaps ancestors) accompanied with date glyphs. You may see the original skeleton and offerings in a reconstructed tomb chamber in the Oaxaca room of Mexico City's Museo Nacional de Antropología. Further burial chambers, including Tombs 103 and 172, were found in the residential complex just to the west. This part of the ancient city may have doubled as a necropolis.

A path takes you along the north side of the North Platform and ends at Building X just above the museum. Some archaeologists see the influence of Teotihuacan in this two-room period-II temple. A basin built into the floor may have caught blood from sacrifices.

This is probably a good time to have a soda and rest in the shade. The only remaining sights are around the parking lot. Just to the north, in the middle of another residential complex lies the entrance to Tomb 7, a construction of the IIIb-IV period. All the treasures and skeletons—Mixtec replacements of the original Zapotec contents—have been removed to the history museum down in the city of Oaxaca. Through a gate you can see the main chamber; no murals decorate its walls.

East of the parking lot lies the I-shaped Small Ballcourt and, on a small rise, the entrance to Tomb 105 amid the ruins of another residence. The walls of the cruciform chamber are covered with murals depicting a procession of nine men and women who may represent Zapotec rulers and their consorts. Unfortunately, the tomb is closed at this writing to protect the murals from deterioration.

MITLA

INTRODUCTION

At the eastern end of the Valley of Oaxaca, the Zapotec site of Mitla is one of the gems of Mesoamerican architecture. The quality of its stonework is rivaled only by the Nunnery at Uxmal. Mitla's stone mosaics are worked into elaborate step-and-fret patterns that cover entire walls. The main buildings are five palace or civic-ceremonial groups built around large patios. The site has barely been excavated, but luckily the ruins are in a good state of repair and were expertly restored in the early part of the century. Ancient Mitla is set among the houses of the modern town, where you can visit an excellent museum of Zapotec pottery and buy bottles of the local specialty, the firewater called mescal.

HISTORY

Mitla has never been thoroughly excavated, so the details of its chronology remain vague. The cliffs to the north and west were the site of some of the earliest settlements in the Valley of Oaxaca, dating to as early as the Late Pleistocene (circa 8000 B.C.). The eastern end of the Tlacolula subvalley is narrow, relatively high (1,688 meters), dry, and subject to occasional frosts; the water supply comes from Río Mitla, which carved out the valley. Early residents were willing to brave the poor agricultural prospects, because the nearby cliffs were made of soft, easily worked stone and contained veins of harder flint that could be chipped into tools. Hunters used these tools to hunt and skin deer and rabbits. They also dined on mesquite pods, prickly pear fruit, and wild berries.

MITLA

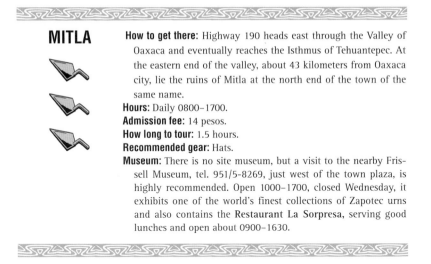

How to get there: Highway 190 heads east through the Valley of Oaxaca and eventually reaches the Isthmus of Tehuantepec. At the eastern end of the valley, about 43 kilometers from Oaxaca city, lie the ruins of Mitla at the north end of the town of the same name.

Hours: Daily 0800–1700.

Admission fee: 14 pesos.

How long to tour: 1.5 hours.

Recommended gear: Hats.

Museum: There is no site museum, but a visit to the nearby Frissell Museum, tel. 951/5-8269, just west of the town plaza, is highly recommended. Open 1000–1700, closed Wednesday, it exhibits one of the world's finest collections of Zapotec urns and also contains the **Restaurant La Sorpresa**, serving good lunches and open about 0900–1630.

The first permanent settlement in Mitla dates to the Early Preclassic (1800–1200 B.C.) and numbered fewer than 12 households. By the late Monte Albán I period (200 B.C.), Mitla's population measured in the hundreds and the town stretched for a kilometer along the south bank of the Río Mitla. The large settlement called Yegüih, of which Lambityeco is a part, dominated the Tlacolula subvalley during this era. Two hundred years later, Mitla erected the civic-ceremonial center now called the South Group and house terraces ex-

DANIELLE GUSTAFSON

the Hall of Columns, antechamber to the high priest's residence

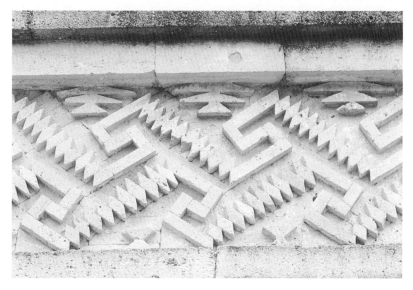

DANIELLE GUSTAFSON

Column Group stone mosaic designs

tended across the north bank of the river. Mitla declined during the Classic-era ascendancy of Monte Albán; that city may have centralized all the valley's resources.

Mitla began to grow again as Monte Albán was gradually abandoned during the IIIb-IV period (A.D. 600–1250). After 1250, Mitla reached its apogee: the Zapotecs built the four building complexes—the Church Group, Column Group, Adobe Group, and Arroyo Group—on the north side of the Mitla river. The town's population rose to 10,000—as large as modern Mitla—stretching for kilometers along both banks of the river. Above rose agricultural terraces and four hilltop fortresses where the population could gather during attacks.

Mitla during this era has been described as the "Vatican of the Zapotecs." The Column Group was the home of the high priest, to whom the Zapotec rulers, then based in Zaachila, had to make regular pilgrimages. Beneath the palaces and temples were supposedly magnificent, treasure-filled tombs for the priests, rulers, and high-status sacrificial victims. Tombs have been found but not the treasures.

Mitla and the rest of the Late Postclassic (A.D. 1250–1520) Valley of Oaxaca have been the subject of intense debate as to whether the region's rulers were Mixtec or Zapotec. The Mixtecs had moved into the valley after the Monte Albán collapse and had married into a number of aristocratic Zapotec lineages, particularly in the Etla subvalley. Now-faded Mixtec murals decorate some of Mitla's walls. By the end of the Late Postclassic, however, many of the Mixtecs had left the valley in search of more peaceable areas to the south. Archaeologists now believe that most of the valley was always controlled by Zapotec rulers who nevertheless had extensive ties to the Mixtec aristocracy by marriage and/or descent. Mitla, then, was Zapotec with a modest Mixtec influence.

Part of the reason for the Mixtec departure was the arrival of Aztec armies in the Mixteca, first under the A.D. 1440–69 rule of Motecuhzoma I. By the late 1480s, the Aztec emperor Ahuizotl had ordered his army into the Valley of Oaxaca itself, where it defeated a Zapotec army at a fortress called Huitzo. In A.D. 1494, they attacked again and sacked Mitla and the Zapotec capital of Zaachila. Aztec and Zapotec-Mixtec armies met again the following year at the fort city of Guiengola on the Isthmus of Tehuantepec (close to Juchitan on Chiapas's Pacific Coast). This time the Zapotecs won; afterward the Aztecs agreed to a treaty and the consummation of a marriage between Aztec and Zapotec lineages. The Zapotec rulers still did not feel safe and moved their capital to the Isthmus of Tehuantepec.

At the time of the Conquest, Mitla and the other Valley of Oaxaca cities had fallen under Aztec domination and paid tribute to Motecuhzoma II. Mitla's palaces and temples remained occupied by Zapotec priests and rulers into the late 16th century.

Today modern Mitla has achieved some measure of prosperity from the tourism and mescal industries. Ancient Zapotec rituals are still performed alongside Catholic ceremonies in the chapel that forms part of the Church Group.

ARCHAEOLOGICAL RECORD

Since the arrival of the Spaniards, Mitla's intricate stone palaces have fascinated historian and treasure-seeker alike. Many of the stories (and perhaps myths) about Mitla were first written down in the 1580 *Relación de Tlacolula y Mitla* by Alonso de Canseco. De Canseco relied on native informants who still lived in the Zapotec city and practiced "pagan" rites; unfortunately, he embellished his account to emphasize bloody sacrifices and hidden treasures. His text became the prime source for the waves of adventurers who visited the ruins during the following 350 years.

Mitla was especially publicized by Guillermo Dupaix, who some 30 years after his travels published his 1834 book on Mexico's antiquities, and by the German explorer Alexander von Humboldt (who never actually visited the site). During the rest of the 19th century, Mitla far outranked Monte Albán in popularity, drawing Désiré Charnay, Viollet-le-Duc, and William Holmes (his map is still used today) among others. Eduard Seler produced probably the most important work of this era; his study of Mitla's murals documented many details that have now disappeared with the passage of time.

In 1901, the pioneer Mexican archaeologist Leopoldo Batres performed some small-scale excavations at the site and restored the Column Group, including many of the mosaics. Mitla's main excavations took place in 1934 and 1935

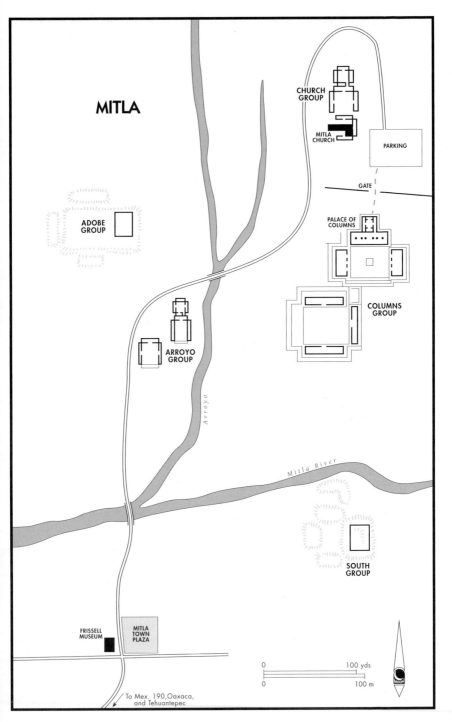

MITLA

CHURCH
GROUP

MITLA
CHURCH

PARKING

GATE

PALACE OF
COLUMNS

ADOBE
GROUP

COLUMNS
GROUP

ARROYO
GROUP

Arroyo

Mitla River

SOUTH
GROUP

FRISSELL
MUSEUM

MITLA
TOWN
PLAZA

0   100 yds
0   100 m

To Mex. 190, Oaxaca,
and Tehuantepec

and were performed by Alfonso Caso and Rubin de la Borbolla (both taking a break from work at Monte Albán). They explored the Column Group, the Church Group, and the Arroyo Group and discovered a number of tombs—all the major ones were unfortunately empty. During the last two decades, the majority of the work performed at Mitla has been confined to restoration. A 1993 INAH project partially excavated and restored the Arroyo Group. One hopes that a major excavation will begin before the pre-Hispanic remains are destroyed by the rapidly growing town.

TOURING THE SITE

The site parking area lies on the north end of the site, next to the large handicrafts market. After buying your ticket and passing through the gate, you head downhill and take a right into the Church Group. This takes its name from the colonial Church of San Pablo, which was built in the middle of the group's south courtyard as a way of literally and symbolically squashing the "pagan" Zapotec religion. The church is worth a visit; a profusion of bright flowers often fills the spare interior, hinting at a non-Christian subtext to the Catholic rites.

The path takes you into Courtyard B at the center of the Church Group. The walls around this square patio are decorated with the ornate step-and-fret friezes that are the hallmark of Mitla's architecture. They are sometimes called *grecas* for their resemblance to Greek stonework designs. Here you see five different patterns running horizontally along the walls; they probably had some symbolic meaning, but we do not know what it was. Three narrow rooms occupy the east, west, and north sides of the courtyard.

A door at the north side of the patio opens into the smaller Courtyard A. Above the doors on the north side of this patio, you see three partial panels of white-on-red Mixtec-style murals. Their style closely resembles that of Mixtec codices. Smaller mural fragments decorate the lintels over the west-side doorways. These murals were the major evidence that Mitla was Mixtec-dominated; today, however, archaeologists believe that "domination" was merely "influence."

If you exit the complex to the west, you see a 17th-century fountain occupying the patio just west of Courtyards A and B. Between Courtyard B and the north wall of the church, you can see a Spanish floral motif carved on a lintel; the Catholic curate once lived in a room here. Now cross Courtyard B and exit through the main entrance. A path takes you to the right (downhill). On the east side of the church you can see pre-Hispanic carved stones in the wall and the "pagan" foundation on which the building rests.

You pass through the gate by the market and then another gate to enter the Columns Group, Mitla's glory. This is built around two large patios. The path first takes you into the sunken Courtyard E. The east, west, and south sides are mostly in ruins; the stones were used to build the Church of San Pablo. In the center of the patio lies a low square platform, probably for an altar.

The north end of the patio is dominated by a long raised structure with three layers of stonework friezes decorating the facades. These intricate designs resemble textile patterns and may replicate motifs found on fabrics belonging to aristocratic lineages (much as tartan patterns refer to one or another Scottish clan).

A wall painted red runs along the base of the structure, and a short, steep staircase ascends to the second level. Here, three doorways open into the Hall of Columns, a long, narrow room whose ceiling was supported by six wide pillars. Mitla's roofs were as much as a meter thick; on top of thick beams lay a kind of early concrete. One wall plaque commemorates President Porfirio Díaz's visit to the site in the early 1900s, while another prohibits the defacing of monuments. According to historical accounts, this section of the Column Group was the temple of the Zapotec high priest. The hall acted as an antechamber housing the main idols, in front of which blood sacrifices were performed.

A door on the north wall runs through a short passage and enters Quadrangle D, also called the Palace. Built around a small, square patio, this secluded structure was the high priest's luxurious residence. Three levels of friezes decorate the patio walls, and further stonework is found on the lintels above the main doorways. Each of these four doors opens into a narrow room whose wall is covered with friezes from about waist level to the ceiling. The west room is the best-preserved; under the restored roof you see friezes running the length of the walls. Remnants of plaster adhere to the stonework; painted red, this was the original veneer on the mosaics. These friezes represent the apogee of late Zapotec art. One day we hope to be able to read them.

After you return to the main patio, a path from its southwest corner takes you into the neighboring Courtyard F. Like Courtyard C of the Church Group, this complex has rooms on the north, south, and west sides, while the east side is open. The entry into the rooms is through narrow doorways capped by massive stone lintels. Only fragments of stonework friezes are visible on the facades. Historical accounts state that this quadrangle was the center of Mitla's administrative area. Here, the Zapotec rulers came to discuss problems and imbibe alcoholic beverages. Beneath their feet lay the tombs of their ancestors.

A hole at the base of the north-building stairway leads down into Tomb 1, which was excavated by Leopoldo Batres in 1901. The tomb shape is cruciform, with a large round column at the center of the arms. According to local myth, if a man hugs this phallic stone, called the "Column of Life," he will have many children (or he will know how many years remain of his existence). The walls are decorated with simple friezes carved from single slabs rather than made from mosaics. What appears to be a headrest lies at the far end of the tomb beyond the column. The tomb was discovered empty; it had been looted decades or even centuries before. Another cruciform chamber, Tomb 2, lies beneath the stairs at the foot of the east building. The walls are again adorned with stonework, but the rest of the interior is bare. Be prepared to stoop if you want to enter either of these tombs.

The Church Group and the Column Group are by far the most important part of the site. Three further building complexes will interest the more devoted archaeological tourist. Due west of the Column Group, lying across the entrance road and at the end of a short unpaved street, stands the Adobe Group, so-called for its construction material. This unexcavated temple mound may be earlier than the two previous groups, dating to A.D. 250–750. The main mound is topped with the dilapidated Calvary Chapel (1674). Inside you find the three crosses representing Calvary, and graffiti and garbage. Behind the mound lies a small plaza with smaller mounds occupying the other three sides. The patio is used as a farmyard.

Down the road to the south lies the Arroyo Group, which borders a narrow gully (arroyo). This recently reconstructed complex is a smaller copy of the Column group. No friezes remain; the main sights are the enormous lintels over the doorways. From the layer of ash that was discovered, archaeologists believe the complex was destroyed by fire. During the colonial era, it was used as a corral and then a garbage dump.

The last area is only for the fanatic. Take the road across the Río Mitla (little more than a stream) and turn left and then another left to arrive at the ruined South Group, Mitla's first ceremonial center. Alfonso Caso dug some exploratory trenches here in the 1930s, but since then no work has been done. Atop the vegetation-covered mound, you can see the remains of a red plaster floor. Like the Adobe Group, the main temple here formed the east part of a complex of four buildings around a small plaza. You have a good view over the Column and Church Groups across the river to the north.

Any tour of Mitla should end with a visit to the excellent Frissell Museum on the main square. Its collection of Zapotec ceramics, particularly funerary urns, is unrivaled.

YAGUL

INTRODUCTION

The ruins of Yagul lie on a fortified ridge 10 kilometers west of Mitla. From here, the Zapotecs could command the valley and protect their population from invaders. The ruins themselves were constructed showing a clear Mitla influence; the eastern end of the Tlacolula subvalley produced its own distinctive Mitla-Yagul-Teotitlan variant on late Zapotec culture. The sights include tombs, a large palace, and the valley's largest ballcourt. The main attraction, however, is the dramatic setting atop a cactus-covered mesa with a view of the valley sweeping away below.

HISTORY

Yagul's Preclassic- and Archaic-era (2000–600 B.C.) occupation was sporadic. The earliest settlement, called Caballito Blanco (White Horse), lies on a small bluff down by the Oaxaca-Mitla road. Around 200 B.C., the inhabitants constructed an arrowhead-shaped temple here that is similar to Monte Albán's Building J.

By the time of the Monte Albán IIIb-IV phase (A.D. 600–1250), the settlement had moved up to the current broad terrace two-thirds of the way up the hillside. The spur for this expansion was the abandonment of Yegüih, a sprawling city (encompassing Lambityeco) on the valley floor a few kilometers to the southwest. This was the unsettled era after Monte Albán's collapse, and Yegüih had no natural defenses. On the mesa top above, the inhabitants built a fortress where they could seek protection from attacks.

Yagul reached its apogee during the Monte Albán V period (A.D. 1250–1520). The largest structure was the Temple of Six Patios, which was constructed with Mitla-style stonework patterns. The ballcourt outdid all others in the region for size and beauty. More than 30 tombs have been found at the site, most decorated with stone mosaics and one containing hieroglyphic inscriptions.

After the Conquest, Spanish administrators forced Yagul's residents to move to the town of Tlacolula just to the west. Yagul is still known as Pueblo Viejo (Old Town) in the region.

ARCHAEOLOGICAL RECORD

In the early 1880s, Adolph Bandelier was the first to explore Yagul and report on his findings. Mexican archaeologist Manuel Gamio rediscovered the site in the early 1950s. In 1953, Gamio and Ignacio Bernal returned to the site and dug some exploratory trenches. They returned the next year with a team that eventually included John Paddock, Robert Chadwick, and Charles Wicke and began a series of excavations that lasted until 1961. The explorations centered around the ceremonial center of the Palace of the Six Patios; they also explored the Caballito Blanco area in the valley below.

TOURING THE SITE

Yagul's parking lot lies just east of the ruins. A path leads uphill to the highest section of the settlement. On your right is the large unexcavated platform called Patio 3. Just beyond, the path takes you up to the Palace of the Six Patios, Yagul's elite residential compound.

This complex is made up of three groups of paired patios aligned along a north-south axis. The closest (east side) pair, Patios C and F, is a near copy of Mitla's Church Group. You enter the larger Patio F, bordered on all sides by narrow rooms, and from here head north into the more secluded Patio C. To the left, or west, lie Patios B and E, followed by Patios A and D at the west side of the complex. Tombs were found beneath the floor of the latter two patios.

Just north of the Palace stands Building J on the northern edge of the terrace. This temple was the highest point in the ceremonial center; on top lie the ruins of a ritual room.

As you return to the other side of the Palace of Six Patios, a path leads down to the complex surrounding Patio 1. The narrow "street" between the two building groups is lined with remnants of stonework *greca* (Greek-style) friezes much like those found at Mitla. The south side of the street is the back wall of the Council Hall, a long one-room structure that occupies the north side of Patio 1.

DANIELLE GUSTAFSON

Palace of the Six Patios

The east and west sides of the patio have been only partially reconstructed. The south side is open, leading out to Mound 5-W, which looks over the valley to the south.

East of Patio 1 stands Yagul's famous ballcourt, the largest in Oaxaca and rivaled in Mexico only by Chichén Itzá's. Like all Oaxaca courts yet found, this one lacks rings on the side walls. Patio 5, totally unexcavated, lies down the hill to the south.

Continuing east, a path leads into Patio 4. This is a plaza lined by four pyramids, mostly unreconstructed; in the center stands a square adoratorio. A metal roof on the east side covers a carved stone believed to represent a frog.

Tombs have been discovered beneath the plaza, at the foot of the pyramid steps and atop the mound to the north. A hole on the west side of the plaza leads down to the Tomb 30, also called the Triple Tomb, which is made up of three chambers. Steps descend to an antechamber; you face a facade decorated with Mitla-style friezes carved on large slabs rather than made from mosaics. The slab propped up to the right was used to seal the doorway. On either side of the door project two small carved heads, relatively crudely executed, that presumably act as guardians. Inside you find the three chambers, each unadorned. They had been looted before the archaeologists arrived.

The last Yagul sight requires a short hike. A path from the northeast corner of the site leads to the summit of the mesa. Partway up, you reach a ruined residential platform in which archaeologists discovered tombs. One is open for visitors; carved glyphs adorn the lintel above the tomb entrance, and the door panel is decorated with a running step-and-fret motif.

On top stand the ruins of the Great Fortress—now little more than a mound of rubble—which was surrounded by protective walls along the edge of the bluff. The archaeologist Robert Chadwick found three early (500-200 B.C.) tombs here. If you walk along the southern lip of the mesa, you can see the remains of the old fortifications (including a lookout point) and have an excellent view of the site and the valley beyond. The hillside was once dotted with small terraces that held farm plots and simple homes.

LAMBITYECO

INTRODUCTION

Lambityeco is one of the smallest sites in the valley but one of the most worth visiting. Its magnificent stucco reliefs, including portraits of a Zapotec lord and lady, provide a more direct sense of contact to the ancient civilization than do the abstruse geometric patterns of sites such as Mitla.

Lambityeco is a tiny part of a much larger (and almost totally unexcavated)

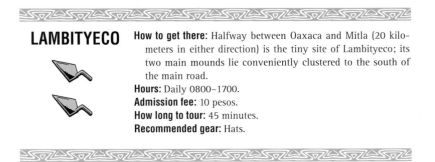

LAMBITYECO

How to get there: Halfway between Oaxaca and Mitla (20 kilometers in either direction) is the tiny site of Lambityeco; its two main mounds lie conveniently clustered to the south of the main road.
Hours: Daily 0800–1700.
Admission fee: 10 pesos.
How long to tour: 45 minutes.
Recommended gear: Hats.

Zapotec city called Yegüih, which spreads across the flat floor of the central Tlacolula subvalley. Covering 75 hectares at its peak, Yegüih's urban area was constructed of dozens of temples and residence areas grouped around small plazas. The part that is called Lambityeco probably contained the largest and most luxurious of these complexes. These reached a brief but glorious apogee between A.D. 600 and 750 and then were suddenly and mysteriously abandoned.

HISTORY

Although Lambityeco has been excavated, the 230 visible mounds that make up the greater settlement of Yegüih have barely been touched by the archaeologist's trowel. The earliest artifacts found so far date to about 700 B.C. The soils here were poor; the main activities seem to have been salt production and the crafting of ceramics from the good clay in the neighborhood.

DANIELLE GUSTAFSON

stucco mask of Cocijo, the Zapotec rain deity, on the dais of a temple platform

Yegüih's occupation was sporadic until about A.D. 600, when the population exploded. More than 75 percent of the hundreds of mounds were occupied during this period; the residents must have numbered well into the thousands. The city probably thrived as a regional market center in addition to its salt and pottery industries.

The three residential complexes that make up Lambityeco were home to five generations of a local aristocratic lineage and four generations of high priests. From stone genealogical registers, we know the names of some of Lambityeco's chiefs; the portraits of Lord I Earthquake and Lady 10 Reed decorate the entrance to a tomb. The offerings found inside, including bat-claw vessels and spiked censers, help define the pure Monte Albán IV style for the Valley of Oaxaca.

Coqui is the title for the chiefs of Zapotec aristocratic lineages at centers such as Lambityeco.

After A.D. 750, Yegüih was mysteriously abandoned. This may have come in response to the unrest that began to trouble the valley during Monte Albán's slow decline. Around the same time, the nearby fortified city of Yagul saw a sudden increase in population. Archaeologists believe that Yegüih's inhabitants emigrated en masse to this new and better-protected location.

Today's Yegüih is gradually being engulfed by the outskirts of Tlacolula. The journey that began in Yegüih, continued in Yagul, and then moved to Tlacolula (Yagul's residents were forcibly moved to the latter town by the Spanish) is finally returning to its starting point.

ARCHAEOLOGICAL RECORD

In his 1953 survey of the valley's archaeological sites, Ignacio Bernal was the first to describe Lambityeco. Excavations began in 1961 under John Paddock of the Institute of Oaxaca Studies and continued on and off through 1975. Since then, no work has been done at the site, and the hundreds of surrounding mounds remain easy pickings for looters.

TOURING THE SITE

After buying your ticket, the first structure you see to the right is Structure 195, the platform-based residence of the *coqui*, or "chief," of Lambityeco. The structure on top is actually the last of six construction stages.

You enter from the west through a small courtyard with an altar in the middle. This proceeds to a raised platform and into another court that acts as the antechamber to a small temple or altar complex, now covered by a metal roof. Beneath floor level at the base of the temple lies the amazing Tomb 6.

You look down into a hole and see the tomb entrance topped with two stucco heads that are portraits of the goateed Lord I Earthquake on the left and his spouse Lady 10 Reed on the right. They are depicted as a distinguished couple in late middle age with ear spools and headdresses. They are parents of the last *coqui* who occupied this house, Lord 8 Death, who was buried in the tomb with his wife Lady 5 Reed. Four other bodies were found inside, possibly his parents and grandparents. As the tomb was sealed up and the entrance was buried, ceramic offerings depicting Zapotec gods were placed in front of the portrait heads.

The altar complex behind is decorated with further stucco reliefs along the top and bottom of the facade. Only fragments remain of the topmost sculptures; the one on the right probably showed Lord 8 Death and Lady 5 Reed. Along the bottom are a pair of remarkable friezes depicting Lord 8 Death's ancestors, probably his grandparents and great-grandparents, in a horizontal position as if they were flying. On the right are Lady 3 Turquoise and Lord 8 Owl, while on the left you see Lord 4 Face and Lady 10 Monkey. Both these couples wear jewelry and other adornment that is similar to that found on the portrait heads.

The secluded patio to the right of this altar complex probably was the actual residence of Lord 8 Death and Lady 5 Reed.

Due south of the *coqui*'s house stands Structure 190, the residence of the *bigaña*, or high priest. This is similar in layout to Structure 195, but it is built on ground level rather than on a platform. You enter through a ruined patio on the west. A metal roof covers the structure on its east side; this is the Cocijo Temple. If you walk around to the other side, you see two large stucco god masks to the left and right of the short staircase. These represent Cocijo, the Rain God and principal Zapotec deity. The face is almost buried under a resplendent headdress that extends in a fan of plumes. He is adorned with large earspools on either side of which you can see his hands. One grasps a lightning bolt while the other holds a vase from which pours a stream of water.

On the west east side of this patio, you see a depression; it is the entrance to Tomb 2, now sealed up. Inside archaeologists discovered seven burials, four of which they believe to have been *bigañas,* the Zapotec high priests. These were found with five ceramic urns representing Cocijo.

The only other structures excavated at the site were a small temple due north of the *coqui*'s house and, due west, the small House of the Golaba. The *golaba* was the Zapotec functionary in charge of collecting taxes and other forms of tribute owed by the population to its rulers. This residence contained a more modest tomb housing five burials, presumably the *golaba* and his ancestors. More than 200 unexcavated mounds lie in the vicinity, most on private lands.

DAINZÚ

INTRODUCTION

The base of a cactus-covered hill in the center of the Tlacolula subvalley is the site of Dainzú, home to a series of dramatic, almost violent, reliefs depicting Zapotec rulers and ballplayers in moments of action. This Late Preclassic center has been only partially excavated. We know, however, that Dainzú had close ties to Monte Albán—the ballplayer sculptures closely resemble the Danzantes at the latter site. Dainzú lies on a tributary of the Río Salado; the rich soils along the shores of this river were the site of at least four other early settlements.

HISTORY

Dainzú's chronology cannot be fully defined until more excavations are performed. The earliest remains found so far date to about 600 B.C. The settlement reached its apogee during the Monte Albán II era (100 B.C.–A.D. 200) when the major structures were built and the population surpassed 5,000. The settlement began to shrink after A.D. 600 and by the end of Monte Albán IV (A.D. 1250) was completely abandoned.

ARCHAEOLOGICAL RECORD

In 1967, Ignacio Bernal discovered a carved stone at the base of Dainzú's hillside. He realized it formed part of the facade of a large structure—Complex A—and began the first excavation. Work continued through 1973 under Bernal, Lorenzo Gamio, José Arturo Oliveras, and others. Since then, only minor exploration and restoration has been performed at the site.

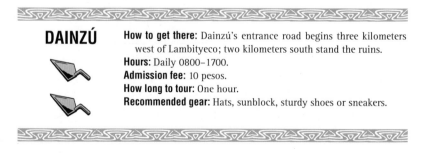

DAINZÚ

How to get there: Dainzú's entrance road begins three kilometers west of Lambityeco; two kilometers south stand the ruins.
Hours: Daily 0800–1700.
Admission fee: 10 pesos.
How long to tour: One hour.
Recommended gear: Hats, sunblock, sturdy shoes or sneakers.

TOURING THE SITE

From the parking area, walk left up the hill to Complex A, the highest-level structure of the ceremonial center. On top you find a platform containing ruined rooms; a staircase heads down the front of the temple. The entire site is aligned east-west, with the temple entrances facing the setting sun. On the south side of the staircase top, you see a vertical shaft that leads down to the entrance of Tomb 2, which was found almost empty.

From here, you descend the stairs to a lower platform and take a second, narrow staircase to the structure's base. A large metal roof covers a wall made of 28 bas-relief carvings whose subjects are worn but still visible. Most of them depict ballplayers frozen in moments of action, while others show warriors in jaguar costume and richly adorned Zapotec rulers. The ballplayers wear wide belts and, it seems, masks to protect themselves from the heavy rubber ball. The Mesoamerican ballgame was a combination sport, gambling pastime, and religious and civic ritual; its practice was obviously central to Dainzú's culture. An old cart track runs along the base of Complex A and continues south by a number of unexcavated mounds.

Due west and slightly downhill of Complex A stands a series of patios and temples called Complexes B and C. To your right lies Complex B, which is a confusing assemblage of pits and buildings that represent at least six different construction stages. In the middle of the top level, you find a small room containing two columns; this is the Yellow Temple, named for the paint on its walls (yellow is rare in Mesoamerican art).

A gate on the north side of Complex B blocks the entrance to Tomb 7.

DANIELLE GUSTAFSON

Complex A at Dainzú

Through the bars you can see an elaborately carved entrance. The lintel is adorned with a frightening mask representing a jaguar (or a bat, say some) while its claws dangle down the jambs on either side. On the floor lies the broken door panel. The tomb contained stone sculptures, broken urns, and bones covered with cinnabar (a red pigment). Just to the north, stairs enter a passage and cut down through earlier stages of the structure's construction.

The stairs exit at the north side of the platform. You can take a left and then walk along the west side of the structure. Just beyond its wide main staircase lies the mouth of the building's drainage system, which used pipes made from clay tubes. The south side of this structure is a relatively small platform called Complex C, a late construction. A patio along its southeast corner contains the entrance to Tomb 3, a relatively simple chamber with niches in the walls. The skeleton found here was accompanied by pottery and greenstone jewelry.

Due west of this building lies Complex J, Dainzú's I-shaped ballcourt, which closely resembles Monte Albán's main ballcourt. The last stage of this structure is late, dating to about A.D. 800. The earliest stages do not appear to have been

THE JUCHITAN ZAPOTECS

The Zapotecs are a collection of Indian tribes loosely bound together by their history, related dialects, and homeland covering most of eastern and southern Oaxaca. They are also linked by a common preoccupation with capitalism, even if on a very modest scale. To the Zapotecs, markets have always been as important as, or even more important than, subsistence farming. Given the arid, hilly terrain in much of the Zapotec region, this makes perfect sense. It is easier to make a living producing crafts for the market than to scrape out a meager existence growing corn on the scrub-covered hillsides. The best example of the Zapotec genius for markets, however, comes from the town of Juchitan on the hot, lush coastal plain at the southern end of the Isthmus of Tehuantepec.

In Juchitan, the women, and in particular the market women, have always been the most powerful economic force. The men do work—they till the fields, build the houses, make the crafts, and fish in the river and ocean—but the women control the town's commercial life through their control of the market. Dressed in their traditional garb, the Juchitan women even look like they have power. Their hair cascades in two long, dark braids, and they wear long, brightly colored (purple, crimson, etc.), ruffled skirts below heavily embroidered blouses. In the florid Zapotec poetry, they are frequently described as queens, and they carry themselves regally as they move about town. As they preside over their stalls in the market, they obviously take great pride in their commercial ability, rows of gold and silver showing with every smile. They sell fruit, coconuts, chocolate, meat, dried shrimp, fish, tamales, candies, canned goods, and even live iguanas that one famous market woman holds on her head. In the past two decades, a number of Juchitan men have found work at a nearby oil refinery and have risen in status. But the power of the Juchitan women persists, not only because of their wily commercial instincts but because of tradition and their sheer force of character.

contemporaneous with the ballplayer reliefs. We do not yet know on what court they played.

Numerous unexcavated mounds lie to the south and west. The valley below contained the fields and huts of Dainzú's agricultural workers. The adventurous might want to take the path that leads from Complex A up to the top of the hill. On the summit lie a number of rocks covered with carvings, including a sacrificial scene. The view is worth it.

ZAACHILA

INTRODUCTION

About 15 kilometers south of Oaxaca, Zaachila was the Zapotec capital during the centuries leading to the Spanish Conquest. Only one of the many mounds dotting this town has been excavated; the locals, who are of Zapotec ancestry, do not appreciate outsiders coming to unearth the tombs of their ancestors. The one expedition that succeeded in exploring here (with the help of the Mexican army) discovered two rich tombs that contained stucco sculptures and some beautifully crafted polychrome pottery offerings. The site does not take long to visit, but it is well worth the trip.

HISTORY

We know Zaachila's history from the partial excavation and from a number of 16th-century historical accounts. The site has been occupied since at least 1400–1150 B.C., when this was a tiny hamlet. The subsequent chronology is unclear, although we do know that the settlement eventually grew into a large village.

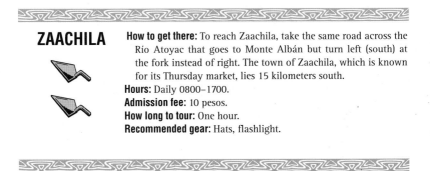

ZAACHILA

How to get there: To reach Zaachila, take the same road across the Río Atoyac that goes to Monte Albán but turn left (south) at the fork instead of right. The town of Zaachila, which is known for its Thursday market, lies 15 kilometers south.

Hours: Daily 0800–1700.

Admission fee: 10 pesos.

How long to tour: One hour.

Recommended gear: Hats, flashlight.

As Monte Albán dwindled during the IIIb-IV period, Zaachila grew. Its population was probably larger than that of the current town. Stone genealogical registers (the most elaborate is in Mexico City's Museo Nacional de Antropología) have given us the names of Zaachila's ruling lineages. There may have been some Mixtec domination during this period (many older texts identify Zaachila as a Mixtec site).

In ancient times, a **necropolis** was a zone set aside for the burial chambers of the elite.

During Monte Albán V (A.D. 1250–1520), however, Zaachila was purely Zapotec, and we have the names of its sovereigns from the early 15th century through the last ruler, Cocijopii, who died in 1563. Zaachila's extravagant Tombs 1 and 2 date to this pre-Conquest era. They held the bones of more than 20 people, probably including 9 Flower and 5 Flower, two lords whose stucco portraits adorn the walls. Zaachila's rulers reigned over a Zapotec empire that contained the entire Valley of Oaxaca and extended as far as the Isthmus of Tehuantepec.

Zaachila's Tomb 1: the dead 5 flower, a Zapotec ruler, on his journey through the land of the dead

DANIELLE GUSTAFSON

In 1494, the Aztecs, who had been threatening the region for decades, attacked and sacked Zaachila and Mitla. The next year, a mixed Zapotec and Mixtec army under their ruler Cocijoeza defeated the Aztecs at Guiengola on the Isthmus of Tehuantepec. Under the treaty that followed, Cocijoeza married Coyolicatzin, the daughter of the Aztec emperor Ahuizotl, and an uneasy truce reigned between the Aztecs and the Zapotecs. The Zapotec rulers moved their seat to Tehuantepec, and the Valley of Oaxaca cities had to pay tribute to Tenochtitlan (perhaps in acknowledgment of the Aztecs' superior power).

The Zaachilans, however, have kept their pride. In the past few centuries, they have taken up arms against the Spanish for being forced to work on plantations and then against the dictatorship of Porfirio Díaz for the same crime. They are still considered one of the most revolutionary of valley towns. In 1947 and 1953, they forced archaeologists to flee, and Roberto Gallegos Ruiz's 1962 expedition succeeded only through military intervention. The unfortunate byproduct of Zaachila's rebelliousness is that government projects and money are sent elsewhere—it is one of the poorest towns in the valley.

ARCHAEOLOGICAL RECORD

The only project to excavate at Zaachila was the 1962 UNAM expedition under Roberto Gallegos Ruiz. He explored the top of Mound A, discovering the two famous tombs, and part of Mound B. These lie on Zaachila's acropolis, which remains mostly unexcavated. The surrounding mounds have been explored only by pothunters.

TOURING THE SITE

You buy tickets at the guardian's hut and then proceed uphill to the top of Mound A. The acropolis is a massive structure aligned along a north-south axis. It supports at least eight mounds—elite residences and temples—as well as patios and plazas. A second large, but lower, mound stands just to the west.

Mound A was an elite residential structure consisting of at least three rooms built around a square patio. Altars occupy the centers of the north and west rooms. The patio also contains the entrances to two tombs. The site guardians accompany you on your explorations of the Underworld.

Stairs on the patio's north side lead down to Tomb 1. They alight in a vestibule; the lintel of the tomb entrance in front of you is adorned with a simple Mitla-style frieze. Small animal heads, perhaps cats, protrude from the top of each jamb (much like the heads outside the Yagul tomb). Red paint still adorns the stone. You step into the antechamber, a small room with niches in the middle of the side walls. Above each niche flies a stucco owl painted white; these birds act as messengers of death in many Mesoamerican religions. The floor of this chamber was filled with pottery offerings, including some of the finest Zapotec ceramics yet found, and a beautiful turquoise mosaic mask. A tiny bowl with a hummingbird perched on the rim is one of the masterpieces of Mesoamerican art (on display in Mexico City's Museo Nacional de Antropología).

Next you enter the tomb's main chamber, where the crumbled skeletons of 11 people were found. Niches, which contained further pottery offerings, penetrate the north, east, and west walls. These walls are also decorated with elaborate stucco figures. Above the niche on the far wall flies a man whose body is the carapace of a turtle. A dragon mask headdress covers his head, and he holds flint knives, perhaps for sacrifices, in either hand. The first figures on the side walls are representations of Mictlantecuhtli, the Zapotec god of the Underworld. Human hearts hang from their shoulders on cords. Beyond, on the west (left) stands a man identified as 5 Flower by a date glyph. He wears a cape and elaborate headdress and carries a bag in his hand. Opposite, on the east wall stands 9 Flower in similar garb. Both figures have seemingly impossible positions for their arms and appear to be walking behind the lord of the Underworld.

The entrance to Tomb 2 lies in the center of the complex's patio. This one is aligned east-west as opposed to Tomb 1's north-south. At the bottom of the steps, another stonework frieze adorns the facade above the tomb entrance. Inside you find an antechamber and main room similar to Tomb 1, only without the stucco reliefs. When archaeologists opened the door, they found the floor dense with bones and pottery, including an amazing polychrome dish with long jaguar claw feet. Finely crafted pieces of gold jewelry were still attached to some of the remains. At least 12 full skeletons were found here as well as a lesser number of partial ones; the Zapotecs frequently rearranged the skeletons to make way for new ones. Rulers also used the femurs of their ancestors as symbols of their divine right to rule.

The tombs are Zaachila's main sights. You can walk to Mound B at the north end of the acropolis, where three unexcavated temples cluster around a patio. Platforms on the lower east and west sides of the acropolis also contain mounds, all unexcavated.

CHIAPAS

Temple of the Cross, Palenque

THE SOCONUSCO COAST

One of the great unsolved puzzles of Mesoamerican archaeology is the origin of Maya civilization. Researchers believe the key to this problem may lie in the southeastern corner of Mexico along the Pacific Coast of Chiapas. From the town of Pijijiapan to the watershed of the Río Naranjo just beyond the Guatemala border, the region between the Pacific beaches and the southern slopes of the Sierra Madre de Chiapas mountain range is known as the Soconusco.

The coastal plain and low hills of the Soconusco are a zone of rich soils, frequent rains, and year-round warm temperatures. In this region of tropical abundance, there was no pressing need to develop intensive agriculture. You could just pick the fruits off the trees, including the all-important cacao (chocolate), which was central to Mesoamerican diet, ritual, and trade.

Many cultures came to the Soconusco for cacao and other tropical goods. The Olmecs, Maya, and Aztecs all either traded with or directly colonized the region. Between the end of the Olmec and the beginnings of the Maya civilization, the Soconusco saw the rise of its own homegrown culture around the center of Izapa. Like the Olmecs, the Izapans based their civic and religious rituals around massive stone monuments and altars. Although these monuments contain similarities to earlier Olmec sculptures, they also display early forms of the religious and political motifs that achieved more complexity in the great Classic Maya centers. Archaeologists believe that Izapa and the surrounding Soconusco region acted as the crucial pivot between Olmec and Maya cultures. Afterward, the Soconusco slowly lapsed into obscurity, its harvest of Mesoamerica's finest cacao its only claim to fame.

THE LAND

Southeast of the Isthmus of Tehuantepec rises the Sierra Madre de Chiapas mountain range, which runs along the length of southern Chiapas. The jagged product of ongoing volcanic activity, this range connects with the Guatemala Highlands to the east. The last major eruption in the region was the 1902 Santa María volcano (near Quetzaltenango, Guatemala), whose subsequent fall of ash caused major damage to the Soconusco's ecology.

The southern slopes of the Sierra Madre (interspersed with occasional cinder cones and outcroppings of volcanic rock) swoop down to the narrow coastal plain of the Soconusco. The soils here are some of the richest in Mexico, made

TUXTLA GUTIÉRREZ

To reach Chiapas's many archaeological sites, most people pass through Tuxtla Gutiérrez, the state capital, which has the area's largest airport, and then head off to San Cristóbal de las Casas and beyond. For archaeological tourists, the capital's one great sight is the exhibit on pre-Columbian cultures at the **Museo Regional de Chiapas** in the park along Calle 5 Oriente.

of mineral-rich alluvial runoff from the mountain slopes. These soils end at the Pacific in a line of estuaries, lagoons, barrier islands, and beaches.

Climate

The zone closest to the ocean is the driest, with the average rain totaling around 1,500 mm a year. Over the mountains, however, moisture-bearing winds from both the Gulf of Mexico and the Pacific collide. In the upper foothills of the Soconusco, some areas receive more than 6,000 mm of rain a year, making them among the wettest spots in Mesoamerica. The dry season (such as it is) runs only from December to February, while the rest of the year rain is almost guaranteed every day between 3 P.M. and 10 P.M.

The temperature is warm and stable, usually around 85°F year-round.

Flora and Fauna

In this damp climate, tropical plant and animal life thrive. The vegetation is lush and always threatening to overwhelm man-made clearings. The many species of tree include chicozapote (rubber), banana, cacao, pitaya palm, coconut palm, calabash, avocado, mamey, balsa, mango, orange, and lime. The most popular crops are the Mesoamerican staple of maize and the European import of sugarcane.

The Soconusco's jungles once teemed with animal life. Unfortunately, these have all but disappeared; this is due first to the Santa María volcano—the massive ash fall asphyxiated many animals and destroyed their sources of food—and subsequent overhunting has killed most of the remaining fauna. The most common animals now are gopher, rabbit, opossum, and iguana. In pre-Columbian times, the animal population included jaguar, tapir, coati, howler monkey, crocodile, and deer. Among the wide variety of bird species were turkey, macaw, parrot, harpy eagle, and the quetzal, whose plumage made the elaborate headdresses of the Maya rulers.

HISTORY

The earliest hunter-gatherers arrived in central Chiapas by about 6000 B.C. In the Soconusco, however, the first traces of human life do not appear until 3000 B.C. These were found at a site called Chantuto in the zone of estuaries and lagoons along the Pacific Coast. This was a temporary seasonal settlement of a small band of hunter-gatherers living mainly off mollusks—archaeologists found large mounds of clamshells at the site.

After 2000 B.C., the land farther inland began to be settled with small agricultural communities built along riverbanks. The crops included an early form of maize and probably manioc; luckily, the land was so rich with fish and fruit that they did not have to rely on what they grew. These people, who belong to what archaeologists call the Barra culture, also produced some of the earliest ceramics yet found in Mesoamerica—beautiful, thin-walled jars and bowls covered with geometric designs. In these villages, researchers also find the first signs of social stratification: small regional centers containing longhouses that acted as residences for the chief and his clan.

By 1500 B.C., the hills of the Soconusco were dotted with large and small villages living off agriculture, abundant wild fruit, and cacao, which grew wild but by this point was certainly cultivated. The most important of these settlements was the site known as Paso de la Amada, where archaeologists have found evidence of large-scale public architecture, possibly a chief's or communal house, and the earliest ballcourt yet found. Built around 1400 B.C., this 260-foot-long court predates the next oldest ballcourt by about 500 years (though rubber balls and depictions of ballplayers dating to about 1300–1200 B.C. have been discovered in Veracruz). By about 1100 B.C., ceramics similar to those found in San Lorenzo, Yucatan, begin to appear, indicating that the site was becoming part of the larger Mesoamerican culture. After the decline of Paso de la Amada after 1000 B.C., the settlement of Izapa would grow to become the dominant force in southern Chiapas.

IZAPA

INTRODUCTION

Tucked into an obscure corner of southeastern Chiapas just up the road from the Guatemala border, Izapa is one of the most important sites in the Maya region. This was not a Maya center. Archaeologists believe, however, that the motifs found here provided the basis for many later Maya civic and religious practices.

IZAPA

How to get there: Izapa lies seven kilometers east-northeast on the road from the town of Tapachula almost at the Guatemala border.

Hours: Daily 0900–1700.

Admission fee: You usually tip the site guardians about 10–20 pesos.

How long to tour: Two hours.

Recommended gear: Hats, sunblock, hiking boots, bottled water, mosquito repellent, rain gear during the rainy season.

Museum: There is no site museum, but in nearby Tapachula, the small Museo Regional del Soconusco in the Antiguo Palacio Municipal on the main plaza contains some important stelae from Izapa. It's open 0800–1600, closed Monday.

Food and accommodations: One of the top hotels in the town of Tapachula is the **Kamico**, tel. 962/6-2640 on Prol. Calle Central Oriente. It is a fancy motel-style lodging on an avenue heading out to the suburbs.

Izapa's ruins, encompassing roughly 80 mounds, are set amid a beautiful, steamy jungle. In the clearings you find dozens of large carved stelae and altars standing in the middle of plazas and at the foot of massive mounds (only a few of Izapa's structures have been reconstructed). The stelae show rulers engaged in rituals and interacting with deities and religious symbols, many of them in the form of animals or plants, such as the holy ceiba tree. After visiting the main building complexes, you can (with the help of the site guardian) sample some of the many tropical fruits found in the surrounding jungle.

H I S T O R Y

Humans first settled at Izapa between 1500 and 1250 B.C. For the first 500 years of its occupation, this was a small village living off simple agriculture, abundant wild fruits, and cacao. The settlement's center was built around Mound 30 on the north side of Group B.

Between 1100 and 850 B.C., Izapa ceramics show the influence of the Gulf Coast, particularly the Olmec styles of first San Lorenzo and later La Venta. Why would the great Olmecs come to the Soconusco? The answer is cacao, whose seed could be used as money and which also could be turned into the favorite drink of Mesoamerican rulers. Although the language spoken by the early Izapans is unknown, archaeologists theorize that it may have been the Mixe-Zoquean tongue whose center is the Olmec heartland. Izapa then was an outpost on the southeastern fringes of the Olmec empire.

Izapa began its transformation from egalitarian village to civic-religious center between 850 and 300 B.C. The Group B complex was still the center, but now large platform mounds rose around its plaza, and the earliest stages of Groups A and C were built. Izapa's role as a border town became increasingly important as to the east rose the early stages of Maya civilization along the Pacific Coast of Guatemala and on up into the Guatemala City area. At the end of this period, around the time of La Venta's collapse, the Izapans carved the first large stone monuments.

CYCLES WITHIN CYCLES: THE MESOAMERICAN CALENDAR

We all live within a calendar cycle. For most readers of this book, the main calendar is based on the 365.25-day solar year, which is divided into 52 weeks made up of seven days apiece. The current era of this calendar began at the birth of Jesus; all of history is defined as either before or after this date. We use the decimal system, so larger groups of years are divided by tens, hundreds, and thousands. Perhaps because of this division, the most significant dates come at the passage between decades, centuries, and millennia. Whether the passage of these calendar milestones provides any definition for modern cultures is a matter of debate: did the arrival of the year 2000 (or 2001) really change anything?

For the residents of ancient Mesoamerica, on the other hand, observance of the calendar system made the difference between life and death. The Universe would literally stop if they did not respond appropriately. They did not live within just one calendar cycle but within many. They followed not only the sun, but the moon, planets, and stars, as well as cycles caused by the seemingly arbitrary laws of mathematics. One of the principal jobs of the priest was to keep track of these cycles and inform the people and rulers about where they stood in the dense ceremonial calendar.

Not all Mesoamerican cultures used the same calendar system. Archaeologists believe that the division common to all of them—and one of the defining attributes of Meso-

america—was the 260-day cycle formed by the rotation of the numbers 1 to 13 through 20 named days (13 x 20 = 260). This calendar was probably invented during the Middle Preclassic (1000–300 B.C.) in the Valley of Oaxaca and was used through the Spanish Conquest.

The early Oaxacans apparently did not use the solar year calendar, which may have been first adopted by the late Olmecs or early Maya in the Isthmus of Tehuantepec region. This 365-day calendar was divided into 18 "weeks" of 20 days each followed by five unlucky days at the end. They did not use leap years, so they did not have a fixed New Year's Day in our reckoning but one which slowly moved over the decades (a fact which complicates the translation of Mesoamerican dates into our calendar).

The 260- and 365-day calendars were also interlocked; after running through the complete sequence of all possible date combinations, it took 52 years before a date would be repeated. Called the calendar round, this was one of the most important cycles of Mesoamerica. At the end of the 52 years, the Aztecs extinguished all fires in their empire and performed the New Fire ceremony to signal the start of this new cycle. This occasion was also marked by intensive building programs; Tenochtitlan's Great Temple was expanded every 52 years.

Just as we (to some extent) believe in the significance of centuries and millennia, the residents of Mesoamerica believed in longer cycles, some stretching back to the beginning of creation. To mark their position in these

Izapa reached its climax during the Guillen phase between 300 and 50 B.C. Contacts with the Olmec region disappeared, and Izapa rose in "splendid isolation." Groups A, B, C, and D reached their present form, and all the great stone monuments were carved during a period of intensified ritual life. Izapa was the dominant center of the Soconusco, and Izapan motifs (such as the long-lipped god) are found in numerous sites heading east all the way to Kaminaljuyú, the early Maya metropolis outside Guatemala City.

cycles, the Classic Maya developed the remarkable Long Count calendar system. This notation marked the exact placement of a day in the calendar cycles that began on August 11, 3114 B.C., the beginning of the current cycle of creation.

Long Count dates are written as a stack of glyphs with the largest number, representing hundreds of years, on top and the smallest—individual days—on the bottom. These dates were noted using the vigesimal system based on multiples of 20.

Twenty days, or *kin,* formed one month, or *uinic.*

Eighteen months formed a *tun,* or year, of 360 days.

Twenty *tuns* became one *katun.*

Twenty *katun* made one *baktun* (almost 400 years) and so on. One remarkable Long Count date found at Cobá is so long that it refers to a cycle 41,341,050 followed by 21 zeros long.

Archaeologists write Long Count dates from left to right with the largest cycles first and the smallest last; the vast majority use the *baktun* as the largest cycle. The August 11, 3114 B.C. date is 13.0.0.0.0, while the last Classic Maya inscription, found at Toniná, is written 10.4.0.0.0. Translated this means 10 *baktuns,* 4 *katuns* and no *tuns, uinics* or *kins*—since that 3114 B.C. day. Most researchers use a computer program to quickly convert Long Count dates into our calendar. The current *baktun* in which we live—the 13th of this cycle—ends on December 23, 2012, the day when the calendar round returns to 13.0.0.0.0. Ominously, the modern Maya do not believe that a new cycle of creation begins at this date; the world as they know it may come to an end.

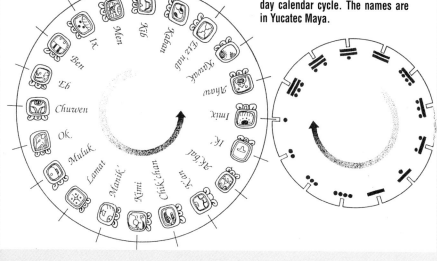

Schematic representation of the 260-day calendar cycle. The names are in Yucatec Maya.

Two characteristics that have not been discovered at Izapa are a writing system and the Long Count calendar. These appear at both the late Olmec center of Tres Zapotes and at Chiapa de Corzo (just northwest of the Soconusco) and in Guatemala. Izapa was apparently too self-contained to accept these products of an outside culture (perhaps the Olmecs).

After 50 B.C., Izapa's growth suddenly stops. The only complex with new construction is Group F, which appears to be the new civic-religious center. The ceremonial use of Groups A through D mysteriously stops, and the ceramic evidence shows strong influence from Guatemala to the east. Izapa may have been conquered by early Maya groups who cut off contact to the north and west.

Between A.D. 100 and 200, the eastern domination appears to end as well. This was an era of severe volcanic activity in western El Salvador; many cultures in southern Guatemala may have been weakened by the effects of lava and ash. After A.D. 250, Group F remains Izapa's center but all the ceramics are local Soconusco style. The population slowly wanes over the following centuries, with a small settlement in Group F and the rest of the site used as a burial place and garbage dump. By the end of the Early Postclassic (A.D. 1200), Izapa was abandoned.

At the time of the Spanish Conquest, the Aztecs had conquered this region of precious cacao trees and named it Xoconochco after one of its larger towns. It then became a province of New Spain, and the Spaniards picked up the addictive habit of chocolate drinking. After the cacao tree was planted around the tropical world, the Soconusco's monopoly on fine chocolate disappeared, and it gradually lapsed into obscurity. In 1790, the Soconusco region was added to the province of Chiapas.

ARCHAEOLOGICAL RECORD

Izapa's first mention in the literature comes in the mid-1930s when José Coffin reported on the site's existence to the Department of Monuments. In 1939, Professor Carlos A. Culebro described Izapa in a paper on Chiapas archaeological sites and named it "Tuxtla Chico." A Carnegie Institution report by Karl Ruppert spurred the visit of Matthew Stirling during his expedition to explore the stone monuments of Southern Mexico (including Tres Zapotes). In 1941, Stirling spent seven days at Izapa clearing and photographing the stones but performing no excavations.

Many Izapan and Classic Maya monuments contain representations, either realistic or highly stylized, of a great tree. This is a ceiba, a towering tree with broad branches that you see in the plaza of many present-day Maya villages. The ceiba represents the **World Tree**, or *axis mundi* (center of the world), that stands at the center of the Maya Universe. Its roots dig down to the Underworld, and its branches rise to the Heavens and point in the four cardinal directions. The most famous World Tree is carved on the lid of Lord Pakal's sarcophagus at Palenque.

The first excavation at Izapa was led by Philip Drucker (Stirling's assistant at the Tres Zapotes dig) who mapped the site and dug 12 stratigraphic trenches. He believed Izapa's apogee came during the Late Classic. This theory was refuted in 1956 by Gareth Lowe of Brigham Young University (BYU); he found large amounts of Late Preclassic refuse and decided the site was far earlier than previously thought. During the 1940s and 1950s, Izapa was also inspected by a number of Mexican archaeologists, such as Román Piña Chan.

Gareth Lowe returned to Izapa in 1961 to lead a major excavation of the site sponsored by the New World Archaeological Foundation at BYU. With the assistance of the Guatemalan archaeologist Carlos Navarrete, the project cleared and mapped the site, uncovered dozens of stone monuments, and explored all the major structures. The project concluded in 1965; Lowe's 1982 report is one of the models of the genre. Since then, no major projects have taken place at Izapa. Aside from the centers of Groups A, B, and F, the jungle has again encroached on the ruins.

TOURING THE SITE

Due north of Izapa towers the Tacaná Volcano (4,064 meters) and further mountains stand to the east. Archaeologists believe Izapa's location could be in alignment with these volcanoes and various astronomical bodies—stars, planets, and the sun—on auspicious days of the year.

The ruins themselves stand just east of the Río de Izapa. The entrance to the main site on the right is poorly marked; if you pass the ruins of Group F on the left or cross the river, you have gone too far. The site entrance lies about a kilometer south of the river. During the rainy season, the road may be impassible because of mud, rocks, or other obstructions. In your car bounce about half a kilometer through the jungle and then turn right into the main part of the site. After about 300 meters, you reach a crossroads; if you continue straight, you will enter Group A.

Take the road to the left into Group B. The hill looming to the left is actually Mound 25, standing at the

Stone monolith and ball may represent a cult of fertility.

DANIELLE GUSTAFSON

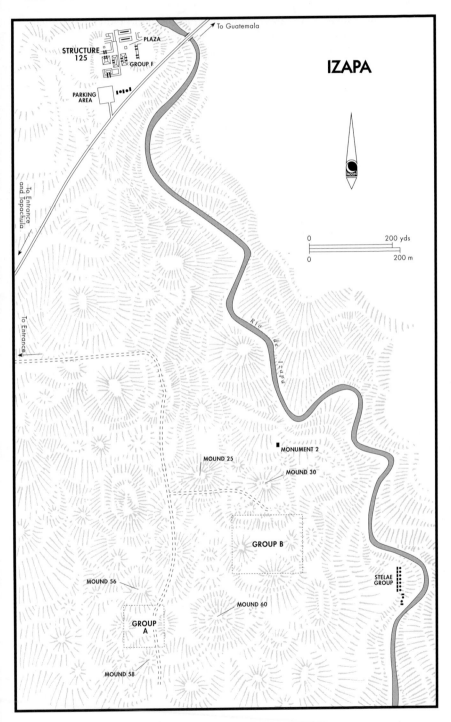

north end of the Group H plaza (now a field) to the south. You enter the clearing that is Group B. The nearby houses belong to the farmers who double as site guardians (they actually own the land); cows and other animals graze on the mounds.

On the north side of this complex lies Mound 30, on top of which stands Mound 30a, an unrestored pyramid that is now just a large grass-covered mound. This structure was the site of Izapa's earliest settlement and remained the civic-religious center through the end of its Guillen phase apogee around 50 B.C. Smaller mounds occupy the south, east, and west sides of the plaza.

Archaeologists found a series of large carved stone monuments and stelae ringing the plaza in front of these temples. Most of those in Group B have been removed. In front of Mound 30 stand three pillars holding three flattened stone balls; these may be male and female symbols representing fertility. The majority of the monuments were stelae depicting mythic scenes and rulers interacting with deities amid lush nature motifs. Researchers also found flat stone altars and what appears to be a carved throne next to the central pillar.

To the northeast of the plaza, a path takes you behind Mound 30 to a banana and cacao tree grove where you see a small roof covering Monument 2. This is a large stone sculpture in the form of a monster's head whose gaping mouth contains a seated figure. The identity of the monster is unknown; it may be a jaguar. The seated figure is also mysterious because its face and other features are worn smooth (or were never finished). Native myth holds that the figure represents a guardian figure who ventures forth in the dark of night.

From Group B, a site guardian can help you bushwhack down to the riverbank. Inside an oxbow lie two rows of 19 small stelae and altars of unknown purpose. In the middle of the river about 100 meters upstream, you see Monument 54 with a crude carving of an otter or perhaps a dog.

Return now to the intersection on the entrance road and park your car. The tire tracks lead south past some humble farmhouses and into Group A. This is another plaza bordered by four temples; along the base of each, small thatched shelters protect many of Izapa's finest stelae and altars. The northernmost structure is Mound 56, in front of which stood six elaborate carvings (some have been removed to museums), each with an oval altar lying in front.

On the left (west) side stands Stela 5, Izapa's most famous monument. The center of this scene is a towering tree, probably a ceiba, representing the Tree of Life. Around this spreads a complicated assemblage of human figures, serpent motifs, and perhaps deities. The exact meaning is the subject of much debate; it may represent the human life cycle from birth to death and beyond. The neighboring monuments are less legible. Tapachula's small anthropology museum contains Stela 25 from here showing a crocodile whose tail grows into a tree; in its branches sits a resplendent bird, probably Vucub Caquix, the all-powerful macaw of the Popol Vuh, the Maya mythological epic. Standing a short way out into the plaza, Stela 6 depicts a squatting composite figure—part jaguar, serpent, and toad—facing up with a miniature canoe balanced on its outstretched tongue.

The eastern Mound 57 is adorned with only one monument, Stela 27, which shows a figure backed up against another tree, while before him crouches a jaguar or dog figure. The stelae on the front of the opposite Mound 55 are too worn to be legible.

Three stelae stood in front of Mound 58 at the south of the Group A plaza.

POPOL VUH: THE MAYA BOOK OF THE DAWN OF LIFE

The Popol Vuh is the great Maya mythological and historical text, the story of the gods, the creation of the Universe, and of humanity from its genesis into historical time. In the early 18th century, a Franciscan friar found a Quiché Maya version of the Popol Vuh in an archive in the highland Guatemala town of Chichicastenango and produced the translation upon which all written versions are based. You see scenes from the Popol Vuh reproduced on sculptures at sites throughout the Maya region. The text's longest story is the tale of Hunahpu and Xbalanque, the Hero Twins who destroy the false gods and make way for the true rulers of the Universe and, at the same time, for the creation of humanity. One of their victories, their defeat of Seven Macaw, appears on the proto-Maya stela found at Izapa in southern Chiapas.

Here is the beginning of the defeat and destruction of the day of Seven Macaw by the two boys, the first named Hunahpu and the second named Xbalanque. Being gods, the two of them saw evil in his attempt at self-magnification before the Heart of the Sky. So the boys talked:

"It's no good without life, without people here on the face of the earth."

"Well then, let's try a shot. We could shoot him while he's at his meal. We could make him ill, then put an end to his riches, his jade, his metal, his jewels, his gems, the source of his brilliance. Everyone might do as he does, but it

should not come to be that fiery splendor is merely a matter of metal. So be it," said the boys, each one with a blowgun on his shoulder, the two of them together.

And this Seven Macaw has two sons: the first of these is Zipacna, and the second is Earthquake. And Chimalmat is the name of their mother, the wife of Seven Macaw.

And this is Zipacna, this is the one to build up the great mountains: Fire Mouth, Hunahpu, Cave by the Water, Xcanul, Macamob, Huliznab, as the names of the mountains that were there at the dawn are spoken. They were brought forth by Zipacna in a single night.

And now this is the Earthquake. The mountains are moved by him; the mountains, small and great, are softened by him. The son of Seven Macaw did this just as a means of self-magnification.

"Here am I: I am the sun," said Seven Macaw.

"Here am I: I am the maker of the earth," said Zipacna.

"As for me, I bring down the sky, I make an avalanche of all the earth," said Earthquake. The sons of Seven Macaw are alike, and like him: they got their greatness from their father.

And the two boys saw evil in this, since our first mother and father could not yet be made. Therefore deaths and disappearances were planned by the two boys. And here is the shooting of Seven Macaw by the two boys. We shall explain the defeat of each one of those who engaged in self-magnification.

The eastern Stela 1 is now in Mexico City's Museo Nacional de Antropología. The central Stela 2 shows Vucub Caquix again, here descending head first into a calabash tree; on either side are two small figures. Researchers believe the latter represent Hunahpu and Xbalanque, the hero twins of the Popol Vuh, the epic text that lies at the center of Maya religion. This is one of their first appearances in Mesoamerican art—another sign that Izapan civilization was a progenitor of the Maya.

This is the great tree of Seven Macaw, a nance, and this is the food of Seven Macaw. In order to eat the fruit of the nance he goes up the tree every day. Since Hunahpu and Xbalanque have seen where he feeds, they are now hiding beneath the tree of Seven Macaw, they are keeping quiet here, the two boys are in the leaves of the tree.

And when Seven Macaw arrived, perching over his meal, the nance, it was then that he was shot by Hunahpu. The blowgun shot went right to his jaw, breaking his mouth. Then he went up over the tree and fell flat on the ground. Suddenly Hunahpu appeared, running. He set out to grab him, but actually it was the arm of Hunahpu that was seized by Seven Macaw. He yanked it straight back, he bent it back at the shoulder. Then Seven Macaw tore it right out of Hunahpu. Even so, the boys did well: the first round was not their defeat by Seven Macaw.

And when Seven Macaw had taken the arm of Hunahpu, he went home. Holding his jaw very carefully, he arrived:

"What have you got there?" said Chimalmat, the wife of Seven Macaw.

"What is it but those two tricksters! They've shot me, they've dislocated my jaw. All my teeth are just loose, now they ache. But once what I've got is over the fire—hanging there, dangling over the fire—then they can just come and get it. They're real tricksters!" said Seven Macaw, then he hung up the arm of Hunahpu.

Meanwhile Hunahpu and Xbalanque were thinking. And then they invoked a grandfather, a truly white-haired grandfather, and a grandmother, a truly humble grandmother—just bent-over, elderly people. Great White Peccary is the name of the grandfather, and Great White Tapir is the name of the grandmother. The boys said to the grandmother and grandfather:

"Please travel with us when we go to get our arm from Seven Macaw; we'll just follow right behind you. You'll tell him:

'Do forgive us our grandchildren, who travel with us. Their mother and father are dead, and so they follow along there, behind us. Perhaps we should give them away, since all we do is pull worms out of teeth.' So we'll seem like children to Seven Macaw, even though we're giving you the instructions," the two boys told them.

"Very well," they replied.

After that they approached the place where Seven Macaw was in front of his home. When the grandmother and grandfather passed by, the two boys were romping along behind them. When they passed below the lord's house, Seven Macaw was yelling his mouth off because of his teeth. And when Seven Macaw saw the grandfather and grandmother traveling with them:

"Where are you headed, our grandfather?" said the lord.

"We're just making our living, your lordship," they replied.

"Why are you working for a living? Aren't those your children traveling with you?"

"No, they're not, your lordship. They're our grandchildren, our descendants, but it is nevertheless we who take pity on them. The bit of food they get is the portion we give them, your lordship," replied the grandmother and grandfather. Since the lord is getting done in by the

(continued)

(continued from previous page)
pain in his teeth, it is only with great effort that he speaks again:

"I implore you, please take pity on me! What sweets can you make, what poisons can you cure?" said the lord.

"We just pull the worms out of teeth, and we just cure eyes. We just set bones, your lordship," they replied.

"Very well, please cure my teeth. They really ache, every day. It's insufferable! I get no sleep because of them—and my eyes. They just shot me, those two tricksters! Ever since it started I haven't eaten because of it. Therefore take pity on me! Perhaps it's because my teeth are loose now."

"Very well, your lordship. It's a worm, gnawing at the bone. It's merely a matter of putting in a replacement and taking the teeth out, sir."

"But perhaps it's not good for my teeth to come out—since I am, after all, a lord. My finery is in my teeth—and my eyes."

"But then we'll put in a replacement. Ground bone will be put back in. "And this is the "ground bone": it's only white corn.

"Very well. Yank them out! Give me some help here!" he replied.

And when the teeth of Seven Macaw came out, it was only white corn that went in as a replacement for his teeth—just a coating shining white, that corn in his mouth. His face fell at once; he no longer looked like a lord. The last of his teeth came out, the jewels that had stood out blue from his mouth.

And then the eyes of Seven Macaw were cured. When his eyes were trimmed back the last of his metal came out. Still he felt no pain; he just looked on while the last of his greatness left him. It was just as Hunahpu and Xbalanque had intended.

And when Seven Macaw died, Hunahpu got back his arm. And Chimalmat, the wife of Seven Macaw, also died.

Such was the loss of the riches of Seven Macaw; only the doctors got the jewels and gems that had made him arrogant, here on the face of the earth. The genius of the grandmother, the genius of the grandfather did its work when they took back their arm: it was implanted and the break got well again. Just as they had wished the death of Seven Macaw, so they brought it about. They had seen evil in his self-magnification.

After this the two boys went on again. What they did was simply the word of Heart of the Sky.

—translated by Dennis Tedlock

Stela 3 depicts a deity or masked priest striding forward while a large serpent deity emerges from between his feet. Another boat-shaped form floats atop the serpent's tongue. Altars carved in the shape of frogs lie in front of Stelae 1 and 2.

Groups A and B are the main complexes of this part of Izapa. In the jungle between them lies the forest-covered Mound 60, at 22 meters the highest pyramid in southern Chiapas. Many more mounds and poorer quality stelae and monuments lie amid the surrounding jungle.

Return to the main Tapachula-Talisman road and go about a kilometer north of the turnoff and you'll see the ruins of Group F immediately to the left. This was the center of Izapa from 50 B.C. until its final abandonment in the Early Postclassic. Its residents reused at least 38 carved stones from the earlier southern part of the site as ritual objects or as building material.

From the small parking lot (the small house here is the residence of the site guardian/owner), you enter the grounds and walk left up the short ramp onto Structure 125. This is a reconstructed platform bearing four small temples on its south side and one large one on the north. The latter pyramid contained a trove of 61 burials and offerings deposited at various times of Group F's occupation. You can see some of the pottery in the Tapachula museum.

Behind the platform lies a square stone base from which rises Monument 4, a square column with a stylized serpent head at the top. This abuts the I-shaped ballcourt, which was decorated with stone monuments, including a throne at the west end, pillaged from the older part of the site. Inset in the ballcourt's north wall is Stela 67, showing a man (perhaps masked) gesturing with some type of baton in his outstretched hands while he sits in a boat floating on water. The stela's top half is broken off.

The ballcourt forms the north end of the plaza containing the small Structure 130, a three-tier platform with stairs to the east and west. The east side of the plaza is bordered by a long platform made up of Structures 128 (on the east end of the ballcourt) and 129.

A thatched roof at the site entrance protects Stela 22 (during rainstorms, this hut may be shared by chicken and ducks), which was discovered during the construction of the nearby highway. This depicts a figure wearing an elaborate mask seated in a boat-shaped trough with water motifs below and a second deity mask floating above. Unfortunately, around 1960 this relief was recarved by a rogue art dealer following his own imagination. Luckily, photographs were taken of the more worn but at least authentic original.

THE USUMACINTA BASIN

The Usumacinta is one of the most important rivers of Mesoamerica. Along its banks, the Classic-era Maya erected a series of cities whose elaborate architecture took full advantage of the region's hilly terrain. Centers such as Palenque and Yaxchilan represented the apex of Maya civilization; from architecture to ceramics, their artworks are some of the most beautiful produced in Mesoamerica. Their temple walls were lined with stone and stucco reliefs containing long hieroglyphic inscriptions. We now can read them: they tell a tale of kingly ritual, war, and self-exaltation—the central leitmotifs of Maya rulership.

Jungle now surrounds those Maya cites. The Usumacinta flows through some of the last untouched rainforest in Mexico, a region known as the Lacandon, made up of hills and flatland. These fast-disappearing forests are habitat to literally thousands of plant and animal species. They are also the home of the Lacandon Maya, a small group of hunter-gatherers who until the 20th century had almost no contact with the outside world. Although they are now settled in permanent villages, the Lacandon still practice Maya rites in ancient centers such as Yaxchilan and Bonampak.

THE LAND

Southeast of the Isthmus of Tehuantepec rises a band of mountains called the Central American Highlands, which runs from the Mexican state of Chiapas to Nicaragua. In Chiapas, the highlands are divided into two by the Río Grijalva valley; the Sierra Madre de Chiapas lies to the south, while on the north rises the Sierra de San Cristóbal. These converge just beyond the Guatemala border and become the Guatemala Highlands.

The headwaters of the Río Usumacinta lie in the mountains of Guatemala. From the upper slopes of a volcano just north of Huehuetenango descend the Río Lacantún and the Río Salinas-Chixoy. The latter river becomes the border between Guatemala and Mexico and about 50 kilometers to the north runs into the Río Pasión entering from Guatemala's Petén Jungle to the east. From here to the Gulf of Mexico, the river takes the name of the Usumacinta.

For the next 120 kilometers, the Usumacinta acts not only as the border between two nations but as the frontier between two geographical areas. To the east extend the broad and incredibly dense forests of the Petén Jungle, home to dozens, perhaps hundreds of Maya centers (including the metropolis of Tikal), and, until recently, an armed guerrilla movement. Immediately to the west abruptly rise the first foothills of the Sierra de San Cristóbal.

The latter region's geology is caused by upfaulted blocks topped with limestone. In some areas you see gentle rolling hills, in others choppy waves of "haystack" hills separated by sinkholes. Chiapas's limestone is highly porous, so many of the streams run underground and caverns are plentiful. The narrow valleys between the hills provide ample protection for Maya settlements (and for an ongoing Mexican armed guerrilla movement). In the larger Classic-era centers, the Maya built their most important temples up the steep hillsides, giving rulers a dramatic platform from which to dominate their people. Because of the roughness of the terrain, the easiest way to move people and trade goods was on canoes paddling up and down the river.

At a spot appropriately called Boca de Cerro, Mouth of the Hills, the Usumacinta emerges onto the broad coastal plain of the state of Tabasco. From here it meanders through a maze of oxbows, lakes, and swamps before spilling into the Gulf of Mexico from a wide, swampy delta formed by both the Río Usumacinta and Río Grijalva. Most of this region is river floodplain; the only safe spots to build cities are on the natural levees along the riverbanks. Here you find not only such late Maya centers as Comalcalco, but the far earlier Olmec city of La Venta.

Climate

From the cool highlands to the steamy coastal plain, the Usumacinta basin contains a number of climatic regions. The highlands have a humid temperate climate. The rainy season runs from May through November, with occasional wintertime Nortes bringing cold drizzles. The average daytime temperature runs 68–80°F while nights are 50–60°F. Frosts and hail are possible in winter.

As you drop in altitude, you pass through a number of intermediary microclimates before reaching the Usumacinta. The lowlands are far wetter and hotter, with temperatures averaging 77°F and up. Rain falls year-round; only February and March may be called "dry"—high humidity is a constant. The southern Tabasco plains are one of the wettest regions of Mexico, beaten only by parts of the Soconusco for annual rainfall. The only cool periods arrive with the December to March Nortes.

Flora and Fauna

The Sierra de San Cristóbal Highlands are covered with a dense pine-oak forest, now somewhat thinned by overlogging. Below the upper canopy, you find a wide variety of shrubs, ferns, mosses, and grasses. As you descend, the pine trees disappear and the forest becomes wholly deciduous, including dogwood and sweet gum.

Dense tropical rainforest lines the banks of the Río Usumacinta. More than 4,000 plant species—over a fifth of all found in Mexico—have been identified

THE LACANDON MAYA

When loggers first entered the rainforests of southeastern Chiapas in the late 19th century, they discovered that the dense jungle was not uninhabited. They encountered small groups of barefoot Indians with long black hair and wearing only short robes. These were the Lacandon, a group of seminomadic Maya who were probably descended from Indians who in the 17th and 18th centuries had fled from Spanish invaders into the jungles along the Río Usumacinta. The Lacandon still worshipped the Maya gods and held regular ceremonies in the temples of Palenque, Yaxchilan, and Bonampak. Because of their isolation, they managed to preserve their traditions well into the 20th century. In the 1940s, however, their lands were encroached by other Maya tribes emigrating from the Chiapas Highlands. In 1971, the Mexican government gave the Lacandon the deed to a large tract of jungle and induced them to settle in a series of small villages. Roads brought modernity in the form of tourists, American missionaries, and consumer goods. Today, most Lacandon practice their own religion while managing to adapt to their new lifestyle. They are still threatened, however, by Chiapas's simmering civil war and increased lawlessness along the Mexico-Guatemala border.

here, from towering mahogany, ceiba, and chicozapote trees to tiny orchids and bromeliads. These are now threatened by logging and encroaching settlement.

Now much depleted because of overhunting, the highland fauna included deer, mountain lion, and wild turkey. The most famous of the birds was the majestic quetzal, whose feathers were traded and used to construct ritual costumes throughout Mesoamerica. You still can see some migrating birds, particularly ducks, but today's highland mammal population has largely dwindled to members of the rodent family.

The lowland jungles contain the richest assortment of wildlife in Mexico. In the Lacandon region, you find 800 species of butterflies, 345 species of birds, 114 species of mammals, and an incredible 67 species of bats. The nighttime forests resound with the roars of howler monkeys. Many of these animals, including bats, harpy eagles, and jaguars, found their place as deities in the Maya pantheon. The best place to see this remarkable fauna is around such jungle sites as Yaxchilan and Bonampak.

HISTORY

One of the great mysteries of Maya archaeology is why the middle and upper Usumacinta region was not settled earlier. The first traces of human settlement yet found are relatively late, dating to the Middle Preclassic (1000–300 B.C.). Either people were not here, or archaeologists have simply not yet found their settlements. This contrasts with all the surrounding regions (central and southern Chiapas, southern Guatemala, Gulf coast, and Yucatan Peninsula) where human remains have been found dating to at least 3000 B.C. and in some cases far earlier.

The earliest Usumacinta basin settlements yet discovered lie along the Río Pasión in Guatemala. The sites of Altar de Sacrificios and Ceibal were first inhabited between 800 and 600 B.C. Their settlers may have entered the region from the Petén jungles to the east. At Ceibal researchers found Olmec-style jades and a carved bone perforator, signs that the region had ties with the Gulf. (Further evidence of Olmec influence in the region is an Olmec rock relief, now destroyed, found at Xoc in the Río Jataté drainage southeast of Toniná).

Altar de Sacrificios, which lies a stone's throw from Mexico at the confluence of the Río Pasión and Río Salinas, grew into a large village with a small civic-religious area around a central plaza. Nevertheless, it was dwarfed by early Maya centers such as Tikal and the even larger metropolis of El Mirador lying to the east in the heart of the Petén Jungle. Altar de Sacrificios, Ceibal, and other Río Pasión sites continued as Maya centers until the 9th-century Classic Maya collapse.

The riverbanks downstream from Altar de Sacrificios were, as far as we know, uninhabited during the Middle Preclassic. By about A.D. 100, a series of small settlements had sprung up along the Usumacinta. Where these immigrants came from is unknown. They could have paddled up the Usumacinta from the Gulf, trekked west across the Petén or hiked across the highlands from southern Chiapas or Guatemala. Their settlements grew into some of the most important in the Maya region—Piedras Negras in Guatemala and Yaxchilan, Bonampak, and Palenque on the Mexico side.

PALENQUE

INTRODUCTION

Poised on the edge of the jungle overlooking the floodplain of the Río Usumacinta, Palenque is one of the most breathtaking sites in Mesoamerica. Researchers have found a trove of archaeological riches here, including the richest and most elaborate tomb discovered in Mexico. Palenque's numerous temples and pyramids are covered with fine sculptures and thousands of hieroglyphs. Epigraphers—specialists in the decipherment of ancient inscriptions—can now read the hieroglyphs; they tell of the dynasties that ruled Palenque from the Early Classic through the site's collapse and mysterious abandonment. The ruined city is set among the steep foothills and dense jungles at the base of the Chiapas Highlands. You can easily spend two days wandering and exploring the site and not see it all. Many unexplored temples lie in the surrounding forest.

The Temple of the Inscriptions was built to house the tomb of Janaab' Pakal I, also known as Pakal the Great, the city's most powerful ruler.

DANIELLE GUSTAFSON

HISTORY

Palenque's success is partially due to its location. It lies in the far northern foothills of the Chiapas Highlands. Here, it could act as a trading post between the Maya country to the south and east and the Gulf cultures to the north and west. The city itself was built on a natural terrace overlooking the Usumacinta plain to the north; on the other three sides, it was protected by the steep, forest-covered foothills. At least six year-round streams provided ample supplies of water. This dramatic setting also gave the Maya a natural amphitheater in which to build their spectacular pyramids—a visitor's first sight of Classic-era Palenque must have been awesome indeed.

Although Palenque is one of the most studied ancient cities in Mesoamerica, it is embarrassing to report how poorly we understand the center's chronology,

PALENQUE

How to get there: The modern town and ancient ruins of Palenque lie on Highway 199 between San Cristóbal and Ocosingo to the south and Highway 186 (running from Villa-hermosa to Campeche) to the north. Palenque's famous ruins lie on the edge of the hills 11 kilometers southwest of town. The road to the entrance of the ruins winds uphill, passing fields and unexcavated mounds. Frequent minibus service departs from downtown.

Hours: Daily 0700–1800.

Admission fee: 30 pesos.

How long to tour: To see only the highlights, it takes a half day. A complete tour of everything will take at least two days.

Recommended gear: Hats, sunblock, bottled water, mosquito repellent, hiking boots.

Museum: One of the best archaeological museums in Mexico, the Palenque museum lies at the base of the hillside. The entrance is part of the site admission. Its collection includes more than a dozen spectacular incense burners found during the recent excavations; the Palace Tablet, which tells of K'an Joy Chitam I's accession to the Palenque throne; and a number of fine stucco portrait heads. There seem to have been relatively few free-standing sculptures at the site; one of the few examples is the damaged figure of a richly costumed ruler on display. Temporary exhibitions are displayed on the second floor, and the complex also houses a good gift shop and snack bar.

Food and accommodations: The town of Palenque is a good base for all the Usumacinta area sites. On the top end, the **Hotel Misión Palenque**, tel. 967/5-0241, fax 5-0300, east of downtown caters to tour groups and offers all the amenities. The less expensive **Hotel Cañada**, Calle Merle Green 14, tel. 967/5-0102, fax 5-0392, is a favorite with archaeologists and set among a grove of shade trees.

DANIELLE GUSTAFSON

stone reliefs of captured and tortured rulers from the sunken patio of the Palace

particularly its origins. What little researchers know is based on Robert Rands' stratigraphic excavations from the 1960s.

The earliest ceramics found in Palenque date to around A.D. 100. The first permanent settlement may have been founded during the following two centuries. It lay on the northwestern frontier of the early Maya Chicanel culture centered in the Petén Jungle. One early center of Palenque was around the Picota Group and the Templo Olvidado (Forgotten Temple) in the forest a kilometer west of the main plaza. Further early ceramics were found in the base of the Temple of the Count and the Temple of the Inscriptions. It is not clear if early structures were built here or if the ceramics were moved here and used as fill for the later temples.

Between A.D. 300 and 600, Palenque was a small regional center with trade ties to the Petén region and to the Chiapas Highlands and the Grijalva Valley just beyond. During this era, Palenque's center shifted from the Picota Group to the present Main Plaza area. The site shared so many cultural and artistic traits with the centers of Piedras Negras, Yaxchilan, and Bonampak lying up the Río Usumacinta that it is evident that they were built by peoples rising from a common ancestry. The Usumacinta acted as the region's superhighway along which people traded not only goods but civic and religious beliefs. At the height of the Classic era, they would use the river to transport aristocratic spouses for neighboring rulers and to carry warriors for ritual battles whose purpose was to seize sacrificial captives.

In the middle of this period, Palenque's written history begins. On March 10, 431, a man named K'uk' B'alam (Quetzal-Jaguar) ascended to the throne. We know this not from contemporaneous accounts but from the dynastic history written two centuries later by the great Palenque ruler K'inich Kan B'alam II (Great Sun Snake-Jaguar). The latter traced his ancestry from the mythic first

THE LORDS OF PALENQUE

This list gives the dates of accession and the names of the rulers of Palenque. The names in parentheses are the original names given them by the archaeologists before they were able to translate the complete name. After K'inich Ahkal Mo' Naab' III, Palenque's lords became less avid about recording the important dates of their reign, and we are missing many of the dynastic details between him and Wak Kimi Janaab' Pakal, the city's last ruler.

1. A.D. 431 K'uk' B'alam I (Bahlum-Kuk I)
2. 435 "Casper"
3. 487 B'utz'aj Sak Chik (Manik)
4. 501 Ahkal Mo' Naab I (Chaacal I)
5. 529 K'an Joy Chitam I (Kan-Xul I)
6. 565 Ahkall Mo' Naab' II (Chaacal II)
7. 572 Kan B'alam I (Chan-Bahlum I)
8. 583 Lady Yohl Ik'nal (Lady Kanal-Ikal)
9. 605 Aj Ne' Ohl Mat (Ah Kan)
10. 612 Lady Sak-K'uk' (Lady Zac-Kuk) also known as Muwaan Mat
11. 615 K'inich Janaab' Pakal I (Pakal II also known as Pakal the Great)
12. 684 K'inich Kan B'alam II (Chan-Bahlum II)
13. 702 K'inich K'an Joy Chitam II
14. 721 K'inich Ahkal Mo' Naab' III (Chaacal III)
15. 742? K'inich Janaab' Pakal II
16. 764 K'inich K'uk' B'alam II (Kuk)
17. 799 Wak Kimi Janaab' Pakal (Cimi-Pacal)

ruler (dubbed "Lady Beastie" by epigraphers) of the present creation through to a semimythic (probably Olmec) king named U-Kix-Chan. From K'uk' B'alam, Kan B'alam II recorded the following 11 generations leading up to himself, and artists depicted the story on hieroglyphic plaques decorating the tops of Palenque's major temples.

The Late Classic Maya era—the height of Maya civilization—begins in A.D. 600. During the following century, the rulers of Palenque commissioned some of the finest Maya artworks known. Most of the great structures you see in Palenque's central area date from this time, including the Palace and the Temples of the Inscriptions, Count, Cross, and Sun. These works were built during the reigns of—and to glorify—the two greatest Palenque rulers.

In A.D. 603, K'inich Janaab' Pakal I, better known as Pakal the Great, was born, and he ascended the throne a mere 12 years later. His great work was the Temple of the Inscriptions, the towering pyramid that he designed as his tomb. The massive stone lid covering his body was carved with a relief showing Pakal descending into the maw of the Underworld. Around its side are glorified portraits of his immediate ancestors, including two women (his mother and great-grandmother) who were apparently Palenque rulers. After Pakal's death in A.D. 683 at the age of 80, he was succeeded by his oldest son, K'inich Kan B'alam II, the ruler who ordered the creation of the complete dynastic history. The purpose of this creation was to legitimize his rule, not only through ancestry but through associating himself with the most powerful forces in Maya religion.

Why did Pakal and Kan B'alam II feel such a need to assert their right to rule? During the 8th century A.D., Palenque grew, both as a city and as the regional power of the northwestern Maya frontier. This did not happen without tension, both internal—could the land support the larger population?—and with

F. Waldeck.

M⁰ Queen & Co Lithog.

an 18th-century drawing of a Palenque relief

its neighbors. Hieroglyphic plaques in Palcnque and at other Maya centers, including the distant Maya superstate of Calakmul, record a history of battles and
destruction. In A.D. 603, Bonampak captured Palenque's standard of war. Eight
years later, Calakmul attacked the city and destroyed Palenque's center.
Palenque in turn captured and sacrificed high-caste warriors from neighbors

such as Pomoná. These records of warfare seem to become more common during the following century, perhaps as a symptom of increasing chaos in the Maya world.

Palenque seemed to flourish during the 70 years following Kan B'alam II's death in A.D. 702. The city reached its height as a regional power, expanding far north into Tabasco. Work continued on the structures around the ceremonial center, including the completion of the Temple of the Foliated Cross and an addition to the Palace. After A.D. 731, however, most construction is halted, and the recording of dynastic history becomes noticeably less grandiose. Palenque's best-known 8th-century ruler (and Kan B'alam II's younger brother), K'inich K'an Joy Chitam II, is famous only for his defeat: in A.D. 711, he was captured by the newly militaristic center of Toniná.

The last calendar inscription found at Palenque dates to A.D. 799. It was discovered on a vase from a second-rate tomb in a residential area just below the main plaza. The glyphs record the ascension to Palenque's throne of Wak Kimi Jannab' Pakal (6 Death ? Shield); the ruler's name is half-Mexicanized (6 Death) and half tries to associate itself with Pakal the Great. This last gasp of Palenque's dynasty did not endure. In A.D. 810, all ritual activity in the center of city stops. The ceramics dating to this era are a foreign intrusion crafted in the style of the Tabasco lowlands to the north. They probably belonged to Putún Maya tribespeople who occupied an abandoned city. They also left behind broken ballgame yokes and markers that were scattered around the main plaza. After A.D. 900, even they had deserted the city, and the temples were engulfed by forest.

DANIELLE GUSTAFSON

Temple of the Sun

ARCHAEOLOGICAL   RECORD

Few Mesoamerican sites have been so extensively studied for so long and by such colorful characters—there is easily enough information for a book on this topic. Rumors about a marvelous city in the Chiapas jungles began to circulate in the mid-18th century. In 1773, the canon of the cathedral at San Cristóbal de las Casas sent his brother to investigate. The brother's report of marvelous ruins reached the authorities in Guatemala City, and in 1784 an expedition embarked from the capital. The 1784 Guatemalan expedition found 215 structures, including a palace; from the sandals on the stucco relief figures, the explorers believed the builders were Romans.

Two years later, a second Guatemalan expedition entered the ruins; they were led by Don Antonio del Río, an artillery officer, and an Italian architect named Antonio Bernasconi. They hired 79 local Indian laborers and burned off the vegetation covering the main plaza. They then explored every temple and broke off pieces of stucco relief that were sent first to Guatemala City and then to the king in Madrid. Del Río believed that Palenque had been built by some early European civilization ("Phoenicians, Greeks, Romans, and others"); he did, however, recognize that Palenque and the ancient cities of Yucatan were constructed by the same peoples.

In 1807, the famous expedition of Guillermo Dupaix visited Palenque. He was accompanied by an excellent artist, Luciano Castañeda, who produced accurate drawings of the site and fanciful reproductions of the most important reliefs. Dupaix believed Palenque had been built by the residents of Atlantis. Nevertheless, his report opened the floodgates for an invasion of foreigners at Palenque.

One of the most eccentric was "Count" Jean Frédéric de Waldeck, of unclear nationality, who in 1832, aged a spry 66, built a hut at the base of the Temple of the Cross and set up house with a local girl. He lived there for 18 months and produced a number of highly romanticized drawings of the reliefs. Waldeck believed Palenque's builders were the Egyptians. Of his main work, *Monuments Anciens du Mérique,* the distinguished Mexican archaeologist Ignacio Bernal wrote: "... its ideas are so absurd as to preclude any intelligent discussion of them."

It became the custom to set up camp for months or years at Palenque. In 1839 the site was visited by the English team of Patrick Walker and John Caddy, who marched through the Petén Jungle from Belize. They had been determined to beat the far more famous duo of John Lloyd Stephens and Frederick Catherwood, who arrived at Palenque in early 1840. Stephens was the writer and Catherwood was the artist, and together they produced *Incidents of Travel in Central America, Chiapas and Yucatan,* a work that combines scholarship with the best of adventure writing. They camped for months at Palenque, clearing the ruins and producing excellent descriptions and drawings of the structures and the numerous reliefs. Unlike many of his predecessors, Stephens believed that it was the ancestors of the native Maya in the area who built the ruins, not some far-off race from across (or below) the oceans.

This expedition was among the last to rely solely on pen and watercolors to record the site (they brought a camera on their subsequent expedition to the Yucatan). In 1858, Désiré Charnay was the first to photograph the site. Two decades later, Teobert Maler brought more professional camera equipment to the site. His example was improved upon by Alfred Maudslay, who in 1890–91 produced a beautiful photographic record of Palenque. Both their heavily illustrated reports are invaluable tools for comparing the present state of the monuments to an earlier, dilapidated, yet more pristine, condition.

In the late 19th and early 20th centuries, Palenque was visited by a number of the early greats of archaeology, including William H. Holmes, Eduard Seler, and Sylvanus G. Morley. In 1922, the Dirección de Arqueología sent Frans Blom to Palenque; he discovered many more buildings and produced a large-scale map of the site but did not excavate. In 1934, the first major excavation of Palenque began under Miguel Ángel Fernández with the assistance of Heinrich Berlin and Roque Cevallos Novelo. During the next 11 years, they cleared the central area of the site, discovered many important reliefs, and restored the Temple of the Sun and part of the Palace.

Miguel Ángel Fernández was succeeded in 1949 by Alberto Ruz Lhuillier, the man who made the most famous discoveries at Palenque. Most of what you see today, particularly around the main plaza, dates to the Ruz era. He initiated a complete investigation of Palenque from the archaeological sequence to the ethnography of the area's modern inhabitants. Among his many discoveries were the aqueduct, the Palace Tablet, and tombs in Temples 13, 14, and 18.

While exploring the top of the Temple of the Inscriptions, Ruz realized that a large stone in the floor probably covered a passageway. He removed it and discovered a staircase crammed with rubble. Its extraction took months; on June 13, 1952, the excavation arrived at six skeletons and an offering lying on top of a huge triangular stone. When they opened it up, they discovered—more rubble. They knew they were digging toward something important, but they had no idea what it was. Two days later, they arrived at a great carved stone that they guessed to be an altar. Unfortunately, they had to stop because the dry excavating season had ended and they had temporarily run out of funds. They returned in November to see what lay beneath the stone. On November 15, Ruz was able to peek underneath and see the heavily adorned skeleton of a Palenque ruler we now know to be Pakal the Great. News of the tomb's discovery brought Ruz—and Palenque—worldwide fame.

Ruz continued excavating at Palenque until 1958. After his death in 1979, his ashes were buried at the foot of the Temple of the Inscriptions. After a gap of a decade, Ruz was succeeded by Jorge Acosta, who worked at the site until he died in 1976. Acosta's project was mostly devoted to cleaning, protecting, and restoring the buildings, although some excavations were performed. César Sáenz continued Acosta's work, restoring parts of the Palace and Temples of the

Inscriptions, Sun, and Foliated Cross. Another preservation project ran from 1982 through 1988 under Roberto García Moll; the project also produced a topographic map of the area.

In 1989, INAH's Chiapas center began a new excavation and restoration program under Arnoldo González Cruz. Their work centered on the Palace, the base of the Temple of the Cross, and the Temple of the Bat in Group III. This project was extended from 1992 to 1994 as one of the Salinas administration's archaeological special projects. The excavations unearthed numerous spectacular finds, including tombs with elaborate offerings and dozens of large, perfectly preserved incense burners in the form of god masks.

Since 1964, Palenque has also been the fixation of Merle Greene Robertson, an American art historian. For decades, she has been photographing every known sculpture at the site. The results of her work are published in four large-format volumes that are an invaluable tool for researchers. Robertson has also hosted the famous Palenque Round Tables, an irregularly scheduled series of symposia dedicated to Maya research. In 1973, the first Round Table was the scene of one of the great breakthroughs in the translation of Maya hieroglyphs; the more recent meetings have attracted overflow crowds of professional Mayanists, students, and enthusiastic amateurs.

Since 1997, the Palenque Project, directed by Robertson and Alfonso Morales, has unearthed some of the most exciting finds in Mexico. Their work centers on the Cross Group, particularly on Temple XIV (just north of the Temple of the Sun) and Temples XIX and XX rising just to the south. The most spectacular discovery was a long, perfectly preserved relief panel on the front of a platform of Temple XIX. On it, the Ahkal Mo' Nahb', flanked by two nobles, personifies the patron god GI and thus lays claim to rulership over Palenque's city-state. Other discoveries include a frescoed tomb in Temple XX, towering incense burners, and a number of large fragments of reliefs. Many of these artworks are now on display in the site museum.

T O U R I N G   T H E   S I T E

From the blissfully shaded parking lot, you enter Palenque's civic and religious center, normally ablaze under the tropical sun, at the west side of the Main Plaza. Along the foot of the hill to your right stand three temples. The first is Temple XII, better known as the Temple of the Dying Moon. On the left pier of the upper temple, you see the carved skeletal mask of a rabbit with large fangs. The Maya associated rabbits with the moon (and deer with the sun); a dead rabbit then corresponded with a dying moon.

Opposite this structure stands the vegetation-covered bulk of Temple XI. Next to the path here lies the tomb of Alberto Ruz Lhuillier (1906–79), the renowned Mexican archaeologist who discovered Pakal's tomb and excavated most of the ceremonial center.

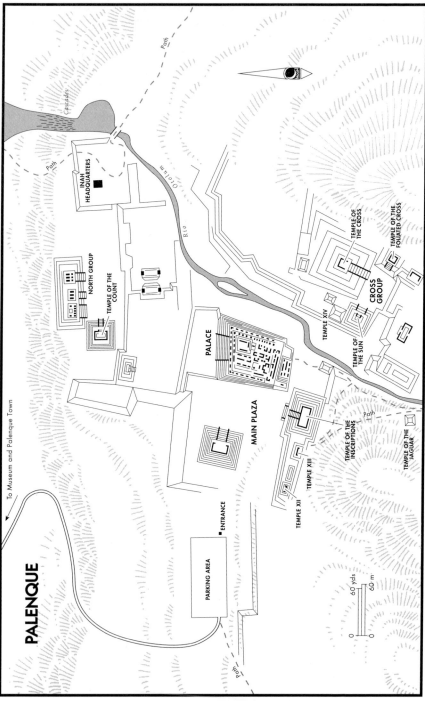

PALENQUE

To Museum and Palenque Town

PARKING AREA

ENTRANCE

MAIN PLAZA

PALACE

NORTH GROUP

TEMPLE OF THE COUNT

INAH HEADQUARTERS

Cascades

Path

Path

Río Otolum

Río

TEMPLE XII

TEMPLE XIII

TEMPLE OF THE INSCRIPTIONS

TEMPLE OF THE JAGUAR

Path

TEMPLE XIV

TEMPLE OF THE SUN

CROSS GROUP

TEMPLE OF THE CROSS

TEMPLE OF THE FOLIATED CROSS

60 yds

60 m

0

0

Continuing east, after Temple XII you come to a lower platform, the small structure of Temple XIII (an elaborate noble tomb containing a richly adorned skeleton was recently found here) covered with a thatched roof and, finally, the massive Temple of the Inscriptions. Like most of Palenque's ceremonial buildings, this 61-meter-tall pyramid was painted a deep red. It was built during the second half of the 7th century A.D. during the last decades of Pakal the Great's reign. The staircase ascends nine (you see this number repeated frequently at Palenque) tiers to the temple on top. The topmost flight of stairs is flanked by two stone reliefs, perhaps representing captives, that strongly resemble those found in the Palace's East Courtyard.

This upper temple is a wide structure with a ruined roofcomb atop a mansard roof. Five doorways enter into one large chamber with elaborate stucco reliefs decorating the piers on either side of the doors. The ones on the far left and right are purely inscriptions, made of rows of now-fragmentary hieroglyphs. The other four depict regal figures in elaborate feathered headdresses standing on monster masks. Each holds a "child" or, more likely, a representation of the serpent-footed K'awiil, also known as God K, who is associated with dynastic change. He is one of the Palenque Triad, a group of three gods whom Palenque's rulers worshipped as their mythic ancestors. The K'awiil serpents extend from the outstretched hands of each standing figure. These are portraits of Pakal and his ancestors; the one on Pier C (third from left) is probably his mother.

Behind these piers, you find a long vaulted room. Its outstanding features are three hieroglyphic plaques, one each on the east and west end and a third on the back wall in the center. The temple takes its name from these tablets. They are a form of royal propaganda that tells the story of Palenque's ruling dynasties culminating in the glorious reign of Pakal himself.

When Alberto Ruz Lhuillier was exploring this temple, he saw that one of the large floor stones had holes in it, as if ropes or pegs could be placed in them and the stone moved. The rest is history. You can now descend the 66 slippery steps to Lord Pakal's tomb. At the bottom, you reach a barred portal looking into the vaulted tomb chamber. The massive sarcophagus lid—one of the most famous sculptures in Mesoamerica—is suspended over the tomb, now empty. Pakal's bones and adornment, including a magnificent jade funerary mask, are now on display in Mexico City's Museo Nacional de Antropología.

Still bearing traces of red paint, the limestone sarcophagus lid depicts Pakal at the instant of his death descending into the gaping mouth of the Underworld (Mayanists utterly reject the astronaut-in-spaceship hypothesis that became popular in the 1970s). Above him rises the World Tree, the center of the Universe, upon which perches the Vucub Caquix, the Celestial Bird, symbolizing the heavenly realm. The lid's sides are carved with portraits of Pakal's most glorious ancestors. The atmosphere down here is thick with humidity and age; it is a relief to return to the outside world.

From the top of the Temple of the Inscriptions, a path leads into the forests behind. If you take the right fork, in about 150 meters you come to the Temple

DANIELLE GUSTAFSON

the Palace, with the four-story Observatory in the center

of the Jaguar, also known as the Temple of the Beautiful Relief. You enter this small, semiruined temple via the second story. Fragments on the wall are all that remains of the beautiful relief. Count Waldeck drew this as a ruler seated cross-legged on a double-headed jaguar throne. Only parts of the throne seat and left claw remain. An interior staircase leads down to a vaulted room (a crypt?) with narrow, T-shaped windows. These are the so-called "Ik" openings found throughout the site; "Ik" probably symbolizes the wind and may be associated with the ruling lineage. Above this temple soar the massive trees of the Palenque jungle.

A trail cuts along the stream, actually the Río Otolum, just below this structure. This is the local Chol Maya trail to their settlement of Naranjo on the other side of hill. The stream is walled here; it was the beginning of the aqueduct that carried water into the center of the site. If you cross the stream and head uphill, you come to a fork in the path. To the right stand the small, semireconstructed Temples XX and XVII. Two more temples lie to the left. The second of these, a two-stage platform set against the ridge, contains an elaborate serpentine stucco relief in its inner room.

From here, you drop into the plaza of the Cross Group, Palenque's second great funerary complex (after the Temple of the Inscriptions). After Kan B'alam II buried his fa-

The **Palenque Triad** is made up of three patron deities, dubbed GI, GII, and GIII. The first, GI the Younger, has been identified as the reincarnation of a god, GI the Elder, who ruled during the previous cycle of existence. GII is the infantile variant of K'awiil, the patron of royal lineages, and GIII is a version of the Jaguar Sun God.

ther and ascended to the throne in the late 7th century, he began the construction of this temple group to proclaim his version of dynastic history and, probably, to act as his tomb. It is named the Cross Group because early explorers thought that the cruciform objects in two of its greatest reliefs were versions of the Christian cross. Researchers now believe they are representations of the Maya World Tree that lies at the center of Universe.

The first structure you come to is the Temple of the Foliated Cross, which is built against the hillside on the east side of the plaza. This was probably the last of the group constructed. (Few researchers agree on the order in which the temples should be visited; as a group, the inscriptions do not seem to conform to our ideas of a linear text.) You take a winding path up the building's unrestored base. Like each of the Cross Group structures, this is topped with a small temple with three doorways, a mansard roof, and a roofcomb. The outer facade of this temple is now gone; the side of the roof bears some fragments of stucco reliefs, and the roofcomb is heavily damaged.

The interior layout is the same at all three Cross Group temples. You enter a wide outer room from which three doorways open along the back. The left and right doors enter small vaulted chambers, while the center takes you to the sanctuary. The latter resembles a one-room temple that guards three elaborate reliefs. Two were on the left and right doorjambs; they were heavily damaged and have been removed. They showed Kan B'alam II before (left) and after (right) his accession to the throne.

On the back wall stands the Tablet of the Foliated Cross depicting the act of accession itself. On the left stands Kan B'alam II, almost naked; opposite him is the smaller figure of his dead predecessor, Lord Pakal, wrapped in twisted cloths. Pakal is about to pass on to Kan B'alam II the symbols of royal power. Between them rises the Foliated Cross, a variant of the World Tree adorned with maize stalks, symbolizing maize as the source of sustenance. It was only through the ruler's interaction with the gods that this staff of life could grow. The inscriptions to the left and right tell of the rituals leading up to Kan B'alam II's accession.

You see a similar scene inside the Temple of the Cross, the large pyramid that occupies the north end of the Cross Group plaza. Its main staircase faces away from the rest of the city, as if to emphasize the elite nature of the ceremonies performed here. You climb five tiers to reach the temple. The front of the temple has collapsed, leaving only two damaged piers bearing fragmentary stucco reliefs. The roofcomb, the highest at Palenque, is in excellent condition. Sculptures originally occupied its niches.

The interior layout is the same as that of the Foliated Cross, only more spacious. The sanctuary's left doorjamb depicts Kan B'alam II in full kingly regalia on January 20, 690, at the end of a 10-day ritual period following his accession. Opposite, the jamb shows God L, the aged cigar-smoking deity who guided Kan-B'alam on his ritual journey. The Tablet of the Cross panel inside the sanctuary again shows Kan B'alam II and Pakal during the accession ritual just before the dead Pakal has handed over the scepter. Between them rises the World Tree (identified as the ceiba), this time in its role as the axis of the Universe, rising from the Underworld to the Heavens with the four directions radiating from it. Palenque's rulers were the intercessors between this hub of mystical powers and their people. The inscriptions on either side recite the dynastic succession, beginning with "Lady Beastie," the mythic first ruler of this Creation, and culminating in Kan B'alam II.

The last, and smallest, of the Cross Group is the Temple of the Sun rising on the west side of the plaza. It acts as a barrier between this complex and the rest of the ceremonial center. You climb 17 steps and then seven steps to arrive at this well-preserved temple. The roof bears pieces of a stucco monster mask relief (similar ones were probably on the Temples of the Cross and Foliated Cross), while on the roofcomb you can see the legs of a large god figure who was seated top center and the remains of a row of smaller gods sitting below. The center two piers depicted standing figures; you can see the remains of headdresses and feet. The left and right piers were glyphic; only one large quatrefoil cartouche remains on the left pier.

The theme of the interior sanctuary is once again Kan B'alam II's ascent to the throne. This time, however, the context is war and sacrifice, the third of a Palenque ruler's duties (after ensuring the orderly progression of the Universe and the growth of crops). To the left and right, the jambs (now removed) contained portraits of Kan B'alam II before and after his assumption of the throne. The back wall contains the Tablet of the Sun, so named because 19th-century archaeologists thought the central figure was a sun shield. Researchers now believe it is a war shield with the face of GIII, the humanoid, jaguar-eared third god of the Palenque Triad. It is suspended on two crossed flint-tipped spears. The spears rise from a bleeding Jaguar and Snake throne, representing war and sacrifice, supported by two gods. To the left stands the figure of the dead Pakal, while to the right is the larger Kan B'alam II holding a manikin of K'awiil (GII in the Palenque Triad). The inscriptions relate an abbreviated dynastic history up to the date when a six-year-old Kan B'alam II was designated heir.

Abutting the north face of this structure, the small, two-tier Temple XIV was probably built by Kan B'alam II successor K'inich K'an Joy Chitam II. It blocks the access to the Cross Group from the rest of the site. On top, a metal roof covers a tablet showing Kan B'alam II in the Underworld. His mother, Lady Tz'akb'u Ajaw, kneels to the left and offers him a K'awiil manikin. Kan B'alam II gestures with his arms and raises his left foot: he is dancing in triumph after a three-year journey through Xibalba, the Maya Underworld, which culminated (like the story of the Hero Twins in the Popol Vuh) with the defeat of the lords of Xibalba.

Archaeologists recently found a burial of 18 skeletons, including a richly adorned aristocrat and some elaborate incense burners (now in the site museum), in the plaza behind Temple XIV and the smaller platform of Temple XV. North of the Temple of the Cross, Group XVI is a complex of eight elite residences built along an east-west axis. Recent INAH excavations here unearthed a number of hieroglyphic tablets and other reliefs.

Abutting the jungle-covered hills just south of the Cross Group, Temples XIX and XX are still being explored by archaeologists with the Palenque Project. You can visit them via a short path that heads up the hill. Many of the amazing objects found in these two structures are now on display in the site museum. In Temple XX, the frescoed tomb that was discovered in early 1999 has been re-sealed until researchers can figure out how to enter the brightly painted room without harming its contents.

From the Cross Group, a path drops and crosses the Río Otolum to Palenque's Palace, one of the most complicated structures in Mesoamerica. This complex of courtyards separated by long "houses" with corridors was the central ritual and perhaps residential space of Palenque's rulers. Many of the rooms contained or-nate benches that were probably used as thrones. On the walls you can see holes for pegs holding tapestries to divide rooms and cover doorways. Based on a three-meter-tall platform, the Palace was built in many stages from the early, now-subterranean structures to the multistory Tower, erected just before the city's collapse.

You approach the Palace from the east. A roof halfway up the right side covers stucco reliefs on the *tablero* face of a tier. Above, five piers are decorat-ed with further reliefs. The left-most contains an inscription made from 36 glyphs, now mostly missing. The rest show standing men richly costumed in plumed headdresses and adornments. On either side are seated figures facing the central character. These scenes probably represent Palenque rulers sur-rounded by their parents or other ancestors. The central pier may depict Pakal, while the next pier to the right shows Kan B'alam II; a young K'an Joy Chitam II stands on the far end.

These piers act as portals to House A on the northeast corner of the Palace. The wall behind them originally held 13 medallions in which were set portrait busts, perhaps of Palenque rulers. Through the doorway you enter a long colon-naded room that opens onto the East Courtyard, the largest of the Palace's open spaces. Across this patio stands House C, while House B and House A-D occupy its south and north sides respectively.

Short staircases descend the four sides of the sunken courtyard; the east steps become increasingly steep as you descend. On either side of the House A stair-case are a series of reliefs dubbed the Nine Grotesques. Because of their mis-matched borders and awkward framing, researchers believe these panels were carved for another site, moved here, and cut down to fit. Of the four half-naked figures on the north side, the two to the left are dwarfs, as is the second from the right on the south side. The latter's right-hand neighbor has a deep hole in his chest and grossly enlarged, probably mutilated, genitals (notice the three large slashes). Archaeologists theorize that this is a procession of humiliated enemy rulers, much like the Danzantes at Monte Albán, and the one on the far right is already dead.

Across the court, more of these panels flank the staircase; six smaller ones depicting rulers in poses of submission are set into the wall on either side. Between the latter, six square panels are carved with four-glyph inscriptions that probably identitify the defeated rulers. The west steps are carved with some of the earliest glyphic inscriptions found at Palenque; they mark the birth in A.D. 603 of an heir to the throne—Pakal the Great.

On the north side of the courtyard, House A-D originally held the Palace Tablet, the most elaborate relief found at Palenque, now in the site museum. Most of it is a lengthy glyphic dynastic history. In the top center, you see three figures celebrating the assumption of the throne by K'an Joy Chitam II. On the left and right are his parents, Pakal and Lady Tz'akb'u Ajaw, holding the symbols of rulership, including a "drum-major" headdress. K'an Joy Chitam II sits cross-legged on the throne in the center.

House C on the west side of the courtyard was probably built by Pakal. The wall of its east corridor is perforated with T-shaped Ik openings; above are a series of stucco monster masks that probably depict the nine gods of the Underworld. A doorway takes you through to the west corridor, which opens onto the West Courtyard. The six piers facing this small plaza are decorated with further reliefs, only partially visible. They appear to show a figure (possibly Pakal) in a plumed headdress seated on a throne and accepting an offering from another figure. The south face of one pier contains a stucco hunchbacked dwarf.

Across the narrow courtyard, the west wall is decorated with a sculptured panel containing a half-buried peccary and, almost hidden by the wall at one end, a sculptured head. Above stands House D, on the northwest corner of the Palace. Like the other Palace structures, this is made of two long rooms divided by a wall (perforated by Ik openings) with colonnades on the east and west sides. The main sights here are the six piers holding reliefs that face the plaza west of the Palace. They depict the rituals of sacrifice. Seated or kneeling figures bow before the fall of an ax being swung by a ruler, probably K'an Joy Chitam II, wearing sacrificial garb. Along the roof above runs a line of 75 glyphs. The reliefs were probably designed to be viewed from the plaza below.

As you return to the West Courtyard, the north side is bounded by the famous, four-story Tower. Unfortunately, the building is unstable and you are not allowed entry. This was built by K'an Joy Chitam II and his successors; the Tablet of 96 Hieroglyphs found here contains the date A.D. 780 and is thus one of the last inscriptions made at Palenque. The exact purpose of the Tower is unclear. The theory that it was used as an observatory received a boost when a researcher discovered that on the summer solstice an Ik opening on the third level cast a perfect shadow on the opposite wall. Others speculate the Tower may have acted as a giant sundial.

A small court opens on the south side of the Tower. The holes in the floor here were Classic Maya toilets. The structures south of the tower, Houses F, G, H, and I, are late constructions of lesser archaeological interest.

On the east side of the Tower court stands House E, whose roof is carved to look like thatching. The room inside is adorned with a copy of the Oval Palace Tablet. Dated A.D. 652, it shows the simply dressed Pakal seated on a double-headed jaguar throne facing his mother, Lady Sak K'uk', holding a "drum-major" headdress. It marks the date and ritual in which Pakal ascended to Palenque's throne. Below the relief originally sat a carved throne. This was illustrated by a number of 19th-century travelers but has long been missing.

The walls of House E are decorated with rows of painted floral motifs whose design is not found anywhere else in the Maya world. Murals and stucco reliefs transform the doorways into the gaping mouths of serpents and bicephalic monsters. A stairway descends into the rooms of the House E basement; we will return to them shortly.

ceramic incense burner

Just east of House E opens a little court; to the left you see the entrance to House B, whose construction postdates the former. Fragments of reliefs dot the walls. The most complete decorates the southeast room; this is an elaborate step-and-fret design around two T-shaped Ik shapes, one an open window and the other closed. The whole assemblage forms a monster mask. The north side of the building overlooks the East Court.

If you return to the House E stairway, at the bottom you find a warren of underground rooms built on an east-west axis. House E's basement was the first of Pakal's constructions in the complex. Passages take you to the south end of the Palace and a series of rooms that represent the earliest stages of Palace construction (other early structures lie under the north staircase). You emerge to daylight on the middle of the southern staircase. To the left lies a stela, one of the few found at the site, lying on its back with a few glyphs visible.

If you stroll around the corner to the right and back down to the northwest end of the Palace, you will see rows of stucco reliefs decorating the tiers. These contain one-meter-high portrait heads of rulers wearing Sun God headdresses with serpent panels on either side. The fourth-level portrait is in the best condition.

It might be a good idea to stop here for the day. The rest of the tour includes lots of walking, mostly in the shade of the forest.

A path leads down the river northeast of the Palace to the INAH headquarters and the old museum. Here a small bridge leads across the river to a fork in the path. The right-hand path takes you about 150 meters to Río Murciélagos (Bat River), which is spanned by a bridge just above Bat Falls. On the other side, you find Group C, an assemblage of about six small platform temples around a plaza. The jungle here is lush and beautiful.

Return to the fork, where the left-hand path descends to the Bat Group (Grupo Murciélagos), a large residential complex built on a series of tiered platforms. A number of tombs were found here. The path continues downhill to the main road. On the way, it passes a series of cascades culminating in a narrow waterfall that drops into a deep natural pool called the Bath of the Queen. It is popular as a local swimming hole, where all are welcome.

You can return to the center of the site via a trail up the east side of the Río Otolum. At the INAH headquarters, turn right and head into the plaza of the North Group, just below the Palace. On the south side of this lies Palenque's only ballcourt, measuring a compact 18 meters in length. The north side of the plaza is occupied by a long platform holding five small and medium-sized temples. Of the tiny easternmost structure only foundations remain. Next comes a larger temple atop a wide staircase. The four piers in front contain the remains of stucco figures, including one of a figure wearing a large chest piece with a scepter in his hand. This is followed by a shrine measuring only four meters square. The last two temples resemble the first large one; the right-hand one contains a glyph block used as a building stone (it is upside down), while its neighbor's front facade is missing. From the sloppy layout and construction, archaeologists believe these were among the last large temples built at Palenque.

On the west side of the plaza stands the Temple of the Count, named after Count Waldeck who, according to legend, made it his residence. This product of Pakal's reign rises in four tiers to a temple topped by the remains of a roofcomb. Three doorways pass into the interior, which, unlike most other Palenque temples, contains only one room. Behind this temple to the south stands Temple X, an early structure facing the Palace.

For the last part of the tour, return to the site parking lot. A path heads west into the forest and one of the least-visited parts of the site. Mounds, many unmapped, loom in the jungle to the north and south. The trail crosses the Río Motiepa, passes the Batres Pyramid on the left, and reaches the small Río Piedras Bolsas at another building complex. It then winds its way to the Picota Group, the center of the earliest Palenque, at the Río Picota about a kilometer from the parking lot. About 100 meters to the southeast rises Templo Olvidado (Forgotten Temple). Built by Pakal, this small temple's design—thin walls, multiple doorways, vaulted rooms—became the model for many later constructions. The path continues west to the Chol Maya village of Naranjo. This region is dotted with unmapped house mounds. Although the perimeters of the site have not yet been explored, researchers believe that ancient Palenque may have contained a population upward of 100,000.

YAXCHILAN

INTRODUCTION

For sheer beauty, Yaxchilan has few rivals. The site is built along the banks and on the hills above the Río Usumacinta amid a dense jungle teeming with animal life. Yaxchilan had a brief but brilliant apogee between A.D. 600 and 800; during this time, its rulers built dozens of elaborate temples decorated with finely carved reliefs. The subject of these reliefs was glorification of the rulers; they are shown playing the ballgame, ritually letting blood, sacrificing captives, and being elevated to the throne. The accompanying glyphs were among the earliest read by Mayan epigraphers; we now know the dynastic and some of the political history of Yaxchilan.

In addition to the site's archaeological interest, the other attractions of Yaxchilan are the adventure of getting there—you can arrive at the site only by light plane or motorized canoe—and the incredible natural beauty. The ruins are shaded by towering trees, including mahogany, cedar, and chicozapote (rubber), draped with vines, bromeliads, and orchids. The river teems with fish and crocodiles, and in the jungle there is the possibility of seeing jaguars, tapirs, agoutis, and boa constrictors. Through the trees fly red macaws, blue-headed parrots,

the roof frieze of Building 33 at Yaxchilan, Bird Jaguar IV's monument to himself

DANIELLE GUSTAFSON

YAXCHILAN

How to get there: For information on reaching these ruins, see the Traveling to Yaxchilan and Bonampak box.
Hours: Daily 0700–1800.
Admission fee: 14 pesos.
How long to tour: You need a half day to see the highlights and at least a full day to see everything.
Recommended gear: Hats, sunblock, bottled water, mosquito repellent, hiking boots, rain gear during the rainy season, bathing suit for swimming in the river.
Food and accommodations: Most overnight visitors sleep in tents near the site headquarters. Simple meals are available here.

chachalacas, royal pheasants, and numerous other birds. The trees are also home to spider and howler monkeys—the latter will keep campers awake at night with their extended screams (they sound like freight trains roaring through the jungle).

HISTORY

Yaxchilan's location must have been a natural attraction for the Maya. It lies on a huge oxbow that punctuates the course of the Río Usumacinta. The river bends around a cluster of steep hills from whose summits they had an excellent view over the Guatemala jungles to the northeast. At the base of the hills, they found a long terrace running along the river well above the high-water mark—the perfect place for a settlement. From here, they could trade cacao, maize, and pelts for jade and other luxury goods with other Classic Maya centers such as Piedras Negras, Bonampak, and Tikal.

Much as at Palenque, the translation of the inscriptions has given researchers a good grasp on Yaxchilan's dynastic history. Many questions remain, however, about the archaeological record. Most of these should be answered by publication of the final report of INAH's Proyecto Yaxchilan.

Yaxchilan may have been settled as early as 300 B.C. Archaeologists have found ceramic material dating back this far but no other traces of early villages. By the 4th century A.D., a small town stood on the banks of the Usumacinta. Its residents lived off farming, fishing, and hunting and traded with other settlements for conch, jade, and obsidian artifacts. According to later dynastic histories, Yaxchilan's first ruler was Yoaat B'alam (Penis of the Jaguar) who may have assumed power in A.D. 359. This lineage proceeded unbroken until the city's 9th-century A.D. collapse.

No structures remain of Yaxchilan's next three centuries. The earliest dated monument yet found is Stela 27 (on Building 9 in the Main Plaza), which was

TRAVELING TO YAXCHILAN
AND BONAMPAK

You can reach Yaxchilan and the nearby site of Bonampak on your own; however, if you do not have much experience in dealing with the jungle, it is highly recommended that you arrange for a visit with the assistance of a Palenque travel agency, either one of these or one of your own choosing:

Viajes Misol-Ha, Juárez 103, tel. 934/50816, fax 50488

Viajes Bonampak, Juárez 65, tel./fax 934/50134

Viajes Toniná, Juárez 105, Local 1, tel. 934/50384, fax 50209

You can either fly—the short, expensive way—or go by land—the long, cheap way. By air, a light plane takes you in to both sites on small, slightly nerve-wracking landing strips. The visits are usually rushed.

By land, the most common tour itinerary begins in the early hours of the morning, when you depart by minibus for an interminable 160-kilometer journey along a rutted dirt road to the frontier town of Frontera Echeverría on the Río Usumacinta. You may have to show passports at several army checkpoints along the way. You then take a powerboat about 20 kilometers downstream to the ruins of Yaxchilan. You usually reach the ruins in the middle of the afternoon and tour them that day.

After camping overnight (the howler monkey screams usually keep you from sleeping), early the next morning you return by boat to Frontera Echeverría and take the minibus back up the road 25 kilometers to the Bonampak turnoff. The bus parks at a Lacandon Maya village; from here, a Lacandon guide leads you on an easy two-hour hike into the ruins. After touring the site for a few hours, you hike back to the bus and take your seats for the long bus ride back to Palenque. You usually arrive in the middle of the evening. The journey is wearing but worth it.

If you feel up to the adventure, you can travel the same route by minibus and hire your own boat at Frontera Echeverría. You should be prepared for delays and carry food and camping equipment.

carved in A.D. 514 and depicts a ruler named Knot-Eye Jaguar I in the act of ritual bloodletting. Further inscriptions give the names of subsequent Yaxchilan rulers and tell of their ties to Piedras Negras, Bonampak, and Tikal. After 537, however, the inscriptions stop, and there is a gap in the record until A.D. 629 (though Stela 2 at the base of the Building 33 staircase seems to have a date of 613).

Yaxchilan underwent a sudden boom beginning in the early 7th century A.D. The earliest surviving structures date to this era—Buildings 6, 7, 13, and 74, all built around the Main Plaza. In A.D. 629, the throne was assumed by Bird Jaguar III, who gained renown 18 years later when he captured an enemy king identified by the glyphs of bat, bird, and frog. Bird Jaguar III also initiated a relatively modest building program that erected Buildings 25 and 26 on the terrace above the Main Plaza and Buildings 39 and 41 in the hilltop South Acropolis.

Bird Jaguar III and his wife, Lady Pakal, produced a son, Izamnaaj B'alam II, also known as Shield Jaguar II, whose long and brilliant rule bears many similarities to Pakal's in Palenque. He was early designated as the successor; Pakal of Palenque captured Bird Jaguar's brother in a battle and noted his relation to the young (perhaps age 11) heir-apparent of Yaxchilan. After capturing his own high-status sacrificial victim, Shield Jaguar became ruler at age 34 on October 20, 681. He ruled for an astounding six decades and died at the age of 95.

Shield Jaguar was a warrior, and he recorded many of his victories on Yaxchilan's temples. His building program included expansion of the South Acropolis, the construction of Building 44 in the Little Acropolis, and the addition of Buildings 23 and 24 to the Main Plaza. Building 23 is his unique achievement: the only known Maya building to glorify a woman. This was his wife, Lady K'ab'al Xook, who came from a powerful Yaxchilan noble lineage. Its lintels depict this noblewoman engaged in many rituals, including bloodletting and helping her husband dress for battle.

The **lintel** or supporting beam, made either of wood or stone, across a door, was often carved with symbolic scenes by the Maya.

Why did Shield Jaguar feel the need to erect this temple in his wife's honor? At age 61 he married a second wife, Lady Ik' Skull (Lady Eveningstar) from the powerful center of Calakmul, who bore him the son destined to be his heir: Bird Jaguar IV. Researchers speculate that Shield Jaguar had to glorify Lady Xook and her powerful family to avoid friction over the naming as successor this son of a foreign wife. Temple 23 is one product of this delicate political balancing act.

It must not have been completely successful, because Bird Jaguar IV did not accede to the throne until 10 years after his father's death in A.D. 742. Leaving monuments is the privilege only of the victors; we do not know who his competitors were. One theory is that Yaxchilan was ruled for a time by a king named Yoaat B'alam II, whom we know only from a sculpture at Piedras Negras in Guatemala. We do know that Bird Jaguar waged a 10-year campaign in which he played the ballgame, communed with the spirits of his ancestors (including his dead father), and, near the end, captured high-status sacrificial victims. He finally assumed the throne on April 29, 752, and erected a magnificent temple, Building 33, decorated with plaques extolling these achievements. He also embarked on Yaxchilan's most ambitious building program, including numerous structures around the Main Plaza.

Researchers do not see this effort as a sign of Bird Jaguar's strength but of his weakness or insecurity. After he finally secured the throne, he and his wife, Lady Great Skull, produced an heir, Iztamnaaj B'alam III, also known as Shield Jaguar III. All the subsequent reliefs produced during his reign pound home the point of Shield Jaguar III's legitimacy as heir and reemphasize his ties with other noble lineages in both Yaxchilan and the neighboring cities. (Apparently Bird Jaguar's own half-foreign parentage was still causing problems.)

The campaign worked, because Shield Jaguar III assumed the throne by A.D. 769. He was another warrior; reliefs not only at Yaxchilan but also at Bonampak and La Pasadita (in Guatemala) record his victories. During his brief reign, he erected Buildings 54, 55, and 58 at the extreme eastern end of the Main Plaza and Building 88 lying a kilometer farther to the east.

Shield Jaguar III was succeeded by his son, K'inich Tatb'u Skull III, who took his name from one of the earliest Yaxchilan rulers. He built only two poorly designed temples, Buildings 3 and 64. The former contains the last dated inscription found at Yaxchilan—A.D. 808—recording a victory in battle. Unfortunately, the scribe did not plan well, because he ran out of space as he moved from left to right and was forced to squash the last glyphs to fit them all in.

Yaxchilan was slowly depopulated during the following decades. All major construction stopped, and small houses were built in the ceremonial spaces. By A.D. 900, Yaxchilan was abandoned and the jungle returned to cover the ruins. Its only visitors were wandering Maya tribespeople, such as the Lacandon, who occasionally returned to the temples to perform the ancient ceremonies.

ARCHAEOLOGICAL RECORD

Dense jungle obscured Yaxchilan's ruins for many centuries. Although there may have been a sighting in the late 17th century, the first certain visitor was Juan Galindo, a Mexican explorer who stopped at the site while navigating the Usumacinta. Mexican loggers harvested around the ruins in the following decades. In 1881, Edwin Rockstroh, a professor at the Colegio Nacional in Guatemala City, wrote a brief description of Yaxchilan.

This report reached the hands of the English explorer Alfred Maudslay, who arrived at the ruins on March 18, 1882. Two days later, the ambitious Désiré Charnay appeared at Yaxchilan. His face fell at the sight of the Englishman—he had been hoping to claim the discovery for himself. The ever-modest Maudslay

DANIELLE GUSTAFSON

entrance of structure 19, also known as the Labyrinth

DANIELLE GUSTAFSON

a portrait of Bird Jaguar IV in a detail of Lintel 3, Building 33

insisted, however, that Charnay take full credit; he was a mere amateur and Charnay a professional. Charnay named the ruins Ciudad Lorillard after his patron, the French-American tobacco magnate. Nevertheless, it was Maudslay's eight days at the site that are more important to archaeology. He discovered dozens of lintels, and his report includes drawings, photographs, and a site map. Maudslay removed eight of the lintels; all but one are now in the British Museum (the eighth was destroyed during the World War II bombing of Berlin).

The next important visitor was the Austrian explorer Teobert Maler. He visited Yaxchilan in 1895, 1897, and 1900, spending five months at the ruins and discovering numerous buildings and monuments, including the South Acropolis, 20 stelae, and 14 lintels. Maler also gave the site its current name, Yaxchilan, after a nearby tributary of the Usumacinta. This may change when the phonetic translation of the city's emblem glyph is finally deduced. Published in his two-volume work on the Usumacinta valley, Maler's report is still a major source for information about the site.

In 1931, the Mexican government named a guardian for Yaxchilan; these guardians have been crucial in protecting the ruins from looters and other vandals. That same year, a Carnegie Institution expedition led by Sylvanus Morley spent a month at Yaxchilan. They did not perform any excavations but produced the basis of the site map that is still used today and discovered many more structures and stone monuments. His results were published in his book, *The Inscriptions of the Petén.*

After Morley, there was a two-decade lapse in investigations at Yaxchilan. Then the archaeological world's interest was relit by three seminal early 1960s articles written by Carnegie's Tatiana Proskouriakoff, the first on Piedras Negras and the next two on Yaxchilan. She studied the lintels and other stone monuments and realized that these were not portraits of mythic beings enacting divine rituals—the dominant theory at the time—but historical texts depicting real people. The date glyphs were divided into periods roughly as long as a human life span. From these, she identified three Yaxchilan rulers, Shield Jaguar I, Bird Jaguar IV, and his son, whom we now know to be Shield Jaguar II. Although it was highly controversial at first, her discovery helped begin the epigraphic revolution that during the subsequent decades rocked the world of Mesoamerican archaeology and overturned many cherished beliefs about pre-Hispanic peoples.

In 1964, more than a dozen Yaxchilan lintels and four stelae were removed to be placed in the new Mexico City Museo Nacional de Antropología. The new interest in Yaxchilan's monuments led Merle Greene Robertson and Ian Graham to document each inscription, the former with rubbings and the latter by drawing and photographing nearly every sculpture at the site. The results of this work have borne fruit in the research of epigraphers such as Linda Schele, David Stuart, and Peter Mathews. They have deciphered Yaxchilan's complete dynastic history and have begun to work out the political interaction between the city and the surrounding region.

In 1972, INAH's Roberto García Moll finally began the first archaeological excavations at the site. The ongoing Proyecto Yaxchilan has cleared, explored, and restored well more than half the 120 buildings. They have discovered numerous tombs and objects and performed stratigraphic excavations to work out the site chronology. The project has published a number of preliminary articles but, so far, not a final report.

TOURING THE SITE

A visit to Yaxchilan begins at the landing strip, which is lined with a half-dozen houses for the site guardians and archaeologists. The riverbank here acts as the landing for the motorized canoes that ply the Usumacinta. The land on the opposite bank is Guatemala. The ruins lie to the east (upstream) of the airstrip along the river terrace and on the hills above.

A path heads east from the airstrip into the jungle, passing a few unexcavated mounds. In about a half kilometer, it reaches Buildings 18 and 19, also known as the Labyrinth, at the western end of the Main Plaza. The earliest stages of this building date to A.D. 600 or before, and work continued here through the end of the 9th century A.D. This wide platform structure is topped with five pyramid-shaped temples and takes its name from an underground warren of vaulted rooms—home to bats and mosquitoes—connected by passages and staircases. Désiré Charnay camped in these unhealthy quarters during his brief 1882 visit. At the far end of this maze, the building opens out onto the Main Plaza; suddenly you are in the middle of ancient Yaxchilan.

If you look behind, you see the remains of an ornate stone facade topped with a roofcomb. In front stand three round altars with eroded glyphs visible along the sides. One is dated A.D. 742, the year of Itzamnaaj B'alam II's death, so they were probably carved to commemorate that event.

Occupying the terrace just above the Río Usumacinta, the Main Plaza is a long rectangular space bounded on all four sides by structures. On the north side (left), the first structure you reach is Building 16, a temple with three doorways facing east. Like all Yaxchilan structures, this is relatively short compared to the soaring pyramids at sites such as Palenque and Tikal. Yaxchilan's builders appear to have preferred expending their labor on elaborate temples rather than massive bases.

Above Building 16's doorways are the first of the dozens of beautifully carved lintels that you will see on this tour. These are portraits of Yaxchilan nobility either sitting or half-reclining (to fit in the narrow frame of the lintel). In their arms they hold double-headed serpents out of whose mouths emerge the upper bodies of K'awiil. Bands of glyphs frame them on either side. The central lintel shows Bird Jaguar IV, while the left and right ones depict noblewomen. The carvings probably represent Bird Jaguar and his wife and mother engaged in ritual bloodletting; the serpents are part of the visions they see during this act. Letting blood to evoke the gods was the duty of Maya nobles; performing this rite also reasserted the legitimacy of their exalted station.

Across a plaza to the east lies Building 14, Yaxchilan's pocket-sized ballcourt, aligned on a north-south axis. Five

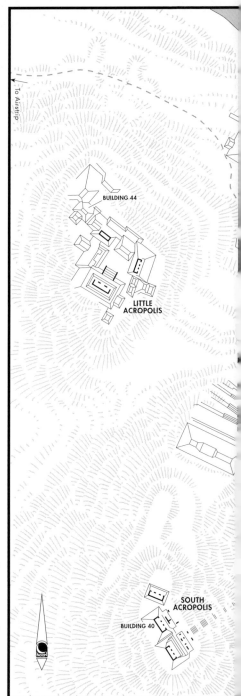

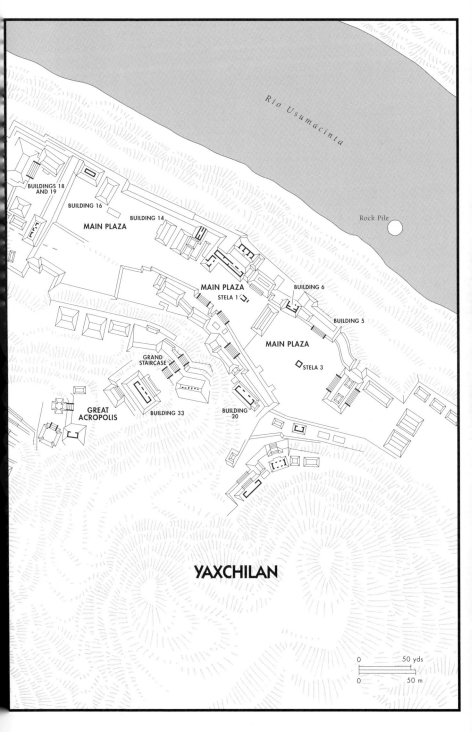

Rio Usumacinta

Rock Pile

BUILDINGS 18
AND 19

BUILDING 16

BUILDING 14

MAIN PLAZA

MAIN PLAZA
STELA 1

BUILDING 6

BUILDING 5

MAIN PLAZA

STELA 3

GRAND
STAIRCASE

GREAT
ACROPOLIS

BUILDING 33

BUILDING
20

YAXCHILAN

0   50 yds
0   50 m

DANIELLE GUSTAFSON

This detail from Structure 33 at Yaxchilan depicts Bird Jaguar IV (right) and an ally holding God K manikin scepters.

circular ballcourt markers were found here; one eroded stone remains under a corrugated roof at the south end of the court. Each showed a seated figure on a throne holding a staff in his arms with monster or god masks emerging from either end.

Just beyond the ballcourt stands an L-shaped platform containing three structures, respectively Buildings 13, 10, and 74. Lintels showing Bird Jaguar IV decorated Building 13; they are now in Mexico City. Further, purely glyphic carvings relating to Bird Jaguar are set into the lintels of Building 10. The lower Building 74 is one of the earliest structures at the site, built during the first half of the 7th century A.D.

The plaza in front of these buildings contains a small grouping of stone monuments. From here, you can look up the hill and see Building 33 peeking through the trees on top. Researchers believe that these sculptures were an extension of the ritual and political imagery flowing down from the hilltop complex. The largest monument is the upright Stela 1. This shows Bird Jaguar IV ritually perforating his penis with blood streaming into a container. A woman, perhaps his wife, kneels in front of him, while tiny figures of his dead parents watch from above. The sides of the stela are carved with standing figures of a man and woman, probably his parents again; further, very worn reliefs decorate the back. On either side of the stela lie stone monuments in the form of a caiman and a jaguar. Three small round altars, numbered 10–12 and carved with eroded glyphs, stand just to the west.

Returning to the north side of the plaza, you come to two Buildings, 7 and 6 respectively, dating to the early 7th century. The Building 6 frieze contains a stucco monster mask peering out from the worn brickwork; two more originally adorned the facade to the left. Above rises the base of a roofcomb.

Next, you arrive at the long, low platform of Building 5; along with the similarly shaped Buildings 8 and 4 to the west and east, this forms a plaza within the Main Plaza. Six steps whose risers are carved with hieroglyphics ascend to a long platform that may never have had a structure. The extremely worn inscriptions comprise the longest text found at Yaxchilan. Researchers believe they relate the dynastic history of the city from the earliest on the top left down to Bird Jaguar IV on the bottom. The latter ruler may have re-carved the last two steps to add his name to the list.

From the top of Building 5, you can look down to the river and see a mound of rocks in the swirling waters. A similar pile lies near the far bank. Researchers believe these were the base for some kind of bridge or perhaps a gate that allowed the city to block traffic and charge a toll. The Usumacinta was the lifeblood of Yaxchilan, the artery on which all goods, captives, and royal visitors traveled.

The **flapstaff** was a ritual staff with fabric attached that was used in kingly dances.

In front of this platform stands Stela 11 under a protective roof. This comes from the South Acropolis on the hilltops to the southwest. In 1964 archaeologists tried to move it to Mexico City, but it was too heavy for light aircraft and became stranded in Guatemala for years until Trudy Blom returned it to Yaxchilan. This remarkable sculpture is one of the many designed to legitimize Bird Jaguar IV's rule. The front shows Bird Jaguar IV and his father (left), Itzamnaaj B'alam II, in an "exchange-of-flapstaff" ritual (a kingly act performed on the summer solstice) just before the latter's death; the sculpture was carved years later to commemorate that event. On the back, Bird Jaguar, costumed as a god, stands over three bound captives, while his dead parents look on approvingly from above. Two years later, Bird Jaguar finally became Yaxchilan's ruler. The relief borders and stela sides are covered with glyphs.

Stela 3 stands in the center of this plaza; it was found next to Building 20 on the terrace just to the north. Again, this relief shows a much earlier king named Bird Jaguar III mutilating his penis—drops of blood fall into a basket—while a man and woman, perhaps his parents, flank him to the right and left. Behind the stela lies Altar 22, a round stone covered with glyphs dating to Itzamnaaj B'alam II's reign.

Stela 3 originally stood on the south side of the plaza as part of a row of five sculptures. Stelae 4, 5, 6, and 7 remain, all showing rulers engaged in ritual mutilation and bloodletting. Three of them are late, depicting Itzamnaaj B'alam III, while Stela 6 (second from the right or west) represents Bird Jaguar III. By moving the latter's monuments here, Itzamnaaj B'alam III was obviously trying to associate his reign with that of the earlier ruler.

On the terrace above these sculptures stands Building 20, which was built by Itzamnaaj B'alam III. A hieroglyphic stairway recording this ruler's battles was discovered in front of this structure; it has been re-buried for its own protection. Building 20's three doorways open into a single room. On the floor sit the sculptured legs and torso of a statue that originally occupied one of the niches in the roof frieze. The latter now contains the reconstructed figures of a man and a woman; the former's face emerges from a serpent's mouth. The guides may erroneously claim this represents the birth of Kukulcan, the Maya version of Quetzalcoatl. This motif is repeated on the Building 20 lintels now in Mexico City; they show Itzamnaaj B'alam III's parents celebrating his birth in a vision serpent ritual in which the son's face and arms protrude from the monster's mouth. Traces of red, blue, and green paint still remain on the facade.

Itzamnaaj B'alam III's father, Bird Jaguar IV, built Building 21 just to the west. This temple contains five doorways opening into three rooms. The three center doors were adorned with carved lintels that now reside in the British Museum. They showed Bird Jaguar with his famous captive, Bird Jaguar bloodletting with his wife to celebrate the birth of an heir (by another wife), and a noblewoman engaged in a vision rite. The interior walls of the temple were originally decorated with stucco reliefs of a serpent monster and five cross-legged figures, all brightly painted. Propped against the wall is Stela 35 depicting an elaborately dressed noblewoman with a bowl in one hand.

The **serpent vision** was a ritual that incorporated bloodletting and drug-taking to induce a vision of a serpent out of whose mouth might come a god or the head of an ancestor.

To the right of this structure stand Buildings 22 (dating to Bird Jaguar IV's rule) and 23. The latter was built by Itzamnaaj B'alam II to venerate his principal wife, Lady K'ab'al Xook, while another, foreign-born wife produced his heir. Unfortunately, its famous lintels—Lady K'ab'al Xook engaged in her wifely and ritual duties, including bloodletting—are now in either the British Museum or the Mexico City Museo Nacional de Antropología.

Between Buildings 21 and 22 ascends the Grand Staircase. From here, you climb the three flights of stairs up to the hilltop Building 33, also called the Palace. About three-quarters of the way up, you see the ruined Buildings 25 and 26 on the left. On the right, a bit farther away, stand Buildings 28, 29, and 30. The last is in the best condition, with traces of stucco decor on the frieze and two interior chambers. All these structures date to the second half of the 7th century.

At the top of the staircase, you find the building complex known as the Great Acropolis. The first structure—the most famous at Yaxchilan—is Building 33, which was built by Bird Jaguar IV in his own honor. Atop a platform stands a wide temple capped with an ornate roof frieze that rises to an elegant roofcomb above. Lacandon Maya still burn copal incense in its interior. A large stalactite, probably from a nearby cave in Guatemala, is set into the platform in front. Its surface is carved with a scene showing three males letting blood with penis perforators; the accompanying glyphs have not been translated but probably date to Bird Jaguar's reign.

The topmost steps on the way up to the three doorways are another hieroglyphic staircase. The 13 risers are carved with scenes of Bird Jaguar IV and his ancestors playing the Mesoamerican ballgame. They lean into a large ball that bounces on steps made from glyphic blocks. The central step (number seven) shows Bird Jaguar himself, while to the left and right are his father and grandfather. The more eroded outside steps depict Bird Jaguar's lieutenants and female relatives. The staircase was carved to commemorate Bird Jaguar's ballgame of October 21, 744, his first politico-religious act after his father's death.

Above Building 33's doorways rises a complicated roof frieze with three niches bearing the traces of seated stucco figures. Above, the ghostly remains of a larger figure seated on a throne (Itzamnaaj B'alam III?) occupy the central panel of the well-preserved roofcomb. Beautiful lintels carved to glorify Itzamnaaj B'alam III's reign cap the three doorways. On the left, Lintel 1 shows Itzamnaaj B'alam III on the day of his accession holding the K'awiil scepter of kingship while his wife stands behind. Next, the central Lintel 2 depicts Bird Jaguar IV on the right and his young son, Itzamnaaj B'alam III, performing a ritual on the fifth anniversary of his rule. This artwork naturally furthered his heir's claim on the throne. Last, Lintel 3 features Bird Jaguar IV on the right facing an important lineage head during another anniversary celebration; both hold beautiful scepters topped with god manikins.

The three doorways enter a long corridor with four alcoves along the back wall and small chambers at either end. The Lacandon Maya still burn copal incense here. In the central alcove sits a headless sculpture that is probably Bird Jaguar IV himself. This figure sits cross-legged with hands on knees; it wears a belt, wristlets, and a wide band around the shoulders. The statue's head lies to one side with a damaged face and a feathered headdress above. According to local legend, when the head is reattached to the body, it will signal the end of the present Creation.

Behind and just below Building 33 lies a small plaza bounded by three small ruined platforms. The two on the west are unique at Yaxchilan in that they have rounded corners. These are all relatively early, dating to Itzamnaaj B'alam II and before.

A path leads downhill to the northwest of Building 33 and then ascends through the forest to a second hilltop complex, known as the Little Acropolis (confusingly, it is actually larger than the Great Acropolis). Here you find a line of eight temples built along an east-west axis facing the river. The most important is the central Building 44, which was erected by Itzamnaaj B'alam II to celebrate his battlefield exploits. This temple faces the river, and the plaza in front was set with six stelae, including a very early one, and hieroglyphs recording his victories (including bound, prone captives) were carved on the staircase leading up to the three doorways. Building 44's three carved lintels depicted Itzamnaaj B'alam II grasping the top-knots of his kneeling captives.

Building 42 at the east end of this acropolis was built by Bird Jaguar IV in his own honor. The temple faces east; its eroded remaining lintel shows the ruler with a chief lieutenant, both richly costumed. Behind this structure lies a small plaza with the remains of Buildings 50 and 51 on its south and west sides.

From here, a path leads south downhill, across a small valley and then up to the South Acropolis, yet another hilltop complex. Here stand three temples, Buildings 39, 40, and 41, the first facing north and the latter two looking northeast. Building 39, the first and lowest, had a line of three stone altars (two remain) at the base of the steps, on top of the steps, and at the back of the central room.

Next comes Building 40, yet another product of Bird Jaguar IV's self-aggrandizement campaign. Three stelae stood on the terrace in front; the glyphic Stela 12 and eroded Stela 13 (depicting an unknown ruler) remain, while Stela 11 portraying Bird Jaguar and his father is now in the Main Plaza. Inside you find the remains of a brightly painted mural with only one delicate profile remaining clear. Building 41, the highest at the complex, is notable only for the remains of a stucco monster mask on its facade. The ruined main staircase to the South Acropolis descends into the jungle below.

The tour of Yaxchilan's principal sites ends here. If you are feeling energetic, you can explore the river terrace east of the Main Plaza's Building 4. A path takes you to a number of constructions dating to the last decades of Yaxchilan's ruling dynasty. The most notable structure is Building 54, erected by Itzamnaaj B'alam III. Unfortunately, the lintels depicting the king engaged in rituals are now in Mexico City. In the surrounding jungle, there remain more than 100 unexplored structures. It would be best to get the advice of the site guardians before hiking off in search of them. At the end of the long day on the ruins, the best refreshment is a swim in the Usumacinta (watch out for the strong currents).

BONAMPAK

INTRODUCTION

Some of the best-preserved Maya murals ever found decorate the walls of a small temple at the site of Bonampak deep in the Lacandon Jungle. In a tale out of pulp fiction, the murals' 1946 discovery seemed to put a "mummy's curse" on the first explorers. Two died and the rest fell into violent squabbling that ruined many reputations. Bonampak's beautiful ruins are quieter now, and a team of specialists has finished restoring the famous murals (exposure to air and humidity caused rapid deterioration). The paintings were recently analyzed using new infrared video cameras, and the results have led to a startling reappraisal of their predominant theme. Bonampak also lies at the heart of the Lacandon homeland; these descendants of the ancient Maya act as guides to visitors hiking in and out of the site (you can also come by air).

BONAMPAK

How to get there: For information on reaching these remote ruins, see the Traveling to Yaxchilan and Bonampak box.
Hours: Daily 0800–1600.
Admission fee: 20 pesos.
How long to tour: Two hours.
Recommended gear: Hats, sunblock, bottled water, hiking boots, mosquito repellent, rain gear during the rainy season.
Food and accommodations: Bring your own.

HISTORY

Bonampak lies in the wide valley of the Río Lacanjá about 20 kilometers south-southeast of Yaxchilan. The Maya built this center on a stream flowing into the Lacanjá from the first foothills of the ridge separating this valley from the Río Usumacinta. The Lacanjá flows southeast into the Río Lacantún, which heads north and meets with the Usumacinta flowing northwest. Nestled against the foothills, Bonampak's site gave it protection from attack, while the flat valley floor possessed water and tillable soil for farming.

The excavation of Bonampak began in 1977, but few results have been published. The earliest ceramics yet found may date to A.D. 100; no structures from Bonampak's first three centuries have been found (as far as we know).

DANIELLE GUSTAFSON

A procession of musicians winds along the walls of Bonampak's Temple 1.

Later dynastic inscriptions name the settlement's first great ruler as Bird Jaguar, who ruled sometime before A.D. 454. During the 6th century A.D., when the site may have been dominated by Toniná, Bonampak's rulers included Fish Fin and Knot-Eye Jaguar.

Bonampak's most famous ruler was its last, Yajaw Chan Muwaan, who came to the throne January 15, 776 (a previous king of the same name ordered the carving of Lintel 6 around A.D. 600). Chan Muwaan's wife and mother of his heir was a sister of Itzamnaaj B'alam III of Yaxchilan. Chan Muwaan celebrated this alliance by accompanying his brother-in-law in a war against a third city-state and then celebrated their victories on the Temple 1 lintels and, inside, in the battle mural of Room 2. Afterward, Bonampak celebrated a brief period of collecting tribute from the vanquished city; in the Rooms 1 and 3 murals, they commemorated the arrival of the vassal lords bearing cacao beans and other objects of value.

Temple 1's dedication date of November 15, 791, is also the last calendric inscription from Bonampak. No further monuments were erected, and, over the next decades, the city was abandoned.

ARCHAEOLOGICAL RECORD

The 1946 discovery of Bonampak led to two deaths, a national scandal, and a protracted campaign of mud-slinging that took decades to wane. In 1898, the Austrian explorer Teobert Maler heard about ruins on the headwaters of the Lacanjá but was unable to visit them. In 1943, a Danish archaeologist named Frans Blom (he and his wife, Gertrude, later opened the famous Na Bolom museum in San Cristóbal de las Casas), possibly acting as a scout for the U.S. military, embarked on an exploration of the Usumacinta area. He briefly hired Karl Hermann Frey, an American draft-dodger and general malcontent, to assist him but soon grew to dislike Frey so much that he fired him. Blom penetrated to within a kilometer of Bonampak but then collapsed of malaria and had to be carried out.

Two years later, a filmmaker named Giles Healey was hired by the United Fruit Company to produce a documentary of the Lacandon Maya. To help him, he hired Karl Hermann Frey and a young war veteran named John Bourne, who also happened to be the heir of the Singer Sewing Machine fortune (Healey apparently hoped—futilely—that Bourne would help with expenses). A few days into the expedition, the party broke up due to mutual hatred: the other two thought Healey was paranoid, while the latter called Bourne a freeloader.

Bourne and Frey returned to the Usumacinta jungle in February of 1946. They were accompanied by two Lacandon Maya guides who took them to the ruins of Bonampak. They saw a plaza, the acropolis, and a fine lintel—but not the famous murals. Apparently, the paintings were unknown to the Lacandon.

After this trip, Bourne drops out of this story—he returned to the U.S.—while Frey presented his findings to INAH in Mexico City.

Three months later, Giles Healey visited Bonampak with the same two guides and discovered the murals, which remain the finest yet discovered in Mesoamerica (only Cacaxtla comes close). The news caused a sensation, not all of it good. Frey returned to Bonampak a few weeks later, saw the murals, and left with a large grudge. By this time, he had renounced his American citizenship and Hispanicized his name to "Carlos Frey." He went to Mexico City and told the newspapers and anyone else who would listen that he was the real discoverer of Bonampak and that Healey and the United Fruit Company were trying to steal the glory from Mexico.

Bonampak and the controversy over its discovery became a cause célèbre in Mexico City. Dozens of Mexican intellectuals, including such celebrities as Diego Riviera and David Siqueiros, subscribed to a fund to send a Mexican expedition to the ruins. While this was brewing, in 1947 a joint Carnegie Institution and INAH expedition under Karl Ruppert and J. Eric S. Thompson spent two weeks at the site drawing the murals and mapping the ruins. The excellent copy made by Guatemalan artist Antonio Tejeda became the basis for most subsequent study of the murals. This project was a smashing success compared to the Frey expedition, which finally left for Bonampak in May of 1949.

Under the sponsorship of the Instituto Nacional de Bellas Artes, this expedition assembled in Tuxtla Gutiérrez. Most of its members were Mexico City residents with absolutely no jungle experience (one journalist was 76 years old!). While the party waited to fly into the site, Frey and two others went ahead in a canoe to transport a generator to the ruins. The official story is that the canoe overturned and Frey drowned while trying to save another man, who also perished. The third was rescued after spending the night in the jungle. Frey's body was recently exhumed because of the construction of a dam, and, according to rumor, it was discovered to have been pierced by a hitherto-unmentioned bullet hole.

A few members of the expedition managed to spend a limited number of hours at the ruins, but on news of the tragedy all returned to Mexico City. A few months later, one of the reporters from this party wrote that the Carnegie Institution expedition had used kerosene to make the murals more visible, not a technique recommended for the long-term preservation of artwork. This was true, but so had members of the Frey group. Charges and counter-charges flew for years, particularly after people realized that the murals were rapidly deteriorating (a Mexican boy scout troop was even blamed). Meanwhile, the story of Herman Frey, the bitter American draft-dodger, was transformed into a tale of jungle adventure and steamy passion (he had a Lacandon mistress) serialized in magazines around the world.

This series of disasters seems to have scared researchers away from Bonampak. It took a decade for the next expedition to arrive. From 1960 to 1962, an

INAH team under Raúl Pavón Abreu worked at the site clearing the main plaza, restoring buildings and building an airstrip and a research headquarters. When they compared the murals with the photos from the late 1940s, they saw that the paintings might soon become illegible. They built a sun roof over the temple to keep the building cool. Unfortunately, that was only partly successful; the main problem seems to have been exposure to air and light.

In 1964, an artist named Rina Lazo painted a full-scale copy of the murals for the new Museo Nacional de Antropología in Mexico City; this has since proved an invaluable tool for researchers. Copies have also been created for the Florida State Museum in Gainesville and for the archaeology museum in Villahermosa, Tabasco.

In 1977, Bonampak became part of the ongoing INAH project run by Roberto García Moll, now called the Proyecto Yaxchilan-Bonampak. They have excavated and consolidated much of the Acropolis and made a number of interesting finds in the main plaza, including the so-called "Queen" sculpture. The main focus of the project, however, has been the protection and restoration of the murals. A special INAH team from the conservation center in Mexico City went over every inch of the paintings to stop their deterioration and, if possible, bring back their original brilliant colors. The back of the temple has also been sealed to keep moisture from leaking into the interior and causing deposits to build up on the walls.

In 1996, a joint Mexican and American expedition led by Mary Miller of Yale University returned to Bonampak to film the murals using the hitherto new technique of infrared video cameras and then analyzing the results with computer-imaging programs. Never-before-seen images suddenly sprang out at them, including hieroglyphs, paintings of dead captives, and gods.

Recently, the helm of INAH's Bonampak project was assumed by Alejandro Tobalin. He and his colleagues have excavated around the small temples near the top of the Acropolis and have discovered a number of tombs.

TOURING THE SITE

The two routes into Bonampak are on foot or via a light airplane. The hiking trail into the site follows the old Maya causeway connecting Bonampak to the Río Lacanjá and the site of Lacanjá on the opposite side. From the site headquarters, you walk south across the airstrip into the Main Plaza. Up the hillside on the far end rise the many stairways and temples of the Acropolis. The causeway ends at the northwest corner of the plaza. Standing just to the east is Building 15, a low platform where the fragmentary Stela 7 lying just south was found. On top of the platform a roof covers a door opening into the base. If you lift the lid and squeeze down the narrow steps, you will see the large sculpture called the "Queen" discovered in 1994. This headless torso (pieces of the head lie nearby) is seated on a platform facing north. It was carved with an elaborate

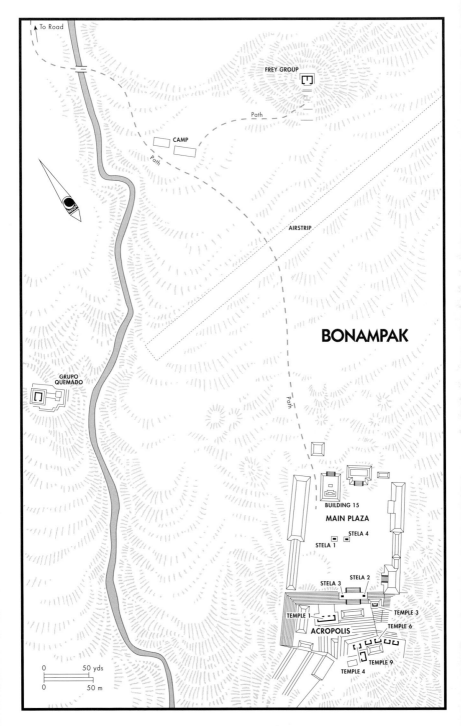

To Road

FREY GROUP

Path

CAMP

Path

AIRSTRIP

BONAMPAK

GRUPO
QUEMADO

Path

BUILDING 15

MAIN PLAZA

STELA 4

STELA 1

STELA 2

STELA 3

TEMPLE 3

TEMPLE 1

TEMPLE 6

ACROPOLIS

TEMPLE 9

TEMPLE 4

0   50 yds

0   50 m

costume upon which traces of red, blue, and green paint remain.

In the center of the plaza stand two stelae. To the west, Stela 1 shows Yajaw Chan Muwaan, Bonampak's last ruler, holding a shield and beribboned spear and standing on a block of glyphs with a large monster mask below. The top third of the relief is missing; it originally stood over four meters tall. To its left stands the highly eroded Stela 4. The east and west sides of the Main Plaza are bounded by long low platforms.

At the south end of the plaza rises the Acropolis, a series of platforms and small temples that ascend the northern end of a long hill. Indeed, they block the ridge so completely that they make it look like a man-made rather than natural creation. In the center of the platform, seven steps take you up to

Temple 1 lintel showing a ruler killing a captive

DANIELLE GUSTAFSON

a small terrace where you find Stelae 2 and 3. On the left, Stela 2 shows a richly dressed Chan Muwaan in a wildly elaborate headdress flanked on the left by his wife, the sister of Itzamnaaj B'alam III from Yaxchilan. On his right stands his mother holding a penis perforator; he is apparently about to begin a bloodletting rite. Stela 3 depicts Chan Muwaan in an another complicated costume facing a kneeling prisoner who wears what appears to be a chest protector made from thick ropes; this is probably the prelude to a sacrifice.

Behind, the central steps ascend to a second, larger terrace. On the right stands the famous Temple 1, also called the Temple of the Paintings, covered by a corrugated metal roof. Like the temples at Yaxchilan, this one has three doorways topped by a roof frieze. No traces of a roofcomb have been found, however, and researchers say that the exterior molding is more Puuc than Usumacinta style. Five niches adorn the roof facade, two on the ends and one over each doorway. The central niche contains the remains of a seated figure, and to the right you can also see a stucco relief of a ruler grasping the hair of a captive below.

Above each doorway, you find a beautiful, deeply incised lintel. Starting from the left, Lintel 1 depicts Chan Muwaan clutching a captive by his topknot. Next, the central Lintel 2 shows his brother-in-law, Itzamnaaj B'alam III, in the same position. Finally, Lintel 3 features Knot-Eye Jaguar, possibly Chan

MAIZE: THE STAFF OF LIFE

In the Christian religion, God made Adam from soil; in the Maya religion, the gods made men from maize dough. To the native Mesoamericans, therein lay their innate superiority to the European invaders: soil was crude and low; maize dough was literally the staff of life, the substance around which all their lives revolved. Maize, or corn, was probably first domesticated in ancient Mexico. The earliest traces of primitive maize cobs come from around 5000 B.C. in the Tehuacan Valley in the present state of Puebla. The main problem with maize as a foodstuff is that it guards its nutritional treasures well underneath a tough skin. Sometime before 1000 B.C., Mesoamericans developed a highly effective method to unlock the nutritional box of each kernel of maize. The process is called nixtamalization: first, the maize kernels were soaked in water, and then wood ashes or lime (the chemical) was added. This mixture was cooked until the combination of heat and chemical sloughed off the transparent skin protecting the meat inside. The cooked kernels were then ground and could be made into literally dozens of types of dishes. After being nixtamalized, the maize released its store of protein and vitamins in an easily digestible form. The Indians of Mesoamerica discovered that they could survive on nixtamalized maize alone. And the combination of maize with squash and beans (the "triumvirate" of Mesoamerican diet) would sustain life for the vast majority of people who did not have regular access to meat or fish. Maize became the central crop of every Mesoamerican culture, and its production and nixtamalization allowed for the growth of small villages into the great civilizations from the Olmecs on. For the Aztecs, tortillas were the primary way in which nixtamalized maize was consumed. These were usually the simple corn tortillas that we see today. Preparation of tortillas was the major task of Aztec women. After preparing the nixtamalized corn, they would grind it with a mano and metate, pat out the tortillas with their hands, and then cook the disks of dough on a round stone called a *comal*. In Tenochtitlan's famous marketplace, vendors sold plain tortillas and a huge array of special types, including tortillas made with honey, squash, cactus tunas, green maize, amaranth seeds, and so on. Aztecs preferred to eat their tortillas with a sauce, beginning with the basic chile and water. The next most popular maize dough creation was the tamale, usually a ball of dough wrapped in the husk from a special variety of maize. As with tortillas, Aztec cooks produced a huge number of variations on the basic tamale, including tamales with nearly every kind of meat, fish, or insect inside. The Maya of southern Mesoamerica preferred not to chew their maize dough but to drink it. The basic Maya foodstuff was *posolli*, which was half-ground maize that was mixed with water and then drunk. The morning meal was usually a maize drink with a little chile sprinkled on top; the breakfast leftovers were blended with more water for lunch; and only in the evening did they have somewhat more solid food such as stews and soups. For a fancier drink, the Maya consumed *atolli*, which was finely ground maize dough often mixed with chile, beans, seeds, roots, or chocolate. After the Conquest, the Spanish adopted *atolli*, which resembled their gruel, but *posolli* remained (and remains) the staple of the purebred, traditional Maya. When the Europeans took maize back to their homelands, they unfortunately did not bring back the process of nixtamalization. In Italy, where poor people turned to maize as a staple, peasants began to come down with a disease they called "corn sickness," later named pellagra or "rough skin." It was not until the early 20th century, by which time pellagra had become rife in Africa, that scientists realized that the disease was caused by a vitamin deficiency. Centuries of human anguish could have been avoided if they had learned a process that is the birthright of every Mexican peasant.

Muwaan's father, sticking a spear into an enemy's chest. From the dying man's mouth runs an S-shaped line of blood droplets.

Each doorway opens into a separate room (unlike at Yaxchilan). The famous murals begin on the doorjambs and continue inside, covering the walls and ceilings above low benches that border the rooms. Until recently, researchers believed that the paintings told the story of the presentation of a new heir, Chan Muwaan's son, to the throne of Bonampak. They thought that Rooms 1, 2, and 3, in that order, were a narrative showing the arrival of the baby at a huge celebration complete with musicians and masked dancers, the battle waged to take captives for ritual sacrifice and, finally, an elaborate ceremony of bloodletting and sacrifice on the steps of a temple.

After analyzing the results of the infrared video imaging project, its director, Mary Miller, and other researchers have overturned that long-accepted theory. The imaging brought to light many unseen features, clarified glyphs, and gave them insight into how the murals were actually painted. Although they have not finished their work, they believe that the murals' theme is not the presentation of an heir but tribute.

Before we turn to the paintings themselves, you should understand how they were meant to be viewed. Much like the action of an ancient Greek play was divided between the chorus and the principal actors, the mural scenes are arranged by their relative importance. The back, or south, wall contains the most important events, while the north wall around the doorway depicts the supporting cast, including the orchestra. The easiest way to view the latter scenes is by sitting on the low bench emerging from the south wall. The lords of Maya tribute states were probably brought here to sit and ponder upon the murals' theme and the power of Bonampak's warriors.

A tour of the murals should begin with the central Room 2, which was the first to be painted. The back and side walls show a bloody battle fought by a mixture of richly dressed and near-naked warriors stabbing each other with long spears amid the blare of trumpets. The central figures are the two warriors in jaguar costumes on the back wall. One, a bearded man with a jaguar-head headdress, grasps a prisoner by his topknot; this is a portrait of Chan Muwaan himself. Itzamnaaj B'alam III of Yaxchilan is probably here as well; this powerful ally appears to have been central to the whole temple's conception. Opposite, the north wall depicts the battle's aftermath, the Bonampak lords presiding over the sacrifice of captives on the steps of a temple. A dead prisoner sprawls on the top center of the steps, while blood flows from the fingers of the captives seated to his left.

Painted a year or two later, Rooms 1 and 3 show the consequences of the battle. Its great victory has given Bonampak a network of vassal states; their noblemen arrive bearing tribute and are greeted with a great celebration. On the upper right (west), a wide throne is the base for three figures, possibly Chan Muwaan himself flanked by two wives. To the left, on the back wall you see a figure carrying a young child (his eye has been gouged out in a ritual mutilation), perhaps the heir to the throne, whose presence researchers now say is less important. The child faces a line of noblemen, all portraits obviously taken from life, dressed in white. Further nobles stand on the upper east wall. White-costumed figures are a rarity in Maya art; researchers believe these are the vassal lords. The accompanying glyphs tell of cacao, shells, and other valuable commodities—exactly the goods that they would be required to pay in tribute.

Below, a procession winds along the walls. Its most remarkable stretch is the north wall, which shows a line of musicians and dancers. Among the latter are men dressed in fantastic costumes representing crayfish with giant claws on their hands, carp, and caimans. The arrival of the tribute was obviously the time for a great celebration. Above them, you see a group of Bonampak lords donning huge quetzal plume headdresses in preparation for a ceremonial dance.

Further celebration is depicted in the Room 3 murals. The stage for this party is the temple steps. Figures wearing elaborate quetzal feather headdresses and amazing skirts that jut like wings perform a dance around the temple; these may be the nobles getting dressed in Room 1. In the center of the scene, you can just make out two men holding the bent body of a captive for sacrifice. The panel on the upper level of the east wall shows noblewomen seated on a large throne letting blood by passing knotted cords through their tongues. The woman seated on the lower left holds the child, perhaps the same as in Room 1, while the girl behind her passes a stingray spine perforator. Along the base of the north wall, another orchestra blows trumpets, while above you see rows of seated and standing noblemen dressed in white; again these are portraits of vassal noblemen who have brought tribute to the rulers of Bonampak.

Not all of the murals' glyph blocks were filled in, leading many archaeologists to believe that some cataclysm caused the artists to put down their brushes and never return to work. Now, however, researchers think that they are essentially finished, and that Bonampak's decline began sometime in the months or years that followed the building's November 15, 791, dedication.

To the left of Temple 1, in the center of the terrace lie the foundations of Temple 2, now obliterated. Next, on the far left stands Temple 3, a small Yaxchilan-style structure with three doorways entering into a single room. The roof above was decorated with a stucco frieze, and the remains of a roofcomb have been found on top. An eroded stela has been erected just to the right.

From here, a staircase climbs to the next level near the summit of the hill. Here you see a line of five small temples, with a sixth standing just behind. These all have one or two doors with a column behind each door. On the right (west), Temple 4 has notched doorways and a roofcomb, the best at the site, rising above. Behind stands the ruined Temple 9, which faces west and contains a bare stela standing in the middle of its room.

Two structures to the left of Temple 4, the central Temple 6 contains the fine Lintel 4 above its doorway. This depicts the first Chan Muwaan—an ancestor of the last Bonampak ruler—clutching a double-headed serpent bar in his arms. From the mouths of the serpents emerge two god manikins. The relief is dated to the early 7th century A.D.. The neighboring Temples 7 and 8 contain large columns and very worn lintels. You may see the remains of copal incense burned by the Lacandon. Recent archaeological excavations around these tombs have unearthed a number of tombs, including one containing a fine stone mirror.

Behind these temples, the hilltop is engulfed in dense jungle teeming with bird life. Numerous unexplored structures lie hidden along the ridge and on the west face of the hillside.

All Bonampak's most important sites lie around the Main Plaza. Diehards may want to explore two outlying building complexes. From the west end of the airstrip, a path heads about 100 meters to the Grupo Quemado (Burned Group). Here you find two small temple platforms around which archaeologists discovered traces of a destructive fire.

Due east of the camp, a path runs 150 meters to a small hill on top of which stands the Frey Group, named after the site's Western discoverer. Under a towering ceiba tree (the Maya World Tree was a ceiba) you see the ruins of a two-room temple standing on top of a semirestored platform. The temple faces south toward the Main Plaza and the Acropolis. The complete extent of Bonampak has never been discovered, and the Lacandon tell tales of further cities hidden in the surrounding hills.

TONINÁ

INTRODUCTION

The very end of the Classic era was a time of battles and instability. As cities such as Palenque and Yaxchilan declined, the militaristic center of Toniná grew to dominate the Usumacinta Basin. Its rulers directed their campaigns from a spectacular civic-religious acropolis built on seven great tiers up the side of a steep ridge above the Valley of Ocosingo. Archaeologists have found well over 200 stone monuments at the site, many of them life-size portraits of rulers in full regalia. The most spectacular find at the site is the "Frieze of the Dream Lords," a huge stucco wall illustrating scenes from the Popol Vuh, the great Maya mythological account. A climb to this complex's summit is an adventure—there are dozens of nooks and crannies to explore—and from the top you have an excellent view of the valley.

HISTORY

A detailed chronology of Toniná's history awaits a coherent final report on the last two decades of excavations. The Ocosingo Valley's oak forests comprise the

TONINÁ

How to get there: The ruins of Toniná stand on a hillside a few kilometers east of Ocosingo, which lies on Highway 199 roughly halfway between Palenque and San Cristóbal de las Casas. Just north of town, a good dirt road heads east up a valley through cattle country. After 10 kilometers, you can look north, to the left, and spot the ruins on the hillside–the top of the Acropolis in the foothills of the valley wall. Another dirt road turns left (north) and runs two kilometers to the site itself.

Hours: Daily 0900–1600.

Admission fee: 20 pesos.

How long to tour: Three hours.

Recommended gear: Hats, sunblock, hiking boots, mosquito repellent, bottled water, rain gear during the rainy season.

Museum: Designed to look like a giant ruin itself, the good new site museum contains a number of the best sculptures discovered during excavations. It stands amid the ruins of a densely populated residential neighborhood dating to the late 6th century.

Food and accommodations: Ocosingo has some basic tourist services, including a few passable restaurants and inexpensive hotels. Your best bet, however, is to head to Palenque 120 kilometers to the north.

limit of the Usumacinta Basin's *tierra caliente* (hot zone); to the north lie the pine-covered Chiapas Highlands. The valley was first settled around A.D. 1. An early center was a site called Mosil west-southwest of Toniná.

The occupation of Toniná proper (as opposed to small settlements in the surrounding hills) may have begun around A.D. 300. Potsherds dating to this era were found on the fifth terrace of the Acropolis. Archaeologists surmise that this complex's upper levels were occupied first. Toniná still was not the largest settlement in the valley; that was the site of Santa Teresa northeast of Toniná.

Between A.D. 600 and 900, Toniná emerged as one of the most important sites not only in the Ocosingo Valley but in the Usumacinta Basin, particularly at the end of this era. The earliest calendric inscription yet found is A.D. 514; for the few next decades, the dates found so far are spotty because of the state of the early monuments. At the end of the 6th century A.D., however, begins a nearly continuous line of inscriptions lasting almost three centuries. Almost all of what you see at Toniná today dates to this era.

The first ruler for whom we have multiple references is K'inich Hix Chapat, who probably came to the throne in 595. Next came the as-yet-unnamed Ruler 2, followed by K'inich B'aaknal Chaak, Toniná's greatest ruler. B'aaknal Chaak became ruler in 688 and presided over a 27-year reign of almost constant conflict with Palenque and other Usumacinta Basin city-states. His first great victory apparently came in A.D. 699, when he dedicated a ballcourt, probably Ballcourt 1, in commemoration of his defeat of Palenque allies. In A.D. 711,

DANIELLE GUSTAFSON

The Frieze of the Dream Lords: a detail from this large stucco relief depicts an upside-down head with its hair falling earthward.

B'aaknal Chaak struck a decisive blow against his principal enemy (only 64 kilometers to the north) by capturing K'an Joy Chitam, Palenque's ruler. A relief at Toniná shows the royal prisoner with his arms tied by ropes and crouching in a position of subservience. This victory led to a massive building campaign to commemorate the event; the Temple of War dates to this era.

Although almost all other Usumacinta religious centers stopped making calendric inscriptions by about A.D. 810, Toniná continued to flourish through the 9th century A.D. The city's great king during this period has been named Ruler 8 by researchers. He seems to have thrived from war and tribute; he called himself "He of Many Captives" and left many reliefs celebrating his military successes. These gave him enough wealth to order the construction of temples and the crafting of the Frieze of the Dream Lords.

The Toniná dynasty lasted until the early 10th century A.D. In A.D. 904, Ruler 10 erected a monument to celebrate his accession to the throne. Five years later on January 15, 909, he erected another sculpture (Monument 101), a portrait of himself marking an anniversary, and then the written record stops forever. This was not only the last monument carved at Toniná but the last Classic Maya monument from the southern lowlands of Mexico, Guatemala, and Honduras. With it, one of the most glorious eras in Mesoamerican history comes to the end. During the following months or years, nearly every monument and sculpture was ritually destroyed or mutilated.

After this collapse, archaeologists have found a gap of about a century in the stratigraphic record. Around A.D. 1000, Toniná was occupied by a foreign group, probably originating in the Chiapas Highlands. They performed sloppy repairs on the Acropolis temples and used it as a necropolis for their dead, sacking the old tombs for offerings. After A.D. 1250, they too disappear and the valley's largest settlement became Tzajalchib to the southwest. When Dominican priests entered the valley after the Spanish Conquest, they forced its residents to move into the towns of Ocosingo and Sivaca.

ARCHAEOLOGICAL RECORD

Toniná was probably never forgotten by the local Maya. Around 1700, a priest named Jacinto Garrido visited and described the ruins. Guillermo Dupaix included Toniná on his great 1808 tour of Mexico's archaeological sites, and illustrations of it appear in his book. John Lloyd Stephens and Frederick Catherwood also visited in 1840 but only briefly described two monuments. In 1859, E. G. Squier bought a collection of jade from Toniná that is now in the American Museum of Natural History in New York City.

Around 1900, the ruins were photographed by Eduard Seler, and officials from Mexico City removed four monuments for the Madrid Exposition in Spain (they are now in the Mexico City Museo Nacional de Antropología). During the following 50 years, archaeologists such as Frans Blom, Oliver La Farge, Heinrich Berlin, Sylvanus Morley, and J. Eric S. Thompson all made short visits to Toniná and unearthed stone monuments.

The first excavations began in 1972 under the joint French expedition of the Mission Archéologique et Ethnologique Française au Mexique and the Centre Nacional de la Recherche Scientifique led by Pierre Becquelin. During

DANIELLE GUSTAFSON

semi-reconstructed temple atop Toniná's Acropolis

four seasons lasting through 1980, this project excavated and explored the major structures of the Acropolis and the plaza below. It also identified and excavated numerous smaller sites in the valley and produced a preliminary chronology from stratigraphic studies. The report, published in four fat volumes, includes an excellent site map.

During the 1970s and early 1980s, the epigraphers Ian Graham and Peter Mathews photographed and drew many of the site's major monuments. This work has been the basis for the translation of Toniná's inscriptions.

In 1981, INAH began an ongoing Toniná project directed by Juan Yadeun Angulo. It has consolidated and restored most of the Acropolis and has made dozens of remarkable discoveries, including the Frieze of the Dream Lords and numerous stone monuments. The final report has yet to be published.

TOURING THE SITE

From the parking area, the path takes you down across a stream and then up to the Main Plaza, with the massive Acropolis looming to the right (north). The first structure you reach is the large Ballcourt 1, measuring 70 meters long with staircases on its north and south ends. This was dedicated in A.D. 699 by B'aak-nal Chaak, the same Toniná ruler who later captured Palenque's king. On the side walls, the ballgame targets were not rings but grisly sculptures of bound captives leaning head foremost.

Set in the center of the court was a round stone showing a seated ruler clasping a double-headed staff (sprouting not serpents' heads but a white flower glyph) in his arms. Maya ballcourts acted as a gateway into the Underworld, and this stone, which has a hollow space beneath, acted as the portal itself. The glyphs mark the man's death and later burial on May 22, 776. Immediately west stands the square Altar of Sacrifices with four short staircases around the sides. Here, archaeologists found a relief depicting the decapitation of a defeated ballplayer.

On the south end of the Main Plaza stands a large temple platform with trees sprouting from its top. Along the north side runs a row of five small pedestals facing the plaza. In front of each was found a circular disk bearing glyphs around the edge, some with figures in the center. They are dated to the 7th and 8th centuries A.D. The cattle pastures to the south and west are dotted with mounds.

From here, walk across the plaza to the base of the Acropolis. At the left of the bottom platform, some corrugated roofs cover loose sculptures collected from around the site. These include circular.glyph stones and the eroded remains of seated or standing stone sculptures.

The Acropolis rises through the trees above. This is a series of seven large terraces, each covered with temples and other structures. Still on the plaza level, just in front of the main staircase lies a small ballcourt built along an east-west

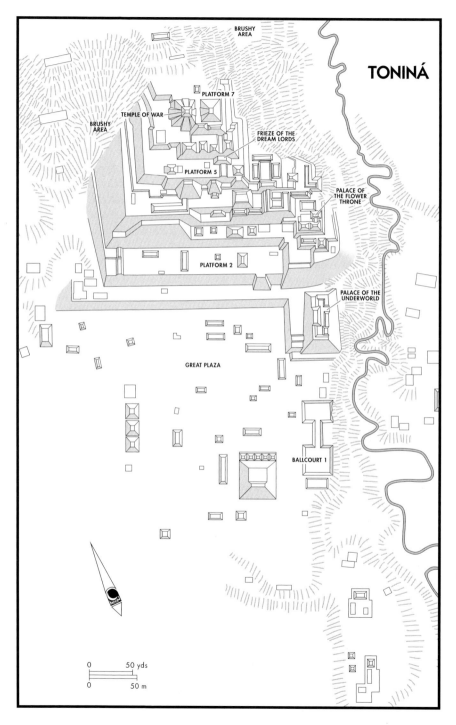

TONINÁ

BRUSHY
AREA

PLATFORM 7

TEMPLE OF WAR

BRUSHY
AREA

FRIEZE OF THE
DREAM LORDS

PLATFORM 5

PALACE OF
THE FLOWER
THRONE

PLATFORM 2

PALACE OF THE
UNDERWORLD

GREAT PLAZA

BALLCOURT 1

0   50 yds

0   50 m

axis. In its floor were set circular stones carved with glyphs celebrating anniversaries and naming rulers of Toniná.

A broad staircase takes you up to the first tier. On the right (east), three vaulted entrances open into a warren of rooms and corridors dubbed the Palace of the Underworld. This was an early (A.D. 500) complex that was covered by later constructions. The archaeologists stored some of their sculptures here, including the magnificent portrait of Ruler 8. Some of the walls are perforated by windows in the form of a Greek cross (like the Red Cross symbol with four arms of equal length).

Returning to the main staircase and climbing to Platform 2, you see a series of small mounds in which archaeologists found numerous sculptures. One of these was Monument 101, the portrait of Ruler 10 that is the last dated sculpture of the Classic Maya. On the right—most of the Acropolis's attractions lie on this side—you find a structure called the Palace of Agriculture (not to be confused with the Temple of Agriculture) built along a north-south axis. After a room containing six columns, you see a thatched roof covering an immense (more than two meters high) stucco monster mask adorned with a mustache and a large hole in its forehead.

On to Platform 3. On its east side stands the Palace of the "Grecas," named after the Greek-style step-and-fret motifs. These designs are constructed on a grand scale out of stone blocks covering a huge sloping wall measuring 21 meters wide and seven tall. The step-and-frets actually double as a staircase, which you can climb, taking you to a small platform. Here, another narrow staircase ascends to a thatched roof covering a throne made of stone and stucco. Its legs are shaped in the form of jaguar paws and one contains the emblem glyph of

DANIELLE GUSTAFSON

view from top of Acropolis

Toniná. On the wall behind, you can see the remains of a stucco relief that may be a large Venus symbol.

From this, the path continues up through a vaulted tunnel to an intermediary platform between levels three and four. This is the Palace of the Flowered Throne, built by Ruler 8. Another thatched roof covers a stucco wall decorated with the scales of a feathered serpent painted red and blue and, below, crossed bones. To the east lies a patio surrounded by small rooms with stucco monster masks visible on the walls. One contains the broken stucco bench that gives the complex its name; the stack of glyphs refers to Ruler 8 "seating" in the building. You can edge along a very narrow passage between the west and east buildings to see (with the aid of a flashlight) further monster masks along the roof frieze.

On the northeast side of this patio, a corrugated roof covers the fragments of a very large stucco wall relief. A monster mask is visible above, while below you see a unique freestanding section, perhaps part of a throne, made of two rounded frames separated by a stack of glyph blocks. The use and meaning of this assemblage has yet to be clarified.

From here, return down the stairs passing the first stucco throne and back to Platform 3. The main staircase takes you up to Platform 4, with low altars, some reconstructed in the center and on the left. On the east side (right), you find a small residential complex faced with a row of columns. Behind lies a patio surrounded by rooms. Corrugated roofs around the outside of this complex protect the remains of stucco wall reliefs.

Back to the center, where you climb the main stairs to Platform 5. On the way up, you see a five-room residential complex on an intermediary terrace. In front of an unexcavated mound a bit to the left, a ladder descends into a hole. Bring a flashlight into the clammy darkness below, where you can see an open sarcophagus with its stone lid lying to one side. Farther west, a thatched roof covers a stucco god mask at the base of the Temple of Water rising on the level above. The opposite side of this platform is occupied by the semiexcavated Celestial Palace built around a patio. At the far eastern end, the Acropolis drops off steeply into the jungle. This is the highest point of the Acropolis's east side; above, the platforms are smaller and lie slightly to the west of the central stairs.

Slightly to the east of this palace, the base of the next tier (the Temple of the Earth Monster lies just above) is the site of the famous Frieze of the Dream Lords, measuring 16 meters by four meters and covered by a protective roof. This enormous stucco relief represents the *wayob'*, otherworldly counterparts to Toniná's rulers who take the form of weird mythological creatures.

Bands of plumes border the four scenes and cross each in a giant "X." In the center of each "X," you see a medallion containing an inverted human head. Of the leftmost relief, you see only a part of a medallion. As you move to the right, the next scene is the best-preserved. The nightmare image of a skeletal "Turtle Foot Death" holds the head of a decapitated captive in his hand; his tongue hangs from his slack mouth. The glyphs identify him as the defeated ruler of

ASTRONAUTS, AFRICANS, AND ISRAELITES

Ever since Spaniards first set foot in the New World, people have been speculating about who was responsible for building the great civilizations of Mesoamerica. The Europeans first thought the pyramids had been built by a race of giants or perhaps Carthaginian sailors or even Atlanteans fleeing the destruction of their mysterious continent. Despite centuries of scientific exploration and literally tons of evidence, these speculations have continued to the present day and are frequently no less fantastic than the wild conjectures of the conquistadors. All these theories have two main problems. Perhaps because of racial bias, they refuse to address the extremely high probability that all the pre-Columbian cultures were built by the ancestors of Mexico's Indian tribes. And instead of studying the scientific evidence before developing a theory, they reach their conclusion first and then search through the evidence for anything that proves it. Here are three theories of Mesoamerican origins that still have wide currency today.

Ancient Astronauts

The main propagator of the theory that astronauts from outer space brought the knowledge that formed the basis of all Mesoamerican cultures is the Swiss author Erich von Däniken. In dozens of books beginning with *Chariots of the Gods?*, von Däniken looked at ancient sites around the world with a mind untainted by careful scientific study. Deeply impressed by the glory years of space exploration, he saw astronauts everywhere he looked. On Lord Pakal's famous tomb lid at the Maya site of Palenque, he saw not a king descending into the Underworld but an ancient astronaut rocketing into outer space. Chalcatzingo's Monument I, which most archaeologists believe depicts a ruler seated in a cave with wisps of wind blowing from its mouth, became to von Däniken a spaceman whizzing through space in his rocket ship.

Excited by these revelations, he proposed a theory that civilization, not just in Mexico but everywhere, came from a group of immensely wise alien astronauts who gave humans the knowledge and technology to rise from cavemen into our supposedly highly advanced modern selves. They then rocketed off into the unknown, leaving behind mementos of their visit in sources as widely separated as the Old Testament, the Nazca lines in Peru, and the Castillo at Chichén Itzá.

As numerous scientists have pointed out, however, von Däniken's theory does not stand up to close scrutiny. Among other faults, he ignored the context of everything he looked at. If you study Maya art, you realize that the motifs on Pakal's tomb lid are repeated in other Palenque temples in situations that could not be interpreted to contain flying saucers. And if you compare the carving at Chalcatzingo to similar designs at other Olmec sites, you realize it could not possibly be a rocket ship.

Though the popularity of von Däniken's work has diminished over the years, the ancient astronauts theory continues to find advocates. Based on great imaginative leaps by its author, the New Age tract *The Mayan Factor* by José Argüelles theorizes that the Classic Maya were "planetary navigators and mappers of the larger psychic field of the Earth, the solar system, and the galaxy beyond."

Nubian Kings

Ever since the first colossal head was unearthed at Tres Zapotes in 1858, writers have proposed that Africans traveled to the New World and helped found the Olmec civilization, considered the "mother culture" of Mesoamerica. In recent years, the most vehement proponent of this theory has been Ivan van Sertima, author of *They Came Before Columbus* among other works. Van Sertima states that between 705 and 664 B.C.

Nubian kings from Egypt's 25th dynasty sailed across the Atlantic and landed on the Gulf Coast of Mexico. Here their superior technology and wisdom overwhelmed the relatively primitive native peoples, who accepted them as their rulers. From this point onward, there were numerous landings of African ships in the New World. Indeed, according to van Sertima, African voyagers were profound influences on nearly every important pre-Columbian culture in the Western Hemisphere.

As with von Däniken, however, the main problem with van Sertima's theory is that he ignores both the context of Mesoamerican artworks and all evidence that contradicts his conclusion. To use just his premises about the colossal heads as an example, the problem is that archaeologists now believe that these statues were first carved at San Lorenzo before 1000 B.C., more than 300 years before the arrival of his Nubian kings. Van Sertima (and many others) have pointed out that the colossal heads have "Negroid" features— thick lips, wide nose, etc. Unfortunately, this ignores the fact that these attributes are also found in peoples far from Africa, such as in East Asia and the Pacific region. If he had spent any time in the Olmec region of Veracruz, he would have noticed that many of the indigenous peoples have those same features—including the epicanthic fold over the eyes seen on the colossal heads but not a common trait in "Negro Africans." And finally, the Nubian rulers of ancient Egypt were depicted as having narrow noses, and in fact were distinctly non-"African" in appearance. There is not space to go into all of van Sertima's arguments; it is sufficient to say that the real refutation of his theory is what the archaeologists have not found: large numbers of objects with an obvious origin in Africa.

Israelites

The belief that the ancient Mexican sites were built by descendants of the Lost Tribes of Israel has been popular for more than five centuries.

The most intricate version of this explanation is the one that appears in the Book of Mormon, purportedly a historical text, which was translated by Joseph Smith and first published in 1830. The Book of Mormon recounts the travels of a group of Israelites (but not the Lost Tribes) who around 600 B.C. sailed west from the Middle East across the Pacific and landed in Central America. They were led by Lehi and his sons Nephi, Laman, and Lemuel. In the New World, they built a city with a temple that copied the Temple in Jerusalem, followed Jewish law, and were acknowledged as rulers by the natives.

After Lehi's death, Laman and Lemuel refused to follow Nephi's rule and fled with half the city's population to set up their own, idolatrous settlement. Conflicts and even open battles between the light-skinned Nephites and the dark-skinned Lamanites mark much of the Book of Mormon. The major exception is the two centuries after about A.D. 30, when the post-resurrection Jesus Christ appeared in the New World and ushered in a period of peace and contentment. But then the old frictions reemerged, while at the same time the Nephites forgot their ancient religion and became rich and decadent. Around A.D. 400, the Lamanites destroyed the Nephites in a series of great battles and thereafter the land reverted to paganism—war, depravity, cannibalism, etc.— until the arrival of the Spanish.

When the Book of Mormon appeared, newspapers and magazines were filled with stories of the discoveries of ancient ruins in the jungles of Mesoamerica. To Joseph Smith and his followers, these could have been the Nephite and Lamanite cities mentioned in the Book of Mormon. They believed that the Native Americans they met on their trek westward were descendants of the dark-skinned Lamanites. They became fascinated by the possibility of proving the veracity of their holy book through archaeological research, beginning a long tradition of Mormon archaeology. One happy result of this quest is that they

(continues)

(continued from previous page)

have produced some of the best scientific archaeologists of recent times (and the source of much information in this book). At the same time, however, their ultimate goal, scientific proof of the Book of Mormon, remains elusive.

Though the Book of Mormon claims to be a historical account, its detailed descriptions are few and open to interpretation. In his *An Ancient American Setting for the Book of Mormon*, the Mormon scholar John L. Sorenson places the book's narration in a context that parallels the great growth of our knowledge about pre-Columbian Mesoamerica. From the first Nephite city, which he says is probably Kaminaljuyu in Guatemala, he finds possible locations for all the important Nephite and Lamanite centers in Highland Guatemala, Chiapas, Veracruz, and Oaxaca. In Mesoamerica's long record of wars and natural disasters, he pinpoints events that could have been those described in the Book of Mormon. Where he falls into difficulty, however, is in the details. The Book of Mormon specifically mentions crops such as wheat, barley, flax, olives, and grapes; animals such as pigs, goats, horses, donkeys, and elephants; and technological products such as iron, steel, glass, and silk. All of these were common in the ancient Middle East, and in the Old Testament, but they were unknown in Mesoamerica. (For a discussion of these and similar anomalies in the Book of Mormon, read Deanne G. Metheny's article "Does the Shoe Fit? A Critique of the Limited Tehuantepec Geography" in *New Approaches to the Book of Mormon,* edited by Brent Metcalfe.)

Mormon scholars also neglect the broader pictures of the cultures described in the Book of Mormon and by modern-day archaeologists. Lehi's descendants were Israelites, followers of the laws of Moses, yet there is no evidence of any Mesoamerican culture practicing what we consider the main attributes of Judaism, including monotheism, worship in the Temple (with its carefully defined attributes), the Torah as the principal religious text, and the cycle of Jewish holy days. And if we look in the Book of Mormon for what archaeologists believe are the main attributes of Mesoamerican cultures—the pantheon of gods, the ballgame, the 260-day calendar system, etc. (not to mention indigenous crops such as corn and squash and animals such as turkeys and jaguars)—we do not see them either. The best that can be said about this religious text is that it does not correspond with any pre-Columbian culture yet discovered.

Pipa', a Maya city near Palenque. Behind the death god's feet, you see the compact form of a rodent, perhaps the First Rat of the North from the Popol Vuh, carrying a bound bag or ball. A skeletal foot missing its body strides to its left.

The next scene is more fragmentary. To the left, you see a figure lying on his back on a throne with his legs in the air; this is Hunahpu, one of the Hero Twins. The great sky bird crouches above him, having just torn off his hand. A jaguar head can be seen above this sun. On the last scene, the only complete figure is the form of a tumbling man leaning backward with his weight on one hand and one leg. He may represent Xbalanque, the second of the Hero Twins. In front of this wall stands a red altar with three holes in the top; numerous bones and offerings were found buried within.

The temples become dense on the top two tiers. The central staircase climbs between the Temple of Seven Rooms on the left and the Hidden Temple on the right. Just to the right of the latter temple, a thatched roof on the west side of the Temple of the Earth Monster (also called the Temple of Agriculture) covers the stucco relief that gives it its name. The monster devours a solar sphere made from stone and set inside a niche formed by its mouth. Inside, you find two vaulted rooms. This structure is topped with a teetering roofcomb constructed in the unique Toniná style, built not as a long line but as a thick square of decoration.

From here, you ascend the steep staircase to the seventh and final platform of the Acropolis. Four structures occupy the top. On your left, you see the small Temple of War, which is capped with another unstable-looking roofcomb. A frieze around the temple's base is decorated with stucco reliefs depicting bound captives sitting on the floor. The temple above contained two vaulted rooms, now ruined.

Behind and to the left stands the Temple of Commerce, a mound still covered with trees. This is the second-highest point at the site and a nice place to rest in the shade and enjoy the view. Its neighbor, the restored Temple of the Smoking Mirror, is the highest point. The ultimate layer of this structure was added during the 9th century A.D., perhaps during the reign of Ruler 10, and represents the last major construction at Toniná. To the right of the stairs, a stucco relief tablet now damaged by water and algae depicts a line of captives with inscriptions along the sides. You can climb to the temple's summit by the main staircase and then by scrambling up the east side. On top, there is a breeze and a stunning view.

CHINKULTIC

INTRODUCTION

The Maya knew how to build their cities for drama. They used hills both to accentuate their temples' contours and to give them commanding views over the valleys below. As at Toniná and Bonampak, Chinkultic's Acropolis is built up a hillside whose steep slopes give it both drama and natural defenses. Although it lies in the Chiapas Highlands and is part of the Río Grijalva drainage, this city is closely related to the lowland culture based around the Usumacinta Basin, with particular similarities to Toniná. Chinkultic grew as a border city, trading between the Maya region to the north and east and the Pacific Coast cultures to the south. After the Acropolis, the most important structure is the recently discovered ballcourt; this was lined with a remarkable series of stelae depicting Chinkultic's rulers celebrating victories over captive foes. A few stelae remain, though most have fallen down and been removed.

CHINKULTIC

How to get there: The large town of Comitán de Domínguez is a good base for exploring Chinkultic and other attractions of this obscure corner of Chiapas. From Comitán, drive 16 kilometers east and just before the town of La Trinitaria take the left turn toward the Lagunas de Montebello. After about 35 kilometers, a sign points left toward the site three kilometers down a rough dirt road (or you can go on to explore the Montebello Lagoons).

Hours: Daily 0900–1700.

Admission fee: 14 pesos.

How long to tour: Two hours.

Recommended gear: Hats, sunblock, hiking boots, bottle water, mosquito repellent, rain gear during the rainy season.

Food and accommodations: Comitán de Domínguez possesses a number of good hotels, including the **Hotel Lagos de Montebello**, Belisario Domínguez 1257, tel. 963/2-1092. For much more scenic (and remote) accommodations, the **Parador-Museo Santa María**, tel. 963/2-3346, 22 kilometers west of Chinkultic (near La Trinitaria), is a countryside oasis. This is a restored early 19th-century hacienda containing rooms decorated with antique furniture and an excellent restaurant.

H I S T O R Y

Chinkultic lies in a saddle of land between the Chiapas Highlands and the mountains of Guatemala. Situated at 1,500 meters in a zone of hills and broad valleys, this region has always been a pathway between the Usumacinta and Petén lowlands to the north and the Pacific Coast to the south. Chinkultic itself overlooks the Valley of the Lost Desires, a subvalley of the Comitán Valley. Just to the north is an inexhaustible supply of water—the lake system called the Lagoons of Montebello. Combined with rich soils, this makes Chinkultic an excellent location for human settlement.

Chinkultic has been only partially excavated, and not all of those results have arrived at publication. Our understanding of the site chronology is fragmentary. The region's first occupation dates to between A.D. 1 and 350, when the site was probably settled by an early Maya group originating to the west in the Grijalva Depression. Already there were trade ties to the north and south. These early residents used the neighboring Cenote Agua Azul (Blue Water Sinkhole) as both a site of ritual ceramic offerings and a garbage dump (later residents depended on it mainly as a reservoir).

From A.D. 350 to about 700, there is a gap in Chinkultic's ceramic record; no sign of human occupation has yet been found for this era. Eight kilometers to the west, the site of La Esperanza was thriving; a beautiful circular ballcourt marker dated A.D. 591 from there is now in Mexico City's Museo Nacional de Antropología.

Much of what you see at Chinkultic today dates to the relatively brief period between A.D. 700 and 900, including the Acropolis and the amazing Group C ballcourt. The ceramic evidence shows strong hints of trade ties to Palenque and other cities in the Usumacinta region. The first dated inscription was carved on Monument 7 in A.D. 780, and this practice lasted for less than a century. As at Toniná, Chinkultic's rulers recorded their dates of accession and great victories on stone monuments; most of the inscriptions, which are relatively eroded, have yet to be translated. At the same time, many other sites arose in the nearby valley, including Tenam Puente and Sacchana.

What followed A.D. 900 is unclear, although evidence shows that occupation continued through about A.D. 1250. The zone of densest settlement was Group C, and additions, including burials and offering caches, were made to the ceremonial buildings on top of the Acropolis. Whether these late residents were Maya or other peoples is not known. After A.D. 1250, the site was abandoned.

ARCHAEOLOGICAL RECORD

Although locals must have known about the ruins for many years, Chinkultic was not identified as an archaeological site until Eduard Seler visited the valley in 1895 and discovered Stelae 4 and 5. Thirty years later, Frans Blom and Oliver La Farge explored the site, found six more stelae, and mapped the Acropolis.

In the late 1960s, Stephen F. de Borhegyi of the Milwaukee Public Museum led a large-scale project with the assistance of Brigham Young University's New World Archaeological Foundation to study the Cenote Agua Azul. He evidently thought that its depths concealed a trove of ritual offerings similar to that found in the cenote in Chichén Itzá. They partially drained the water and sent divers down to plumb the deepest portions; they found mounds of broken pots, most dating to Chinkultic's earliest occupation, but no great treasures.

After Borhegyi's untimely death in an auto accident, the New World Archaeological Foundation under Gareth Lowe continued investigations at the site, mapping the ruins, clearing Group C, and digging test-pits in Group A. This

TENAM PUENTE RUINS

On the trip back to Comitán, stop at the newly opened ruins of **Tenam Puente,** built at roughly the same time as Chinkultic. It contains two ballcourts and a number of temples. These you reach by turning left eight kilometers east of Comitán, heading through Ejido Francisco Sarabia, and ascending to the hilltop site six kilometers south from the turn. It's open daily 0900–1630; free admission.

DANIELLE GUSTAFSON

Complex A, Acropolis

was continued by an INAH project led by Roberto Gallegos Ruiz, which completed the cenote study and consolidated part of the ballcourt and the temples at the top of the Acropolis, clearing debris and preserving the area from further deterioration. In 1973 and 1976, Carlos Navarrete of Universidad Nacional Autonoma de Mexico (UNAM) continued the restoration work on the Group C ballcourt and on the Acropolis. Since then, no significant work has been done except for maintenance.

TOURING THE SITE

The site is in a long valley lying on a north-south axis. At the north end of the valley, you see the end of a forest-covered line of hills that runs to the west. Chinkultic's Acropolis occupies the easternmost summit of this ridge. These hills also block the flow of the line of lakes that form the headwaters of the Río Comitán; they make a great loop around these hills before flowing to the west-southwest.

You enter the site at its south end. The layout is much like Toniná's, with a large plaza below covered with temples and ballcourts, while the Acropolis rises up the hillside to the north. As you walk north, on your right you pass a tree-covered platform built from large stones and then a semireconstructed three-tier temple. You enter the Main Plaza bounded on the north, east, and west sides by mounds, mostly unexcavated. A square platform stands in the middle. You can see the summit of Acropolis on the hillside to the north. To the left and right lie two lakes, respectively the Tepancuapan and Chanujabab Lagoons.

From the three mounds on the plaza's north side, walk down to the river. During the rainy season, you may have to wade, because the bridge does not go all the way across. From here, walk up the hill to the left, passing the unreconstructed mounds of Group A. The path zigzags up the hillside to the Acropolis; the main staircase has not been reconstructed. At one point, a small path heads a few steps to the right, leading you out onto a lookout over the Cenote Agua Azul. This large limestone sinkhole is bounded on all sides by steep, often precipitous slopes. It was the main water supply for Chinkultic; numerous broken water jars, and offerings, were found in its depths.

The main path continues to the top past trees covered with bromeliads and Spanish moss. The front of the Acropolis platform is lined with three small square altars. Late burials and offering caches were found in and around these structures. Propped up against the right-hand altar stands the fragmentary Monument 9. This is highly reminiscent of Toniná's Frieze of the Dream Lords. You can see a sun disc containing a head; from this radiates a band like the feathered "X" at Toniná, while from behind it emerges a head. The border is lined with an inscription.

Behind these altars, the semiruined main temple is built in three or four stages with one or two rooms on top. From here, you have a breathtaking view of lakes (filled with bass and other fish), cornfields, and hills covered with a mixed pine and deciduous forest. You can see how the end of the ridge is punctuated by the cenote's huge sinkhole and how this terrace perches precariously on its western rim. On the east side of the platform stands a low, three-tier temple. Beyond, a path leads to another lookout over the cenote.

Returning all the way back down the hill and through the Main Plaza to the entrance, a path heads west 100 meters to Group C. On your right lies the complex of tree-covered mounds called the Palace. Here you see the first of many stelae, a worn representation of a standing figure, under a thatched roof. You enter a north-south plaza containing Chinkultic's Great Ballcourt. This I-shaped court is unique in that its north end is far larger than its south; almost all others are strictly symmetrical.

The west side of the ballcourt is formed by a long platform. On top stand four stelae under protective roofs. The best is Monument 4, the second from the left, showing a standing man wearing a large headdress and carrying a staff in one hand and a ritual bag in the other. Another, lying on its back, depicts a victorious ruler standing over what is perhaps a captive. You find further stelae on two ruined platforms just to the left of the ballcourt's north end. The clearest is Monument 3, which shows a standing figure with a worn or intentionally erased face looming over two small supplicants at his feet. Many of the Group C stelae appear to be dated to the late 8th century A.D.; their carving may have been ordered by one dynamic ruler.

The surrounding countryside is covered with unexplored mounds.

COMALCALCO

INTRODUCTION

Comalcalco lies about 160 kilometers northwest of Palenque in the humid coastal plain of Tabasco. It is included in this chapter because there are strong indications that Comalcalco was an extension of Palenque-region culture—its buildings are almost exact copies of structures such as the Temple of the Cross. Comalcalco is unique among Maya sites in that its temples were built out of brick rather than stone because of the lack of the latter on the Tabasco plain. Thousands of these bricks were inexplicably scratched with designs, varying from crude graffiti to glyphic inscriptions. Although Comalcalco lacked the fine Palenque stonework, they were great artists with stucco. A large monster mask and a tomb lined with reliefs are some of the many stucco artworks found at the site.

HISTORY

Despite years of investigation, we know very little about Comalcalco's chronology. The region appears to have been settled around 800 B.C., when this was the easternmost border of the Olmec region. This early occupation lasted until about A.D. 100. Comalcalco's main period of occupation began during the Early Classic,

Temple 1, Comalcalco, constructed of unusual kilned brick

DANIELLE GUSTAFSON

COMALCALCO

How to get there: These ruins stand on the outskirts of the town of the same name, which lies on the steamy Tabasco lowlands 20 kilometers from the Gulf of Mexico. You can reach them either from Villahermosa heading northwest via Jalapa and Cupilco or by heading 40 kilometers north from Cárdenas on Highway 187. Once you arrive in Comalcalco town, follow the signs to the ruins.

Hours: Daily 1000–1700, with the last entrance at 1600. It is best to visit the ruins at the beginning or end of the day, when the heat is not so oppressive.

Admission fee: 20 pesos.

How long to tour: Two hours.

Recommended gear: Hats, sunblock, sturdy shoes or sneakers, lots of bottled water. (The 19th-century explorer Charnay noticed that the region was so humid that locals kept their salt in liquid form.)

Museum: There is a good museum at the site entrance.

Food and accommodations: Comalcalco contains two good hotels, the **Copacabana**, tel. 933/4-1932, and the **Kaoma**, tel. 933/4-1964, both on Av. Juárez downtown. The best food is found at the roadside grilled fish restaurants between Comalcalco and Jalapa.

when the first stages of the main buildings were erected. Some of the site's many stucco reliefs date to this era. The center reached its height between A.D. 750 and 800, with the massive expansion of the ceremonial center. Because of the many similarities between the architectural styles of Palenque and Comalcalco, archaeologists believe the latter was an outpost of Palenque's state. After Palenque's fall, refugees fleeing the dying capital may have made Comalcalco their new home. There is evidence that it continued as a regional center of the Chontal Maya—the main indigenous group in the area today—through A.D. 1250. Occupation dwindled during the following century, and by A.D. 1350 Comalcalco was abandoned.

ARCHAEOLOGICAL RECORD

The first to describe Comalcalco was Désiré Charnay, who spent two weeks at the site in 1881. He noticed that the houses and main street of the nearby town were all built with bricks from the ancient ruins. Luckily, something remained of the temples.

In 1892, Captain Pedro H. Romero performed the first excavations at the site, digging into the Great Acropolis and uncovering its construction method. In

1925, the Tulane Expedition to Middle America led by Frans Blom and Oliver La Farge visited Comalcalco and discovered a tomb that had been recently looted. The walls held intact stucco reliefs, which you can still see today. Blom and La Farge also described the unique Comalcalco practice of scratching designs on the bricks.

The next excavations were conducted in 1956 and 1957 by Gordon Ekholm of the American Museum of Natural History, mostly around the Palace and the Great Acropolis. This project produced a summary but never a final report. A decade later, Carlos Navarrete published his book on the engraved bricks of Comalcalco, which discussed their patterns, symbolism, and use in construction. Around the same time, George Andrews led a summer project from the University of Oregon that produced a complete site map. Their architectural studies are the basis for the theory linking the site with Palenque.

Between 1972 and 1982, a Mexican expedition led by Ponciano Salazar spent 10 years investigating the site and restoring its major structures. When the final report of this project is published, our knowledge of the site's history will be greatly improved. In 1988, a project centering on the North Plaza unearthed a funerary urn and associated burial.

TOURING THE SITE

You approach the site from the west, on a road that may run on top of an ancient causeway. At the entrance, you find a good site museum containing a selection of the famous decorated bricks. Some are adorned with small raised reliefs of lizards and other animals, while on others the design has been scratched with a tool. These patterns were added to the bricks before their firing; afterward, they were placed with the decorated face hidden from view. Almost 10,000 of these bricks have been found among the ruins. Experts are divided on whether these are mere graffiti or artworks with some religious symbolism. (More imaginative researchers see the patterns as proof that Comalcalco was settled by Roman Christians, Libyans, or Mesopotamians—despite the utter lack of corroborating evidence.)

You enter the ruins just west of Comalcalco's ceremonial center. On your left lies the North Plaza; at its west end stands Temple 1, a 12-stage pyramid built from flat reddish bricks. Because of their fragility, you are not allowed to climb to the two-room temple on top. To the left of its staircase, the corner is adorned with a stucco relief depicting a huge bird. Both the mortar between the bricks and the stucco are made from a mixture of sand and carbonized oyster shells. The plaza is built along an east-west axis bordered to the north and south by two lines of temples; only the two westernmost have been consolidated. The room layout on top of all three of these temples is an almost exact copy of the room plans found in Palenque's Cross Group. A low mound occupies the plaza's east end.

DANIELLE GUSTAFSON

stucco mask of the Sun God, Temple of the Mask

South of this plaza stands the Great Acropolis, the largest architectural grouping at the site, built around another plaza. On its north side stand three temples facing south. The easternmost (far left) structure is the three-tier Temple 6. At the foot of its staircase, a window covers a large stucco monster mask wearing plugs in its ears and an ornate headdress.

Its similar but slightly larger neighbor, the central Temple 7, contains stucco relief fragments lining the main staircase and on panels just to its right. The first- and second-tier reliefs depict rows of seated figures, probably rulers, wearing headdresses and wide belts. The top relief is harder to see—it may represent a serpent—and the decorations on either side of the staircase are illegible. Temple 8, the westernmost in this line, has not been explored.

Returning to Temple 6, take the ramp up the grass-covered main platform of the Great Acropolis. Built along a north-south axis, the top of this massive structure contains at least seven temples and the long line of rooms called the Palace. This path leads to Temple 5 at the southern end of the platform. From here, a path winds down the west face of the temple to the vaulted entrance of the Tomb of the Nine Chieftains.

When Frans Blom and Oliver La Farge explored this tomb in 1925, it had already been looted; human bones and red-stained beads were found on the floor. The tomb walls are decorated with nine stucco relief figures, three each to a wall. These richly dressed men appear to be dancing; they may represent the Nine Lords of the Underworld whom the dead encounter on their journey.

On the south side of Temple 5, a flight of stairs takes you back up to Temple 4 on top of the Acropolis. Once again, its temple is laid out in the Palenque

style; a tomb adorned with more stucco reliefs—they have since been looted—
was discovered beneath the floor. From here, a path leads along the eastern
edge of the platform. On your left lies the Sunken Patio, with the long line of
the Palace structure beyond.

At the northeast corner of the ruins begins a roped pathway leading south
back through the palace. You first pass Structures 1 and 2—notice the large
water tank, called a *chultun*—and then enter the Sunken Patio. Pieces of the
floor have been removed to expose the Acropolis's drainage system made from
interlocking segments of ceramic pipe.

This tour ends with a stroll through the Palace, which runs up the center of
the Great Acropolis. Like the Palace at Palenque, this structure is made from a
central wall with long vaulted galleries on either side. A colonnade looks over
the plaza to the west. No decorations have been found, but archaeologists believe this was capped with a roof frieze adorned with a roofcomb above.

The surrounding cattle pastures contain dozens of grassy mounds. Because of
the heat, humidity, swampy ground, and mosquitoes (not to mention ticks!), a visit
to these is recommended only for the diehard. Many of the trees in this area are
cacao; Tabasco produces more chocolate than any other state in Mexico.

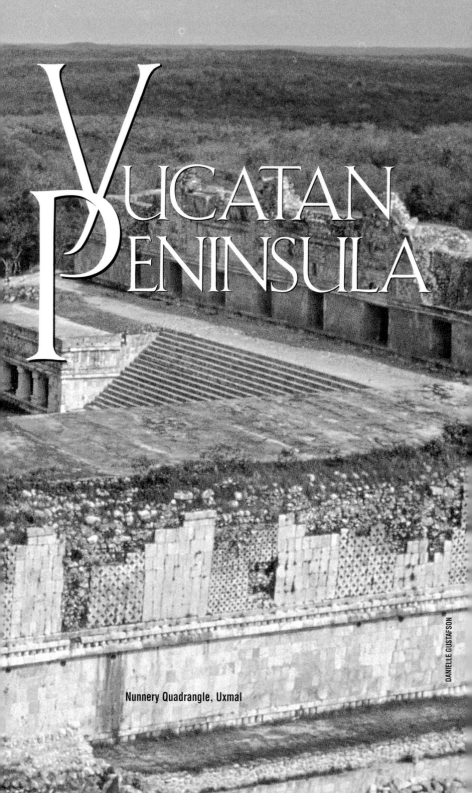

Yucatan Peninsula

DANIELLE GUSTAFSON

Nunnery Quadrangle, Uxmal

The Yucatan Peninsula, comprising the states of Yucatan, Campeche, and Quintana Roo, is something of a paradise for archaeological tourists. It not only possesses all the attributes of a tropical Eden—bright sun, warm weather, beautiful forests, and broad beaches—it also contains hundreds of archaeological sites, including some of the most remarkable in Mexico. Dozens of these have been restored and are accessible to visitors.

Yucatan was a homeland of the ancient Maya. Hundreds of thousands of their descendants, the Yucatec Maya, live in the region today. Many still occupy traditional villages where turkeys and pigs scavenge along the roadside and the women wear the customary *huipiles*—white dresses with embroidered fronts. The memory of their heritage remains strong, particularly along the Quintana Roo coast. In the late 19th century, these Maya rebelled against the Mexican government and in the so-called Caste War managed to carve out a state governed by traditional Maya principles that remained independent for three decades.

Between A.D. 400 and the Spanish Conquest, their ancestors built a series of beautiful cities whose fine stonework and elaborate murals are among the masterworks of Mesoamerican art. The ceremonial centers of Calakmul, Uxmal, and Chichén Itzá became the hubs of empires that spread for thousands of square kilometers and had ties as far away as central Mexico. The first two of these cities declined with the Classic Maya collapse, but Chichén reached its height in the following centuries. After its fall, the power devolved to centers such as Mayapan. In the early 16th century, the first Spanish explorers found a series of rapidly growing ports, such as Tulum, along the Quintana Roo coast. Controlled by Putún Maya traders, these centers thrived for decades after the Conquest, until their populations were decimated by European diseases.

TRAVELING TO YUCATAN

Most visitors arrive by air to the Yucatan Peninsula, landing at Mérida or Cancún. By road, the most common route into the region is Highway 186 from Villahermosa; you can also enter from Belize just south of Chetumal. Yucatan is one of the most heavily touristed regions of Mexico, with hundreds of hotels and a complete array of services.

THE LAND

The Yucatan Peninsula is a broad limestone shelf that has risen relatively recently from the sea floor. It is bound on the west and north by the Gulf of Mexico and on the east by the Caribbean Sea. Its southern boundary runs roughly from Belize City to the Campeche port of Champotón. From west to east, it is bordered by the Campeche coastal plain, the Petén Jungle, and the Maya Mountains in Belize.

The northern third of the peninsula is a pitted karst plain with almost no surface water because of the porosity of the limestone. The exceptions are the limestone sinkholes known as cenotes that connect with underground water channels. All the Mesoamerican centers of this region were built on or near cenotes. The abundant limestone gave them a near limitless supply of soft building stone that they could carve with their flint tools. The maximum elevation of the land is 40 meters; it slopes gradually from south to north and then into the sea. The west and north coasts are ringed by broad lagoons that were an important source of pre-Columbian salt. Beyond, the shores are ringed by a shallow bank that extends many kilometers into the Gulf.

The southern border of this region is along a ridge of hills rising to 130 meters called the Sierrita de Ticul. These hills possess some of the most fertile soils of the peninsula and became home to the Puuc Maya culture centered around Uxmal. To the south rises a hilly karsted zone that slowly ascends to about 300 meters at the southern border. There is slightly more surface water here, but supplies were still short enough that the inhabitants built clay-lined reservoirs called *aguadas*. From the Sierrita de Ticul south, you find many large and small caverns that were used to reach water and as ritual spaces. The Quintana Roo coast lies along some geological fault lines, giving rise to low cliffs and many small coves (used as ports by seagoing Maya traders). Offshore lies the second largest barrier reef in the world (after Australia's Great Barrier Reef), which heads south along the Belize coast to Guatemala.

Climate

The Yucatan Peninsula's climate is tropical, with warm or hot weather likely year-round. The only exception are the December–March Nortes, which bring

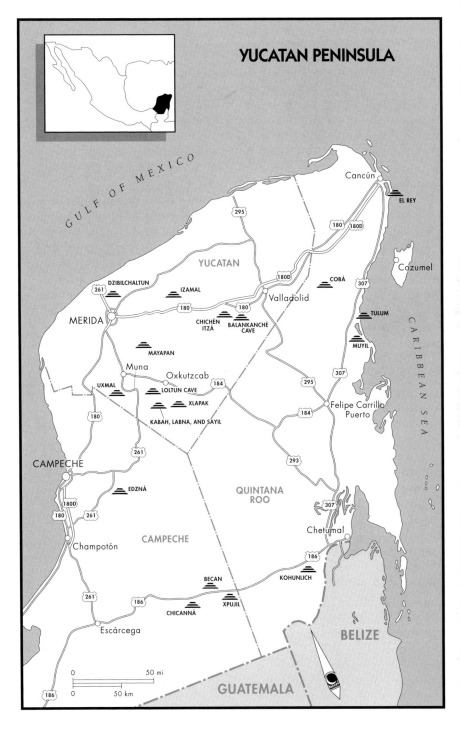

YUCATAN PENINSULA

GULF OF MEXICO

CARIBBEAN SEA

Cancún

EL REY

180

180D

Cozumel

YUCATAN

295

180D

COBÁ

307

DZIBILCHALTUN

261

IZAMAL

Valladolid

TULUM

MERIDA

180

180

CHICHÉN ITZÁ

BALANKANCHÉ CAVE

MUYIL

MAYAPAN

Muna

Oxkutzcab

295

307

UXMAL

LOLTUN CAVE

184

XLAPAK

180

Felipe Carrillo Puerto

KABAH, LABNA, AND SAYIL

184

261

293

CAMPECHE

EDZNÁ

QUINTANA ROO

307

180D

Chetumal

180

261

CAMPECHE

186

Champotón

BECAN

KOHUNLICH

261

186

XPUJIL

CHICANNÁ

BELIZE

Escárcega

50 mi

0

0   50 km

186   GUATEMALA

days of cool drizzle from North America. The peninsula's driest region is the northwest corner, which receives 500 mm of rain a year, while the southern border in Campeche collects almost three times that amount. Unless augmented by the quenching Nortes, the dry season runs from November through May, with March and April being the driest and dustiest (the forests look brownish and parched). The rainy season means regular afternoon storms, varying from quick showers in the north to downpours in the south. Many of the site access roads in the Río Bec region are impassable from July through September. The Yucatan Peninsula also lies in the path of autumn hurricanes. In 1988, Hurricane Gilbert damaged a few archaeological sites and temporarily closed the resorts of Cancún and Cozumel.

Flora and Fauna

The north and west coasts are bound by palm trees and then, around inshore lagoons, huge expanses of mangrove. Inland begin the forests, starting with dry scrub and evergreen in the northwest and gradually moving to tall tropical rainforest in the south. Much of the rainforest is made up of ramon, chicozapote, caoba, and cedar. In the south, the forest alternates with small regions of semiopen savanna. The forest blooms in a riot of deep green and bright flowers during the rainy season; at the end of the dry season, it feels like a tinderbox—brown, dusty, and crackling in the heat.

As in the rest of Mexico, the Yucatan Peninsula's fauna has been severely depleted by the rapid advance of human habitations. Offshore and in the saltwater lagoons, you find a wide variety of sea life, including oysters, crabs, snook, sharks, rays, manatees, and turtles. Huge flocks of flamingos still feed in the north-shore lagoons around Río Lagartos. The forests once teemed with whitetail deer, peccaries, armadillos, rabbits, jaguars, spider monkeys, and snakes. The bird life includes ocellated turkeys (domesticated turkeys are ubiquitous in villages), pheasants, toucans, guacamayas, parrots, and, on the coasts, pelicans. Around the archaeological sites you can usually see families of motmots, and iguanas make homes in many of the ancient ruins.

HISTORY

Humanity came early to the Yucatan Peninsula. In 1977, archaeologists discovered a trove of bones belonging to extinct animals, including early horses, in the Loltun Cave near Uxmal in the Puuc region. The bones were dated to around 8000 B.C., and among them were chipped stones that may have been tools. During the millennia that followed, the Puuc region became home to semipermanent campsites belonging to early hunter-gatherers.

These Archaic settlements gradually developed into permanent villages in the Early Preclassic (1800–1000 B.C.). Although these villages probably ranged over the entire peninsula, the best evidence for them comes from northern Yucatan,

MERIDA MUSEUM

Outside the archaeological sites, the peninsula's best museum is Mérida's **Museo de Antropología y Historia** in the old Palacio Canton at the corner of Paseo de Montejo and Calle 43, open Tues.–Sat. 0800–2000 and Sunday 0800–1400. The palace, built in 1909–11 for the former governor of Yucatan, General Francisco Canton Rosado, makes for an interesting contrast with the exhibits.

where the residents had access to rich supplies of salt and marine protein in the form of mollusks and crabs. Here, the earliest center was Komchen, which during the Middle Preclassic (1000–300 B.C.) spawned the much larger regional power of Dzibilchaltun. Here, researchers already see traces of social stratification, including a ceremonial center grouped around a raised platform.

Throughout the peninsula, there is evidence of contact with the central and southern Maya regions based in the Petén Jungle and on the Pacific Coast beyond. This influence was felt most strongly in the southern region closest to the Maya heartland. The villages that grew at Edzná, Calakmul, Xpujil, and Becan showed clear ceramic evidence of ties to the south. By the Late Preclassic (300 B.C.–A.D. 250), this influence spilled over into the construction of the first monumental architecture.

The dominant culture of the Late Preclassic was the Chicanel, which began in the Petén and spread north through Yucatan. Along the northern Petén and southern Yucatan Peninsula lay a line of massive cities built around large, often massive, ceremonial centers. The main platform of El Mirador, just south of the Mexican border, dwarfs Teotihuacan's Pyramid of the Sun in volume. The hallmark of these cities was tiered pyramids faced with stucco; the tiers were adorned with giant masks, either portraits of rulers or monsters representing various gods. Giant masks glared forth from all of these cities, including Uaxactun, Tikal, Nakbé and, in Belize, Lamanai and Cerros just south of Chetumal. By the Early Classic, this style had spread north into southern Quintana Roo and Campeche to sites such as Balamkú and Kohunlich.

KOHUNLICH

INTRODUCTION

Lying amid a beautiful grove of cohune palm trees, the little-visited site of Kohunlich is home to a series of remarkably well-preserved stucco god masks. These likely represent an extension of the Chicanel style from northern Belize,

KOHUNLICH

How to get there: To reach these ruins, drive 61 kilometers due west of Chetumal, turn south at the entrance road, and continue 10 kilometers to the site.

Hours: Daily 0800–1700.

Admission fee: 30 pesos.

How long to tour: Two hours.

Recommended gear: Hats, sunblock, bottled water, sturdy shoes or sneakers.

Food and accommodations: Although no tourist services are offered near the ruins, Chetumal, Quintana Roo's capital, has a number of good, air-conditioned tourist hotels.

which you can see on the southern horizon. Many of the later structures are built in the style of the Río Bec region lying in the state of Campeche 40 kilometers to the west. Archaeologists have yet to unravel the knotty question of Kohunlich's chronology and its relationship to these two important cultures. In the meantime, the site is a pleasant place to stroll among the ruins and admire the rich flora and fauna of this obscure part of Mexico. The surrounding countryside contains dozens of unexplored sites; during the Classic era, this was one of the most densely populated parts of the Yucatan Peninsula.

HISTORY

Little substantive information about Kohunlich has been published. Very preliminary ceramic studies indicate that the site was occupied at least from A.D. 450 on. Many (but not all) researchers believe that the god masks on Structure I date to the Early Classic (A.D. 250–600). The first ceramics phase runs from A.D. 450 to 600, after which comes a gap until 800. The last phase, corresponding to the terminal Xcocom period in the Río Bec region, lasts until A.D. 1050. By A.D. 1200, Kohunlich was abandoned.

ARCHAEOLOGICAL RECORD

Locals called the ruins "Kohunlich" after the cohune palm found around the site. "Cohune" is a Miskito name, a sign of the close ties between this region and the coastal areas of Central America lying to the south.

In the early 20th century, Kohunlich was named Clarksville (the British had a strong presence here and in neighboring British Honduras) after a nearby lumber camp. In 1912, an American archaeologist named Raymond Merwin exploring southern Yucatan and nearby Belize and Guatemala first described the ruins of Kohunlich. Then the site was forgotten for a half century until the late 1960s, when a local named Ignacio Ek stumbled on the work of looters who had exposed one of the Structure I god masks and were obviously planning to remove it. He reported his discovery to the local schoolteacher, who took him to see the governor in nearby Chetumal (Quintana Roo was very lightly populated back then). After appointing Ek the site guardian, the governor called Mexico City and soon an INAH team arrived at Kohunlich.

Between 1969 and 1981, Victor Segovia of INAH led an expedition that cleared and excavated the ruins and constructed a new road into the site. They also restored a number of the temples, most notably Structure I, which they covered with a huge thatched roof for protection. The results were published in a few short reports and in a lavishly illustrated but less than comprehensive volume whose introduction was written by the president of Mexico.

In 1993 and 1994, work resumed at Kohunlich as part of the Proyecto Sur de Quintana Roo (the expedition also excavated and consolidated the nearby sites of Dzibanché and Kinichná). At Kohunlich, they excavated three of the residential areas and performed restoration work in the rest of the site. No results have been published aside from some preliminary reports.

TOURING THE SITE

The road approaches the ruins from the northeast. It lies on a series of low hills; the depressions on either side are filled with the long, feathery fronds of the cohune palms. If you walk due east through the site, on the far side of the Main Plaza you come to the hill capped by Structure I. This four-stage pyramid is the earliest structure found at Kohunlich.

Structure I, also called the Pyramid of the Masks, is covered by an enormous thatched roof. Its steps face west across the plaza. On each tier, the panels on either side of the staircase are decorated with god masks measuring 2.5 meters tall. Two masks remain on the left and three on the right. These masks represent human faces in the guise of K'inich Ajaw, a version of the solar deity. The oversized eyes adorned with symbols relate to the Sun God, while the other features, including the mustaches and large lips, are more clearly human. This figure wears an elaborate headdress with deity masks above and below (both with jaguar features, perhaps symbolizing the sun of the day and the night sun of the Underworld) and huge earplugs on either side. Enough differences exist between the faces to suggest that these are portraits representing the deified ruling dynasty of early Kohunlich.

These masks were built on the first, Early Classic stage of the pyramid. They were covered by a second, poorly preserved stage built around A.D. 700. On top, you find the remains of a two-room temple. To the west, you have an excellent view over the site, while the view east over rolling hills to Belize is unfortunately blocked by the roof. A mound group lies about 500 meters due east.

After descending the pyramid and returning toward the Main Plaza, on your

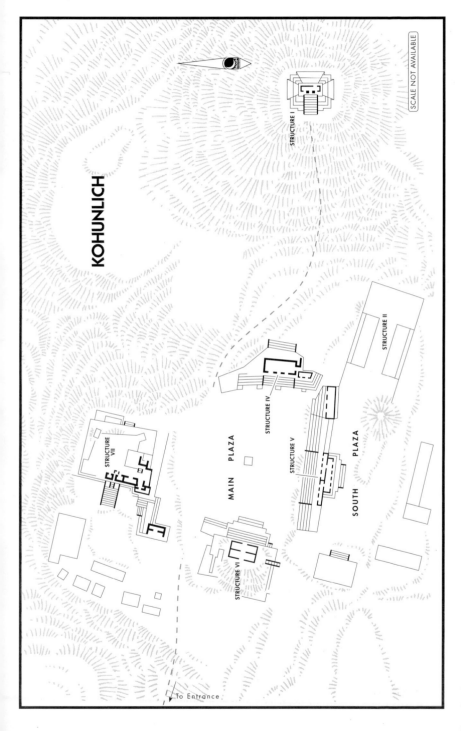

KOHUNLICH

SCALE NOT AVAILABLE

STRUCTURE I

STRUCTURE II

STRUCTURE IV

STRUCTURE V

STRUCTURE VII

STRUCTURE VI

MAIN   PLAZA

SOUTH   PLAZA

To Entrance

DZIBANCHÉ AND KINICHNÁ RUINS

After touring Kohunlich, you may want to explore the recently opened sites of Dzibanché and Kinichná. Both lie north of the Chetumal-Escarcega road. Heading back toward Chetumal, take the left turn a few kilometers east of the Kohunlich road. These two Early Classic cities are built around enormous pyramids. In the surrounding forests and pas-

tures, you can see numerous unexplored temples—a mother lode for both archaeologists and looters. Both are open 0800–1500 daily and there is no admission fee.

You can also continue west to the Río Bec sites, though visiting all these sites may take two days.

---

left you see Structure II, the remains of an I-shaped ballcourt. The west side of the court opens onto the South Plaza, also called the Merwin Plaza (named after Raymond Merwin, the early 20th-century archaeologist who first described Kohunlich). The north, south, and west sides of this plaza are bound by platforms—long, one- or two-room temples. Many of the doorjambs are rounded, in a clear reflection of Río Bec style. Archaeologists believe most of these structures were built after A.D. 600. A large residential complex lies amid the trees to the west.

The north side of this plaza is bordered by the long Structure V. Opposite, this temple-platform opens onto the Main Plaza. This is also called the Plaza of the Stelae after the three plain stelae that were found on the steps leading up to Structure IV on its east end. Opposite stands the elegant Structure VI, whose beautifully restored two-room temple also possesses Río Bec–style rounded doorjambs.

On the north side of the main plaza, you find Structure VII, also called the Acropolis, Kohunlich's largest building complex. The south and east walls of this massive structure are decorated with Río Bec–style false pyramid

DANIELLE GUSTAFSON

a stucco sun god mask, perhaps doubling as a royal portrait, from the Pyramid of the Masks at Kohunlich

staircases. The main steps ascend the Acropolis's west side and, after passing through a narrow doorway, take you into a large patio. The tall, vaulted rooms surrounding this court are once again decorated with rounded jambs and false columns, all from Río Bec. At the platform's southwest corner, an L-shaped addition projects into the plaza to the west. To the west of the Acropolis stands a large, late (A.D. 600–1200) residential complex whose residents apparently specialized in crafting ritual objects made of shell.

THE RÍO BEC REGION:
XPUJIL, BECAN, CHICANNÁ

INTRODUCTION

The Río Bec region sites of southeastern Campeche are so closely interrelated that they should be considered together. These sites are the most accessible of dozens—including the sprawling ruins of Río Bec itself—that occupy this area of rolling forests and marshy savannas. They lie at the crossing of two major trade routes: between the Bay of Chetumal and the Gulf Coast and between the Chenes and Puuc regions to the north and the Petén Jungle to the south. During the Late Classic, the Río Bec centers blossomed into a distinct regional style characterized by enormous monster mask doorways and towers simulating

THE RÍO BEC SITES

The three ruins of Xpujil, Becan, and Chicanná lie just across the Campeche border, 58 kilometers west of Kohunlich and 119 from Chetumal. In the other direction, it is a 153-kilometer drive through a very remote part of Mexico to Francisco Escárcega, a dusty but bustling crossroads town.

In this area of the Río Bec, well over two dozen sites lie within a 30-kilometer radius.

From the town of Xpujil itself, a bad dirt road (impassable during the rainy season) runs south to a town from which a guide can take you on bicycle to the widely scattered ruins of Río Bec itself. You can buy soda in Xpujil town and possibly find a spare room if you wish to spend the night; however, most people tour all three sites in a day and return to Chetumal.

temples with impossibly steep staircases. While these show evidence of influence from both the Puuc and the Petén, they are so sharply stylized as to be impossible to confuse for anything else. After emerging from a long trek through the forest, pre-Columbian visitors must have been awed by these weird towers, toothed doorways, and massive palaces.

HISTORY

Archaeologists believe the Río Bec region was first settled by immigrants from the south around 600 B.C. These early residents, who relied on slash and burn agriculture, had close cultural connections to the Petén region, particularly the regional center of Uaxactún. The Río Bec region was probably chosen as a settlement for two reasons: good soil for farming and a location on the trade route between northern Belize (home to a number of important early sites) and the Gulf Coast cultures linked with the Olmec.

The area's ties with the Petén became even stronger between 300 B.C. and A.D. 250, when the Chicanel culture radiating from the Guatemala jungles spread throughout the Maya region. After 50 B.C., the first permanent ceremonial structures were built at Becan and Chicanná. These include Becan's Structure XXVII (a low but ornate platform) and the 10-meter-high platform inside Structure IV. Becan's protective ditch dates to the end of this period, a sign that an era of warfare frequently threatened the city.

After A.D. 250, there is an apparent hiatus at Becan and Chicanná. Most monumental construction stops, and new foreign influences suddenly appear in the ceramic record. Archaeologists see northern Maya influences first in the region and then strong traces of Teotihuacano presence. One theory is that these cities may have been taken over by an elite allied with that central Mexican power. Another is that the Río Bec sites waned during the rapid rise of the nearby Maya superpower of Calakmul. Becan and the smaller cities may have been defeated in battle—researchers have found many fragments of human bones dating to this era.

During the 8th and 9th centuries A.D., the Río Bec region reached its apogee after the collapse of Calakmul's power. The Río Bec culture developed its distinctive architectural style, one that is linked to the Puuc and Chenes styles farther north. Its hallmark is the square tower with rounded corners that appears to copy the towering pyramids of the Petén. The main difference is that the tower is a simulacrum: the stairs are impossibly steep, and the temple on the top is solid rock (some contain a narrow stairway for priests). These towers generally appear as part of a three-structure complex, with towers on either end and a monster mask doorway into a temple in the center.

During these centuries, the regional population rose dramatically, aided by sophisticated terraced farming watered by aqueducts and reservoirs. More than three dozen Río Bec region sites have been identified so far, extending as far as

Kohunlich 50 kilometers to the east. Due south of Xpujil, the site of Río Bec it-self may actually be a conglomeration of at least 13 separate small centers. The region's rulers did not leave any inscriptions—no stone reliefs of any kind have been found—so we do not know their names, dates, or lineages.

By A.D. 900, monumental construction had stopped at Becan and Chicanná. Crude dwellings invaded the ceremonial center, and garbage filled the rooms of the palaces. Its residents abandoned terraced agriculture and reverted to the less productive slash and burn method. Once again, archaeologists see signs of in-fluence from the north, possibly from Putún Maya originating on the Tabasco coast. The Putún were great seagoing traders, and their canoes may have opened a more rapid route from the Caribbean to the Gulf Coasts, by paddling around Yucatan rather than trekking across. Once the trade route was closed, the Río Bec region lost its connections with the outside world.

The ceremonial centers of Becan and Chicanná were abandoned after A.D. 1050. A sporadic presence continued until about 1400—archaeologists have found Late Postclassic censers strewn about the sites—but this may have been pilgrims or just local farmers.

ARCHAEOLOGICAL RECORD

The French explorer Maurice de Périgny discovered a site he named Río Beque during a 1906–07 expedition through the central Maya lowlands. It is not known why he gave it that name—no river named "Bec" has ever been found (the region has almost no running water). His description of the ruins includes a solid tower with rounded sides. Researchers believe this is part of Group A at the site of Río Bec.

In 1912, Raymond Merwin and Clarence Hay, both Harvard archaeology graduate students, visited the region and discovered further ruins near de Périgny's structure. These are probably Río Bec Groups B through F. During the 1930s, four Carnegie Institution expeditions led by Karl Ruppert explored the area, surveying and photographing the ruins and discovering the sites of Becan and Xpujil. Ruppert published the results in a 1943 report. Tatiana Proskouri-akoff drew a magnificent reconstruction of Xpujil for her 1946 work on Maya architecture; this sparked the interest of many researchers in the Río Bec area.

The next major project in the region was the 1969–71 joint National Geo-graphic and Tulane University project led by E. Wyllys Andrews IV. During the exploratory work leading to this project, Jack Eaton discovered the ruins of Chicanná and outlying groups of Xpujil. Andrews's expedition centered on the ceramic and lithic chronologies of Becan; the expedition produced an exhaus-tive chronology of the site and explored many of the ruins, particularly Struc-ture IV. David Webster led a team to clear and excavate the protective ditch surrounding the ruins.

From 1972 to 1974, this project was followed by a joint National Geographic and University of Tennessee expedition under Prentice M. Thomas to study settlement patterns around Becan, Xpujil, and Chicanná. Around the same time, INAH continued excavation work on Becan and restored Structure IV.

In 1979, INAH's Centro Regional del Sureste began an ongoing project—since 1984 named the Proyecto Arqueológica Frontera Sur—to explore and restore the Río Bec region sites. Led by Ramón Carrasco, this project has excavated and consolidated Xpujil, Becan, and Chicanná and is now working at Río Bec itself. The results have been published in Carrasco's 1994 book on Chicanná and in summary reports.

XPUJIL

INTRODUCTION

Just across the Campeche border (some maps erroneously put it in Quintana Roo), Xpujil is the first of the pure Río Bec-style sites you encounter on the road between Chetumal and Escarcega. Although small, Xpujil (shpoo-HEEL) is a lesson in Río Bec architecture. Here you see the main temple complex, containing three well-preserved towers with simulated pyramid staircases built up the steep sides. The central doorway is carved in the shape of a gigantic monster mask—a motif found at all Río Bec sites. Xpujil lies just south of the road; you can easily see its main sights in less than an hour.

TOURING THE SITE

Just beyond the tiny crossroads town of Xpujil, you see the ruins of the same name standing just south of the road. Although this Classic Maya center apparently extended over many square kilometers, only two building groups are visitable (the rest lie among dense scrub forests interspersed with rainy season swamps).

To the west, you cannot miss the towers of Structure I, the amazing building complex that was reconstructed in Tatiana Proskouriakoff's famous drawing. Three square towers with rounded sides rise from a long platform built along a north-south axis. The tallest and best-preserved tower occupies the center, set slightly back, while shorter towers stand on either end. You can see remains of the false staircases on the upper levels. On top of each tower stands a simulated temple with a solid roofcomb above; the central temple is the most complete. The staircases are set with fragmentary monster masks, perhaps representing

XPUJIL

How to get there: Just west of the town of Xpujil, the ruins stand on the south side of the main road.

Hours: Daily 0800–1700.

Admission fee: 14 pesos.

How long to tour: 45 minutes.

Recommended gear: Hats, sunblock, bottled water, sturdy shoes or sneakers.

felines, while the temple "doorway" of the center tower is carved in the form of a giant serpent mouth.

Between the two end temples are three doorways opening between rounded jambs that simulate columns. The panels beside them and the frieze above were decorated with an elaborate stone mosaic, now collapsed. Behind each door, you find two tall vaulted rooms.

From here walk around to the back via the left side of the structure. In the base of the south tower, you see a narrow doorway opening into a steep staircase that leads up to a doorway on the north side of the structure. This may have been a secret passageway used by priests.

Behind Structure I, you can see another simulated staircase ascending the back of the central tower. Beside them rise at least a dozen false tiers that increase the illusion that this is a Tikal-style pyramid. Near the top, a nearly intact feline mask is set into the steps. The temple above is adorned with another serpent mask around a false door.

Structure 1, east side

Return to the east side of this building; the east side faces a small plaza. Opposite stands a residential complex on a raised platform. Continuing east, in the woods behind the temple, the intrepid explorer will find further residential complexes and another small plaza.

BECAN

INTRODUCTION

Lying a few kilometers west of Xpujil, Becan is one of the largest sites in the Río Bec area. The ruins are surrounded by an enormous dry moat—one of the few found in Mesoamerica—which forced the concentration of the main temples and palaces in a relatively confined area. Based merely on the size of the structures, Becan must have been one of the most powerful cities in the region—it would have taken a huge labor force to build them. These are built in the classic Río Bec style but with far less emphasis on the false pyramids and more on large complexes of rooms that bear some resemblance to the palaces of the Puuc. Becan is constructed around four large plazas. Fewer than half of these have been cleared and restored; you can spend enjoyable hours clambering around steep mounds shaded by the towering forest.

TOURING THE SITE

From the parking area, you take the wide path west to the ruins. Just beyond the guardian's hut, you pass over the dry moat via one of seven ancient accesses to Becan. The moat was apparently used for defense only during the Early Classic; later inhabitants used it as a garbage dump.

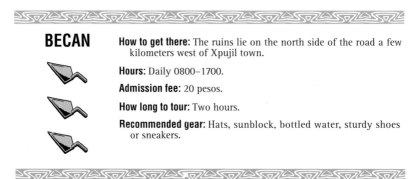

BECAN

How to get there: The ruins lie on the north side of the road a few kilometers west of Xpujil town.

Hours: Daily 0800–1700.

Admission fee: 20 pesos.

How long to tour: Two hours.

Recommended gear: Hats, sunblock, bottled water, sturdy shoes or sneakers.

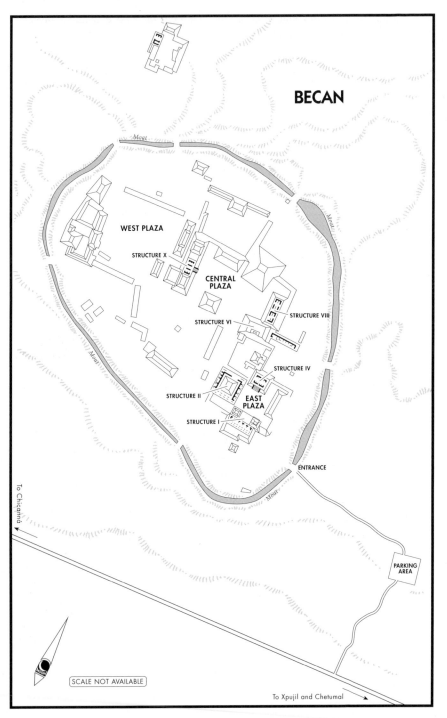

BECAN

WEST PLAZA

STRUCTURE X

CENTRAL PLAZA

STRUCTURE VIII

STRUCTURE VI

STRUCTURE IV

STRUCTURE II

EAST PLAZA

STRUCTURE I

ENTRANCE

Moat

To Chicanná

PARKING AREA

SCALE NOT AVAILABLE

To Xpujil and Chetumal

The first structures you reach are built around the East Plaza, actually an enormous platform lying at the southeast corner of the ruins. Decorated with pseudo-stairways and rounded corners, the two huge towers of Structure I loom over the south side of the plaza. This massive complex actually faces south toward the road. Below the towers are two levels of rooms, 10 on the top and 14 on the bottom. Jambs in the form of false columns decorate the doorways. A wide stairway climbs to the platform top just east of Structure I, whose north side has no opening on the plaza.

On the east side of the East Plaza stands the long mound of Structure III, which probably supported a row of rooms. Opposite rise the semiruined tiers of Structure II; between the doorways you see checkerboard stone mosaic panels. The temple probably contained 20 rooms on the east and west sides.

Structure IV, the most restored building at the site, stands on the north side of the plaza. The interior of this temple contains Structure IV-Sub, one of the earliest monumental buildings found at Becan. You climb a steep staircase up four tiers to the wide temple on top. Just to the right of the door remain some fragments of stucco decorations; a monster mask probably encircled the doorway. This doorway opens onto a patio surrounded by seven vaulted rooms; simple stone mosaic patterns decorate the walls.

The north side of Structure IV descends on three tiers to a smaller courtyard. These tiers form another residential complex with more than two dozen rooms. At the base of the building, one of the doorways is decorated with the remains of a serpent mask; its tongue forms the doorstep. Further stone checkerboards are visible on the low Structure V-A on the east side of this courtyard. Archaeologists found a seated stucco figure and three stucco monkey masks here, some of the few representational sculptures discovered in the Río Bec area.

The north side of the courtyard is bounded by the large platform of Structure VI. A vaulted tunnel runs about 75 meters west from the south base of this building

Note the ruined corbel vaults at the summit of Becan's Structure VIII

CALAKMUL

About 40 kilometers west of Becan, a new paved road heads down to the important site of Calakmul, the center of a Maya "super state," about 60 kilometers to the south. Thought to possibly be one of the largest of Maya structures, the site was once home to more than 60,000 people. For more information, contact the very helpful **State of Campeche Office of Tourism** in Campeche City, at Plaza Moch Couoh, Av. Ruiz Cortines, tel./fax 981/6-6767. It's open Mon.–Fri. 0900–2100, Saturday 0900–1900, Sunday 0900–1300.

through to the Central Plaza on the other side. This open space is the largest plaza at the site.

On the plaza's east side, you see Structure VIII, a smaller copy of Structure I. A wide staircase ascends to a monster mask doorway (now ruined) between twin pseudo-temple towers. A much-eroded stela stands on top of the steps. The doorway takes you back through three rooms to the east side of the temple. This was another residential complex with nine rooms on this level and further rooms tunneling into the lower level.

The ruined Structure IX, the tallest pyramid at Becan, stands on the north side of the Central Plaza. It may have been a direct copy of one of the steep pyramids found at Tikal. To the west lies Structure X, a lower temple containing an excellent serpent mask around its doorway. You can still see traces of red paint in the cracks. Above stand the remains of a roofcomb. The temple contains 12 rooms on the top and lower levels.

To the north of this building lies another series of ruined platforms built around a plaza. To the west, you find a small ballcourt and the West Plaza, which is also surrounded by unexcavated mounds. The largest is the building complex of Structure XIII on the plaza's west side.

From here, the adventurous can cross the dry moat just beyond this plaza's northwest corner and walk about 150 meters due north to the small building group of the Mundo Perdido (Lost World) built around a courtyard.

CHICANNÁ

INTRODUCTION

During the Classic era, the Río Bec area was so densely populated that it is impossible to draw clear boundaries between the ancient centers. Chicanná, a medium-sized site lying west of Becan, may have been an extension of the latter city. It is best-known for its beautifully preserved serpent mask doorway; the

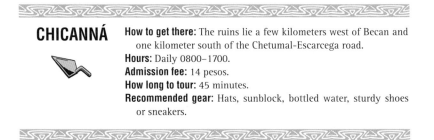

CHICANNÁ

How to get there: The ruins lie a few kilometers west of Becan and one kilometer south of the Chetumal-Escarcega road.
Hours: Daily 0800–1700.
Admission fee: 14 pesos.
How long to tour: 45 minutes.
Recommended gear: Hats, sunblock, bottled water, sturdy shoes or sneakers.

best time to visit is the late afternoon, when the setting sun dramatically highlights its features. The other great sight is Structure XX, a two-story temple with one serpent mask doorway stacked on another. Chicanná's main buildings are confined to a small area—you can tour them in less than an hour—while Structure XX lies a short hike away.

TOURING THE SITE

The ruins lie slightly less than a kilometer south of the Chetumal-Escarcega road. Just south of the parking area, you see the four structures of Group A clustered around a small plaza. Your eyes are immediately drawn to Structure II on the east side of the plaza.

The central doorway of this one-story temple is surrounded by an enormous serpent mouth—a row of jagged teeth covers the lintel. Above the door protrudes the serpent's nose, while on either side you see the spirals of its eyes. Further rows of teeth adorn the doorjambs and extend along either side of the platform step—actually its protruding lower jaw—in front. To the left and right, this giant mask is bordered by rows of small stylized serpent heads in profile. The two side doorways were topped by stone reproductions of traditional thatched Maya huts (the same motif is repeated at Uxmal and other sites); the one to the left is the best preserved. Inside Structure II you find eight small vaulted rooms.

The south side of the plaza is bordered by the long mound of Structure IV, while opposite stands Structure III. The west half of this building is a low, semi-reconstructed pyramid; on the right, you see attached columns flanking two doorways into an elite residential structure. On the west side of the plaza rises Structure I, a classic Río Bec complex of two pseudo-pyramid towers on either side of a serpent mask doorway. The panels between the doorways are decorated with stone mosaics very much like the ones at Xpujil and Becan. Inside, you find 10 vaulted rooms.

Three further building complexes lie at the end of paths heading in different directions. Seventy-five meters to the southwest, you find Group C, a palace

god mask around doorway of Chicanná's Structure II

complex with small serpent head profiles on the facade and a short glyphic inscription painted in red just above and to the right of the main doorway.

Return to Group A, and another path heads 80 meters southeast to Group B. Here, the facade of Structure VI still contains some serpent-head profile panels on either side of the door. Above rises the remains of a roofcomb. Inside, you find seven vaulted rooms and, behind, a ruined platform. More unreconstructed mounds lie to the east and west.

Finally, a path leads from the back of Group A's Structure I about 300 meters to Group D. Here stands the unique Structure XX, a two-story temple built on a square floor plan. The main facade is the south, which is decorated with serpent masks surrounding both the first- and second-story doorways. Through the lower mask, a ruined stairway ascends to the upper temple. The upper facade corners are adorned with long-nosed masks in the style of the Chenes region to the north. The temples' north and south sides, which are less well preserved, contain some fragmentary serpent head profile panels; their doorways probably also had serpent masks as their borders. Inside, the temple contained at least a dozen rooms facing in the four directions.

EDZNÁ

INTRODUCTION

The ruins of Edzná lie 50 kilometers southeast of Campeche City; their architecture represents the southern extent of the Classic Maya architectural style known as the Puuc. Before the Puuc entered the area, however, Edzná was home to a thriving population who built the most extensive canal and irrigation network in the Maya region. They turned the rich soils of their valley into one of the most productive agricultural regions in Yucatan, supporting a population measuring in the tens of thousands from the Early Classic on. The Late Classic Puuc period was a time of monumental construction; the central building was the massive palace called the Building of Five Stories. From here, the ceremonial center extended in every direction with pyramids, palaces, and ballcourts, many decorated with stelae and hieroglyphs. The campesinos (peasant farmers) of the region are probably direct descendants of Edzná's builders; they keep up many ancient traditions, including shamanistic cures for medical or psychiatric problems.

HISTORY

Edzná lies in a wide, flat valley in the drainage of the Río Champotón. Good soils and a stable supply of water probably brought the first settlers here. The valley's first permanent residents entered the area about 400 B.C.; they were part of the great migration of peoples from the Petén Jungle to the north of Yucatan.

The earliest Edzná (400–250 B.C.) was a small agricultural settlement at the northern end of the current site. In addition to farming, they used the clay soils to create ceramic pots and built *aguadas*—artificial ponds with raised sides—to store water in the dry season. Despite the settlement's small size, it was part of the widespread lowland Maya trade in obsidian tools originating from a single source in the Guatemala Highlands.

Between 250 B.C. and A.D. 150, Edzná underwent a period of phenomenal growth, reaching its maximum population and extent. The key to its success was the construction of the huge system of canals and reservoirs. The problem with Edzná's location was that during the rainy season, the water did not drain but merely pooled, drowning the plants and turning the landscape into mud. During the dry season, of course, there was not enough water. The hydraulic system allowed them to channel the rainy season torrents into reservoirs, saving the crops, and store it for the dry season. The aqueducts stretched for many

EDZNÁ

How to get there: The coastal city of Campeche is your best base for seeing the ruins of Edzná, which lie about 45 kilometers to the east-southeast. Take Highway 180 east to Highway 188 and turn right, following the signs for Edzná. You can also reach the site via Highway 261 heading south from the Puuc region.

Hours: Daily 0800–1700.

Admission fee: 20 pesos.

How long to tour: Two hours.

Recommended gear: Hats, sunblock, bottled water, sturdy shoes or sneakers.

Food and accommodations: Campeche possesses the nearest food and hotels, including the waterfront **Hotel Baluartes**, on Av. Ruíz Cortines, tel. 981/6-3911. It has 104 rooms and includes a sidewalk café, a dining room, and a pool.

kilometers, the longest being the 12-kilometer canal from the ceremonial center south to the Río Champotón.

This huge project could not have been completed without thousands of laborers and decades of work. Researchers believe this Late Preclassic city was the product of urban planning under the reign of one or two powerful monarchs. With sophisticated terraced farming replacing slash and burn agriculture, the city could feed a far greater population than any of the nearby towns. Edzná rose to dominate western Campeche, but this was not achieved without strife. Edzná's Fortress was built and surrounded with a moat in a very short time at the end of this period. Although archaeologists have found no evidence of a battle fought here, this large complex was certainly built for defensive purposes.

After A.D. 150, Edzná mysteriously shrinks and large-scale construction stops. It is not known if this hiatus was caused by an invasion or by an ecological disaster spurred by overpopulation and the deforestation of the valley. The residents nevertheless continued their trade ties with the Petén region to the southeast.

In A.D. 600, monumental construction suddenly resumes around the ceremonial center. It is likely that this was caused by the entrance of some new group to the city, because trade with the Petén stops and new ties are forged with the Río Bec area and northern Yucatan. Between A.D. 600 and 750, the first stages of the Great and Little Acropolises were erected and the first dated stelae were carved. The hieroglyphic staircase at the base of the Building of Five Stories is dated A.D. 731. The population grew around the ceremonial center but never extended to the limits of the Late Preclassic City—the Fortress had long been abandoned. The old hydraulic system may have been clogged with silt and unable to function well.

The Edzná that you see today was built between A.D. 750 and 950. This was when the ceremonial center acquired the characteristics of the Puuc style originating in the Sierrita de Ticul to the north. The sequence of construction here has not been adequately studied. The dated stelae continue to at least A.D. 810, but the last of them are not carved in the Classic style and may be influenced by the Putún Maya to the southwest. The latest radiocarbon date, A.D. 925, comes from a hearth on Structure 20 and indicates the approximate end of this era at Edzná.

During the Postclassic, Edzná was sporadically occupied by farmers and visited by occasional pilgrims who left incense censers. It was probably these pilgrims who moved many of the stelae to the base of Structure 419-3 on the Little Acropolis.

ARCHAEOLOGICAL RECORD

Edzná was probably never forgotten by the local Maya. In 1906, campesinos reported the existence of the ruins to the local government, but this report was forgotten amid the tumult of the Mexican Revolution that soon followed.

Ceramic sequencing is a method of determining a site's age. Stratigraphic layers of ceramics—usually potsherds found in piles of ancient refuse—are used to gauge the main phases of the site and its relation to neighboring sites.

In 1927, Nazario Quintana Bello, the state archaeologist of Campeche, was the first to explore and describe the ruins. He was quickly followed by an expedition from Mexico City under Enrique Juan Palacios that studied the Building of the Five Stories and unearthed a number of stelae. Hot on their heels, a Carnegie Institution expedition led by Sylvanus Morley discovered 17 more stone monuments. The site was dubbed "Etzná," later changed to the current spelling.

Archaeologists did not return to the ruins until 1943, when an INAH expedition under Alberto Ruz Lhuillier (later discoverer of Pakal's tomb at Palenque) and Raúl Pavón Abreu spent almost three months exploring the main structures and digging test pits to unearth a preliminary ceramic sequence. Between 1958 and 1962, Pavón Abreu worked at the site consolidating and restoring some of the central structures, particularly the Building of the Five Stories.

In 1968, immediately after their work at Comalcalco, George F. Andrews and his students from the University of Oregon visited Edzná and on the spur of the moment decided to map the site. At this time, the valley was covered with a thick forest interspersed with marshes and small openings of savanna. From an old aerial photo, they noticed a line of vegetation heading due south from the ruins to a swamp close to the Río Champotón. They realized that this was an ancient canal and that the city was set among a huge system of aqueducts and *aguadas* (small reservoirs with raised sides). The expedition also discovered that Edzná was far larger than previously thought, sprawling for many square kilometers across the valley floor.

Between 1970 and 1972, an INAH team under Román Piña Chan and Raúl Pavón Abreu explored the Great Acropolis, excavating a small temple and continuing restoration on the Building of Five Stories.

The discovery of the hydraulic system sparked the interest of Ray Matheny and a team from the New World Archaeological Foundation (Brigham Young University). They received permission to explore the canals and dig test pits to help define the ceramic sequence. When they arrived at Edzná, however, they discovered that a Mexican government agriculture program was busy deforesting the valley and flattening all the mounds at the north end of the site in order to create farmland. They informed the governor that the site was being destroyed and were given authority to conduct emergency salvage work, halting the bulldozers for a couple of weeks.

Their budget allowed them to complete only a limited number of their goals. They were able to do sufficient excavations for the ceramic sequence, but they did not have enough time to complete the study on the hydraulic system. Nevertheless, they discovered 44 large and small canals, 84 reservoirs, and one moat. Lying south of the ceremonial center, the moat circled an Early Classic building complex they named the Fortress, complete with lookout mounds at each corner. The results were published in a series of excellent reports issued in the late 1970s and early 1980s.

The next large-scale expedition (Román Piña Chan led two short seasons in 1975 and 1976) at Edzná began in 1986. Funded by the United Nations High Commission on Refugees and the Mexican Commission for Aid to Refugees, this ongoing project has focused on the excavation and restoration of the ceremonial center, particularly the Great and Little Acropolises. The work has been directed by first Luis Millet Cámara and now by Antonio Benavides Castillo, both of the Campeche INAH office. The workers are Maya refugees from the Guatemala Highlands who have fled the civil war there. It is not known if the recent peace treaty will lead to their return to Guatemala.

TOURING THE SITE

You enter the ruins from the northeast. The path takes you into the Main Plaza, with the Great Acropolis looming to the left. From the Main Plaza extend two *sacbeob*—raised Maya causeways—to the northwest and west. The building to your right as you enter is the Platform of the Knives, a large residential complex named after the trove of flint blades found there. The plaza's west side is bounded by the long platform called the Nohoch-Ná (Great House), which resembles a similar platform at Dzibilchaltun. On top of its long staircase, you find two rows of square columns flanking an interior wall.

On the east side of the plaza, a grand staircase ascends into the Great Acropolis, a collection of at least 10 structures standing on a raised platform that measures about 170 meters to a side. Medium-sized pyramids topped by temples

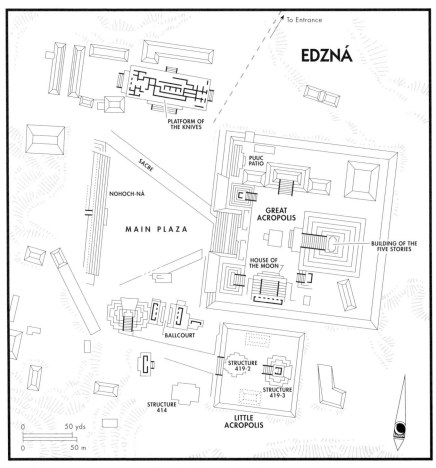

EDZNÁ

To Entrance

PLATFORM OF
THE KNIVES

SACBE

PUUC
PATIO

NOHOCH-NÁ

GREAT
ACROPOLIS

MAIN PLAZA

BUILDING OF THE
FIVE STORIES

HOUSE OF
THE MOON

BALLCOURT

STRUCTURE
419-2

STRUCTURE
419-3

STRUCTURE
414

LITTLE
ACROPOLIS

0   50 yds
0   50 m

flank the stairs to the left and right, and in the center you see a square altar platform. Beyond stands the massive Building of the Five Stories, also called the Palace.

This structure faces west and is aligned so that on May 1 and August 13—when the sun reaches its zenith at this location—the setting sun blazes directly into its rooms. This alignment probably related to planting times. A grand staircase ascends the center of the west face to a temple topped with a ruined roofcomb. The risers of the first four steps at the base are carved with a hieroglyphic inscription that is as yet untranslated. On either side of the staircase, you see doorways that enter into rows of tall vaulted rooms.

The building above resembles the great palace structures found in both Becan and in the Puuc region. The architects varied the doorways; those on the second and third tiers are plain, while the ground-floor doors are divided by two square columns. Each of the fourth-level doorways is supported by one round column. On the first and second floors, a passageway penetrates under the staircase to connect the two sides. The fifth-level temple contains three rooms; the back wall of the central room contained a stela, now removed, which was illuminated by the rays of the setting sun at its zenith.

Returning to the Acropolis's plaza, in its northwest corner you find the Puuc Patio, a newly rebuilt temple with red columns and decorations along the staircase. The small courtyard here contains several stelae under thatched roofs. The best of these is Stela 21, dating to the 8th century, depicting a standing ruler wearing a headdress and a very complicated belt surrounded by glyphs. Artistically, its appearance is not nearly so fine as the reliefs produced in the Usumacinta region at the same time. The patio is cut off from the rest of the plaza by the Northwest Temple.

On the south side of the plaza rises the aggressively reconstructed House of the Moon (the restorers used so much concrete that it looks like a blockhouse with a few old stones in it). Its seven-tier base is the platform for a wide temple with a large center room and one small one on each end. Its neighbor just to the west is the Southwest Temple, which faces east.

From here, take the staircase back to the Main Plaza. On its south side, you see on the right the South Temple and the small Ballcourt just to the east. The latter contains the remains of one ring on its west wall. After walking through the ballcourt, just beyond you come to Structure 418, a low platform whose first stage dates to the earliest phase of Edzná monumental construction.

On the left (east) you see Structure 414, also called the Temple of the Masks. The stairway facing you is flanked by two stucco masks that roughly resemble those found at Kohunlich, only smaller. With their enlarged eyes, they probably

Edzná's Building of the Five Stories served as both an elite residence and as the central ritual structure.

DANIELLE GUSTAFSON

represent aspects of the solar deity, perhaps the rising and setting suns. These may be rulers in the guise of the Sun God; they also have mutilated upper teeth, and huge earplugs lie on either side of the faces. Both date to the Terminal Pre-classic, Edzná's first great apogee.

To the east, a path leads into the Little Acropolis, a five-meter-high platform measuring 70 meters to a side. Fragments of stelae lie under a roof just to the left of the staircase. On top, you find four small temples, two of them unreconstructed, oriented to the points of the compass. Structure 419-2 stands just above the staircase; researchers found pieces of stucco sculpture around its sides. Structure 419-3 on the east side is decorated with reliefs along its staircase; the temple on top was made from stones from earlier structures, including broken reliefs. It may date to as late as the Postclassic (A.D. 1200–1530). These late inhabitants of Edzná collected the stelae from the rest of the site and placed them around this complex.

THE PUUC REGION:
UXMAL, KABAH, SAYIL, LABNÁ, XLAPAK

INTRODUCTION

In the southwestern corner of the state of Yucatan, a region of lush, rolling hills is home to the Puuc; this distinct Terminal Classic Maya culture flourished here from the late 8th to the early 10th centuries. The Puuc is best known for its architecture, which some researchers believe is a direct heir to the Río Bec and Chenes styles to the southeast. The hallmark of the architecture is a finely cut stone facade, often including mosaics and other reliefs, fitted onto a rubble and lime core. The greatest works of Puuc building are Uxmal's Nunnery and House of the Turtles. Outside the region, you can also see examples of Puuc style at Edzná (Building of the Five Stories) and at Chichén Itzá's Nunnery.

Although the Puuc apogee was short, lasting less than 150 years, archaeologists are only now realizing the power of this culture. Recent settlement surveys have revealed more than 200 Puuc sites within their heartland—not counting such outposts as Edzná and Chichén. Large centers such as Uxmal and Sayil

HISTORY OF CHILAM BALAM

Much of what researchers know about northern Yucatan during the Postclassic era is based on the *Books of Chilam Balam*. This 16th-century text was written by Yucatec Maya priests in Spanish script and records the past, present, and future of their world. Chilam Balam (whose name probably means Interpreter of the family name Jaguar) was a Maya prophet living around A.D. 1500 who most famously foretold that foreigners from the east would bring a new religion.

Unfortunately for archaeologists, the books' historical information is recorded by *katun,* a period of roughly 20 years, and the *katun* cycle runs 256 years and then begins again, so separate events dated by a *katun* of the same name could actually have occurred centuries apart. This style of Maya historiography has contributed to some of the great, ongoing debates of Mesoamerican archaeology, such as the identity of Chichén Itzá's builders.

were linked by *sacbeob,* Maya causeways running many kilometers. Around Kabah, Sayil, Labná, and Xlapak (a region of more than 200 square kilometers) there was essentially no break between settlements—human habitation was continuous. At its height in the late 9th century, the Puuc's population must have measured in the hundreds of thousands.

HISTORY

The flat plain of northern Yucatan is bordered on the south by the Sierrita de Ticul, a 160-kilometer-long ridge running from northwest to southeast. Nearly all the Puuc sites lie in the region immediately south of this ridge. This region is divided into two geological zones. Uxmal is in the northern Santa Elena district, which is made up of gently rolling limestone valleys and hills. To the south, cone-shaped karst hills and abrupt ridges are the distinctive features of the Bolonchen district, home to Kabah, Sayil, and many other sites.

The Maya settled in the Puuc for the soils, which are the best in northern Yucatan. The region's main drawback is the lack of surface water; there are none of the cenotes you find in the land to the north of the Sierrita de Ticul. The main water sources were caves such as Loltun and *aguadas* and *chultunes*—two types of small man-made reservoirs. The ancient Maya must have spent an incredible amount of energy finding, channeling, and storing water.

The complete chronology for Maya settlement in the Puuc is unclear. Despite years of work in the region, very few stratigraphic excavations have been completed and the results published. This has led to vigorous debates about the origins, apogee, and end of the Puuc culture. These debates become even more complicated when you add them to the controversy over Chichén Itzá and its relationship to the Maya and central Mexico.

Early hunters passed through the area between 9000 and 3000 B.C. in search of wild game, including mastodons, camels, and extinct horses. They left bones and stone tools in Loltun Cave and then disappeared. There followed 2,000 years with no apparent human habitation.

Archaeologists believe immigrants returned to the area in the Middle Preclassic (1000–300 B.C.) and settled at Uxmal and other sites. By the Late Preclassic (300 B.C.–A.D. 250), Uxmal's residents had built some small ceremonial platforms but the settlement remained small. Uxmal was dwarfed by centers such as Dzibilchaltun, lying near the crucial northern salt-producing lagoons, and Edzná, which was reaching its apogee to the south. Some time during this era, an elite delegation from Kaminaljuyú near today's Guatemala City came to Loltun Cave and carved the ruler relief at its entrance.

During the Early Classic (A.D. 250–600), the dominant Puuc center was Oxkintok, lying at its northwestern corner. Its residents developed a regional architecture that researchers call "Proto-Puuc"—crude but containing the seeds of the later Classic Puuc style. At the end of this period, Uxmal's early monumental architecture also shows the influence of the Chenes culture, which lay just to the south of the Puuc and was an intermediate stage between the Río Bec and Puuc cultures.

By the beginning of the Late Classic in A.D. 600, all the major Puuc sites were occupied, including Kabah, Sayil, Labná, and Xlapak. In their ceremonial centers, temples were erected in the "Early Puuc" style. The hallmark of this style was a relatively crude stone veneer laid over a rubble core and covered with stucco ornamentation. One of the best examples of Early Puuc is the Building of Five Stories at Edzná—the style may have first emerged here.

Around A.D. 780, the Puuc emerged as the dominant culture of northern Yucatan. As a reflection of this new power, civic and religious buildings were built across the region in the new Classic Puuc style. These structures were faced with finely cut stone veneers and decorated across the top with stone mosaics and reliefs. Atop doors and from the corners protruded long-snouted masks, sometimes dozens of them, that are traditionally identified with Chac, the Maya Rain God. This interpretation has never been certain, however, and a number of archaeologists now believe that these masks represent Uitz, the mountain monster (throughout Mesoamerica, temples are identified as symbolic mountains). From Uxmal in the northwest to Kabah in the southeast, the Puuc centers were linked by a system of causeways that ran right to the heart of the ceremonial precincts.

Although Uxmal is the largest Puuc site, it may not have emerged as the regional capital until the end of the 9th century. For the first century of the Puuc apogee, centers such as Kabah, Sayil, and Nohpat (between Uxmal and Kabah) had ceremonial centers as large as or larger than Uxmal's. Between A.D. 895 and 907, Uxmal underwent a burst of monumental construction that included the House of the Governor and the Nunnery Quadrangle. Dated inscriptions from these structures identify their builder as a ruler named Lord Chac.

Lord Chac's reign was brief but glorious: he covered Uxmal's buildings with remembrances of his rule. Many late Puuc reliefs depict warriors and battles; the era was apparently one of war and unrest. Lord Chac's last monument, dated A.D. 907, is also the last yet found in the Puuc region. During the next 50 years, all the major Puuc region sites were abandoned (some researchers say this did not happen until after A.D. 1000).

The Puuc era was followed by the apogee of Chichén Itzá. The question is, did Chichén's rise predate Uxmal's fall? A number of terminal Uxmal structures, including the Nunnery Quadrangle, contain "Mexican" motifs such as double-headed feathered serpents. Some researchers speculate that Uxmal's elite had strong contacts with the Mexicanized Putún Maya based in Tabasco as well as with the Itzá who ruled Chichén. During the mid-10th century, the Itzá may have allied themselves with the Putún and attacked and defeated the Puuc armies. This mystery can be unraveled only by more excavations.

Sporadic occupation continued at Uxmal and the other major Puuc sites for the next two centuries, but by A.D. 1200 they were abandoned. Sometime during the Postclassic—the dates in their histories vary widely—a Maya group calling themselves the Xiu settled at Uxmal and claimed that they were the descendants of the old ruling lineages. They almost certainly were not, but the Xiu nevertheless managed to become an important force in pre-Conquest northern Yucatan. At the end of 15th century, they abandoned Uxmal and made a new headquarters in the town of Mani just to the north of the Puuc. Uxmal was abandoned for good but never forgotten.

ARCHAEOLOGICAL RECORD

Uxmal's first reference in a post-Conquest document was written by the Maya themselves. In 1557, the Xiu lords met at Mani and drew a map of their realm that contained Uxmal. The site is also mentioned in a number of 16th-century Maya histories, including the famous *Books of Chilam Balam.*

The Catholic Church also knew Uxmal well; it was a favorite destination on the grand tour of pagan idolatries. In the 16th and 17th centuries, various priests included descriptions of Uxmal in their works on pagan religion. One of them, Fray López de Cogolludo, bestowed the names on its main structures—the House of the Governor—that are still used today. He named the Nunnery Quadrangle because he thought it resembled "a cloister, where virgins lived." (Given the current political climate, it is highly likely that these names will be changed to something less charged.)

In 1835, the ruins were honored by the visit of the eccentric Count de Waldeck, who also spent many months at Palenque. He believed that the site was built by an Asiatic people and that the long-snouted masks depicted elephants. Waldeck was followed in 1841 and 1843 by a far more respected expedition led by John Lloyd Stephens and Frederick Catherwood. They camped in the House of the Governor and drew and explored the ruins. Among their many discoveries is the two-headed jaguar throne from the House of the Governor's platform. They also removed one of the wooden lintels from the latter building and exhibited it in the United States. It was later destroyed by fire. On their second expedition, Stephens and Catherwood explored the surrounding hills and discovered the sites of Kabah, Sayil, and Labná.

The publication of Stephens's books and Catherwood's engravings drew a stream of visitors to the Puuc. These included Désiré Charnay (accompanied by his camera), Charles Etienne Brasseur de Bourbourg, William H. Holmes, and Teobert Maler, who produced some of the finest photographs of Uxmal. Many of Maler's photos were reprinted in Eduard Seler's detailed 1917 study of Uxmal.

In 1930, an expedition led by Frans Blom of Tulane's Middle American Research Institute began the first excavations at Uxmal. This project was funded by the organizers of the 1933 Chicago World's Fair to collect artifacts and information for Mexico's exhibit. In 1941 and 1942, further Uxmal excavations were performed by a Carnegie Institution team led by Sylvanus Morley. The work of both these projects centered around the main structure of the ceremonial center. During the 1930s and 1940s, Harry E. D. Pollock, also of Carnegie, explored both the Puuc and Chenes regions and performed an in-depth architectural survey of dozens of sites, including the main Puuc ones.

The Mexican government has spent far more money on restoration of Uxmal than on excavation. The first restoration project (even then with the clear intent of drawing tourism) began in 1927 on the House of the Governor. By the end of the 1950s, all of the major Puuc sites were open for visitors. Since then, most of their major buildings have been consolidated and rebuilt.

Although a few of these projects have also included architectural or archaeological studies—notably Alberto Ruz Lhuillier's 1947–53 work on the Ballcourt, the Pyramid of the Magician, and the Nunnery—most of them have emphasized restoration over excavation. The principal work at Kabah, Labná, Sayil, and Xlapak was performed under either Ruz or César Saenz. Many of the most recent archaeological discoveries have been made by accident, such as the discovery of painted stucco fragments during the installation of the sound and light show on the House of the Governor. All restoration and excavation work is now being administered by INAH's Yucatan Regional Center based in Mérida.

Since the late 1970s, the most groundbreaking Puuc region projects have focused on settlement patterns. This era begins with Edward Kurjack and Silvia Garza Terrazona's study of Puuc settlement and geology. In the 1980s, Paul Gendrop and George Andrews published separate surveys of Puuc region architecture. More recently, Alfredo Barrera Rubio has investigated the patterns of habitation at Uxmal, and Jeremy Sabloff and Nicholas Dunning have performed in-depth studies of the Sayil settlement and of the Puuc region in general.

In 1992, Ian Graham added Uxmal to his Corpus of Maya Inscriptions series, including an excellent map of the ceremonial center. Jeff Kowalski of Northern

Illinois University is considered one of the most knowledgeable investigators of Uxmal; he has published important works on Uxmal's House of the Governor and Puuc settlement patterns.

UXMAL

INTRODUCTION

Situated in a rolling valley just south of the Puuc ridge, the site of Uxmal represents one of the high points of Maya architecture. The harmonious design and fine execution of its structures—the Nunnery Quadrangle, House of the Gover-

UXMAL

How to get there: Uxmal lies on Highway 261 running between Campeche and Mérida. The latter is the nearest major urban area, about 65 kilometers to the north. Numerous Mérida tour operators run daytrips to Uxmal and the neighboring sites.

Hours: 0800–1700.

Admission fee: 30 pesos.

How long to tour: You need a half-day to see the highlights and a whole day to see everything.

Recommended gear: Hats, sunblock, hiking boots, bottled water, mosquito repellent.

Museum: There is a good site museum in the entrance complex.

Food and accommodations: Near Uxmal's ruins stand three good hotels; all accept credit cards.

The expensive, charming **Hacienda Uxmal**, tel. 99/25-2122 in Mérida, fax 25-7022, offers a/c, TV, tropical gardens, pool, restaurant with a fixed-price menu, bar, and gift shop. A café across the way offers lighter meals.

At the site entrance try the **Villa Arqueológica**, tel. 99/29-7053 in Mérida or from the U.S. 800/258-2633, one of many in the chain owned by Club Med; it comes complete with a shallow pool and a library.

The **Misión Uxmal**, tel. 99/24-7308 in Mérida, 800/437-7275, offers a/c, a pool, and a dining room.

The only budget accommodation is the **Rancho Uxmal**, tel. 99/2-0277, three kilometers north; it offers 26 rooms with fans, a pool, and a restaurant.

The only restaurants are at the hotels (fairly pricey) or in the site entrance complex; for classic Yucatecan cuisine, drive to the nearby town of Ticul (65 kilometers south, about an hour), home to the famous **Los Almendros** restaurant near the Cinema Ideal.

nor, etc.–have influenced many modern Mexican architects. At the very end of the Classic era, Uxmal rose to become the dominant power in northern Yucatan. Researchers have identified some of the rulers, among them the powerful Lord Chac, and are beginning to work out the dynastic history. The ruins are set among a dense forest that comes alive with wildlife at night. Uxmal lies less than two hours from Mérida; you will also find three good hotels within walking distance of the ruins.

TOURING THE SITE

The site entrance lies just east of the ruins; this is not some small guardian's hut but a medium-sized mall containing gift shops, cafeterias, and a museum. The highpoint of the latter is Stela 14 showing Lord Chac topped by a pyramid-shaped feathered headdress; he stands on a double-headed jaguar throne like the one found in front of the House of the Governor. From here, a walkway leads uphill to the ceremonial center, which was originally ringed with a defensive wall, now in ruins.

The main structures are built on a rough north-south axis. The archaeoastronomer Anthony F. Aveni has discovered that they are also aligned to the position of the sun and, especially, the planet Venus on certain important dates of the Maya calendar. The House of the Governor and the Nunnery Quadrangle were apparently built in alignment with Venus, while the Pyramid of the Magician has a perfect position for viewing the sun rising and setting on certain auspicious dates.

The oval base of Uxmal's Pyramid of the Magician is probably the product of 20th-century restoration.

DANIELLE GUSTAFSON

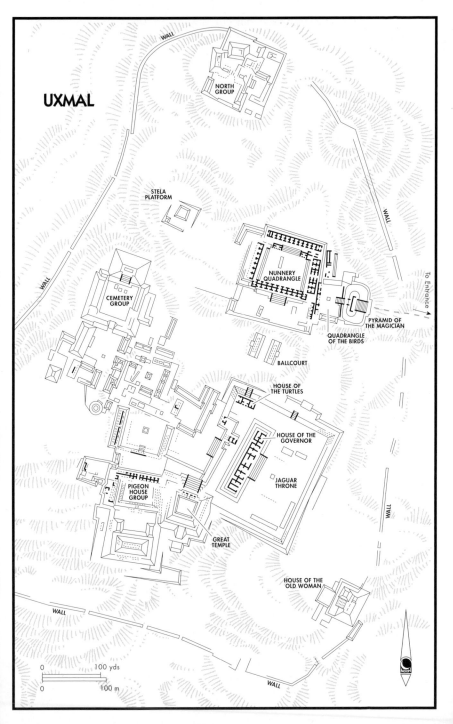

UXMAL

NORTH GROUP

WALL

STELA PLATFORM

CEMETERY GROUP

NUNNERY QUADRANGLE

To Entrance

PYRAMID OF THE MAGICIAN

QUADRANGLE OF THE BIRDS

BALLCOURT

HOUSE OF THE TURTLES

HOUSE OF THE GOVERNOR

JAGUAR THRONE

PIGEON HOUSE GROUP

GREAT TEMPLE

HOUSE OF THE OLD WOMAN

WALL

WALL

WALL

WALL

0   100 yds

0   100 m

MOON

Rising 37 meters from the top of the path stands the unique Pyramid of the Magician, also called Pyramid of the Dwarf. This structure takes its name from a Maya legend collected in the 19th century. John Lloyd Stephens was told that the dwarf, who had been hatched from an egg by an old woman, was challenged by Uxmal's king to build a pyramid overnight. The dwarf built this pyramid and became Uxmal's ruler himself. Sculptures of dwarves have been found at the site; however, they are a common feature of Maya art and occur many other places as well. The legend almost certainly postdates Classic-era Uxmal.

(Another version of this story says that the dwarf, who lived in Kabah, stole a magical drum and rattle from his grandmother, an old wise woman. A prophecy said that whoever played the instruments would become king of Uxmal. When Uxmal's ruler heard the rumble of the dwarf's music-making, he grew afraid and challenged him to a contest. Whoever could break four basketfuls of *cocoyoles* [a nutlike fruit] over his head would become the new king. The dwarf and his grandmother fashioned a strong plate to place on his skull. The king broke open his skull and died; the dwarf passed the contest unscathed. He became king of Uxmal and built the House of the Governor for his grandmother and the Pyramid of the Magician for himself.)

The Pyramid of the Magician has a large elliptical base that is a subject of controversy. There are no similar bases in Mesoamerica, leading a number of archaeologists to doubt that this reconstruction is accurate. A steep staircase ascends over three tiers to the east side of the temple; a chain on the left side helps you keep your balance. (Those with a fear of heights may want to skip the exploration of this structure.) About three-quarters of the way up, you come to a hole that enters into a small vaulted room that is home to two columns and a colony of bats. This was the topmost temple of the stage II structure. Archaeologists have discovered that the pyramid was built in five construction stages, and this one probably dated to the 8th century.

The staircase continues to the top. Here stands the pyramid's stage V temple, a Classic Puuc design. The east side, with two doorways, is rather plain. If you walk around to the west side, you find the main doorway flanked by stone mosaics in the form of crosshatched matting. Mats were associated with power; Maya lords often referred to themselves as the "Lords of the Mat." Niches above contain the bases of two stone figures. The lower facades of the north and south ends are decorated with rows of attached columns, another of the hallmarks of Puuc architecture. You have an excellent view over the site and into the Nunnery Quadrangle lying just to the west.

From here, short staircases ascend on either side of the stage IV temple, a two-story structure rising from a lower level of the west facade. Long-snouted masks decorate the sides and corners of this temple. In between are intertwined serpent borders and crosshatched stone mat panels. The west face of this temple contains a gaping doorway surrounded by an enormous Chenes-style serpent mask that closely but not exactly resembles those found in the Río Bec region.

The doorjambs are decorated with glyphs, and within you find a line of three rooms of descending size. Nineteenth-century graffiti adorns the walls.

One of the steepest climbable staircases in Mesoamerica descends the rest of the way to ground level. Even when you grasp the rusty chain, this can be a heart-palpitating experience. A long-snouted mask panel is set into the top of the staircase, and further masks look out from either side. Researchers found an earlier staircase beneath this one and a stone sculpture of a man's head looking out from a serpent's mouth (the misnamed "Queen of Uxmal" now in Mexico City's Museo Nacional de Antropología).

The staircase alights in the recently reconstructed Quadrangle of the Birds. The Lower West Temple built out from the base represents the earliest stage of the pyramid's construction; rows of attached columns adorn its facade. In the center of the patio stands a round stela with smooth sides; it probably was a sacrificial stone. The complex takes its name from the roof friezes along the buildings that line the quadrangle. These friezes simulate the thatched roof of a Maya hut with stone bird reliefs attached to it. The other, semiruined buildings around the plaza are decorated with rows of attached columns along the roof frieze.

From the birds, a path takes you up into the southeast corner of the famous Nunnery Quadrangle. This patio is not a perfect rectangle but is skewed apparently to align the buildings with the planet Venus. Each of the four long palace-type structures is adorned with beautifully reconstructed and highly complicated symbolic friezes. Some of these contain elements such as feathered serpents and masks of Tlaloc that many researchers believe are evidence of links between central Mexican cultures and the Puuc. This complex was probably built in one concerted effort between A.D. 895 and 906—the last peak before Uxmal's fall.

Standing on a low platform atop a low flight of steps, the East Building is penetrated by five doorways entering into a complex of 14 rooms. The capstone of the northwest room (all the way on the left) is painted with the date A.D. 906, the last found at Uxmal. Stacks of three long-snouted masks adorn the corners and the panel above the central doorway. Crosshatched stone mosaic matting forms the background of the rest of the frieze. Above the four outer doorways and on either side of the central mask panel, you see stone reliefs repeating a complicated pattern. Eight double-headed serpents lie on top of each other, with the smallest on the bottom and the longest on the top. In the center of the top two serpents, you see a reticulated owl sculpture; this bird is associated with warfare and sacrifice in Maya religion.

The North Building is the highest and largest of the Nunnery complex. On either side of its staircase stand low temples. On the left, the Venus Temple has a long-snouted mask on each corner and, above the four columns standing in the entrance, a frieze decorated with a lattice grid and five panels decorated with the W-shaped Venus symbol. Stela 17, containing a long but very eroded hieroglyphic inscription, is set into the middle of the staircase.

Thirteen entrances—one on each end and 11 along the south facade—enter into the North Building's 26 rooms. Above, the frieze is not complete but remains an amazing network of symbolic elements. The background is once again the stone matwork, here broken up by a step-and-fret motif. Above each doorway alternates stacks of four long-snouted masks and relief replicas of thatched Maya huts. Their false doorways once held stone sculptures of rulers; below them you see jaguar sculptures, while along each thatched roof undulate three double-headed serpents. The topmost frieze above each hut is decorated with the goggle-eyed mask of Tlaloc. Further stone figures were attached to the frieze between the doorways; most of them represent bound captives. You can see the remains of many more figures along the back side of this structure.

The West Building is a not-quite-exact reflection of the East Building opposite. Inside lie 14 rooms reached by seven doorways. Once again, you see the stacks of masks, Maya huts, step-and-fret motifs, and mat grids behind. Undulating along the facade are two immensely long feathered serpents, each with a man's face coming out of its mouth and rattles on its tail. Above the central doorway, a stone roof in the form of a feathered canopy covers the figure of God N, the aged god of the Underworld, with the body of a turtle. Small reliefs of human or animal figures are interspersed along the facade. The back of the West Building remains in ruins.

Opposite, the South Building is the lowest of the complex. Its center is penetrated by a great vaulted gateway that opens into a large plaza to the south. On either side lie 16 rooms, with entrances to both the north and south. The north facade is decorated with a lattice grid and, above each doorway, thatched hut

DANIELLE GUSTAFSON

two-headed jaguar throne next to the Governor's Palace

reliefs topped with long-snouted masks. The south facade has not been reconstructed. A plaque states that this complex was explored and consolidated by the Department of Monuments in 1937 and 1938.

Jeff Kowalski believes that the four buildings of the Nunnery, each set at a different height, represent the four main levels of the Maya Universe. Decorated with double-headed feathered serpents (gods of the sky), the North Building represents the Upper World. Opposite, the South Building, the lowest, corresponds to the Underworld with nine doors representing that sphere's nine levels. The East and West Buildings are the Middle World in its two aspects as the rising sun (east) and setting sun (west). In building this complex, Lord Chac positioned Uxmal as the center of not just political power but of religious symbolism. The Nunnery was a kind of Puuc Vatican representing the symbolic center of the Maya Universe.

Between the Nunnery Quadrangle and the House of the Governor lies a large plaza containing the Ballcourt. Lying rather alone at the center of the ceremonial center, this 34-meter-long court was obviously very important to Uxmal's rulers. To the east and west stand tall platforms for viewing the game. Two circular rings originally protruded from the walls; only a replica of one remains on the west side.

The rings were decorated with a partial inscription containing a date. Although some date them to A.D. 649, many researchers believe they should be read A.D. 905 and that the other glyphs refer to Lord Chac, the last great ruler of Uxmal. Along the side of the court are fragments of a feathered serpent sculpture—another sign that the court dates to Lord Chac's late and perhaps Mexican-influenced reign. Small ballplayer sculptures have also been found in the Nunnery Quadrangle.

South of the Ballcourt rises the massive platform of the House of the Governor, measuring 170 by 140 meters and rising from nine to 12 meters off the ground. If you draw a line from the south entrance to the Nunnery, through the Ballcourt, and up to the platform, you notice that it runs right into the center of the House of the Turtles, a small structure at the northwest corner of the platform. This alignment was certainly on purpose; processions probably passed along this route.

The main entrance to this complex is via a staircase on the platform's northeast side. You ascend to a plaza on the east side of the House of the Governor. Here lie the ruins of four small platforms and a square altar with stairs on each side. On top of this altar stands Uxmal's famous two-headed jaguar throne. These were a common symbol of Maya rule; you see them on the Oval Palace Tablet at Palenque and a one-headed version within Chichén's Castillo. Buried below, archaeologists found a rich offering containing 913 pieces, including jade earrings, beads, ceramic pots, and obsidian knives.

Just to the west leans the Pillory column, named because researchers thought it was some sort of sacrificial—or maybe phallic—stone. Now archaeologists believe that this is actually a stela that was originally painted to represent the

World Tree. From the House of the Governor's central doorway, you can draw a line east-southeast directly across the Pillory and jaguar throne, and it will hit the main mound of a site named Nohpat lying on the horizon. A *sacbe* (raised Maya causeway) connected the two centers along this route. This sight line also coincides with an important point of the Venus cycle—the entire complex seems to have been oriented to that planet.

Running more than 100 meters in length, the House of the Governor is one of the longest palace-type structures in the Maya world. It stands on its own platform rising almost seven meters. On the east side, you climb a grand staircase to the structure itself. The palace is divided into three parts: a wide central section and two smaller ones on each end. Between these parts are two tall, transverse vaults that originally cut through the structure but were later walled up to form extra rooms. The 25 interior rooms are built with some of the tallest vaults in the Maya lowlands.

Above the doorways rises the most ornate frieze in the Puuc region, made from more than 15,000 carved pieces of stone. In an incredible touch of architectural refinement, the facade leans slightly outward so that the reliefs would catch more sunlight, both direct and reflected up from the white stone flooring below. The frieze incorporates many of the symbolic elements found at the Nunnery into one great complicated yet beautiful facade.

The background once again comprises crosshatched matting and running step-and-fret designs. Up and down along the facade zigzags a serpentine line of long-snouted masks; further mask stacks adorn the corners (and also the corners at the base). Researchers have counted 103 of these masks on the structure. The most important image lies above the central doorway on the east side. Here you see another inverted pyramid of double-headed serpents; from the center of them emerges a portrait of a ruler, now missing, surrounded by a huge plumed headdress. This was probably Lord Chac. Rows of hieroglyphs formed the double-headed serpent bodies. Further human figures were interspersed along the facades on either side; at best, you can see their headdresses and parts of their bodies.

Lying just north of this palace, the House of the Turtles forms a strong contrast to that elaborate structure. Architects and archaeologists—their taste heavily influenced by the Modern tradition—admire the House of the Turtles' simplicity and "gem-like precision." Its east, west, and south facades are penetrated by three doorways apiece, while only one door opens to the north. Inside lie six rooms. The exterior frieze is stark in comparison with its neighbor—just a long row of attached columns. Above, the cornice is decorated with a row of stone turtles, over 40 of them, attached at intervals along the facade. Turtles are associated with rain; this may have been the center of a rain cult.

The southwest corner of this huge platform is attached to the Great Temple. Only the front of this earlier structure (built at the beginning of the 9th century) has been reconstructed. The grand staircase ascends nine tiers to the so-called Temple of the Macaws on top. The latter structure contains step-and-fret designs on its lower facade—the upper is ruined—and long-snouted masks on the corners. Faces emerge from some of the mask mouths. Stone macaw or parrot reliefs give the temple its name; these may be associated with an aspect of the Sun God. Inside the center door, you find a large, long-snouted mask which was used as a step into a ruined room beyond. The top of the pyramid also contained three other temples, now just piles of stones.

From here, you can either scramble down the west face of the pyramid or descend the staircase and walk west into El Palomar, the Pigeon House Group, dating to around A.D. 850. This is actually a building complex built around three courtyards ending at the tall mound of the South Temple. The group takes its name from the row of temples between the north and central court-yards. These are topped with a row of nine triangular roofcombs that John Lloyd Stephens and Frederick Catherwood took to be pigeon houses. A vaulted passageway takes you into the central courtyard. Numerous unexcavated buildings lie in the dense scrub to the west, including a circular structure dis-covered in the 1980s.

If you return to the Ballcourt, a path heads 200 meters west to the Cemetery Group. This is another ruined temple complex built around a plaza. The tem-ples to the west are the best-preserved, including one with a simple roofcomb. The group takes its name from the four square altars standing about half a meter high in the middle of the plaza. The sides of each are decorated with reliefs depicting skulls, crossed bones, and a shieldlike emblem that is actually a "death's-eye" symbol. A row of glyphs runs across the top of these reliefs; they refer to a noblewoman named Lady Kuk who may have lived at the end of the 9th century. From here, a path leads 200 meters northeast to the Stela Plat-form, which contains more than a dozen very worn stelae; the best are now in the site museum.

These are the main sights of Uxmal's ceremonial center. If you have time and energy, you may want to visit four more building groups at the south and north ends of the site. Due north of the Nunnery, the North Group is a complex of more than 10 structures, all in ruins and overgrown, built around a series of courtyards. Further, smaller complexes lie in the bush to the south.

South of the Pigeon Group lies the Chimez Group, containing a two-story palace adorned with step-and-fret motifs and an attached column frieze. From the southeast corner of the House of the Governor platform, a path takes you to the Chenes Structure, built with a Chenes-style serpent mask around the doorway.

The path then branches to the nearby House of the Old Woman (the grand-mother of the famous dwarf). On the northwest corner of a large pyramid mound stands a small, two-story temple topped with the remains of a roofcomb. Dating to the 8th century, this early structure was partially enveloped by the later pyramid, which may never have been completed. Below, further structures were built around a courtyard. A "garden" of short, squat phallic stones lies just to the northwest.

Three hundred meters to the south, a path takes you to the Temple of the Phallus, a low temple built on an east-west axis. It is named after the phallus-shaped rainspouts protruding from the roof. Only a few are visible; most of the building is in ruins.

KABAH

INTRODUCTION

From Uxmal, a 30-kilometer-long raised Maya causeway runs southeast through the site of Nohpat and continues to the Puuc center of Kabah. The causeway enters the latter city through a beautiful freestanding vaulted gateway. Kabah was always one of the most important Puuc sites; further causeways connected it with the densely populated hill country to the south and east. Although the ruins appear small, they actually extend for many unexplored square kilometers into the forest. The ceremonial center has been cleared and partially restored, but no excavations have ever been performed here. Kabah's main attractions include a palace and the Codz Poop, a remarkable temple covered from ground to roof with more than 250 long-snouted masks.

TOURING THE SITE

Kabah is one of the few sites in the region to be extensively mapped. You park on the west side of the road and cross to the guard's house opposite. A storage shed here contains a stone figure with weirdly fashioned hands from the Codz Poop's facade; you can see ritual scarification around its eyes and mouth. After paying admission, head to the right toward the large platform that is the base for the main temples and elite residences. You climb 22 steps and alight on the

KABAH

How to get there: Kabah stands 10 kilometers south of Santa Elena, or 14 kilometers south of Uxmal, on Highway 261.
Hours: Daily 1000–1700.
Admission fee: 14 pesos.
How long to tour: One hour.
Recommended gear: Hats, sunblock, bottled water, sturdy shoes or sneakers.

platform in front of the amazing Codz Poop temple. In front lies a small platform whose sides are lined with glyphs. The Codz Poop is a half-ruined structure built along a north-south axis on top of a second platform. It consists of a front section of 12 rooms and five doorways, while behind lies a courtyard with further rooms along its sides.

From the floor to the top of the (mostly ruined) frieze, the facade is covered with long-snouted masks, about 250 of them, with extremely hooked noses. More masks lie below each doorway, and their noses become the step in. The noses may have acted as the base for lamps—this glowing facade must have been awesome in the Classic Maya night. The jambs of a doorway on the left are decorated with 9th-century reliefs showing battle scenes with warriors fighting and killing captives. Their dress is not in the style of the Classic Maya,

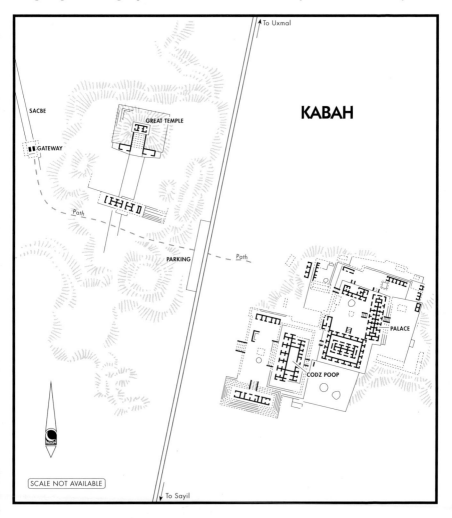

DANIELLE GUSTAFSON

detail of Codz Poop facade

and they carry central Mexican atlatls (throwing sticks used to propel a dart). Some researchers say these reliefs depict the Toltec invasion of Yucatan, but others believe this supposed intrusion came a century later. Inside, you find tall vaulted rooms that are home to flocks of swallows.

To the east of the Codz Poop stands a ruined elite residence with a relatively plain facade. This forms the south part of a courtyard containing at least three *chultunes*—Maya cisterns (11 more have been found around the platform)—and a round stela.

The ruined Palace stands at the east side of this courtyard. This is a large residential complex containing 34 vaulted rooms on two levels and a roofcomb on top. Along the lower facade and upper frieze, you see rows of attached columns, here with raised bands around the middle. These may represent the reed walls of traditional Maya huts; the bands are the cording used to bind them together. The adventurous may want to explore a path heading east into the forest; at the end lies another ruined palace.

The second half of the site lies to the west of the road. From here, a path heads over a hill; on your right, you see the pyramid called the Great Temple, now a pile of rubble. The remains of a four-room structure lie on top (ascent is forbidden). On the other side of the hill, the path descends to Kabah's famous six-meter-high vaulted gateway standing on a low platform. From here, the causeway heads about 15 kilometers as straight as an arrow to Nohpat, where it curves slightly and continues to Uxmal. The forest is filled with unexplored mounds.

SAYIL

INTRODUCTION

Sayil lies among beautiful forest-covered limestone hills seven kilometers due south of Kabah. The wildlife of this region, particularly birds and butterflies, is remarkably abundant and colorful. Although almost no excavations have been performed here, the ruins cover at least five square kilometers of temples, palaces, and hundreds of house mounds—be prepared to walk! The main structures are connected by a one-kilometer causeway; these include the enormous three-story Great Palace complex containing 94 rooms. Sayil was occupied since the Early Classic; however, almost all the monumental structures were built in the brief period between the end of the 8th and the middle of the 10th centuries.

TOURING THE SITE

You enter the ruins from the north. About 100 meters south of the entrance stands Sayil's Palace. It lies at the north end of the central causeway linking the main ceremonial structures. The Palace is an enormous three-story building enclosing 94 rooms. The west side is better preserved than the east; a large central staircase ascends to the eight-room temple on top.

The ground floor is mostly ruined; the second level contains the most elaborate decoration. Pairs of bulging columns stand in most of the doorways, and on either side are panels of banded attached columns. Further banded columns adorn the roof frieze. On the corners and along the frieze protrude large long-snouted masks with great teeth curving down. Between them, stone mosaic reliefs depict the "diving god" figure that is also seen at sites such as Tulum and Cobá; it may represent God E, the maize deity. Undulating serpents flank this

SAYIL

How to get there: About four kilometers south of Kabah on Highway 261, a road turns left (east) to Sayil, then heads to Xlapak, Labná and Loltun Cave.

Hours: Daily 0800–1700.

Admission fee: 14 pesos.

How long to tour: 90 minutes.

Recommended gear: Hats, sunblock, mosquito repellent, bottled water.

DANIELLE GUSTAFSON

the Palace, Sayil

relief. The narrow temple on the top level is a late addition to the structure, designed in an austere late Puuc style. From behind this structure, you have a good view of the hills to the north, where a two-door temple peeks out from among the trees.

From the Palace, you can walk south along the *sacbe* to the Mirador Temple lying about 300 meters south. The pyramid base of this structure has not been rebuilt; on top stands a ruined five-room temple with a plain facade and a well-preserved roofcomb rising above. One hundred meters south of this temple, a thatched roof protects Stela 9, a crudely carved figure possessing a grossly enlarged phallus, obviously associated with a fertility cult.

Returning to the Mirador, a path heads 200 meters west to the Temple of the Hieroglyphic Jamb. Here, you see three rooms half-buried in rubble. The jambs of the north entrance are carved with a hieroglyphic inscription.

A path runs south and joins with the ancient causeway again. At the south end of the *sacbe* stands the two-story South Palace, mostly ruined, with banded attached columns adorning the south facade and frieze. These are interspersed with broken long-snouted masks and other animal masks. Numerous ruined temples and house mounds lie in every direction.

LABNÁ

INTRODUCTION

Labná lies in a small valley among the Bolonchen district hills. For some reason, these forests attract droves of scintillating blue morpho butterflies in the fall, when they may be seen along areas of moisture such as streambeds. The site's layout resembles Sayil's—palace complexes built along a north-south causeway—but the buildings are closer together and better-preserved. Labná is one of the earliest Puuc-region sites; it reached its height during the second half of the 9th century. The ceremonial center contains two restored building complexes decorated with many Classic Puuc motifs, such as Maya hut reliefs, long-snouted masks, attached columns, and step-and-fret designs. These were probably built during the reign of one or two powerful leaders.

TOURING THE SITE

You enter the ceremonial center at the northwest side of the Palace Group. This complex is built on a large platform and consists of about a dozen narrow structures haphazardly built around a series of patios. It was probably built in a series of stages between the late 7th and late 9th centuries.

The eastern face of this archway at Labná is surrounded by Puuc stonework.

DANIELLE GUSTAFSON

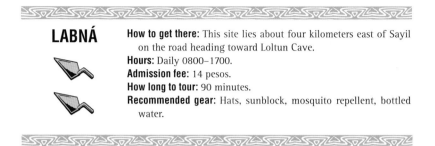

How to get there: This site lies about four kilometers east of Sayil on the road heading toward Loltun Cave.
Hours: Daily 0800–1700.
Admission fee: 14 pesos.
How long to tour: 90 minutes.
Recommended gear: Hats, sunblock, mosquito repellent, bottled water.

The main structure is the Palace itself, standing on the east side of the platform with 42 rooms on the lower level and 28 above. The facade is decorated with attached columns along the top and bottom and built into the corners. Above the west corner protrudes a long-snouted mask—one of the largest and most elaborate in the Puuc—from whose face protrudes a serpent head. Inside the gaping serpent's mouth stands a portrait head, probably of a ruler. The Palace contains low vaulted rooms reached by five doorways. On the semiruined second level, you can see a large *chultun.*

From here, walk south on the *sacbe* about 200 meters to the Mirador (Observatory) Group. Just on your right, you see Labná's famous arch standing between the plaza at the causeway's end and the courtyard of a building complex to the west. It stands on a low platform with a step-and-fret motif running along the frieze and a low roofcomb on top. If you walk through the gateway, you see doorways on either side facing west. Above each doorway stand diminutive replicas of Maya huts with matting patterns flanking them. You can see the remains of blue quetzal plumes painted above their tiny false doors. Long-snouted masks decorate the corners. The buildings around this plaza remain in ruins; a small round altar lies a few steps into the courtyard.

To the east of the causeway stands Labná's "Observatory"—it is not known if it actually functioned as this—facing south atop a ruined pyramid. You have an excellent view of the surrounding hills. Above the plain facade rises an enormous roofcomb. As recently as a century ago, the stones jutting from this structure held dozens of stucco sculptures. The interior contained four rooms; only one is still standing.

The last restored structure in the ceremonial center is the Temple of Columns, lying about 100 meters east of the palace. Standing on a low platform, this L-shaped structure takes its name from the hundreds of attached columns running along the frieze.

XLAPAK

INTRODUCTION

This tiny site halfway between Sayil and Labná is worth visiting for just one structure, the elegant Structure 1 adorned with masks and stone mosaic reliefs. What you see today is actually only a fraction of this Classic Maya center; small temples and house mounds extend deep into the surrounding forest.

TOURING THE SITE

From the parking area, you walk about 200 meters south to Group 1. Here stands Structure 1, also known as the Palace. The north facade is the finest, with three doorways and attached columns at each end. The corners and center of the magnificent roof frieze are decorated with stacks of three long-snouted

masks. Between them the frieze contains wide step-and-fret designs as well as attached columns. Inside lie nine vaulted rooms.

The south facade is half-ruined; over the center door, you see a stack of only two masks, perhaps representations of the god Tlaloc, with rows of serrated teeth. Their noses are upturned, unlike the vast majority of long-snouted masks. Just to the south, you can see the top of a *chultun,* an ancient Maya water tank. Beyond lies another ruined building.

From here, a path heads about 250 meters west to Group 2. The main structure here is a ruined temple built on a north-south axis. You can see rows of attached columns and an undulating serpent along the frieze. A colony of bats makes its home in a cave a few steps to the south.

This fine facade on the south side of Structure I at Xlapak is an example of Puuc architects' mastery of stonework. The masks on the corners may represent mountain monsters.

DANIELLE GUSTAFSON

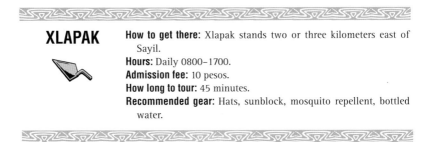

XLAPAK

How to get there: Xlapak stands two or three kilometers east of Sayil.

Hours: Daily 0800–1700.

Admission fee: 10 pesos.

How long to tour: 45 minutes.

Recommended gear: Hats, sunblock, mosquito repellent, bottled water.

The ruined Group 3 lies 100 meters north of here. Its only sights are one or two doorways surrounded by short sections of an attached column facade.

LOLTUN CAVE

INTRODUCTION

After hours touring the Puuc sites under the steamy Yucatan sun, the cool of the Loltun Cave is a welcome relief. This cave system contains some of the earliest human remains found in Southern Mexico, possibly dating to 10,000 years ago, and tantalizing traces of contact with other Mesoamerican areas during the eras that followed. The rooms are also spectacular, culminating in the circular Loltun room; swallows wheel around thick vines and beams of sunlight fall through an opening in its ceiling.

HISTORY

Humankind came early to the Loltun Cave, which lies a few kilometers south of the town of Oxkutzcab in the northern Puuc region. Archaeologists have found the bones of extinct mastodons, bison, camels, horses, and wolves dating to around 9000 B.C. at the lowest levels of the Huechil Grotto. It is not proven that early hunters were responsible for their demise; most of the obvious stone tools date to 5000–3000 B.C. Early occupants probably used the cave not as a year-round residence but as a seasonal campsite. In addition to shelter, the cave provided two important resources to its early residents—clay and water. The first ceramics appear around 1600 B.C., and their manufacture continued without a break through the Spanish Conquest. Many of these early bowls and vases were used as religious offerings. As the symbolic womb of many gods, the sun, and the planets, caves were central to Mesoamerican religions. Loltun Cave was almost certainly an important pilgrimage destination. The strongest evidence is

LOLTUN CAVE

How to get there: Loltun Cave lies 32 kilometers from the turnoff to Sayil off Highway 261. From Uxmal, it is quicker to reach Loltun directly by heading 50 kilometers southeast on Highway 184. After Oxkutzcab, follow the signs.

Hours: Daily 0900–1700, with tours at 0900, 1100, 1300, and 1600. Because of the size, darkness, and dangers of the cave, all visits must be accompanied by a guide. (Caves seem to inspire great flights of the imagination; what you hear from the guides may not reflect current archaeological thought.)

Admission fee: 17 pesos.

How long to tour: 90 minutes.

Recommended gear: Hiking boots (the cave floor is wet), bottled water.

Food: There is a good, open-air restaurant at the site exit.

the relief of the Loltun Warrior at the site entrance. Carved in the style of Izapa in southern Chiapas, this was probably the portrait of a Late Preclassic ruler who visited Loltun from that important proto-Maya city.

During the Classic era (A.D. 250–900), the cave's religious use declined, while the extraction of its water and clay increased greatly. Archaeologists have found thousands of broken water-carrying jugs and storage jars, as well as grindstones carved from the cave's rock walls. During the last three centuries of this era, the cave saw its most intensive use as the main water source for the nearby Puuc center of Idzteil. After the Puuc collapse, the surrounding population dwindled, and the cave was used less and less. Although they look more primitive, many of the crude pictographs may date to the subsequent Late Preclassic era. The cave was forgotten except by local Maya after the Conquest. During the 19th-century Caste War, Maya revolutionaries camped here and built defensive walls facing the cave entrances.

ARCHAEOLOGICAL RECORD

The first (amateur) archaeologist to explore the Loltun Cave was Edward H. Thompson, the American Consul at Mérida, who during 1888 and 1890 expeditions discovered many artifacts and paintings. Around the same time, Teobert Maler visited the cave and photographed and drew many glyphs and paintings. They were followed by Henry Mercer, who in 1895 made a marathon expedition to 29 Yucatan caves in 60 days seeking evidence of prehistoric man. He dug three large trenches in Room 3, finding many animal bones but no ancient fossils. In 1960, the speleologists Jack Grant and Bill Dailey explored the entire cave system and discovered many new rooms. The first modern excavation began in 1977 under Norberto González Crespo of INAH. The work centered on the Huechil Grotto, where the archaeologists made many spectacular discoveries, including dozens of stone tools and the bones of extinct mammals.

TOURING THE SITE

Loltun Cave is aligned on a rough east-west axis covering 850 by 500 meters. At its east end, the Nahkab entrance is formed by the ancient collapse of a limestone roof into the chamber below. Just before you enter the cave itself, you see on the rock face to the left of the stairs the famous Loltun Warrior relief. This eroded carving, showing a ruler clad in a massive belt and headdress and holding a mace, is executed in the style of Izapa, the Late Preclassic Maya center on the southern Chiapas coast. A stack of glyphs floats just above and to the left.

The Nahkab entrance takes you to the beginning of the Main Gallery, which runs more than 400 meters to the west. The guides call the first room the Grindstone Room after the stone metates found here (they actually are scattered throughout the cave). You also see small wells called *ha chultunes* used to store water. A rosette-shaped petroglyph is carved on the left wall.

This room opens into the Cathedral, measuring 20 meters wide and 45 meters high. The guides will point out rock formations shaped like corn, a heart, and the Virgin of Guadalupe. At the end of this room, a stone is the base of the Head of Loltun, a crude sculpture with wide lips and sagging ears discovered elsewhere by speleologists in 1960. Next you enter the Room of the Ha Chultunes containing a number of natural cisterns. The floor is slippery with mud,

Loltun head sculpture

so watch your step. The Main Gallery's narrowest point is the Pass of the Wind, which was artificially narrowed by pre-Columbian inhabitants to intensify the breeze. You may see cave crickets hopping around on the ground. From here, you pass into the Hall of the Columns. When you strike some of the rock columns here, they produce high and low sounds—Lol and Tun—that guides claim sound the cave's name. The following Child's Room contained the burial of a 10-year-old boy, now in the Mérida anthropology museum. The walls are adorned with the first of many rock paintings. Here, you see hand silhouettes in black paint whose symbolic meaning remains a mystery. Next, you enter the Grand Canyon, an enormous room measuring 45 by 100 meters with large stones tumbled on the floor. In the following Room of the Stalactites, the guide will point out two formations, Man's Temptation and Woman's Temptation, whose descriptions I will leave up to your imagination. You then turn into a gallery decorated with more black hand silhouettes (one with six fingers), a glyph, and the crude profile of a Maya personage. This opens into the spectacular Room 3, also called the Room of the Inscriptions, the largest of the cave system, measuring 105 meters long. The roof has partially collapsed, leaving two large holes to the sky through which swallows, motmots, and bats flutter in and out. With its huge stalactites and trailing vines, the chamber is intensely photogenic, particularly at midday when rays of sunlight pour straight down. Archaeologists have found 32 rock glyphs carved on its walls and 41 small water-storage tanks, including one called the Baptismal Font. The largest glyph is the one identified as Chac on the left wall. From here, you turn south to Room 1, also named the Loltun Room, and the cave exit. Trenches here were built as defenses during the War of the Castes (some say these may be only water channels). On the southern side of this chamber, a ledge is the entrance to the Huechil Grotto (off-limits to tourists), the site of the famous discoveries of extinct mammal bones. You climb 76 slippery steps past trailing vines into the sunlight. An excellent restaurant serving Yucatecan specialties lies just beyond the cave outlet.

DZIBILCHALTUN

INTRODUCTION

Lying on the hot, dry plain between Mérida and the coast, Dzibilchaltun is not one of the most attractive Yucatan sites. Nevertheless, it is one of the earliest and most important. The key to its success lay in its location close to the salt-producing lagoons of the Yucatan coast. Salt was precious in Mesoamerica, and Dzibilchaltun used it to build an early and far-reaching trade network that traded salt for such commodities as food and obsidian. During the Preclassic and the last centuries of the Classic, this trade allowed Dzibilchaltun to become the most powerful center in northern Yucatan. The site declined after the Classic era but remained a pilgrimage destination; the famous offerings called the Seven Dolls date to this era. Even though it was largely abandoned, the Spanish took Dzibilchaltun's religious power so seriously that they built a large chapel in the center of the ruins.

HISTORY

Dzibilchaltun lies as close as possible to the coast—22 kilometers—while staying just inside the northern limit of the zone of passable soils and sufficient rainfall for agriculture. As the city developed from trading salt extracted from the coastal lagoons, they found that the soils could not sustain their population, making the trade routes even more important for supplying food. It was on this delicate balance that Dzibilchaltun grew into one of the powers of the northern lowlands.

The site was first settled around 800 B.C. by immigrants from the south, possibly originating along the southern Gulf coast. Except for potsherds found at Loltun Cave and in the Mani Cenote, Dzibilchaltun's ceramics represent the earliest found in northern Yucatan. These fragments were found throughout the site but most copiously at two centers a few kilometers from Dzibilchaltun's ceremonial center around the Xlacah Cenote. The first was the Mirador Group lying 7.4 kilometers to the south-southwest; here, six raised platforms with temples on top were built around a raised plaza by 500 B.C. Komchen, six kilometers northwest of the cenote, burgeoned later but by the end of the Middle Preclassic (300 B.C.) covered as much as one square kilometer. The salt trade was just beginning at this time and Dzibilchaltun's inhabitants lived by hunting game, fishing for marine mollusks, and engaging in small-scale farming.

DZIBILCHALTUN

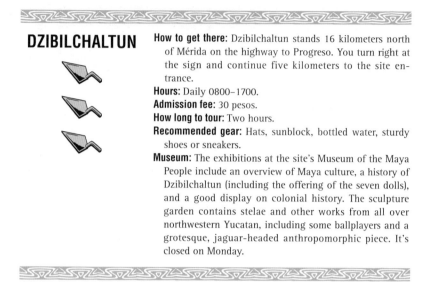

How to get there: Dzibilchaltun stands 16 kilometers north of Mérida on the highway to Progreso. You turn right at the sign and continue five kilometers to the site entrance.

Hours: Daily 0800–1700.

Admission fee: 30 pesos.

How long to tour: Two hours.

Recommended gear: Hats, sunblock, bottled water, sturdy shoes or sneakers.

Museum: The exhibitions at the site's Museum of the Maya People include an overview of Maya culture, a history of Dzibilchaltun (including the offering of the seven dolls), and a good display on colonial history. The sculpture garden contains stelae and other works from all over northwestern Yucatan, including some ballplayers and a grotesque, jaguar-headed anthropomorphic piece. It's closed on Monday.

During the Late Preclassic (300 B.C.–A.D. 250), Komchen became the center of the salt trade and the largest center in northwestern Yucatan, covering two square kilometers with upward of 1,000 buildings. Most of these were houses, of course, but Structure 500 measured 70 by 75 meters and eight meters tall—massive for the time. Growth also continued at the Mirador Group, only on less spectacular a scale. At the end of this era, however, the boom suddenly ended for unknown reasons. It is thought the salt trade probably fell under the sway of an inland center, perhaps Izamal. Both Komchen and the Mirador Group were all but abandoned for the next half millennium, though two small structures, one in the style of Teotihuacan, were built in the Mirador Group.

By A.D. 700, the zone around the Xlacah Cenote became the center of Dzibilchaltun. In slightly more than a century, it went from a negligible population to a city of 8,000 structures sprawling over 19 square kilometers. Housing as many as 40,000 inhabitants, it was one of the largest communities in the northern lowlands. From the center radiated eight *sacbeob* (Maya causeways) that were the beginning of the great salt trade routes. Its principal structures, such as the Temple of the Seven Dolls, were built in the style of the southern lowlands with traces of Palenque styles as well.

Between A.D. 830 and 1000, the Puuc style came to Dzibilchaltun; the major buildings were covered with thin Puuc-style veneers. The population remained stable but fewer new ceremonial or elite structures were built; Structure 36 at the northeast corner of the Central Plaza was the last. Toward the end of this era, Dzibilchaltun began a slow decline, and the population gradually dwindled. The salt trade may have been taken over by the huge city of Tiho-Mérida—which rose 14 kilometers to the south.

The era between A.D. 1000 and 1200 was one of abandonment. This was probably accelerated by the rapid ascendancy of the militaristic state based at Chichén Itzá. During the Late Postclassic (A.D. 1200–1530), the population was small; there was, however, a revival of ceremonial activity in the old temples. The most famous example of this is the offering of seven crudely made dolls that gave the temple its name. Dzibilchaltun's ritual role probably continued after the Conquest. Even though the population was tiny, Spanish priests still felt they had to construct a large chapel here at the end of the 16th century.

DANIELLE GUSTAFSON

headless sculpture of a male holding a symbol of office

ARCHAEOLOGICAL RECORD

Dzibilchaltun was never forgotten by locals and Mérida residents who came to swim in the cenote. Archaeologists did not think it worth studying until 1941, when Alfredo Barrera Vásquez took George Brainerd and E. Wyllys Andrews IV of the Carnegie Institution to visit during their survey of northern Yucatan sites. They did a preliminary survey of the site and dug exploratory trenches revealing the surprising length of Dzibilchaltun's occupation.

Andrews moved to the Middle American Research Institute at Tulane University and in 1956 returned to the site to begin nine seasons of excavations supported by INAH's regional center and the National Geographic Society. This project excavated all the major structures at Komchen, the Mirador Group, and around the Xlacah Cenote. This cenote itself was plumbed by divers. The project

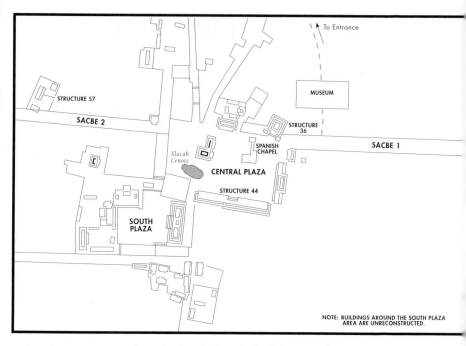

NOTE: BUILDINGS AROUND THE SOUTH PLAZA AREA ARE UNRECONSTRUCTED.

issued numerous reports, and, after Andrews's death in 1971, the comprehensive final report was written by his son, E. Wyllys Andrews V.

Since then, most Dzibilchaltun excavation and restoration work, including projects at Komchen and the Mirador Group, has been performed by the INAH regional center. The site was an Archaeological Special Project between 1992 and 1994; led by Rubén Maldonado C., the project excavated and restored buildings around the Central Plaza and the Temple of the Seven Dolls and rebuilt Sacbe I. They also built the spacious Museum of the Maya People just north of the Central Plaza.

TOURING THE SITE

You approach the ruins from the north. At the site entrance stands a small complex housing the ticket office, a gift shop, and a restaurant. From here, a path takes you left along a shaded path to the museum and to the main path leading to the ruins.

A path exits onto Sacbe 1, the main east-west raised causeway linking two important building groups. You take a left and walk about 300 meters toward the Temple of the Seven Dolls. In front of this structure opens a wide plaza in the center of which stands the small platform of Structure 12. A smooth stele stands on top. This is one of 20 unmarked stelae found at the site; archaeolo-

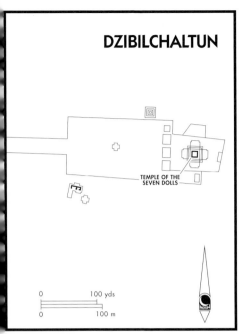

DZIBILCHALTUN

TEMPLE OF THE
SEVEN DOLLS

0   100 yds

0   100 m

gists believe they may have been covered with stucco and then incised with glyphs and other decorations.

At the east end of the plaza, three small temples stand in front of the Temple of the Seven Dolls. Numerous offering caches, including many shells, were found buried in their bases. Rising just to the east of the Temple of the Seven Dolls, Structure 1 is a low, square, two-tiered platform built around A.D. 700 with entrances facing the cardinal directions. About a century later, the building was filled with rubble and covered with a larger pyramid, which now has been almost totally removed by archaeologists.

The four staircases rising on each side climb to a square temple with four doorways and—a rarity in Mesoamerica—square windows in some of the walls. Crude geometrical god masks protrude from the upper facade above the doors and on each corner. This frieze was originally covered with an elaborate stucco relief that included entwined serpents and added much detail to the god masks. On top stands a unique square cupola in lieu of a roofcomb.

The four doorways pass into a square chamber. Numerous graffiti, including silhouetted hands, were found on the walls and floors. In the middle stands a square sanctuary, which you enter via short staircases facing east and west. The top of the sanctuary rises into the cupola. Sometime between A.D. 1200 and 1520, Maya pilgrims burrowed through the later pyramid and opened the old temple. They restored the interior with new floors and resumed ritual activity. As part of this, they buried in the sanctuary floor seven crudely made clay figurines (now in the site museum).

To reach the next building complex, you have to retrace your steps west along Sacbe 1—wear a hat! Just beyond the museum path, it enters the Central Plaza. On your right stands the late 9th-century Structure 36, a four-tiered pyramid that may have been the last major structure built at Dzibilchaltun. Stone from Structure 39 just beyond was used to build the Spanish chapel standing in the middle of the plaza. This was a type of open-air chapel common in 16th-century Mexico; the priests converted such crowds of Maya that it was easier to build a roofless enclosure where they could worship. Its walls contain stele fragments and pieces of Puuc veneer.

The next building group on the north side of the plaza is a complex of four small temples built around a patio. On the east side, Structure 38 contains one of the earliest vaulted temples (Str. 38-Sub) found at Dzibilchaltun, dating to A.D. 700–750. Only the staircase remains of the later building; the early temple is a one-door structure with a simple frieze around the top.

The south side of the Central Plaza is bounded by the 130-meter-long Structure 44, one of the longest buildings in northern Yucatan. On top is one narrow 117-meter temple divided into only three long rooms; 35 doorways look out onto the plaza.

At the southwest corner of the Central Plaza, you find the region's favorite swimming hole: the Xlacah Cenote. The top level of this limestone sinkhole is home for schools of sailfin mollies, cichlids, and other small fish. Sloping to the west as it descends, the cenote reaches a depth of 44 meters. In the late 1950s, divers brought up thousands of water jug fragments and stone, wood, and bone artifacts, a few carved with glyphs. They also found a half-dozen skeletons. Unlike the cenote at Chichén Itzá, however, this was not used as a receptacle for human sacrifices—the skeletons show no sign of violent death. The Maya probably realized that corpses would ruin their water supply.

This ends the tour of the main sights; you will need to bushwhack to reach the outlying building complexes. West of the cenote, the uncleared Sacbe 2 runs about a kilometer to a ruined plaza similar to the Seven Dolls group. About 200 meters down the causeway, you see on your right Structure 57, also called the Standing Temple, actually a four-room Puuc-style residence. Another path heads south from the cenote through an unreconstructed plaza (mounds on the north, east, and west sides) to Structures 95 and 96, two Puuc temples that had long-snouted masks on their facade. From here, two *sacbeob* run south and west to further temple groups, all in ruins.

IZAMAL

INTRODUCTION

Halfway between Mérida and Chichén Itzá, Izamal was one of the great powers in northern Yucatan from the wane of Dzibilchaltun to the rise of Chichén. During the Late Classic, its rulers probably controlled the immensely lucrative salt trade; they had the wealth and power to build the largest temple-platform on the peninsula. Its looming pyramids threatened the Spanish priests so much that they razed one and built one of the largest church-and-convent complexes in southern Mexico on its foundations. Izamal's great temples have been only partially restored—they lie among the downtown blocks of the modern town—but are worth a short visit, more to remember what was destroyed than to see what remains.

IZAMAL

How to get there: To reach the town of Izamal from Mérida, you can either take the scenic route via Highway 80, passing through towns such as Tixkokob, Cacalchen, and Tecantó, or speed east on the multilane Highway 180 to the Kantunil exit (70 kilometers from Mérida), from where you head 17 kilometers north to Izamal.
Hours: Daily 0800–1700.
Admission fee: Free.
How long to tour: 90 minutes.
Recommended gear: Hats, sunblock, bottled water, sturdy shoes or sneakers.

HISTORY

Although a long string of explorers and archaeologists have passed through the site, they have barely scratched the surface of the ruins. Its location among bustling streets and residential blocks makes scientific study that much more difficult; many ancient structures have certainly been destroyed.

Very preliminary ceramic studies indicate that Izamal was occupied from at least the Late Preclassic (300 B.C.–A.D. 250), rising in the wake of Dzibilchaltun to the west. The earliest levels of the ceremonial structures date to the Early Classic (A.D. 250–600), and they reached their height between A.D. 600 and 900. During this time, *sacbeob* were built extending in the four directions, the longest reaching Aké 32 kilometers to the west. This indicates that they were the center of a city-state that controlled the surrounding region.

From A.D. 900, Izamal underwent a long, slow decline, controlled first by Chichén and then by the aggressive rulers of Mayapan. Historical documents report that the city was also the shrine of the gods Itzamna and Ix Chel, important gods of healing, and pilgrims from around the Maya region flocked to it through the Spanish Conquest. In 1552, Franciscan priests erected the enormous Santa Virgen de Izamal church on the remains of one of its principal temples.

ARCHAEOLOGICAL RECORD

Pre-Hispanic Izamal could never be forgotten, even though Diego de Landa, bishop of the church at Izamal, crushed 5,000 Maya idols and 97 irreplaceable codices in a mostly successful attempt to destroy the pagan religion. This act shocked even his superiors across the Atlantic; to atone, he was forced to write the *Relación de las Cosas de Yucatan,* one of the best accounts of Yucatec Maya culture and history. Izamal also appeared in histories written by Maya priests and chieftains, particularly the numerous *Books of Chilam Balam*.

During the 19th century, Izamal's massive temples were visited by John Lloyd Stephens and Frederick Catherwood, who documented an enormous god mask on the side of one temple that was later destroyed. The first (small) excavations were performed by the ubiquitous Désiré Charnay in the 1880s. Dozens of explorers and archaeologists followed, including William H. Holmes and Sylvanus G. Morley of the Carnegie Institution.

The only excavation since then was a 1968 INAH project under Victor Segovia Pinto that restored part of the huge K'inich Kak Moo platform and dug some stratigraphic pits on a smaller structure. From 1978 to 1986, Izamal was part of INAH's Proyecto Aké, which studied the settlement and *sacbe* networks between the regional centers. No work has been done since then.

TOURING THE SITE

Begin your tour on Izamal's main square. On its south side rises the massive, yellow Santa Virgen de Izamal church and convent, which was built with Maya stones. According to historical accounts, this church rests on the foundations of a Maya temple named the P'ap'hol-chaak, of which no traces remain (nobody has yet dug beneath the church's floors). In 1993, Pope John Paul II blessed this church in the name of the ethnic groups of Latin America. The church and convent are worth a tour; some carved Maya stones lie in a storeroom and you can also see a portrait of Bishop Diego de Landa, who tried to destroy the Maya reli-

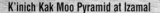

K'inich Kak Moo Pyramid at Izamal

DANIELLE GUSTAFSON

gion and then wrote one of the great works on Maya history and culture as a way of atonement.

From the convent's entrance, you can see the enormous K'inich Kak Moo temple looming two blocks to the north of the square. It is a short walk to its base, which measures 200 meters to a side and rises 36 meters. With a volume of 700,000 square meters, this is the largest structure on the Yucatan Peninsula. A staircase climbs to the top of the platform, which is semicleared and strewn with rubble. At the north side rises a smaller, 10-tiered pyramid; from its summit, you have an excellent view of the church, town, and surrounding henequen fields.

To the east of the square stands the ruined Itzamna pyramid; the stairs leading up have recently been restored. A smaller temple rises from the large platform bases. It is named after Itzamna, a ruler turned divinity after his death; his touch could apparently heal the sick. Opposite, on the west side of the square, you see the smaller Kabul temple. On its side stood the famous, now destroyed, god mask drawn by Frederick Catherwood. Itzamna's miraculous hand was apparently buried within. Further ruined platforms lie south of the church. The roads to Aké (west) and Kantunil (south) run along the old *sacbeob.*

CHICHÉN ITZÁ

INTRODUCTION

At the end of the Classic and the beginning of the Postclassic eras, the flat plains of northern Yucatan were dominated by the powerful city of Chichén Itzá. The rulers of this highly militaristic city captured the trade and tribute routes of Dzibilchaltun, Tiho, and the Puuc region to the south. With this wealth, they built a sprawling urban area around a ceremonial center of towering pyramids and endless rows of columns. Chichén's Castillo has become one of the icons of ancient Mexico, while its Ballcourt and Temple of the Warriors represent Mesoamerican architecture at its most elaborate. Stone reliefs on many of these structures depicted the most important aspects of their culture: war, the bloody rituals of the ballgame, and a form of government in which power was shared between brothers.

Since the 1920s, archaeologists have been painstakingly restoring Chichén Itzá to its ancient glory. It has now become one of the principal tourist attractions of Mexico, with a highway connecting it to Mérida and Cancún and a grand new museum/mall complex at the entrance. Every year at the spring and autumn equinoxes, crowds numbering in the tens of thousands are drawn to a great ritual celebrating the ancient Maya, modern Mexico, and international

Chichén Itzá's largest structure, the Castillo, is the centerpiece of the park-like site.

CHICHÉN ITZÁ

How to get there: These famous ruins lie on Highway 180, now a multilane toll road, 118 kilometers east of Mérida and 168 west of Cancún.

Hours: Daily 0800–1700.

Admission fee: 30 pesos.

How long to tour: You can see the highlights in a half-day, the whole site in one day.

Recommended gear: Hats, sunblock, bottled water, mosquito repellent, sturdy shoes or sneakers.

Museum: There is a good museum in the site entrance complex.

Food and accommodations: Three very good hotels stand just outside the site's south entrance: the **Mayaland,** U.S. tel. 800/235-4079; the **Hacienda Chichén Itzá,** tel. 99/24-2150 in Mérida, which was Edward H. Thompson's archaeological base camp; and the comfortable **Villa Arqueológica,** tel. 99/100-34 or from the U.S. 800/258-2633. Many restaurants and less expensive accommodations are in the town of Pisté three kilometers west.

tourism as a shadow in the shape of the Kukulcan, the Feathered Serpent, slithers down the side of the Castillo.

What this pageantry obscures is that archaeologists actually know very little about Chichén's history. Mayanists are arguing two theories of the site's chronology. The traditional view holds that Chichén was a Maya city strongly influenced by the Puuc region. In the late 10th century, it was conquered by a Toltec army that brought many Mexican traits to Yucatan, including the cult of Kukulcan, also known as Quetzalcoatl, the Feathered Serpent. During the last two decades a revisionist theory has emerged stating that the Toltecs never invaded Yucatan; its adherents believe that from founding to collapse Chichén was dominated by the Itzá Maya, a group with links to central Mexico. Only further excavations will settle this debate.

HISTORY

The question of Chichén Itzá's history is one of the knottiest problems in Mesoamerican archaeology. The main difficulty is that no comprehensive excavations have been performed since the 1930s, and stratigraphic studies are severely lacking. Researchers have gleaned many clues from the numerous 16th-century Maya histories written by both Spanish priests and Maya chiefs. Unfortunately, taken as a group they contain many contradictions, and experts cannot agree on how to read their dates.

The traditional theory is based mainly on historical accounts and on the great difference its adherents see in the early and late phases of Chichén's art and

At Chichén Itzá, from the top of the Temple of the Warriors, the Group of 1,000 Columns stand like soldiers in the midday sun.

architecture. At present, there is no evidence for occupation before A.D. 800 (it is highly likely, however, because the Sacred Cenote was such an important water source). During the mid-9th century, construction began on a series of ceremonial buildings in the Old Chichén part of the site. Although they are missing the fine Puuc veneer, their architecture shows evidence of strong influence from that region to the west, including many long-snouted masks along the friezes. Many of the lintels were decorated with glyphic inscriptions giving the names of groups of brothers who apparently shared supreme power. This early Chichén was built by the Itzá or perhaps the Putún Maya, both known as traders originating on the Gulf coast.

In A.D. 987, Topiltzin Quetzalcoatl, the king of the far-off city of Tula, was ejected from the Toltec capital. According to semi-mythic accounts, he set sail on a raft into the Gulf of Mexico. That same year, so state 16th-century Maya histories, a king calling himself "Kukulcan" (Yucatec Maya for feathered serpent) arrived on the shores of Yucatan. He probably landed at Isla Cerritos, an island settlement on the north coast containing masses of central Mexican trade goods, including obsidian. Topiltzin fought his way inland, defeating all who opposed him, and ended his campaign with his conquest of Chichén Itzá. This city he made his capital, building a great new ceremonial precinct in the style of Tula with *chac mools,* warrior columns, feathered serpents, and an immense central Mexican ballcourt. Reliefs scattered throughout the city tell the story of his victory through pictures—no glyphic inscriptions have been found from this era—showing bearded Toltecs slaughtering Maya warriors. This city dominated northern Yucatan for 200 years, until it was destroyed and abandoned shortly after A.D. 1200.

Supporters of the revisionist theory of Chichén's history do not see great differences between the early and late phases of the city and take the historical accounts with a grain of salt. Its adherents have not settled on one comprehensive explanation; they vary from those who see a Toltec influence to those who insist the city was always purely Maya. One account of the latter view begins in the 9th century when the northern peninsula was controlled by the Puuc to the west and Cobá in the east. Into this area came the Itzá, Maya traders with strong links to central Mexico, who wanted to build their own empire. They fought their way from Isla Cerritos toward Yaxuná, an important city that was connected to Cobá by the longest causeway in the Maya world. When they failed to capture Yaxuná, they settled about 20 kilometers to the northwest by the side of the Sacred Cenote.

Both the "old" and "new" parts of this Itzá Chichén rose in a relatively short time, perhaps 200 years. This city was planned, with no great breaks between the construction of the southern and the northern zones. The buildings and reliefs did have Mexican motifs, such as also appear at Uxmal, but they remain predominately Maya. Indeed, those "Mexican" motifs—the cult of the Feathered Serpent, *chac mools,* etc.—may have actually been developed here and then exported along the Itzá trade routes to Tula. The lords of Chichén may have founded that central Mexican city rather than the other way around! Some time around A.D. 1100, Chichén was abandoned. Other cities, such as Mayapan, rose to take its place, but they were never more than weak reflections of Itzá glory.

ARCHAEOLOGICAL RECORD

Rising from the flat plains of central Yucatan, Chichén Itzá could never be forgotten. In the 16th century, Bishop Diego de Landa included it in his account of pre-Conquest Yucatan history and culture. It was also mentioned by the Maya versions of their history contained in the various *Books of Chilam Balam.* In 1688, the priest López de Cogolludo asserted that Chichén and other Yucatan sites were the product of its native inhabitants, not the Phoenicians or Carthaginians as some said.

In the late 17th century, Chichén Itzá became part of a cattle and henequen (a plant whose fibers were made into rope) plantation, and the hacienda building was built just south of the ruins. John Lloyd Stephens and Frederick Catherwood visited and described the site on their 1841 trek across the peninsula. Stephens describes his arrival thus:

> *At four o'clock we left Pisté, and very soon we saw rising high above the plain the Castillo of Chichén. In half an hour we were among the ruins of this ancient city, with all the great buildings in full view, casting prodigious shadows over the plain and presenting a spectacle which, even after all that we had seen, once more excited in us emotions of wonder.*

Shortly after their visit, in 1847 the hacienda was burned by Maya revolution-aries at the beginning of the Caste War. This struggle scared away explorers for more than a decade. The first excavations were performed in 1875 and 1876 by Augustus Le Plongeon, who discovered the famous *chac mool* (now in Mexico City) at the site. Of his published work, the distinguished archaeologist Ignacio Bernal said: "[His] books and theories are the wildest fantasies and quite use-less." He was followed by many familiar faces, including Désiré Charnay, Alfred Maudslay, and Teobert Maler, who in 1891 excavated the top of the Temple of the Tables.

The Sacred Cenote was an object of particular fascination because of the legends concerning the sacrifice of virgins in its murky depths. Charnay tried but failed to dredge the cenote. In the late 1890s, Edward H. Thompson, an en-thusiastic amateur archaeologist who was the American Consul at Mérida, bought the site and rebuilt the hacienda. With the help of Harvard's Peabody Museum, he built a large dredge apparatus on the side of the sinkhole and from 1904 to 1909 pulled up a trove of artifacts from its depths. The haul also included a wooden scepter inlaid with turquoise and a human skull formed into an incense burner. Thompson also performed small-scale excavations on many of the main structures.

From 1924 to 1940, the Carnegie Institution performed the only comprehen-sive excavations at Chichén. Much of what we know about the site history is due to their researches. Their work centered on the Temple of the Warriors, the Caracol, and the Market. They also returned to the cenote for further dredging.

Mexican government archaeologists have been working at the site since 1926. Most of their work has emphasized consolidation and restoration; few of their reports have been published. In 1961 and 1967, INAH divers returned to the cenote armed with a device like a great vacuum cleaner to scour the bottom. They brought up some remarkable engraved gold plates and dozens of skele-tons, probably sacrificial victims, but only a handful of them were female (ex-perts did not have the means to determine if they were virgins). Since 1993, the Chichén Itzá Archaeological Project under Peter Schmidt has partially excavat-ed and restored the Temple of the Tables, the east side of the 1,000 Column Plaza, and the group around the High Priest's Grave. Among the recent discov-eries are a series of warrior reliefs in the Temple of the Tables and tombs in a platform next to the High Priest's Grave.

TOURING THE SITE

There are two entrances to the ruins, the main one to the northwest by the Great Ballcourt and a less-crowded gate just north of the Hotel Mayaland. The main entrance is through a mall complex containing the site museum and a restaurant, craft market, and bookstore selling a selection of archaeological books. From both these gates, you enter Chichén's Main Plaza; in the center stands the Castillo, the pyramid where this tour will begin. It is best to start early to beat the heat and the crowds.

The Castillo is a great square pyramid measuring 56 meters to a side. Four stairways climb nine sloping tiers to a three-room temple on top. At the base of the north-face staircase, a doorway opens onto a stairway ascending to the buried temple atop the earlier stage of the pyramid. Usually lines are waiting to get in. After climbing 61 steps up a hot and steamy passageway, you reach the old temple. Jaguars and entwined serpents adorn the frieze around the door. Inside, the one-room temple contains two amazing sculptures that were excavated from the Temple of the Chac Mool within the Temple of the Warriors. The door is guarded by the best-preserved *chac mool* in Mexico, with eyes, teeth, and toenails made from shell. Behind stands a single-headed jaguar throne, the traditional seat of Maya rulers (you see them at Palenque among other sites). This is painted red with green jade discs representing its spots. Beneath the throne, archaeologists found an offering cache containing an iron pyrite mirror surrounded by turquoise and shell mosaics forming four square-nosed serpent heads.

The fresh air is a relief. From here, walk left to the Castillo's west staircase, the only one that is still climbable. On either side of the stairs stand great serpent heads whose plumed bodies flank the staircase all the way up. A chain gives a handhold for the nervous. On top, entrances face the four directions. The west doorway is adorned with warrior reliefs on the jambs. Inside, you find tall vaulted (smelly) rooms. The north entrance was the main one, with two columns carved in the form of serpents guarding the door and decorated lintels. Inside, the sanctuary contains two square columns decorated with more figures, probably warriors. The Castillo's platform gives one of the best views of the site, particularly over Old Chichén and the circular Caracol building to the south.

On the vernal and autumnal equinoxes, the Castillo is the focal point of the huge "Kukulcan" celebrations drawing tens of thousands of Mexicans and tourists from all over the world. In 1928, a laborer working on the pyramid's reconstruction noticed that on these dates at the rising and setting of the sun the corner of the structure casts a shadow supposedly in the shape of a serpent—Kukulcan—on the side of the staircase. The site supervisors, who were beginning to promote Chichén as a tourist destination, immediately realized the marketing potential of this phenomenon. Since then, the celebration has grown into a massive gathering exalting the wisdom of the ancients and the glorious ancestry of the Mexican race. Archaeologists, however, have always been dubious about this shadow. Although the Castillo almost certainly had an astronomical alignment, the pyramid may not have been built to produce this effect, which may have been created by the modern restoration.

In the plaza north of the Castillo stands the square Venus Platform, with four staircases ascending four meters to a flat top. Serpent heads jut from either side of the top steps. The platform takes its name from the side *tableros;* the main panels depict a face, supposedly Venus, emerging from the jaws of a plumed

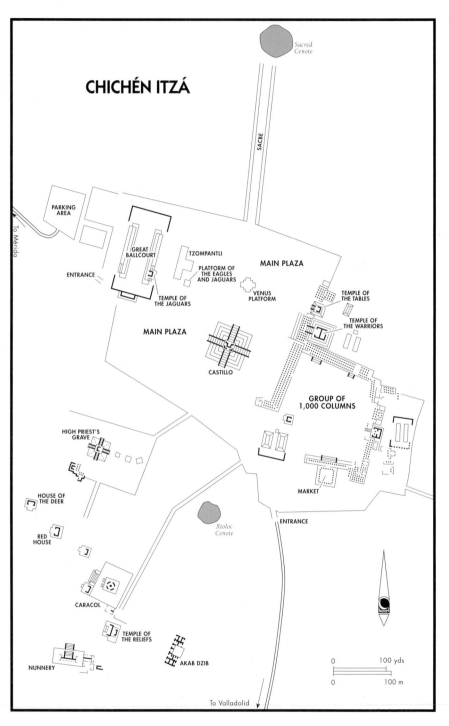

monster face, perhaps a serpent, with a two-part tongue and jaguar claws. The relief above is the body of the plumed serpent whose head emerges from the stair sides. Buried within this platform, Augustus Le Plongeon found the *chac mool* now in Mexico City's Museo Nacional de Antropología.

On the border of the plaza due east rises the famous Temple of the Warriors. This zone of the ancient city was known for its colonnades; the first, comprising four rows of about 16 square columns, stands in front of this temple. Their columns are carved with reliefs representing warriors, captives, and priests, all marching forward as if in a procession of stone.

This procession may lead up the steps of the Temple of the Warriors, which is a square structure, 40 meters to a side, rising in three *talud-tablero* tiers. The middle *tablero* is decorated with a running jaguar and eagle motif, probably representing the two main warrior orders at Chichén—the same are found at Tula and Tenochtitlan. As at the Venus Platform, serpent heads protrude from the side of the top steps. On top of them crouch little standard-bearer sculptures whose hands originally gripped wooden poles.

The first sculpture the procession would meet on top of the platform is the *chac mool* facing west across the plaza. This was probably a sacrificial stone; hearts were placed on the dish resting on its stomach. The walls of the temple behind are decorated with stone heads emerging from serpent mouths and long-snouted masks—both leitmotifs of the Puuc region—at the corners and on either side of the doors. Two amazing feathered serpent columns guard the doorway with gaping mouths at their bases and rattles on top. The temple was divided into two rooms, vaulted in the front and with a flat ceiling behind. Square columns carved with more striding figures held up the roof. Along the back wall, you see a low bench that is supported by little Atlantean (Atlaslike) figures of the type you also see at Tula.

Within the Temple of the Warriors, archaeologists found remains of the Temple of the Chac Mool, which was built slightly off the later structure's plan. Here, they discovered the *chac mool* and throne now displayed within the Castillo.

If you return to the ground level, just to the north of this structure you see the Temple of the Tables, which was recently excavated. Propped up on the ground stands a long relief from the temple frieze depicting jaguars romping among strange-looking trees. On top, you find two rooms with warrior columns and more Atlantean figures holding up a bench in back. Four offering caches were found in the base of the temple; contents included a jade pectoral.

South of the Temple of the Warriors lies a plaza surrounded by the Group of 1,000 Columns. Many on the northern colonnade are carved with further reliefs, and among them you find a circular altar carved with eagles and jaguars devouring hearts—another motif seen at Tula. This procession of columns runs around the west side of the plaza to the Market, which occupies its southern border. Researchers only guess that this wide platform was used as a marketplace. Its central staircase passes through a portico—notice the panel to the left showing a string of captives—into a sunken courtyard surrounded by 24 tall columns. From here, a path heads 50 meters east to the Steambath, a modest structure with a vaulted room. A small ruined ballcourt extends to the north. Another ballcourt lies just west of the Market.

It is time for some shade. Walk north across the Main Plaza passing the Castillo and Venus Platform. In the middle of the plaza's northern border, the forest opens up along Sacbe 1 heading to the Sacred Cenote, also called the

ARCHAEOASTRONOMY

Monumental architecture and city planning provide one of the best examples of the difference between modern Western cultures and ancient Mesoamerica. Most cities in Europe and the Americas are oriented to the local landscape and, roughly, toward the four cardinal directions. In Mesoamerica, landscape and the four directions do have a role, but one of the prime components for the design of pre-Hispanic cities and civic-religious buildings is their orientation to the sun, planets, and stars.

Ancient Mesoamerica was divided into many religions, but they all seem to have shared a similar cosmology. Like a tall stack of pancakes, the Universe was divided into 22 layers, 13 above and nine below (the Earth counts as the top of the Underworld and the bottom of the Heavens). The Heavens contained the moon, sun, planet Venus, and constellations—all manifestations of gods—ascending to the topmost male-female creator god at the 13th level. There was no division of the Heavens and the Earth into the sacred and the profane; it was all sacred and all interconnected.

The Universe was unstable, however, and for human beings to continue to prosper, they had to attune themselves to the movements of the Heavens. Sacred time ordered their existence from planting and harvesting to war, sacrifices, and ritual bloodletting. Failure to follow these cycles could stop the rains, blight the crops, and, perhaps, stop the passage of night into day. The main role of priests was to watch the skies at night and record the rise and fall of the heavenly bodies. They became so expert at this that they developed accurate calendars, not just of the solar year but of the moon, planet Venus, stars, and perhaps even eclipses. Astronomical tables are the main subject of the four surviving Maya codices; they were more precise than any found in the European or even Arab world at the time.

One of the most important priestly tasks was the planning of cities. Researchers believe that many of the main features of these cities were aligned with the appearance of a heavenly phenomenon at a certain propitious date. A priest watching the skies saw the rise of a bright star or planet above a prominent mountain on the horizon and declared that an imaginary line between himself, the hill, and the bright planet would become the city's main axis. For instance, the great grid of Teotihuacan appears to have aligned to the appearance of the Pleiades star group above the Cerro Colorado to the west on a day in 150 B.C., about the time archaeologists believe the city was founded.

Once this first orientation to the stars or planets was in place, construction of the ceremonial center began. Almost every one of the major centers contained a structure that was a replica of their cosmological vision. The Aztec Great Temple was built in 13 tiers representing the stages of heaven; Earth was the platform on which the temple rested. Researchers believe the Nunnery complex at Uxmal may also duplicate the Universe on Earth. The highest struc-

Cenote of Sacrifice. After a stroll of about 200 meters, you reach the rim of the cenote, where you find a small snack bar, gift shop, and the ruins of some small Maya structures. The cenote measures 60 meters in diameter; its limestone walls drop 22 meters to the murky green water's surface, and the bottom lies 6–12 meters below.

The cenote has been a pilgrimage destination for more than a millennium—archaeologists found a crude rubber offering doll dating to the early 1900s in

ture, the North Building, has 13 doorways, while the low South Building opposite has nine doorways, the same number as the levels of the Underworld. Some of these structures also probably symbolize the creation myth of the Universe; the cave underneath Teotihuacan's Pyramid of the Sun was the womb from which the original gods emerged.

Among the many significant dates in the astronomical calendar, the most important were the solar zeniths—when the sun was directly overhead—occurring in late April and mid-August in much of Mexico. The first zenith passage marked the time to begin clearing the fields for planting, while the second signaled the arrival of rain and winds. Many Mesoamerican temples, such as the Building of Five Stories at Edzná, were built so that rays from the setting sun at the solar zenith shone directly onto a sculpture on the rear wall. At centers such as Xochicalco and Monte Albán, priests built underground observatories through which beams of sunlight blazed at noon on the zenith.

While nearly every major Mesoamerican structure was aligned to the skies, the priests also built a special class of structures whose role appears to have been as observatories. The most famous of these is the circular structure atop the Caracol at Chichén Itzá. Researchers were long puzzled by the asymmetrically placed doors in each ring of the tower—some ascribed it to sloppy design. The popular science writer Anthony F. Aveni has shown that these doors line up to a number of important "heavenly" events, such as the sunset at the summer sol-

stice. Most of the alignments relate to the planet Venus, the brightest object in the nighttime sky after the moon, which was important throughout Mesoamerica. Venus is particularly portentous at Chichén because it is the celestial manifestation of Kukulcan, the city's principal deity. Another probable observatory is Monte Albán's Building J, which breaks with the main north-south alignment of the site to aim at the rising of the star Capella on the solar zenith date.

If the heavens could bring structure to Mesoamerican cultures, they could also rock them to their foundations. In 1512, three comets unheralded by priestly astronomers appeared in the nighttime sky. Because they were unexpected, Nezahualpilli, the ruler of Texcoco and a reputed magician, interpreted them as portents of doom for whole kingdoms, including Motecuhzoma's Aztec empire. The last Aztec emperor took them seriously. In a tribute to the power of astronomy over the earthy realm, he lamented:

O almighty god in whose hands lies the power of life and death over mortals. How can you permit that after the passing of many powerful rulers, it should fall to my lot to witness the terrible destruction of Mexico, and that I should suffer the death of my wives and children and live to see myself dispossessed of my great kingdoms and principalities and of my vassals and of all that the Mexicans have conquered by their strong right arm and by the valour and spirit that lies within their breasts? What shall I do? Where shall I hide?

DANIELLE GUSTAFSON

the Caracol, with the Castillo in the background

its depths. Although it was used as a water source, its primary function seems to have been as a place of ritual (and perhaps a garbage dump). The ritual was to hurl offerings into its waters. These offerings included precious objects, such as gold disks engraved with scenes of kingly battle, and sacrificial victims. Many of the human remains found here—mostly men—had been clubbed in the head before being offered to the gods. With an ice-cold soda in your hand, you can sit in the shade and contemplate their fate.

If you return to the Main Plaza and turn west (right), the first structure you reach is the Tzompantli, the 60-meter-long skull platform, possibly an import from central Mexico. It takes its name from the four layers of stone skulls along its sides; archaeologists presume that real skulls were skewered on wooden racks above. On either side of its staircase, relief panels represent warriors and eagles devouring hearts. A plumed serpent twines along the frieze above.

Just to the south of this structure stands the small Platform of the Eagles and Jaguars, a four-sided *talud-tablero* building. The *tablero* reliefs depict jaguars and eagles eating hearts, while above them you see reclining deified warriors. Serpent heads protrude from the top sides of the staircase.

To the west lies Chichén's famous Great Ballcourt, one of 13 at the site and the largest found in Mesoamerica. You approach the long platform at the east side of the court, with a wide ruined staircase flanked by serpents facing you. At the south end of this platform rises the two-story Temple of the Jaguars, a late addition to the structure. A stone jaguar throne stands in front of its entrance. Behind the two columns, the walls and vaulted ceiling of the room beyond are covered with reliefs. The scene is hard to make out but includes a battle and a procession of armed dignitaries. The upper room is unfortunately off-limits. Its walls are decorated with a huge and complicated (and fading) mural showing an enormous battle on the outskirts of a Maya village. This room looks out from between two squat serpent columns over the ballcourt.

Above, the facade is adorned with feathered serpent heads, jaguars, and "shields," among other motifs.

If you walk around the corner, you enter the vast court, measuring 168 meters by 70 meters. This is built in the central Mexican style with vertical walls set with carved rings. Along the base of the wall runs a sloping panel whose centers are carved with elaborate reliefs depicting the final ceremony of the ballgame. In both scenes, rows of players stand to the left and right facing the center. In the middle is the giant ball itself with a skull inside. To the left stands a player holding a knife in one hand and a severed head in the other. Facing him kneels the source of that head, a vanquished player with snakes representing blood spurting forth from his neck (some sort of plant seems to emerge from here as well). All the players wear their complicated game "uniforms," and numerous symbolic motifs float in between them. On either end of this panel, you see further carvings, including serpents. You have a good view of the Temple of the Jaguars from here.

At the north end of the Great Ballcourt rises the North Temple atop a short, steep pyramid. Its top is off-limits, but behind two circular columns you can see remains of reliefs outlined with red paint. These depict lush scenes of nature with trees and birds. Further carvings adorn the jambs and the sides of the staircase. The wide South Temple, a long structure faced with six carved warrior columns, stands at the opposite end of the court.

The last leg of our tour covers the site's Old Chichén zone, so-called because all archaeologists agree that it predates the Main Plaza and surrounding structures. One hundred meters south of the Castillo, a path (actually a *sacbe*) heads out of the Main Plaza. About 150 meters farther, you come to a platform that is a smaller copy of the Venus Platform, but not as well-made. This is part of a line of three platforms, including a round one and a reddish structure with a twined serpent along its top wall and six carved columns above (two tombs were recently found within).

These structures stand in the plaza fronting the High Priest's Grave, also called the Ossuary, rising to the west. This small pyramid may have been the model for the Castillo. Archaeologists have found a natural cave below its foundations—the probable reason for its location. Four staircases flanked with plumed serpents climb seven tiers to a one-room temple. Inside, you find four square warrior columns. The ground around the pyramid base is strewn with stone carvings from above. Archaeologists have rebuilt part of the temple facade just to the southwest.

As you continue south, the next structure on the path is the Red House, also called the Chichanchob, facing west. The temple stands atop a sloping platform; three doorways open into a long room with three smaller chambers beyond (the plan resembles some of Palenque's temples). Above, the roofcomb is decorated with three large, long-snouted masks. The structure takes its name from traces of red paint on a long glyphic inscription inside along the east vaulted roof. The text gives the name of some early Chichén rulers: Yax-Uk-Kauil, Kakupakal, and Hun-Pin-Tok. The Red House faces a small plaza, on the north side of which stands the similar House of the Deer, named after a now-destroyed mural.

The path continues about 150 meters to the Nunnery, a long, low palace bearing many Puuc and/or Chenes motifs. This was actually two separate buildings that were joined by a later construction. At the east end, you see the stunning entrance to the East Annex, with a huge serpent mouth around the doorway, a seated ruler surrounded by plumes above, and stacks of long-snouted masks. The north face of the Nunnery is dominated by a huge staircase rising to a late temple built on top of an eight-room Puuc-style residence with stone mosaic facades.

To the east of this complex stands the "Church." The lower facade is simple, while above rises a wildly ornate frieze of step-and-fret motifs, long-snouted masks, and serpent designs. Niches on each side of the central mask contain small seated figures. In the light of the setting sun, the whole facade glows a beautiful pink. The building just to the northeast is the Temple of the Reliefs, facing west with two rows of columns on top and two rooms behind. From here, a path runs 100 meters east to the Akab Dzib, a wide Puuc-style residence with more than a dozen rooms and long-snouted masks along the top frieze. One of the interior doorways contained a lintel carved with a seated ruler and a long inscription including a date, probably A.D. 869.

The last structure on this tour is the Caracol (Snail) standing just to the north of the Temple of the Reliefs. This is a large platform measuring 67 meters by 52 meters on top of which, at a slightly skewed angle, stands another platform with hollow stone heads facing out from along its wall. The latter structure is crowned by the circular Observatory, which is separated from the platform by a sort of moat. J. Eric S. Thompson, the preeminent Mayanist for most of the 20th century, described it as "a 2-decker wedding cake on the square carton in which it came." Around its frieze, long-snouted masks look out in the four directions (but skewed about 10°); small faces peer from between their eyes. Inside, you find another circular structure containing what appears to be a solid masonry column in the middle (like a missile in a silo). Archaeoastronomers have proved that the Observatory's windows are aligned to important positions of the planet Venus and to the sun's rise and set at its zeniths and on the summer solstice. From the platform, you have an excellent view toward the Castillo looming over the trees to the north.

This ends our tour of the main Chichén sights. Many more structures lurk in the surrounding forest. The best lie along a path, actually Sacbe 7, heading south from the Nunnery. In about 2.5 kilometers, you come to the Temple of the Four Lintels and the Temple of the Three Lintels, both classic Puuc structures adorned with reliefs. Closer to the ceremonial center, to the west of this path lie the Main Southeast Group and the Temple of Sculptured Jambs.

BALANKANCHÉ CAVE

INTRODUCTION

Caves are sacred ground throughout Mesoamerica; it was in their depths that rulers communed with their gods. Lying six kilometers east of Chichén Itzá, the cave of the Balankanché (sometimes spelled Balamkanché) was a sacred ceremonial space for that city's Mexicanized, perhaps Toltec, elite—the word "Balankanché" means "jaguar throne." In 1959, archaeologists discovered a hidden series of rooms containing dozens of perfectly preserved incense burners shaped like the head of Tlaloc, the central Mexican Rain God. No images belonging to Maya gods have been found here—this cave was apparently a kind of VIP room reserved for central Mexicans. Local Yucatec Maya shamans continue to hold ceremonies in its sacred spaces.

HISTORY

According to preliminary excavations, the cave has been intermittently used since at least the Late Preclassic (300 B.C.–A.D. 250). The most intense concentration of ceramic artifacts comes from the end of the Classic and the beginning of the Early Postclassic, about A.D. 850–1100. The cave's use drops off sharply after the fall of Chichén Itzá. Almost all the artifacts are whole or fragmentary incense burners and other offerings, such as miniature grindstones. This indicates that Balankanché's function was almost always as a ritual space and not as a dwelling.

ARCHAEOLOGICAL RECORD

Balankanché was always known to the local Yucatec Maya. In 1932, a Carnegie Institution study under A.S. Pearse explored the cave while searching for rare cave fauna. Among the cave's natural inhabitants are blind fish, schools of cave shrimp, and a kind of venomous arthropod. A Carnegie Institution archaeological expedition followed and dug some test pits at the cave entrance and inside. The great treasures remained hidden, however.

In 1959, José Humberto Gómez, a local tour guide who made the study of the

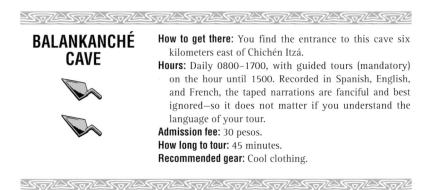

BALANKANCHÉ CAVE

How to get there: You find the entrance to this cave six kilometers east of Chichén Itzá.

Hours: Daily 0800–1700, with guided tours (mandatory) on the hour until 1500. Recorded in Spanish, English, and French, the taped narrations are fanciful and best ignored—so it does not matter if you understand the language of your tour.

Admission fee: 30 pesos.

How long to tour: 45 minutes.

Recommended gear: Cool clothing.

cave his hobby, discovered that one of the walls was actually sealed with crude masonry. When he knocked it down, he discovered that the cave extended for hundreds of meters farther. He explored and stumbled on large assemblages of perfectly preserved clay and stone offerings clustered around natural rock formations. He reported his find to his employer, Fernando Barbachano of the well-known Barbachano Travel Service in Mérida, who notified the authorities. Almost immediately, an archaeological team was assembled.

The excavation was led by E. Wyllys Andrews IV of Tulane University, who was on his way to digging Dzibilchaltun, aided by INAH and the National Geographic Society. They mapped the new caverns, studied the offering groups, and collected surface pottery fragments from throughout the system. Early in their work, a local shaman contacted them and informed them that they had dis-

incense burners, miniature manos, and metates in Balankanché Cave

DANIELLE GUSTAFSON

turbed the cave deities, who must be propitiated. The shamans led the archaeologists in a 17-hour Maya ritual accompanied by frequent swigs of an indigenous grog. The major danger during the exploration was lack of oxygen; unlike the Loltun Cave, Balankanché has only one entrance, so they could work for only a few hours at a time before returning to the outside. The project was wrapped up in five weeks (Andrews had to go to Dzibilchaltun); the report contains a recording of the shaman's incantation. Since then, the major work at the cave has been making the system more accessible to tourists.

Mano and metate are the two stone parts of a corn-grinding device. The metate is the curved tray that the kernels are placed on; the mano is an oval stone that is rubbed across the metate to grind the grain.

TOURING THE SITE

On the border of the parking lot, you see the ruins of a few small structures built around the cave entrance. From the cave entrance, you descend about 10 meters and then walk due south about 350 meters. Your stroll is accompanied by a fairly awful taped musical and spoken soundtrack purporting to dramatize the cave's ritual use. The air is steamy and hot.

The path ends at a large circular room, a kind of natural theater with caverns branching to the east and west. In the center stands a huge limestone stalactite running from floor to ceiling surrounded by the Group I offering. These are made up of 29 incense censers, all with pinched waists. Some are studded, while others bear the goggle-eyed mask of Tlaloc, the central Mexican Rain God. The pots lie in hollows carved from stalagmite formations rising from the floor. A stone incense burner is carved with a little warrior holding an atlatl (throwing stick). He appears to wear a face mask of human skin; if so, this would make him a representation of Xipe Totec, the central Mexican flayed god. You also see a few miniature manos and metates—grindstones—and two red handprints on the central column.

The walkway continues to the left into the larger Group II room. In front of one wall drops a row of stalactites that acts as a backdrop to a group of six (originally 19) studded and Tlaloc-faced censers. These were filled with ashes and beads made from jade, bone, and shell. Small grindstones lie in front.

In the next chamber (the last open to the public), the Group III offering lies on the banks of an underground stream. These include dozens of tiny grindstones and a few more incense burners. Smaller offerings were found in the caverns beyond and along the passageway heading west of Group I.

MAYAPAN

INTRODUCTION

The centuries following the fall of Chichén Itzá were a time of unrest and movement. Tribes wandered around the Maya lowlands seeking homes in which to build new dynasties. The most powerful of these tribes was the Itzá group that built Mayapan, the dominant Postclassic center of northern Yucatan. They surrounded their city with a wall—a tribute to the times—and built their main structures in emulation of Chichén. Their architecture never reached the heights of that of their predecessors, however; archaeologists have called them "drab" and "a flash in the Mayapan." (The contrast between the glorious historical accounts and the shabby reality admittedly influenced their opinions.) In A.D. 1450, racked by internal dissension, Mayapan too was abandoned. After visiting Chichén or Uxmal, touring Mayapan is an object lesson in poor city planning.

HISTORY

Within Mayapan's city walls lie 26 natural cenotes—an abundant source of water. Settlers were attracted to this site as early as the Late Preclassic (300 B.C.–A.D. 250), but their villages remained small for more than a millennium.

After the fall of Chichén, in the 13th century A.D., a group of Itzá wandered over Yucatan seeking a new home. They settled at Chichén itself for a few years but between A.D. 1263 and 1283 moved to Mayapan and made it the seat of their lineage. Mayapan quickly rose to become the most powerful city-state in northern Yucatan, raiding Izamal among other neighbors. In A.D. 1380, an inter-

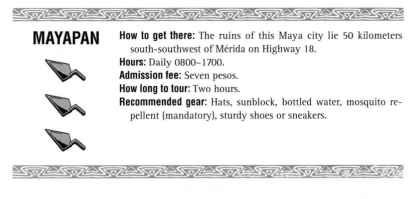

MAYAPAN   **How to get there:** The ruins of this Maya city lie 50 kilometers south-southwest of Mérida on Highway 18.
Hours: Daily 0800–1700.
Admission fee: Seven pesos.
How long to tour: Two hours.
Recommended gear: Hats, sunblock, bottled water, mosquito repellent (mandatory), sturdy shoes or sneakers.

nal revolt toppled Mayapan's rulers and a group of the Cocom lineage assumed power. Around A.D. 1440, they in turn were ousted by the Xiu lineage (the foreign interlopers who had settled at Uxmal), but the dissension was too much, and by A.D. 1450 Mayapan was abandoned. The Itzá resumed their wandering life and ended up on an island in Lake Petén in Guatemala. There, they defended a remarkable pure Maya state until they were finally overthrown by the Spaniards in 1697.

ARCHAEOLOGICAL RECORD

BOB RACE

Mayapan was the most famous Maya city in 16th-century native and Spanish historical accounts, including *Books of Chilam Balam* and Diego de Landa's version. The name supposedly means "banner of the Maya," referring to the region controlled by Mayapan. The early chroniclers took the name "Maya" and applied it to the millions of native inhabitants populating the lands from southern Mexico all the way to Costa Rica.

In 1841, John Lloyd Stephens and Frederick Catherwood spent a day at Mayapan. Two decades later, Brasseur de Bourbourg explored and mapped the ruins, including the city wall. He discovered Stela 1 and was the first to note that Mayapan's Temple of Kukulcan was a copy of Chichén's Castillo.

After Augustus Le Plongeon visited in 1881, there is a long gap until Sylvanus G. Morley's 1918 tour. This began the era of Carnegie Institution investigations at the site. In 1938, R. T. Patton produced the first full-scale map of the entire city and ceremonial center. Four years later, George Brainerd spent two weeks at Mayapan digging stratigraphic trenches as part of his work on Yucatan's ceramic sequences.

The Carnegie Institution's work culminated in the 1952–57 project led by Harry E. D. Pollock with the assistance of Ralph Roys, Tatiana Proskouriakoff, and A. Ledyard Smith. Their work included mapping, excavations, architectural investigations, and studies of the early historical accounts, all collected in an excellent 1962 report.

Since 1996, the Proyecto Mayapan, directed by Carlos Alberto Peraza Lope, has restored many of the structures in the site's Central Plaza and made a number of important discoveries. Among these are murals in the Temple of the Painted Niches and the Room of the Frescoes, as well as some remarkable stucco reliefs of decapitated warriors on the south side of the Castillo.

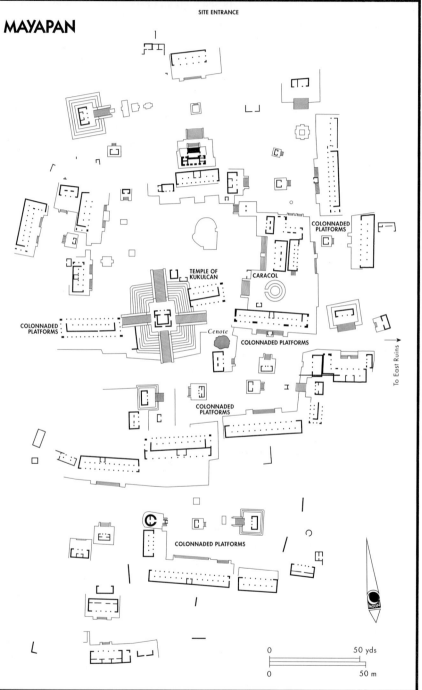

MAYAPAN

SITE ENTRANCE

COLONNADED
PLATFORMS

TEMPLE OF
KUKULCAN

CARACOL

COLONNADED
PLATFORMS

Cenote

COLONNADED PLATFORMS

To East Ruins

COLONNADED
PLATFORMS

COLONNADED PLATFORMS

0   50 yds
0   50 m

TOURING THE SITE

You enter the ruins from the north. House mounds are scattered on either side of the road; the remarkable 1957 city map resembles a slightly skewed pizza with nearly every square inch pocked with at least 10 tiny dwellings.

Seventy-five meters to the south of the parking lot, you enter the ceremonial center. The recent reconstruction has greatly improved the appearance of the buildings, though archaeologists still call them lesser copies of those at Chichén Itzá. One problem faced by the city's builders was that the stone in Mayapan's immediate vicinity is poor; researchers believe they may have scavenged their veneer from neighboring settlements.

You enter a small plaza; on the west stands a four-stage platform with a small temple on top. Two awkwardly carved serpent columns guard its doorway. Next, you walk past low colonnaded platforms to another plaza, at the south side of which rises Mayapan's most famous structure, the nine-tiered Temple of Kukulcan.

This is a smaller, shoddier version of the Castillo at Chichén Itzá. Staircases rise on all four sides to a square three-room temple, with two serpent columns facing north from the main doorway. From the summit, to the south you can see the Sierrita de Ticul—the hills on the northern border of the Puuc region—and the chimneys of a few henequen plantation haciendas. An earlier pyramid has been found within, and a carbon 14 test performed on a platform below its base established a date of A.D. 1015, before the arrival of the Itzá. Perhaps it is

DANIELLE GUSTAFSON

Mayapan's Castillo before the recent reconstruction

because of the reconstruction, but the temple's angles do not look true, and the staircases do not line up. Another problem with the Temple of Kukulcan's presentation is that it is not given room to breathe; low colonnaded halls are built up against its base to the east and west—in the latter case blocking the staircase. The great Maya tradition of city planning seems to have been lost at Mayapan.

Along the south side of the Castillo, you see corrugated roofs covering the recently uncovered stucco reliefs of decapitated warriors. Where the heads would be you see a niche large enough to hold a skull—perhaps real decapitated heads were placed here!

As you head east, a platform holds the Caracol, a spiral structure built around a solid core that is presumed to be a copy of Chichén's observatory.

Many of the other ceremonial center structures are long hallways faced with colonnades. According to historical accounts, these were used as council halls for lineage groups and as schools and dormitories for youths being trained in their adult responsibilities. If you head east from the Caracol, in about 100 meters you come to a small platform with a smaller round structure on top. A few more temple platforms lie in this area, as do dozens of house mounds.

COBÁ

INTRODUCTION

Before the Itzá invasion, the northern Yucatan Peninsula was divided between the Puuc in the west and the great city of Cobá near the Quintana Roo coast. Cobá is most famous for its *sacbeob,* the raised causeways that ran to the farthest reaches of its realm; one extended 100 kilometers due west to Yaxuná. The site itself is set among a network of small lakes—a rarity in Yucatan—between which cut the straight causeways linking the temple groups. Unlike most other northern centers, Cobá is built in the "orthodox" style of the Petén Jungle: steep pyramids surrounded by Classic Maya stelae such as found at Tikal and other southern sites. Cobá's glory was ended by the Itzá, who captured the city around A.D. 1000. It gradually dwindled into a pilgrimage center; ceremonies are still performed in the temples today.

HISTORY

Water drew the first settlers to Cobá in the Late Preclassic (300 B.C.–A.D. 250). Here, they found higher rainfall than on the coast and a group of five small lakes teeming with fish. During the Early Classic (A.D. 250–600), their village grew into a regional center with strong ties to the Petén Jungle to the south.

Cobá reached its apogee during the end of the Late Classic period (A.D. 600–900). It grew into the dominant center of northeastern Yucatan, with a network of causeways, probably the longest in the Maya world, connecting it with many important satellite towns. Its empire probably covered well over 4,000 square kilometers. It built at least five Petén-style temple groups around the lakes and began recording important events on stelae, the first dated A.D. 623. One of these stelae contains a remarkable date recording the beginning of the current Maya era—3188 B.C.—which ends after 13 cycles of 400 years on December 23, 2012. Dikes and dams protected the precious water in the lakes; the surrounding country supported a population of 40,000–60,000—the largest in the northern lowlands.

Between A.D. 900 and 1000, like many Classic Maya centers, Cobá began to decline. The effort of competing with the Itzá at Chichén and building that 100-kilometer causeway may have put too much strain on its resources. The Itzá eventually took over Cobá and used it as a civic-ceremonial center (with a smaller population), building numerous temple shrines around its main pyramid groups.

After Chichén fell, the regional powers were Mayapan and some Quintana Roo coastal centers who used Cobá as a pilgrimage destination. When Tulum rose after Mayapan's abandonment, its rulers erected some small and poorly made temples on top of the pyramids. The region was mainly abandoned by 1546, although a few farmers and hunters continued to live in the area and perform rituals on their ancestors' great constructions.

ARCHAEOLOGICAL RECORD

In the 19th century, the east coast of the Yucatan Peninsula—the present State of Quintana Roo—was the wildest place in Mexico. It was covered by impassable

COBÁ

How to get there: Most visitors reach this Quintana Roo site via the road heading 42 kilometers northwest from Tulum. You can also take a paved road from Nuevo X-Can on Highway 180 about halfway between Valladolid and Cancún.

Hours: Daily 0800–1900 in the summer; 0700–1800 in the winter.

Admission fee: 30 pesos.

How long to tour: Three hours, more if you want to explore.

Recommended gear: Hats, sunblock, bottled water, mosquito repellent, hiking boots.

Food and accommodations: The Restaurant El Bocadito in tiny Cobá town rents simple rooms, but the best accommodation by far is the Villa Arqueológica, tel. 987/420-87, from the U.S. 800/258-2633, which contains some ruins on the grounds.

forest; no roads connected it to the rest of the country; and a group of Yucatec Maya revolutionaries had formed their own state here. The first intrepid adventurers to brave these forests and reach Cobá were José Peón Contreras and D. Elizade, who explored and sketched the ruins in 1886. They were followed in 1891 by Teobert Maler and his excellent camera.

The first excavations were performed between 1926 and 1930 by a Carnegie Institution expedition led by J. Eric S. Thompson, Harry Pollock, and Jean Charlot. They mapped the ceremonial center, explored the *sacbeob,* and discovered most of the stelae known from the site. Around the same time, Professor Alonso Villas Rojos explored the entire 100-kilometer length of the *sacbe* from Cobá to Yaxuná.

The next period of investigations began in 1974 under INAH's Centro Regional del Sureste. The *sacbeob* were once again a focus of interest, and they also produced (with the help of the National Geographic Society) a large-scale map of the ancient city. In 1975, they began the excavation and restoration of the major pyramids and returned in 1980 to dig test pits for stratigraphic studies. In 1983 and 1984, a joint INAH and UNAM team led by Antonio Benavides and Linda Manzanilla performed a study of Cobá's residential zones that is the most in-depth work to date on the ancient Maya "proletariat." Since then, almost all of the work performed at the site has been salvage and consolidation.

TOURING THE SITE

The parking area lies by the side of Lake Cobá, the largest of five lakes at the site, just southeast of town. The lake may flood the entrance road during the rainy season. About 50 meters to the right of the entrance rises the Cobá Group, the most important temple complex found at the site.

You first come to two poorly preserved stelae under a thatched roof behind which is a large stepped platform that is the base of the Iglesia (Church), also called the Cobá Pyramid. In front stands the worn Stela 11 with only a grid that once held glyphs. According to local lore, these stelae were carved by a tribe of dwarves who were Cobá's first inhabitants.

The Iglesia has been only partially restored; its sides were originally covered with polychrome stucco decorations, possibly including god masks. You climb about 75 worn steps (slippery in the rain) and then scramble the rest of the way to a late Tulum-style temple on top ("shoddy" according to archaeologists). An offering found here contained a censer and miniature grindstone in the style of those found in the Balankanché Cave. If you look to the northeast, you can see the Nohoch Mul temples rising over the forest about two kilometers away. On the way down, you see the remains of some rooms—late additions—on either side of a landing about 15 steps from the bottom.

Behind the Iglesia lies a large assemblage of ruined buildings still covered with forest. On its east side, you find two ruined buildings and then a vaulted

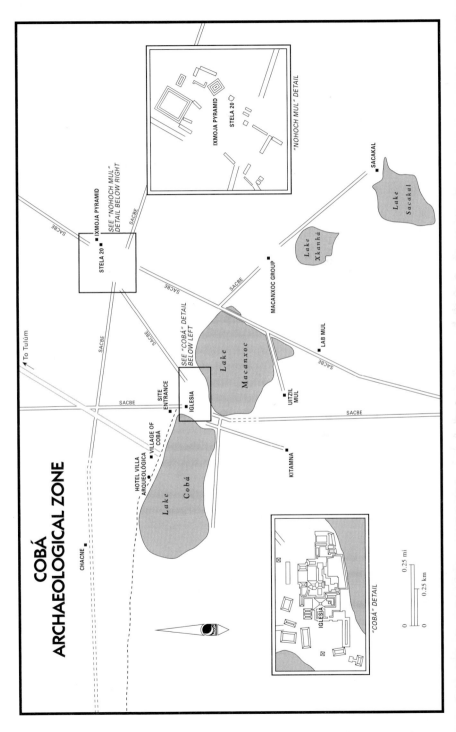

COBÁ
ARCHAEOLOGICAL ZONE

To Tulúm

CHACNE

HOTEL VILLA
ARQUEOLÓGICA

VILLAGE OF
COBÁ

SITE
ENTRANCE

IGLESIA

SACBE

SACBE

SACBE

SACBE

SACBE

SACBE

SACBE

SACBE

STELA 20

IXMOJA PYRAMID

SEE "NOHOCH MUL"
DETAIL BELOW RIGHT

SEE "COBÁ" DETAIL
BELOW LEFT

Lake
Cobá

Lake
Macanxoc

MACANXOC GROUP

Lake
Xkanhá

Lake
Sacakal

SACAKAL

LAB MUL

UITZIL
MUL

KITAMNA

"NOHOCH MUL" DETAIL

IXMOJA PYRAMID

STELA 20

"COBÁ" DETAIL

IGLESIA

0   0.25 mi

0   0.25 km

Iglesia pyramid steps

hallway running under a staircase. From the top of this stairway, a path runs over the mounds and then down the hillside to the shore of Lake Macanxoc, the second of Cobá's lakes. You can see the remains of the Uitzil Mul temple group bulging above the opposite shore.

Return to the Iglesia; on its north side stands a small overgrown ballcourt aligned on a north-south axis. You can see a fragment of one ring on the west side and, opposite, the remains of a vaulted room on top of the platform. Next, a thatched roof covers a heavily eroded circular altar.

From the ballcourt, a path heads right toward the other main temple groups. After about a kilometer, you come to a fork in the road. The left takes you to the Nohoch Mul, while the right leads to the Macanxoc Group and the Temple of the Pictures. This tour will follow the latter path. A one-kilometer walk along an ancient causeway takes you to the Macanxoc Group. Along the way, the path is crossed by numerous leafcutter ant trails.

The path arrives at the famous Stela 1, covered by a roof. One of eight stelae found here, this one shows a Cobá wearing a headdress and carrying a large ritual staff in his arms. He stands on two bound captives bending over in submission, while two more captives lie in supplication to the left and right. Around the edges are lines of worn glyphic inscriptions. Behind rise the unreconstructed temple mounds of the Macanxoc Group, one with a second ruler-and-captives stela at its base. From the top of the largest mound, you can see the Nohoch Mul Group through the trees to the north. To the south lies the small Lake Xkanhá. Five more worn stelae stand in a little clearing about 75 meters south of the Macanxoc Group.

You return a short way down the plaza and then turn left to the Temple of the Pictures. This is a group of about five tiered platforms built around a plaza with the remains of colonnaded temples on top. Most of these structures date to the Early Postclassic (A.D. 900–1250). On top of the Temple of the Pictures itself stands a late, Tulum-style temple with the remains of blue and red murals, including glyphs, on the frieze and lintel. The walls are darkened by smoke. Most of the murals were removed in the 1970s for placement in an as-yet-unbuilt Cobá museum. On the ground in front of this temple, archaeologists found more than a dozen altars and stelae dating from the Tulum era.

THE YUCATEC MAYA

As the tourist buses speed by on the straight highways of the Yucatan Peninsula, the air-conditioned passengers might notice outside their windows trim little houses with thatched roofs and whitewashed walls. Each house sits in a yard containing fruit and shade trees and surrounded by stone walls. Turkeys and almost always a pig or two are running loose in the yard, and the hurrying tourists might glimpse the lady of the house, an Indian woman wearing a *huipil*, a white dress with elaborate embroidery around the square collar. Men are visible too, perhaps walking down the bumpy street between the house plots with hoes on their shoulders. Though the peninsula has been taken over by tourism and *maquiladora* factories, it remains the homeland of the Yucatec Maya.

Most Yucatec Maya villages and small towns are built around a Catholic church, frequently massive and fortresslike, dating to the early colonial era. Despite this presence, Christian beliefs play only a small part in the local Maya religious system. Life in these villages revolves around the milpa, the cornfield just beyond the outskirts. The milpa is ruled by a series of willful, powerful gods who are the "owners" of the wind, the rain, the soil, and the corn itself. To propitiate these deities and gain a good harvest, the farmers consult the town h-men, or shaman, who tells them what prayers, ceremonies, and offerings are needed. The five Rain

Gods are the most frequent recipients of offerings, though the Maya also perform rites to the "great father bee" (beekeeping is common), the deer and geese gods, and the protector deity of each town. The h-men is also consulted when sorcery is suspected and to cure illnesses using his wide knowledge of native botany.

Given Yucatan's history, it is amazing that these beliefs have persisted. After the Conquest, the Spaniards forcibly converted the Yucatec Maya while making every effort to destroy their native culture; the Maya were then stripped of their political and economic power and worked as slaves on the Spanish haciendas. There were many attempts at revolt, most successfully in the War of the Castes beginning in 1847. Maya rebels began attacking haciendas in eastern Yucatan and then, with an army that had grown into the tens of thousands, marched toward the capital of Mérida. Local troops and later the Mexican army eventually turned the tide and pushed the Maya back into the unexplored jungles of what is now Quintana Roo. Here, the Indians built a traditional Maya state around the cult of the Talking Cross in the town of Chan Santa Cruz (now called Felipe Carillo Puerto). Their independence lasted until they were finally defeated by Mexican troops in 1901. There nevertheless remain Yucatec Maya, particularly in southern Quintana Roo, who are unhappy with rule from Mexico City. If incited, the Talking Cross could speak again.

Along the path heading west from this group, you encounter two more stelae showing standing figures holding staffs. This path runs into the main road to the Nohoch Mul Group. About 300 meters to the northeast, you encounter two ruined pyramids with three stelae lying in the plaza between them.

Finally, you arrive at a small temple platform marking the outskirts of the Nohoch Mul Group. The platform holds Stela 20, the best-preserved at the site, again showing a ruler standing on two captives with two more crouching on either side.

To the left, 40 meters behind, stands the massive Ixmoja pyramid, rising 42 meters, the highest at the site. Only its top, stairway, and right side have been consolidated. A broken stela bearing glyphs lies just to the left of the stairs. As you climb, you reach a small landing holding a broken stela under a thatched roof. On top stands a small temple built in the late Tulum style, with diving gods and small and shoddy temples. Along its facade were three niches containing stucco reliefs of diving gods (the same as those found at Tulum). In Cobá, they are associated with Ah Muzen Cab, the local deity who rules over the production of honey, a Cobá specialty. The small doorway leads into a simple vaulted room. From the top, you have an excellent view over the forest and pyramid ruins extending to the southwest.

Many more ruins extend into the surrounding forest. In two, the remains of residential structures lie behind the Villa Arqueológica Hotel.

TULUM

INTRODUCTION

On a cliff overlooking the crashing waves of the Caribbean, Tulum possesses one of the most spectacular locations in Mesoamerica. This was a Maya port of trade serviced by giant seagoing canoes of the type seen by Columbus on his last voyage. The traders carried not only goods (particularly cacao beans) but new forms of religion and political organization from central Mexico. The walls of Tulum's temples are decorated with murals in the "international" style of sites such as Mitla, i.e., pancentral Mexican style; they even include four-legged animals that probably represent horses. The latter is a sign that Tulum continued as a Maya city until decades after the Spanish Conquest. Today, Tulum is one of the most visited sites in Mexico, host of thousands of tourists a day arriving from Cancún and other resorts—arrive early!

HISTORY

Tulum stands on a row of steep cliffs next to a small cove that doubled as a landing area—its port. It was always linked with the settlement of Tancah, which lies a few kilometers to the north. The region was first settled around 300 B.C. by coast-dwellers who ate marine mollusks and turtles. Because of their seaside location, these inhabitants always remained more open to outside influences than those dwelling inland, at Cobá for example.

Around A.D. 770, a new influence appears in the region's ceramic record. Seagoing traders added Tulum-Tancah as a trading port on their route from the Gulf Coast to the southern Caribbean coasts of Belize and Guatemala. These were probably the Putún Maya long-distance merchants who also influenced Uxmal and many other northern Yucatan settlements. Although it lies only 40 kilometers to the northwest, it is unclear if Tulum ever fell within the Late Classic empire of Cobá. Archaeologists have found a Classic-era stela at Tulum but believe that it was carved elsewhere and transported here centuries later.

Through the Early Postclassic, Tancah was always the dominant settlement and Tulum a small village. After A.D. 1200, Tulum underwent a boom. Many of its early temples bear similarities to the Itzá structures of Mayapan. This influence disappears around A.D. 1440, when once again you see the strong hand of central Mexico appearing on the coast. Bright Mixtec-style murals were painted on Tulum's temple walls, perhaps by artists imported from central Mexico. Their subject matter, however, is purely local: rows of Maya gods.

During this period, Tulum reached its highest point as a trading center, enclosing a population of around 600 with a huge defensive wall. Its rulers built many additions to Tulum's main temples; for some unknown reason, they are extremely poorly made—they seem to have forgotten the techniques of fine Maya architecture. They also traveled to Cobá and erected more small and

TULUM

How to get there: Tulum's popular ruins lie on Highway 307 about 130 kilometers down the Quintana Roo coast from Cancún and 95 kilometers north of Felipe Carillo Puerto.

Hours: Daily 0800–1900 in the summer; 0700–1800 in the winter.

Admission fee: 30 pesos.

How long to tour: Two hours.

Recommended gear: Hats, sunblock, bottled water, sturdy shoes or sneakers.

Food and accommodations: A number of spartan beachfront "hotels" (usually wooden huts) are south of the site; for higher-end accommodations with running water and 24-hour electricity, you will have to head north to Akumal. There are a number of inexpensive restaurants in Tulum town.

shoddy temples on top of its largest pyramids. In A.D. 1518, the expedition of Juan de Grijalva sailed up the coast and noted a city with white towers like Seville—almost certainly Tulum. The port lasted decades after the Conquest, and it was probably abandoned after European diseases decimated its population.

ARCHAEOLOGICAL RECORD

The first explorers to describe Tulum were once again John Lloyd Stephens and Frederick Catherwood on their 1841 expedition across Yucatan. They saw brightly colored murals covering both the inside and outside of many of the temples. The region's obscurity and the modest scale of the ruins stemmed further exploration until early in the 20th century. In 1924, a Carnegie Institution team under Samuel K. Lothrop began the first of three seasons at Tulum studying its architecture and murals and exploring Tancah. Their photos of the massive forest covering the temples are an incredible contrast with today.

From 1937 to1940, the Expedición Científica Mexicana surveyed the entire territory of Quintana Roo and discovered dozens of ancient ruins. Miguel Ángel Fernández of this party spent four seasons at Tulum studying and restoring the murals, which had greatly faded since Stephens's day. In 1955, William T. Sanders of the Carnegie Institution dug some ceramic stratigraphic test pits at Tulum and Tancah and worked out a preliminary chronology for the region.

The last major study was Arthur Miller's 1972–76 Tancah-Tulum project sponsored by Dumbarton Oaks. He excavated many of Tancah's structures and, with the help of Felipe Dávalos, recorded every mural they could find at the two sites. Since then, almost all the work at Tulum has focused on restoration and making the ruins more accessible to tourists.

TOURING THE SITE

The entrance has been moved away from the site. Now you have to pass through a large new artisans' market and walk one kilometer or, for about eight pesos, take a small trolley to the ruins.

Tulum is surrounded by a four-meter-tall wall measuring 380 meters on its west side and 170 meters on the north and south. The site's east side is bordered by cliffs and then the sea. You enter through a gate in the center of the western wall; you can see that the wall is wide and may have doubled as a causeway.

Many of Tulum's temples are built along "streets" running on a north-south axis. Facing you in the first street is the famous Temple of the Frescoes, also called Structure 16. This is a two-story shrine-within-a-shrine building. The first story faces west with four squat columns guarding the door. Three niches above the door contain little seated god figures and, in the center, the first of many diving god sculptures found at Tulum. To the left and right, the corners of

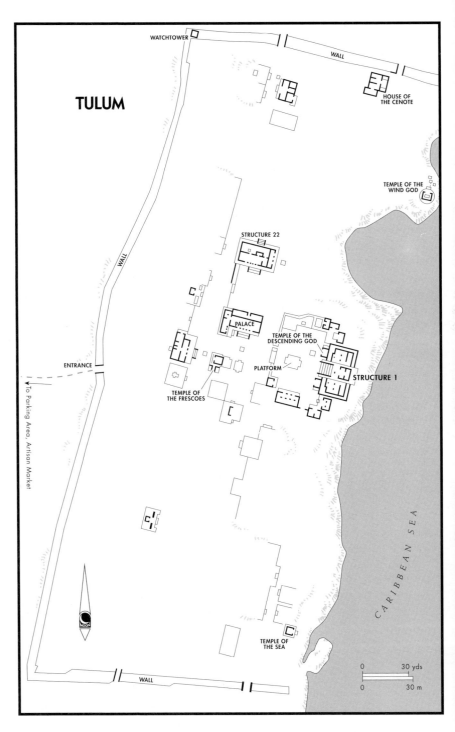

TULUM

this building are shaped into remarkable god masks, perhaps representing an aged deity with closed eyes (i.e., dead).

The inside is off-limits to visitors. A small doorway opens into the interior shrine. The walls of this structure are covered with barely visible murals painted in shades of blue and showing rows of Maya gods. The second floor is a one-room temple with another seated god figure in the niche above its door. Red hand paintings adorn the side of the facade.

This temple faces the House of the Chultun, named after the water-storage chamber over which it is built. To the north of the Temple of the Frescoes stands the Palace, also called Structure 21, with four rooms and a long colonnade. Next you come to Structure 22, with another diving god over an interior entrance; this is a second wide platform with its main entrance facing south through a colonnade.

From here, walk up the hill to the main civic-ceremonial precinct. Because of the crowds, much of this area is off-limits to tourists to protect the structures. A number of small and medium-sized buildings, some dangerously eccentric, stand around a small plaza. They are dominated by Structure 1, also called the Castillo, which stands just before the cliffs to the east. This is a wide temple, whose earlier stage, Structure 1-sub, has been partially covered by the main staircase and the temple on top. Small one-room structures flank the steps. On top stands a temple that contained the three diving god figures above each doorway. Only one remains. Serpent columns originally separated the doorways. You can see an eroded mask on the left corner similar to the ones on the Temple of the Frescoes. Behind, you can see the waves of the blue Caribbean Sea and an occasional shark.

Just to the south of the Castillo, the Temple of the Stela is a small building inside of which archaeologists found sculpture fragments. The square platform in the plaza's center is used to re-create Maya dances. To its north stands the Temple of the Descending God, which faces west with a distinctly cockeyed look. Its platform is earlier than the small temple on top, which was built with a pronounced sag to the right. Its doorway does not line up with the platform's staircase. The building is named after the stucco sculpture of the diving god above the door. Further "international" style murals adorn the interior, but entrance is forbidden.

The land descends to a sandy cove just north of the ceremonial precinct. People come here to dabble their feet, but waves and sharks make it dangerous for swimming. On the north side of the cove stands a small structure called the Temple of the Wind God, named because it rests on a circular platform (associated with wind in some Mesoamerican cultures). The breeze is constant here. Just beyond stand three small shrines.

Just inside the northeast wall of the site rises the House of the Cenote above the entrance to a limestone sinkhole, obviously the Maya center's main water source. A tomb was found beneath the floor of the house—you can see the hole—and just beyond is a gateway through the wall. If you want do a bit of scram-

a view toward Tulum's ritual center, with the Castillo rising in the middle

bling, you can climb to the watchtower at the northwest corner of the wall. On the south side of the site most of the structures remain in ruins. The best is the one-room Temple of the Sea facing the Caribbean in the southeast corner.

MUYIL

INTRODUCTION

South of Tulum, the road to Felipe Carrillo Puerto angles inland through the forests. Archaeologists believe the unexplored interior of Quintana Roo contains dozens, perhaps hundreds, of Maya towns and cities. They cite as an example the medium-sized center of Muyil (sometimes identified as "Chunyaxché"–

MUYIL

How to get there: These ruins stand just east of the highway, 24 kilometers south of Tulum.
Hours: Daily 0800–1700.
Admission fee: 17 pesos.
How long to tour: 45 minutes.
Recommended gear: Hats, sunblock, mosquito repellent.

actually the Maya settlement just down the road), which stands by the roadside 25 kilometers south of Tulum. During the Late Postclassic, this was obviously an important town with more temples and a larger population than Tulum. The building of this road exposed at least 10 other Maya centers within 15 kilometers. How many more lie off in the jungle?

HISTORY

Like many other east coast sites of the Yucatan, Muyil was first settled in the Late Preclassic (300 B.C.–A.D. 250) and remained occupied more or less continuously through the Conquest. Archaeologists have theorized that it became part of Cobá's Late Classic empire but have not found any *sacbe* connecting the two centers. Most of what you see today dates to the Late Postclassic (A.D. 1250–1531), the era of Muyil's greatest population.

the Castillo at Muyil

DANIELLE GUSTAFSON

ARCHAEOLOGICAL RECORD

Muyil appears on late 18th-century Spanish maps. From 1926 on, it was visited by a number of archaeological survey expeditions that explored the temples and prepared preliminary maps. In 1987 and 1988, the first excavations were performed by a Middle American Research Institute (Tulane University) project led by Walter R. T. Witschey. They have prepared a site map, explored the *sacbe*, and excavated some of the major temples and dug ceramic test pits.

TOURING THE SITE

After parking by the roadside, you enter the ruins and encounter a group of three small crumbling pyramids. In front of one stand the remains of a columned room with traces of blue paint around the door frame. Just to the south opens a small plaza dominated by Muyil's Castillo. This is a steep, unreconstructed pyramid rising to a ruined temple with a unique circular turret on top. The stones on the side are loose, making an ascent dangerous.

From the first three temples, a path runs north to Temple 8, a well-preserved one-room temple atop a sloping platform. Dozens of further structures lie to the north amid the trees along the side of the road.

As you return to the three temples, another path, actually a *sacbe,* heads due east into the forest. About 75 meters on, you encounter a ruined platform holding a tiny one-room shrine. A cave just to the right of the path was probably a quarry for limestone building blocks; it is now home to a colony of bats.

From here, the *sacbe* continues through the bush about 350 meters and ends at a tiny structure. This may have been the Late Postclassic landing area for the canoes that still ply the Muyil Lagoon; its banks now lie about 100 meters farther east. This lagoon is the terminus of a network of lagoons and channels that eventually flow into the Caribbean. At least 10 Maya settlements were built along its banks. Archaeologists believe Muyil may have been a crucial link on a trade route running between the coast and the interior.

EL REY

INTRODUCTION

It is hard to believe it, but the tourist metropolis of Cancún is dotted with archaeological sites. Most of these are tiny, such as the small shrines or temples on the grounds of the Sheraton and the Pok-Ta-Pok golf course (next to the third green). Cancún's largest archaeological zone—and one of its hidden treasures—is El Rey at Punta Nisuc on the south end of the hotel strip. During the Late Postclassic, this was an important trading settlement where seagoing Putún

EL REY

How to get there: The entrance to this site lies just east of the Days Inn El Pueblito hotel, Blvd. Kukulcan, km. 17.5, at the south end of Cancún's hotel zone.

Hours: Daily 0800–1700.

Admission fee: 22 pesos.

How long to tour: One hour.

Recommended gear: Hats, sunblock, bottled water.

Food and accommodations: The Days Inn El Pueblito, tel. 98/85-0797, fax 85-0731, U.S. tel. 800/325-2525, Blvd. Kukulcan, km. 17.5, lies at the south end of Cancún's hotel zone. This hotel happens to be one of the better medium-priced accommodations in the hotel zone.

Maya merchants exchanged cacao beans and ritual items for raw materials such as turtle shell. El Rey contains more than a dozen restored temple platforms covered with iguanas basking in the sun.

HISTORY

Because of the lack of archaeological work, very little is known about El Rey's chronology. Although all the structures you see today date to the Late Postclassic (A.D. 1250–1530), researchers believe that the site was settled by the end of the Classic era (A.D. 900).

ARCHAEOLOGICAL RECORD

In 1841, as they were beginning their trip home, John Lloyd Stephens and Frederick Catherwood spent the night at "Nesuc" but did not see any ruins. The next day, they saw a few other Cancún temples, such as they were:

> Early in the morning we were again under way, and coasted to the point of Kancune, where we landed in front of a rancho then occupied by a party of fishermen. Near by was another great pile of skeletons of turtles. The fishermen were busy within the hut mending their nets, and seemed to be leading a hardy, independent, and social life, entirely different from any we had seen in the interior. A

DANIELLE GUSTAFSON

a view of El Rey's main thoroughfare, with a modern pyramid in the background

short walk brought us to the point, on which stood two dilapidated buildings, one entirely fallen, and the other having dimensions like the smallest of those seen at Tuloom. It was so intensely hot, and we were so annoyed by millions of sand-flies, that we did not think it worth while to stay. . . .

In 1877, they were followed by Augustus Le Plongeon and his wife, who described the ruins of a city called "Nizucte"—almost certainly El Rey. Le Plongeon believed that many of the tiny shrines lining the shores were built by a race of dwarves. The others, such as William H. Holmes, who visited Punta Nisuc were not impressed. A site map and short description did appear in *The American Egypt* (1909) by Arnold Channing and F. J. T. Frost.

In 1954, William T. Sanders of the Carnegie Institution opened some small test pits at El Rey as part of his northern Yucatan ceramic survey. The first larger-scale excavations and restorations were performed by INAH's Ernesto Vargas Pacheco and Pablo Mayer Guala in 1977 and 1978. To date, they have published only preliminary reports.

TOURING THE SITE

The ruins are built around three plazas aligned on a north-south axis parallel to the road. The low sandy ridge to the east gave its residents a bit of protection from hurricanes and other Caribbean storms. To the west extends the Nichupte Lagoon, which was probably the main highway for travel (by canoe) between El Rey and other Maya settlements.

El Rey's stone structures are home to dozens of basking iguanas who have become blasé about visitors. The path runs north between two lines of raised platforms, some bearing the remains of columns.

The best-preserved buildings stand around the middle plaza. As you enter it, you pass on the left Structure 4, a wide platform holding 18 columns. The east and north sides of the plaza are bordered by an L-shaped row of platforms. On your right stands Structure 3-B, a small temple with two doors and two vaulted rooms within. The site is named after the sculpture of *el rey* (the king) believed to come from this temple. A second platform temple stands opposite on the east (lagoon) side of the plaza.

Beyond Structure 3-B rises a ruined pyramid connected to another platform and colonnade along the north side of the plaza. From here, you can look north to a third plaza containing more ruined platforms. Off on the northern horizon floats a modern, pyramid-shaped hotel—a temple of the modern cult of tourism.

Dove-Cotes Building, Uxmal

Resources

AN ALPHABETICAL
LIST OF SITES

CULTURES OF
MEXICO

Sites of occupation, grouped by culture

SITES BY ERA

ARCHAEOLOGICAL SITES AND AREAS

Major occupation by cultures, listed alphabetically by location

Atzcapotzalco: Tepanec 68, 74–75

Becan: Maya 337–340

Bonampak: Maya 290–300

Cacaxtla: Olmeca-Xicallanca 112–118

Ceibal: Maya 258

Chalcatzingo: Olmec   124–130; Teotihuacano 126

Chiapas: Barra culture 6, 244; Maya 244, 258–259

Chicanná: Maya 340–342

Chinkultic: Maya 311–315

Cholula: Tolteca-Chichimeca 104–110

Coast of Veracruz: Olmec 173–178

Coatlinchan: Acolhuas 68

Cobá: Maya 404–410

Colhuacan: Toltec 58

Comalcalco: Maya 316–320

Culhuacan: Culhua 73

Dainzú: Zapotec 232–235

Dzibanché: Maya 331

Dzibilchaltun: Maya 7, 375–380

Edzná: Maya 343–349

El Rey: Maya 417–419

El Tajín: Totonac 182–191

Great Temple (Mexico City): Aztec 70–84

Ihuatzio: Tarascan 157–158

Izamal: Maya 380–383

Kabah: Maya 363–365

Kaminaljuyú: Maya 7

Kinichná: Maya 331

Kohunlich: Maya 327–332

Labná: Maya 368–369

Lambityeco: Zapotec 228–231

La Venta: Olmec 6, 178

Loltun Cave: Maya 371–374

Malinalco: Aztec 139; Matlazlincan 138–139

Mayapan: Maya 11, 400–404

Mitla: Aztec/Mixtec/Zapotec 218–225

Monte Albán: Mixtec 211; Zapotec 208–211

Muyil: Maya 415–417

Northern Mexico: Chichimec 161–166

Palenque: Maya 7, 259–276

Paquimé: Mogollon   167;   Toltec 166–171

Puuc Region: Maya 349–371

Quiahuiztlan: Totonac 191–195

Río Bec Region: Maya 332–342

San Lorenzo: Olmec 6, 178

Santa Cecilia Acatitlán: Aztec 95–96

Sayil: Maya 366–367

Tenam Puente: Maya 313

Tenayuca: Chichimec 66–70

Tenochtitlan: Aztec 11, 14, 70–84

Tlatelolco: Aztec 84–94

Toniná: Maya 300–311

Tres Zapotes: Olmec 179–182

Tula: Aztec 59; Coyotlatelcos 57; Nonoalco 57; Toltec/Tolteca-Chichimeca 57–59

Tzintzúntzan: Purépecha 150–153; Wacúsecha 150–153

Usumacinta Basin: Maya 255–259

Uxmal: Maya 354–363

MESOAMERICAN INTERNET SITES

Here is a list of the best and most comprehensive Internet sites for both specialists and amateurs interested in the major sites and cultures of ancient Mexico.

Mesoamerican Archaeology Page

http://copan.bioz.unibas.ch/meso.html

> This site is the most important page for files, links, software, resources, and reports relevant to Mesoamerican and other pre-Columbian cultures.

Instituto Nacional de Antropología e Historia

www.arts-history.mx/ligas/inah.html

> Better known as INAH, the Instituto Nacional de Antropología e Historia is the Mexican government organization in charge of the protection, excavation, and study of all of Mexico's ruins. Its website contains information on nearly every site open to the public and news about the latest discoveries.

Museo Nacional de Antropología

www.arts-history.mx/museos/ext/antropologia.html

> This site gives a room-by-room tour of one of the world's greatest anthropology museums and includes images of many of the most famous Mexican discoveries. In Spanish only.

Mesoamerican Photo Archives

http://studentweb.tulane.edu/~dhixson

> Here you find excellent photographs and descriptions of about 10 major Mexican sites and a good links page.

Ancient Mesoamerican Civilizations

www.angelfire.com/ca/humanorigins/index.html

> This website offers a basic introduction to Mesoamerican culture through descriptions of its religions, writing systems, forms of government, and calendars.

Teotihuacan Home Page

http://archaeology.la.asu.edu/teo

> This Arizona State University website contains a detailed description and map of Mexico's largest ancient city and articles about the most recent discoveries at the Pyramid of the Moon under the joint ASU and INAH program. At the linked Feathered Serpent Site (http://archaeology.la.asu.edu/teo/fsp/index.htm), you

find an excellent report on this major structure and the sacrificial burials and offerings found during the 1988–89 excavations.

Museo del Templo Mayor
http://archaeology.la.asu.edu/tm

One of the best site museums in Mexico, the Museo del Templo Mayor is described here in a bilingual tour.

Mesoweb
www.mesoweb.com

If you are interested in the great Maya site of Palenque and the ongoing archaeological excavations there, this well-organized site is a must. It contains regular updates on the discoveries, all heavily illustrated, and numerous links and cutting-edge scholarly articles on many aspects of Maya history and culture.

GB Online's Mesoamerica
http://pages.prodigy.com/GBonline/mesowelc.html

Biased toward the ancient Maya, this website provides clear descriptions of Mesoamerican writing systems, calendars, and ceramics. It also contains discussion of individual Maya sites and modern-day Maya issues, and a links page.

Rabbit on the Moon
www.halfmoon.org

For a more lighthearted take on the Maya, visit the Rabbit on the Moon site. In addition to serious descriptions on Maya writing, calendars, and architecture, it offers Maya computer games and even a Maya makeover: "Be attractive the Classic Maya way!"

Virtual Palenque
www.virtualpalenque.com

This site offers Quicktime movie tours of the major structures at Palenque, all narrated by Dr. Thomas Guderjan.

SUGGESTED READING

If you are interested in reading further about Mexico's pre-Hispanic cultures, there are thousands of books and periodicals filled with useful information. Many of these are in Spanish, of course. The following list is confined to English-language titles; you can track down many of the Spanish- and English-language works. Large public and university libraries are a good place to start, and museums with Mesoamerican art collections also often have libraries open to the public.

The best general introductions to Mesoamerica's cultures are Michael D. Coe's *Mexico: From the Olmecs to the Aztecs* (London and New York: Thames & Hudson, 1994, 4th edition) and *The Maya* (London and New York: Thames & Hudson, 1993, 5th edition). The most recent theories on Mesoamerican religion are presented in Mary Miller and Karl Taube's dictionary-form *The Gods and Symbols of Ancient Mexico and the Maya* (London and New York: Thames & Hudson, 1993). Mary Miller's *The Art of Mesoamerica: From Olmec to Aztec* (London and New York: Thames & Hudson, 1996, 2nd edition) presents an art historian's view of ancient art and architecture. For the latest information on Maya genealogies and the interrelations between their city-states, Simon Martin and Nikolai Grube's copiously illustrated *Chronicle of the Maya Kings and Queens* (London and New York: Thames & Hudson, 2000) contains the state-of-the-art information. Robert Sharer's *The Ancient Maya* (Stanford: Stanford University Press, 1994, 5th edition) is a weighty summary of archaeological research on the Maya based on Sylvanus Morley's classic volume of the same name. Although it is slightly out-of-date, many of the most authoritative archaeological studies are contained in the multivolume *Handbook of Middle American Indians* (Austin: University of Texas Press, 1964–76 and 1981–1992) edited by Robert Wauchope and later Jeremy Sabloff.

Other good guidebooks to Mexican sites are Joyce Kelly's *The Complete Visitor's Guide to Mesoamerican Ruins* (Norman, OK: University of Oklahoma Press, 1982) and her recent *An Archaeological Guide to Mexico's Yucatán Peninsula* (Norman, OK: University of Oklahoma Press, 1993), which includes descriptions of dozens of minor sites. Another source is C. Bruce Hunter's *A Guide to Ancient Mexican Ruins* (Norman, OK: University of Oklahoma Press, 1977), although it needs updating in some areas.

Dozens of scholarly journals publish articles on Mexican archaeology; among the best is *Ancient Mesoamerica. National Geographic* occasionally contains articles on the latest discoveries, particularly in the Maya world. If you read

Spanish, you should consult *Arqueología* published by the Mexican government's Instituto Nacional de Antropología y Historia (INAH) for up-to-date information on excavations. INAH has also published guidebooks to the major ruins and dozens of folding "miniguides" to the smaller sites.

A number of researchers have written fascinating books on Mesoamerican themes that are not attached to any one site. During the last two decades, the translation of Maya hieroglyphs has led to a revolution in thought about Mesoamerican culture. Michael D. Coe's *Breaking the Maya Code* (London and New York: Thames & Hudson, 1992) is a participant's view of this groundbreaking work. His recently published *Reading the Maya Glyph* (London and New York: Thames & Hudson, 2001) gives beginners the key to decoding Maya hieroglyphs in a travel-size format. Anthony F. Aveni has proved that almost all Mesoamerican temples were aligned to the sun, planets, and stars; his *Skywatchers of Ancient Mexico* (Austin: University of Texas Press, 1980) is the best book on the study of archaeoastronomy. Dozens of works of Mesoamerican literature have been translated into English; the most influential is Dennis Tedlock's translation of the *Popol Vuh* (New York: Simon & Schuster, 1985), the great Maya mythic history. Sophie Coe's *America's First Cuisines* (Austin: University of Texas, 1994) explores the foods of the Aztecs, Maya, and Incas and how they were influenced by the arrival of Europeans.

The published works on specific ruins vary widely depending on region and site. Even though excavations have been performed at nearly every site included in this book, only a fraction of the results have been published. For example, centers such as Teotihuacan and the Great Temple have been described in a wealth of reports, while the results from major sites such as Palenque and Yaxchilan are mostly unknown, except to the excavators. The following is a list on the best English-language studies on the ruins described in this book.

Teotihuacan has been a focus of investigations for more than a century. The best recent book is *Teotihuacan: Art from the City of Gods* (London and New York: Thames & Hudson, 1993) by Kathleen Berrin and Esther Pasztory. Eduardo Matos Moctezuma's *Teotihuacan* (New York: Rizzoli International, 1990) is a heavily illustrated introduction to the site. In 1973, René Millon revolutionized the study of this site by the publication of his remarkable *The Teotihuacan Map* (Austin: University of Texas Press, 1973), which showed the true extent of the ancient metropolis. Edited by Richard Diehl and Janet Berlo, *Mesoamerica after the Decline of Teotihuacan* (Washington, D.C.: Dumbarton Oaks, 1989) contains discussions on the late Coyotlatelco occupants of the ruins and on a number of other important central Mexican sites, as well as articles on the Late Classic and Early Postclassic eras.

The best book on Tula is Richard Diehl's *Tula* (London and New York: Thames & Hudson, 1983). In *The Toltecs* (Norman, OK: University of Oklahoma Press, 1977), Nigel Davies unravels the complicated history of Tula's rise and fall as seen by later ethnohistorical accounts.

Dozens of good books have been written about the Aztecs and their dual cities of Tenochtitlan—built around the Great Temple—and Tlatelolco. The best introduction is Richard F. Townsend's *The Aztecs* (London and New York: Thames & Hudson, 1992), which includes their basic history as well as chapters on religion and social classes. Inga Clendinnen's *Aztecs* (Cambridge, England: Cambridge University Press, 1991) is a fascinating re-creation of Aztec religion and how it is inextricably linked to society. Another important work on Aztec religion and philosophy is Miguel León-Portilla's *Aztec Thought and Culture* (Norman, OK: University of Oklahoma, 1963), which includes the texts of many Aztec prayers. Nigel Davies's *The Aztecs* (Norman, OK: University of Oklahoma Press, 1973) is the last chapter of his trilogy on the Valley of Mexico's ethnohistory from Tula to Tenochtitlan.

The Great Temple has been the subject of many books, but the best is Eduardo Matos Moctezuma's *The Great Temple of the Aztecs* (London and New York: Thames & Hudson, 1988) written by the man who excavated it. Doris Heyden gives a short course on Aztec religion and the temple in *The Great Temple and the Aztec Gods* (Mexico City: Editorial Minutiae Mexicana, 1984).

Aside from the general introductions mentioned at the beginning of this bibliography, very few English-language works focus on the Valley of Puebla. An article by Geoffrey McCafferty in *Ancient Mesoamerica, 7* (Cambridge, England: Cambridge University Press, 1996) is the best summary of research on Cholula. You can find Ellen Baird's article on Cacaxtla in *Mesoamerica after the Decline of Teotihuacan* mentioned above.

Chalcatzingo, the Olmec outpost in the Valley of Mexico, was excavated by David Grove. He describes his findings in *Chalcatzingo* (London and New York: Thames & Hudson, 1984) and in the more detailed *Ancient Chalcatzingo* (Austin: University of Texas Press, 1987). Kenneth Hirth's detailed multivolume study, *Ancient Urbanism at Xochicalco* (Salt Lake City: University of Utah Press, 2000), is by far the best work on that site.

Those "barbarous" interlopers in West Mexico, the Tarascans, were long ignored by the archaeological establishment. Helen Pearlstein Pollard rights that wrong in her excellent *Tariacuri's Legacy* (Norman, OK: University of Oklahoma Press, 1993).

Most archaeological reports skimp on detail. An exception is Charles Di Peso's eight-volume tome on *Casas Grandes* (Dragoon, AZ: Amerind Foundation, 1974), the largest work to date on northern Mexico. For a more up-to-date view of the North's archaeology, the best book is *The Casas Grandes World* (Salt Lake City: University of Utah Press, 1999), edited by Curtis F. Schaafsma and Carroll L. Riley.

The Olmec heartland along the coast of Veracruz has been the focus of many exciting studies in the last few decades. Michael D. Coe and Richard Diehl's two-volume *In the Land of the Olmec* (Austin: University of Texas Press, 1980) describes their excavations at the important early center of San Lorenzo. An exhibition catalog, *The Olmec World* (Princeton, NJ: Princeton University Press, 1996) contains important articles on the latest theories about Olmec religion and society. Matthew Stirling's *Stone Monuments of Southern Mexico* (Washington, D.C.: U.S. Government Printing Office, 1943) includes the most important description of Tres Zapotes.

Although there exist a number of Spanish-language books on El Tajín—such as those written by Jürgen Brüggemann—the only one in English is S. Jeffrey K. Wilkerson's excellent guide, *El Tajín* (Veracruz: Universidad Veracruzana, 1986).

The Valley of Oaxaca is one of the most active areas in Mexico for archaeological work. Good introductions to the region are Ignacio Bernal's guidebook, *Oaxaca Valley* (Mexico City: INAH-SALVAT, 1985), and Marcus Winter's *Oaxaca, the Archaeological Record* (Mexico City: Editorial Minutiae Mexicana, 1989). Kent Flannery and Joyce Marcus include the latest research on the Zapotecs and Mixtecs in their book, *The Cloud People* (New York: Academic Press, 1983) and then reinterpret the Zapotecs using new theories of archaeology in *The Zapotecs* (London and New York: Thames & Hudson, 1996). John Paddock's classic work, *Ancient Oaxaca* (Stanford: Stanford University Press, 1960), is out-of-date but still contains many valuable insights.

The excavations results from the fascinating Chiapas coast site of Izapa are reported in Gareth Lowe's definitive *Izapa: An Introduction to the Ruins and Monuments* (Provo, UT: New World Archaeological Foundation, 1973). Garth Norman gives a detailed description of the site's many monuments in *Izapa Sculpture* (Provo, UT: New World Archaeological Foundation, 1982).

During the last two decades, a revolution has overturned many of the theories about Classic Maya history and culture. Linda Schele, a professor at the University of Texas, was a key figure in this uprising. In 1986, she and the art historian Mary Miller curated an exhibition at the Kimbell Art Museum in Fort Worth to illustrate the new conceptions; their catalog, *The Blood of Kings* (New York: George Braziller, 1986), was the first book-length exposition of these ideas. Since then, Schele published two fascinating and accessible books using the latest research to reinterpret many Maya sites and their religion: *A Forest of Kings* (New York: Morrow, 1990) with David Freidel and *Maya Cosmos* (New York: Morrow, 1993) with Freidel and Joy Parker. *A Forest of Kings* is particularly helpful when studying the Maya centers of Chiapas and Yucatan. Until her death in 1998, Schele hosted yearly Maya Hieroglyphic Workshops at the University of Texas; the volumes of their collected papers contain many of the latest findings.

Much of recent work on the Maya has been based on the publication of the *Corpus of Maya Hieroglyphic Inscriptions* (Cambridge, MA: Peabody Museum, Harvard University, 1975-). This is an ongoing project by Ian Graham, Eric Von Euw, and Peter Mathews to document all the glyphic inscriptions found in the Maya region—an endless task considering that more are discovered every week.

Another important source for research on the Maya is in the proceedings of the Palenque Round Tables. This is an irregularly scheduled symposium founded in 1973 and hosted by Merle Greene Robertson. The first Round Table led to one of the great breakthroughs in the translation of Maya hieroglyphs.

Merle Greene Robertson has also written the best English-language book on Palenque. Her four-volume *The Sculptures of Palenque* (Princeton, NJ: Princeton University Press, 1983–1991) contains photographs and descriptions of every major building and artwork at the site. The best summary of the history of Palenque and Yaxchilan is contained in Schele and Freidel's *A Forest of Kings*. Carolyn Tate's *Yaxchilan* (Austin: University of Texas Press, 1992) is a detailed description of the site's architecture and monuments. The authoritative book on Bonampak is Mary Miller's *The Murals of Bonampak* (Princeton, NJ: Princeton University Press, 1985), which almost certainly will be superseded by her next book.

Despite the intense interest in the archaeological sites of the Yucatan Peninsula, only relatively large-scale excavations have been performed on its sites and even fewer complete reports published. Most of what we know is due to the Middle American Research Institution's (MARI) work at Dzibilchaltun and in the Río Bec area and to the New World Archaeological Foundation's Edzná project. The MARI Río Bec project focused on the site of Becan; the results were published in MARI reports *41, 43, 44* and *45* (New Orleans: Middle American Research Institute, Tulane University, 1976, 1977, 1978, 1981) by David Webster, Joseph Ball, James Stoltman, and E. Wyllys Andrews V respectively on earthworks, ceramics, stone tools, and settlement patterns. Ray Matheny issued the results of his Edzná work in *Investigations at Edzná, Campeche, Mexico* (Provo, UT: New World Archaeological Foundation, 1983).

For information on the Puuc region, the best sources are Jeff Karl Kowalski's Uxmal study, *The House of the Governor* (Norman, OK: University of Oklahoma, 1987), and his short but informative *Guide to Uxmal and the Puuc Region* (Mérida: Editorial Dante, 1990). The Spring 1994 issue of *Ancient Mesoamerica* contains an excellent article on Puuc settlement patterns that summarizes the most recent theories about the region.

The definitive book about Dzibilchaltun is *Excavations at Dzibilchaltun, Yucatan, Mexico* (New Orleans: Middle American Research Institute, 1980) by E. Wyllys Andrews IV and E. Wyllys Andrews V. The latter author also wrote an excellent guide to the site: *Dzibilchaltun* (Mexico City: INAH, 1978).

Shockingly, there is no book in English, Spanish, or any other language that one can recommend for the important city of Chichén Itzá. Most of the English-language works focus on Edward H. Thompson's work in the Sacred Cenote. The best description of the city—and one version of its history—is contained in *A Forest of Kings*. The story of the nearby Cave of Balankanché is told in *Balankanche, Throne of the Tiger Priest* (New Orleans: Middle American Research Institute, 1970) by E. Wyllys Andrews IV. Chichén was succeeded by Mayapan; the results of its excavation are published in *Mayapan* (Washington, D.C.:

Carnegie Institution, 1962) by Harry E. D. Pollock, Ralph Roys, Tatiana Prosk-ouriakoff, and A. L. Smith.

The most important site in Quintana Roo is the sprawling city of Cobá. The best work in English on the site is William J. Folan's *Coba: A Classic Maya Metropolis* (New York: Academic Press, 1983). Finally, not enough has been written on Quintana Roo's coastal sites. Tulum's artwork was studied by Arthur Miller, who published his results in *On the Edge of the Sea: Mural Painting at Tancah-Tulum* (Washington, D.C.: Dumbarton Oaks, 1982).

SPANISH PHRASEBOOK

PRONUNCIATION GUIDE

Spanish is a more phonetic language than English, but there are still occasional variations in pronunciation.

Consonants

c – as 'c' in "cat," before 'a', 'o', or 'u'; like 's' before 'e' or 'i'
d – as 'd' in "dog," except between vowels, then like 'th' in "that"
g – before 'e' or 'i', like the 'ch' in Scottish "loch"; elsewhere like 'g' in "get"
h – always silent
j – like the English 'h' in "hotel," but stronger
ll – like the 'y' in "yellow"
ñ – like the 'ni' in "onion"
r – always pronounced as strong 'r'
rr – trilled 'r'
v – similar to the 'b' in "boy" (not as English 'v')
y – similar to English, but with a slight "j" sound. When standing, alone it's pronounced like the 'e' in "me."
z – like 's' in "same"
b, f, k, l, m, n, p, q, s, t, w, x – as in English

Vowels

a – as in "father," but shorter
e – as in "hen"
i – as in "machine"
o – as in "phone"
u – usually as in "rule"; when it follows a 'q' the 'u' is silent; when it follows an 'h' or 'g', it's pronounced like 'w', except when it comes between 'g' and 'e' or 'i', when it's also silent (unless it has an umlaut, when it is again pronounced as English 'w'.

Stress

Native English speakers frequently make errors of pronunciation by ignoring stress—all Spanish vowels—a, e, i, o and u—may carry accents that determine which syllable of a word gets emphasis. Often, stress seems unnatural to nonnative speakers—the surname Chávez, for instance, is stressed on the first syllable—but failure to observe this rule may mean that native speakers may not understand you.

NUMBERS

0 - cero	11 - once	40 - cuarenta
1 - uno (masculine)	12 - doce	50 - cincuenta
1 - una (feminine)	13 - trece	60 - sesenta
2 - dos	14 - catorce	70 - setenta
3 - tres	15 - quince	80 - ochenta
4 - cuatro	16 - diesiseis	90 - noventa
5 - cinco	17 - diesisiete	100 - cien
6 - seis	18 - diesiocho	101 - ciento y uno
7 - siete	19 - diesinueve	200 - doscientos
8 - ocho	20 - veinte	1,000 - mil
9 - nueve	21 - veinte y uno	10,000 - diez mil
10 - diez	30 - treinta	1,000,000 - un millón

DAYS OF THE WEEK

Sunday - domingo
Monday - lunes
Tuesday - martes
Wednesday - miércoles
Thursday - jueves
Friday - viernes
Saturday - sábado

TIME

While Mexicans mostly use the 12-hour clock, in some instances, usually associated with plane or bus schedules, they may use the 24-hour military clock. Under the 24-hour clock, for example, las nueve de la noche (9 P.M.) would be las 21 horas (2100 hours).

What time is it? - ¿Qué hora es?
It's one o'clock - Es la una.
It's two o'clock - Son las dos.
It's two o'clock - A las dos.
It's to three - Son tres menos diez.
It's ten past three - Son tres y diez.
It's three fifteen - Son las tres y cuarto.
It's two forty-five - Son tres menos cuarto.
It's two thirty - Son las dos y media.
It's six A.M. - Son las seis de la mañana.
It's six P.M. - Son las seis de la tarde.

It's ten P.M. - Son las diez de la noche.
Today - hoy
Tomorrow - mañana
Morning - la mañana
Tomorrow morning - mañana por la mañana
Yesterday - ayer
Week - la semana
Month - mes
Year - año
Last night - anoche
The next day - el día siguiente

USEFUL WORDS AND PHRASES

Mexicans and other Spanish-speaking people consider formalities important. Whenever approaching anyone for information or some other reason, do not forget the appropriate salutation—good morning, good evening, etc. Standing alone, the greeting hola (hello) can sound brusque.

Hello. - Hola.
Good morning. - Buenos días.
Good afternoon. - Buenas tardes.
Good evening. - Buenas noches.
How are you? - ¿Cómo está?
Fine. - Muy bien.
And you? - ¿Y usted?
So-so. - Más o menos.
Thank you. - Gracias.
Thank you very much. - Muchas gracias.
You're very kind. - Muy amable.
You're welcome - De nada (literally, "It's nothing.")
Yes - sí
No - no
I don't know. - No sé.
It's fine; okay - Está bien.
Good; okay - Bueno.
Please - por favor
Pleased to meet you. - Mucho gusto.
Excuse me (physical) - Perdóneme.
Excuse me (speech) - Discúlpeme.
I'm sorry. - Lo siento.
Goodbye - adiós
See you later - hasta luego (literally, "until later")

More - más
Less - menos
Better - mejor
Much, a lot - mucho
A little - un poco
Large - grande
Small - pequeño, chico
Quick, fast - rápido
Slowly - despacio
Bad - malo
Difficult - difícil
Easy - fácil
He/She/It is gone; as in "She left," "He's gone" - Ya se fue.
I don't speak Spanish well. - No hablo bien el español.
I don't understand. - No entiendo.
How do you say . . . in Spanish? - ¿Cómo se dice . . . en español?
Do you understand English? - ¿Entiende el inglés?
Is English spoken here? (Does anyone here speak English?) - ¿Se habla inglés aquí?

TERMS OF ADDRESS

When in doubt, use the formal usted (you) as a form of address. If you wish to dispense with formality and feel that the desire is mutual, you can say Me puedes tutear (you can call me "tu"). Mexicans also, however, use the familiar form vos, which requires slightly different verb forms (see the sidebar on "El Voseo").

I - yo
You (formal) - usted
you (familiar) - tú
He/him - él
She/her - ella
We/us - nosotros
You (plural) - ustedes
They/them (all males or mixed gender) - ellos
They/them (all females) - ellas
Mr., sir - señor
Mrs., madam - señora
Miss, young lady - señorita
Wife - esposa
Husband - marido or esposo
Friend - amigo (male), amiga (female)
Sweetheart - novio (male), novia (female)

Son, daughter - hijo, hija
Brother, sister - hermano, hermana
Father, mother - padre, madre
Grandfather, grandmother - abuelo, abuela

GETTING AROUND

Where is . . . ? - ¿Dónde está . . . ?
How far is it to . . .? - ¿A cuanto está . . . ?
from . . . to . . . - de . . . a . . .
Highway - la carretera
Road - el camino
Street - la calle
Block - la cuadra
Kilometer - kilómetro
North - norte
South - sur
West - oeste; poniente
East - este; oriente
Straight ahead - al derecho; adelante
To the right - a la derecha
To the left - a la izquierda

ACCOMMODATIONS

¿Hay cuarto? - Is there a room?
May I (we) see it? - ¿Puedo (podemos) verlo?
What is the rate? - ¿Cuál es el precio?
Is that your best rate? - ¿Es su mejor precio?
Is there something cheaper? - ¿Hay algo más económico?
Single room - un sencillo
Double room - un doble
Room for a couple - matrimonial
Key - llave
With private bath - con baño
With shared bath - con baño general; con baño compartido
Hot water - agua caliente
Cold water - agua fría
Ducha - shower
Ducha eléctrica - electric shower
Towel - toalla
Soap - jabón
Toilet paper - papel higiénico
Air conditioning - aire acondicionado

Fan - abanico; ventilador
Blanket - frazada; manta
Sheets - sábanas

PUBLIC TRANSPORT

Bus stop - la parada
Bus terminal - terminal de buses
Airport - el aeropuerto
Launch - lancha; tiburonera
Dock - muelle
I want a ticket to . . . - Quiero un pasaje a . . .
I want to get off at . . . - Quiero bajar en . . .
Here, please. - Aquí, por favor.
Where is this bus going? - ¿Adónde va este autobús?
Roundtrip - ida y vuelta
What do I owe? - ¿Cuánto le debo?

FOOD

Menu - la carta, el menú
Glass - taza
Fork - tenedor
Knife - cuchillo
Spoon - cuchara
Napkin - servilleta
Soft drink - agua fresca
Coffee - café
Cream - crema
Tea - té
Sugar - azúcar
Drinking water - agua pura, agua potable
Bottled carbonated water - agua mineral con gas
Bottled uncarbonated water - agua sin gas
Beer - cerveza
Wine - vino
Milk - leche
Juice - jugo
Eggs - huevos
Bread - pan
Watermelon - sandía
Banana - banano
Plantain - plátano
Apple - manzana

Orange - naranja
Meat (without) - carne (sin)
Beef - carne de res
Chicken - pollo; gallina
Fish - pescado
Shellfish - mariscos
Shrimp - camarones
Fried - frito
Roasted - asado
Barbecued - a la parrilla
Breakfast - desayuno
Lunch - almuerzo
Dinner (often eaten in late afternoon) - comida
Dinner, or a late night snack - cena
The check, or bill - la cuenta

MAKING PURCHASES

I need . . . - Necesito . . .
I want . . . - Deseo . . . or Quiero . . .
I would like . . . (more polite) - Quisiera . . .
How much does it cost? - ¿Cuánto cuesta?
What's the exchange rate? - ¿Cuál es el tipo de cambio?
May I see . . . ? - ¿Puedo ver . . . ?
This one - ésta/ésto
Expensive - caro
Cheap - barato
Cheaper - más barato
Too much - demasiado

HEALTH

Help me please. - Ayúdeme por favor.
I am ill. - Estoy enfermo.
Pain - dolor
Fever - fiebre
Stomach ache - dolor de estómago
Vomiting - vomitar
Diarrhea - diarrea
Drugstore - farmacia
Medicine - medicina
Pill, tablet - pastilla
Birth control pills - pastillas anticonceptivas
Condom - condón, preservativo

INDEX

MUSEUMS

S

ACKNOWLEDGMENTS

This book could not have been written without the help of dozens of people and institutions. I would particularly like to thank the Mexican Government Tourism Office in New York, the Mexican Secretariat of Tourism, Danielle Gustafson, Linda Manzanilla, Alfred Bush, and Mary Miller. At the Metropolitan Museum of Art's Goldwater Library, the staff was incredibly helpful and patient with a perennial repeat customer.

WE WELCOME YOUR COMMENTS

Things inevitably change. Your comments and suggestions to help us stay on top of it are helpful and more than welcomed. Please forward your two cents on a card or drop us a line via email.

Archaeological Mexico
Avalon Travel Publishing
5855 Beaudry Street
Emeryville, CA 94608 USA
email: atpfeedback@avalonpub.com

ABOUT THE AUTHOR

In the mid-1980s, Andrew Coe followed a trail that led from the athletic clubs of New York City's South Bronx to the giant wrestling arenas of Mexico City. He was on the track of *lucha libre,* the weird and spectacular world of masked Mexican wrestlers. At the same time, he rediscovered Mexico. The son of two anthropologists, experts on the culture and food of Mesoamerica, he had been taken to visit dozens of ancient Mexican sites as a child. Now he would realize the incredible connections between pre-Columbian cultures and modern Mexico—even in the masks and rituals of *lucha libre.* After composing a semi-  nal article on Mexican professional wrestling, he went on to write guidebooks to Mexico, Mexico City, and Cuba, as well as articles on Latin American popular culture. He also wrote a history of Americans in Hong Kong, China. This guidebook is his way of finishing the story by returning to the sites of his childhood, as well as many others. Andrew Coe lives in Brooklyn, New York, with his wife, Jane, and son, Henry Buster Coe.

AVALON
TRAVEL
publishing

How far will our travel guides take you? As far as you want.

Discover a rhumba-fueled nightspot in Old Havana, explore prehistoric tombs in Ireland, hike beneath California's centuries-old redwoods, or embark on a classic road trip along Route 66. Our guidebooks deliver solidly researched, trip-tested information—minus any generic froth—to help globetrotters or weekend warriors create an adventure uniquely their own.

And we're not just about the printed page. Public television viewers are tuning in to Rick Steves' new travel series, *Rick Steves' Europe*. On the Web, readers can cruise the virtual black top with *Road Trip USA* author Jamie Jensen and learn travel industry secrets from Edward Hasbrouck of *The Practical Nomad*.

In print. On TV. On the Internet.

We supply the information. The rest is up to you.

Avalon Travel Publishing

Something for everyone

www.travelmatters.com

Avalon Travel Publishing guides are available at your favorite book or travel store.

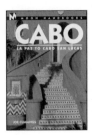

MOON HANDBOOKS provide comprehensive

coverage of a region's arts, history, land, people, and social
issues in addition to detailed practical listings for accommodations, food, outdoor recreation, and entertainment. Moon
Handbooks allow complete immersion in a region's culture—
ideal for travelers who want to combine sightseeing with
insight for an extraordinary travel experience in destinations
throughout North America, Hawaii, Latin America, the
Caribbean, Asia, and the Pacific.

WWW.MOON.COM

Rick Steves shows you where to travel and how to travel—
all while getting the most value for your dollar. His Back
Door travel philosophy is about making friends, having fun,
and avoiding tourist rip-offs.

Rick has been traveling to Europe for more than 25
years and is the author of 22 guidebooks, which have sold
more than a million copies. He also hosts the award-winning
public television series *Rick Steves' Europe.*

WWW.RICKSTEVES.COM

ROAD TRIP USA

Getting there is half the fun, and Road Trip USA guides are your ticket to driving
adventure. Taking you off the interstates and onto
less-traveled, two-lane highways, each guide is filled with
fascinating trivia, historical information, photographs, facts
about regional writers, and details on where to sleep and
eat—all contributing to your exploration of the American
road.

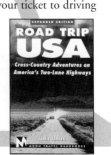

*"[Books] so full of the pleasures of the American road,
you can smell the upholstery."*
~BBC radio

WWW.ROADTRIPUSA.COM